PRAISE FOR
AMERICA FOR AMERICANS

"As Erika Lee brilliantly shows, xenophobia has forever been an integral part of American racism. Forcing us to confront this history as we confront its present, *America for Americans* is essential reading for anyone who wants to build a more inclusive society."

—Ibram X. Kendi, *New York Times*–bestselling author of *How to Be an Antiracist* and *Stamped from the Beginning*

"*America for Americans* is unflinching and powerful. Through extensive research and crystal clear prose, Erika Lee has masterfully tracked the phenomenon of xenophobia and its devastating effects on this nation's democracy and its people. Spurred on by unscrupulous politicians and key segments of the press, the cadence of fear, racism, and policy violence has rained down on immigrants since the colonial period and wreaked havoc on America's laws and claims of moral and human rights leadership. This is a must-read for all who need and want to understand how the 'leader of the free world' came to ban a religion, violate asylum laws, and lock babies in cages."

—Carol Anderson, *New York Times*–bestselling author of *White Rage* and *One Person, No Vote*

"Erika Lee's *America for Americans* is an insightful, thought-provoking book that helps us understand why the United States, a 'nation of immigrants,' could be the home to such longstanding and powerful anti-immigrant movements. Anyone who wants to fully understand why Americans are so divided over border walls, asylum policy, and sanctuary cities must read this outstanding book."

—Tyler Anbinder, author of *City of Dreams: The 400-Year Epic History of Immigrant New York*

"America's xenophobic underbelly is laid bare by Erika Lee's meticulous chronicle, which begins well before 1776, when 'swarms' of Germans in the American colonies were labeled 'scum' and 'criminals,' and then details how those same hateful descriptions have been applied to Irish, Italians, Chinese, Japanese, Mexicans, Muslims, and others. This fascinating, timely, and important book makes it possible for us to stop repeating history and instead to build bridges based on our shared immigrant experiences."

—Helen Zia, author of *Last Boat Out of Shanghai* and *Asian American Dreams*

"*America for Americans* is an intellectual tour de force wrapped in a vibrant, accessible narrative. Erika Lee reveals how hostility toward foreigners has profoundly influenced popular imagination and public policy, beginning with agitation over German settlers in early America. The exclusionist rhetoric, practices, and policies so prevalent today are nothing new, but echo back centuries of marking the boundaries of belonging. A timely, eloquent meditation on immigration, Lee's book demonstrates why history matters in understanding the contemporary resurgence of xenophobia and makes plain its shameful consequences (past and present) for individuals and the nation."

—Vicki L. Ruiz, author of *From Out of the Shadows: Mexican Women in Twentieth-Century America*

"The most comprehensive and chilling history of anti-immigrant sentiment in America ever written. With narrative authority and analytic precision, Erika Lee shows how xenophobia has shaped America more than the ideals embodied by the Statue of Liberty. An indispensable and sobering guide to the politics of our own time."

—Gary Gerstle, author of *American Crucible: Race and Nation in the Twentieth Century*

"A 'nation of immigrants,' America badly needs a history of xenophobia, and in *America for Americans*, Erika Lee delivers. By distinguishing nativism from xenophobia, she shows how Native Americans and Africans were transformed into foreigners and how that xenophobia fueled racist attacks against immigrants. Neither natural nor inevitable, xenophobia is always promoted by those who benefit from it, and in this courageous book, Lee names the beneficiaries."

—Donna Gabaccia, emerita professor of history, University of Toronto

AMERICA
FOR
AMERICANS

Also by Erika Lee

The Making of Asian America: A History

Angel Island: Immigrant Gateway to America
(with Judy Yung)

*At America's Gates: Chinese Immigration During the
Exclusion Era, 1882–1943*

AMERICA
FOR
AMERICANS

A HISTORY OF XENOPHOBIA
IN THE UNITED STATES

ERIKA LEE

BASIC BOOKS

New York

Basic Books
Hachette Book Group
1290 Avenue of the Americas, New York, NY 10104
www.basicbooks.com

Printed in the United States of America

First Edition: November 2019

Published by Basic Books, an imprint of Perseus Books, LLC, a subsidiary of Hachette Book Group, Inc. The Basic Books name and logo is a trademark of the Hachette Book Group.

The publisher is not responsible for websites (or their content) that are not owned by the publisher.

Print book interior design by Amy Quinn.

The Library of Congress has cataloged the hardcover edition as follows:

Names: Lee, Erika, author.
Title: America for Americans : a history of xenophobia in the United States / Erika Lee.
Description: First edition. | New York : Basic Books, 2019. | Includes bibliographical references and index.
9781541672598 (ebook) | ISBN 9781541672604 (hardcover)
Subjects: LCSH: Xenophobia—United States—History. | Immigrants—United States—History. | Minorities—United States—History. | National characteristics, American—History. | Nationalism—United States—History. | United States—Race relations—History. | United States—Emigration and immigration—History.
Classification: LCC E184.A1 (ebook) | LCC E184.A1 L4135 2019 (print) | DDC 305.800973—dc23
LC record available at https://lccn.loc.gov/2019016168
ISBNs: 978-1-5416-7260-4 (hardcover), 978-1-5416-7259-8 (ebook)

LSC-C

10 9 8 7 6 5 4 3 2

In loving memory of my mother, Fay Huie Lee

CONTENTS

	Introduction	1
Chapter 1:	"Strangers to Our Language and Constitutions"	17
Chapter 2:	"Americans Must Rule America"	39
Chapter 3:	"The Chinese Are No More"	75
Chapter 4:	The "Inferior Races" of Europe	113
Chapter 5:	"Getting Rid of the Mexicans"	147
Chapter 6:	"Military Necessity"	183
Chapter 7:	Xenophobia and Civil Rights	221
Chapter 8:	"Save Our State"	251
Chapter 9:	Islamophobia	289
	Conclusion	321
	Acknowledgments	*339*
	Archives and Collections	*345*
	Notes	*347*
	Index	*397*

INTRODUCTION

It's a beautiful midsummer day in Jersey City, New Jersey, and I am on a boat heading to the Statue of Liberty and the Ellis Island National Museum of Immigration. My shipmates reflect America's diversity. There are South Asian grandmothers wearing saris and baseball caps, and Chinese women holding umbrellas to shield themselves from the hot sun. A white father explains to his squirming children how their great-great-grandfather came to the United States a century ago from Austria. The mood is cheerful. An African American family records a video. "Everyone excited to see the Statue of Liberty?" the mother asks. The kids all yell, "Yes!"

A soothing woman's voice welcomes us on board and begins a brief history lesson. She informs us that we're heading to Ellis Island, the "main gateway into America." Our journey, we're told, "recalls the voyages" of approximately twelve million immigrants who "passed through these waters on their way to Ellis Island—and a new life."

I am trying to share in this patriotic celebration of Ellis Island, a place that serves as a symbol of America's welcome to immigrants, but I keep thinking about another message I've heard that day. The 2016 Republican National Convention has just ended, and the GOP platform, put forward by Donald Trump, was one of pure xenophobia. Ever since launching his presidential campaign, Trump had pledged to beef up

1

border security, ban Muslim immigrants, deport eleven million undocumented people living in the United States, and build a massive wall along the country's southern border with Mexico. And now that he was the official Republican presidential nominee, his extreme views were being repeated by a growing number of voters and politicians.

Riffing on the convention's opening theme—"Make America Safe Again"—speaker after speaker painted a terrifying portrait of America under siege by immigrant criminals, terrorists, and gang members. Former New York City mayor Rudy Giuliani claimed, for example, that Democratic presidential nominee Hillary Clinton supported "open borders" that would admit Syrian refugees posing as "operatives who are terrorists," who were "going to come to Western Europe and here and kill us." US senator Jeff Sessions from Alabama falsely claimed that 350,000 people succeeded in "crossing our borders illegally each year." He also blamed immigrants for taking away jobs from Americans.[1]

Most of the statements made by Trump and other convention speakers were either patently false or grossly misleading, but none of that seemed to matter. The number of undocumented immigrants cited by convention speakers was much too high, and these claims ignored the larger trend of an overall decline in undocumented immigration. Studies also reported that immigrants, including those who were undocumented, were less likely to commit crimes than people born in the United States.[2] Yet the crowd inside the Quicken Loans Arena went crazy for Trump's message. During his seventy-five-minute speech, in which he identified immigration as one of the greatest threats to the United States and promised to restore America's "immigration security," he was repeatedly interrupted by cheers, applause, and chants of "Build the wall!"[3]

I can't forget the angry tones and raised fists as I alight on Ellis Island and walk through the museum exhibits. We learn about earlier chapters in our anti-immigrant history, but we are meant to understand them as just that: history that is over and done with. By the time visitors get to the museum gift shop, we are encouraged to banish this ugly past from our minds and celebrate our immigrant roots instead. In true American fashion, we do this by buying something. *Team Italy* or *Team Poland* T-shirts, snow globes of the Statue of Liberty or the Leaning Tower of Pisa. The Ellis Café, however, takes different inspiration, offering menu items like the All-American Angus Cheeseburger and the Freedom Burger. Between the gift shop and the café, it seems that we can buy both immigrant and all-American identities that happily coexist. But I know that it is not that simple.

I am struggling to figure out how these two Americas fit together.

There is the United States that is known as a nation of immigrants. Three-fifths of all the world's immigrants settled in the United States from the beginning of the nineteenth century to the beginning of the twentieth; over the course of the twentieth century, the United States remained the world's largest immigrant-receiving country, and into the start of the twenty-first century, it still admitted more immigrants than any other country—over a million per year. More than eighty million have arrived in the last two hundred years alone. The United States has also historically led the world in resettling refugees, bringing in three million since 1980. Americans celebrate this United States by referring to their "nation of immigrants," a country that values immigrants and offers a haven for refugees. Even as this story has obscured a violent history of invasion, native dispossession, and slavery, defining the United States as a nation of immigrants continues to be a popular way of reaffirming America's acceptance of racial and ethnic diversity. This is the America that my grandparents—immigrants from China—knew and loved. They braved long transpacific journeys and worked long hours as domestic servants, in Chinese restaurants and in laundries, so that their children and grandchildren could have a chance to claim the promised American dream.[4]

But the United States is also a nation of xenophobia. Even as it has welcomed millions from around the world, it has also deported more immigrants than any other nation—over fifty-five million since 1882.[5] Americans have been wary of almost every group of foreigners that has come to the United States: German immigrants in the eighteenth century; Irish and Chinese in the nineteenth century; Italians, Jews, Japanese, and Mexicans in the twentieth century; and Muslims today. Americans have labeled immigrants threatening because they were poor,

practiced a different faith, were nonwhite. They have argued that immigrants were too numerous, were not assimilating, were taking jobs away
from deserving Americans, were bringing crime and disease into the
country, had dangerous political ideals, were un-American, or even hated
America. The United States has passed discriminatory immigration laws
and detained, incarcerated, and expelled immigrants. It has exploited and
segregated the foreign-born, allowing them to be *in* America but not accepted as fully American.

This is also the America that my grandparents knew well. They
managed to enter the country when the Chinese Exclusion Act (which
was enacted in 1882 and lasted until 1943) barred most Chinese from
the United States. One of my grandfathers came in with false papers and
was detained in the prisonlike barracks of the Angel Island immigration
station in San Francisco. Today, some people would call him an "undocumented immigrant" who courageously risked all to come to the United
States despite unfair immigration laws; others would term him an "illegal
alien" who broke the law, challenged our border security, and thus deserved detention or worse. The exclusion laws also forced many families
to live apart from each other, including my grandmother's family, who
were separated for three generations.

Our story is not unique. Immigrant families remain separated from
each other by harsh laws, and an estimated eleven million immigrants,
like my grandfather, have either no documentation or the wrong kind of
documentation. They live their lives in the shadows, ever fearful of sudden deportation.

The books that line my shelves offer many explanations for why we
have targeted various immigrant groups in the past. Historians, sociologists, political scientists, and journalists explain that xenophobia rises
and falls along with economic, political, and social crises; war; and rapid
demographic change. In particular, they say, high immigration combined
with an economic downturn fuels xenophobia. War exacerbates hostility.
Nearly all of these books focus on a specific immigrant group and the corresponding anti-immigrant campaign—the anti-Catholic movement, the
efforts to exclude Chinese, the mass deportation of Mexicans, post-9/11

Islamophobia. In reading about one episode, it's difficult to draw connections to other anti-immigrant campaigns that preceded or followed it, or even between those that were happening at the same time. Nor are there many studies that allow us to understand these xenophobic movements in relation to each other or to Native American and African American history.[6] My initial reading leaves me with an impression that xenophobic episodes flared up at specific times in specific places and then died down.

Generally speaking, xenophobia is also treated as an exception to America's immigration tradition. Anti-immigrant campaigns were unfortunate episodes promoted by paranoid extremists in an otherwise welcoming nation, we're told. There is a consensus that xenophobia triumphed in the 1920s, when the United States legalized a discriminatory immigration quota system that favored immigrants from northern and western Europe over all other groups, a policy that nearly closed the door on immigration for over forty years. Yet with the civil rights movement, many scholars have explained, xenophobia waned. When it has resurfaced in the last fifty years, it has been a momentary blip or an aberration in America's inevitable march toward immigrant inclusion and equality.[7]

Because I was educated within this tradition, my initial reaction to Donald Trump's positions on immigration varied from constant astonishment and dark humor to righteous anger and helplessness. I, like many others, did not really take him seriously. I believed that in post-Obama America, his campaign would be another one of those aberrations in America's history, a cautionary tale of how Americans needed to remain vigilant against injustice, but nothing that would truly resurrect the darkest chapters of American history. I did not think xenophobia could win in 2016.

I was wrong. I did not fully understand how central xenophobia has been to the making of the United States, and how effective it has been in American politics. I failed to recognize both its power and resilience. I was unprepared for this America.

This stark realization drove me to reexamine the long history of xenophobia in the United States. My journey took me to archives from coast to coast to study sources dating from the colonial era to today. I've examined immigrant songs and government documents, cartoons and hate crime statistics, newspaper articles, speeches, and tweets. Early in my research, I stumbled upon President Theodore Roosevelt's 1916 "America for Americans" speech in which he exhorted immigrants to fully assimilate, abandon any loyalty to former homelands, and reject hyphenated identities. They were to pledge their allegiance to a "nationalized and unified America," a "straight Americanism" that was "unconditioned and unqualified," and an "America for Americans." A more extreme version of this speech was promoted in a 1920s pamphlet published by the Knights of the Ku Klux Klan (KKK). Claiming to speak for "all true Americans," the Klan condemned the "flood of foreigners" who took advantage of the United States, pushed her "native born" aside, and retained allegiance to foreign flags. This pamphlet was also titled "America for Americans"; its red, white, and blue cover featured a white-robed-and-hooded Klansman brandishing an enormous American flag astride a similarly styled horse. Finally, in 1925, best-selling author and eugenicist Madison Grant used the now familiar white nationalist rallying cry "America for Americans" to report that native white Americans were being "submerged" by an "influx of foreigners." He warned that strict immigration restriction, even the suspension of *all* immigration, might soon be necessary. The Roosevelt speech, the

Jewish Federation Council of Greater Los Angeles' Community Relations Committee Collection, Special Collections and Archives, Oviatt Library, California State University, Northridge.

Klan pamphlet, and the Grant article are all documents from an era that historians have identified as a high point of xenophobia, but their messages resound across the centuries: immigrants are a threat to the United States; white Americans are the only "true Americans"; and vigilance and regulation, through the KKK's campaign of racial violence, Grant's immigration restriction, or Teddy Roosevelt's coercive "Americanism," are the only ways to protect an "America for Americans."[8]

History shows that xenophobia has been a constant and defining feature of American life. It is deeply embedded in our society, economy, and politics. It thrives best in certain contexts, such as periods of rapid economic and demographic change, but it has also been actively promoted by special interests in the pursuit of political power. It has influenced elections and dictated policies. It has shaped American foreign relations and justified American imperialism. It has played a central role in America's changing definitions of race, citizenship, and what it means to be "American." It has endured because it has been an indelible part of American racism, white supremacy, and nationalism, and because it has been supported by American capitalism and democracy.

Xenophobia has been neither an aberration nor a contradiction to the United States' history of immigration. Rather, it has existed alongside and constrained America's immigration tradition, determining just who can enter our so-called nation of immigrants and who cannot. Even as Americans have realized that the threats allegedly posed by immigrants were, in hindsight, unjustified, they have allowed xenophobia to become an American tradition.

COMING FROM THE Greek words *xenos*, which translates into "stranger," and *phobos*, which means either "fear" or "flight," *xenophobia* literally means fear and hatred of foreigners. But this literal translation obscures its broader meaning and impact. To fully understand the significance xenophobia has had on American life, it is important to recognize what it is, who it targets and why, what it does, and why it has endured.

There is no single or uniformly agreed-upon definition of xenophobia in academia, human rights discourses, or international law.[9] And although xenophobia is often loosely characterized as individual prejudice, animosity, or bias toward foreigners, it is in fact much more. It is an ideology: a set of beliefs and ideas based on the premise that foreigners are threats to the nation and its people. It promotes an irrational fear and hatred of immigrants and demonizes foreigners (and, crucially, people considered to be "foreign"). It defines immigration as a crisis, likening the movement of peoples to an invasion of hostile forces requiring a military-like response. It is born from a narrow and exclusive definition of who is American—and who is not. It is easily weaponized during times of change and anxiety, but it exists and flourishes during times of peace *and* war, economic prosperity *and* depression, low *and* high immigration, and racial struggle *and* racial progress.

Native Americans and African Americans were the country's first "others," and xenophobia was forged by America's enslavement of Africans, the seizure of native land and resources, the removal or elimination of indigenous peoples, and the violence and denial of equal rights that accompanied both slavery and settler colonialism. How immigrants have fit into this racial environment of settlers, slaves, and indigenous peoples has shaped Americans' attitudes toward them from the colonial era to the present. Describing certain immigrant groups as *savages* or as *violent*—two terms used to dehumanize Native Americans and African Americans, for example—was a way of singling out these arrivals as similarly racially inferior and therefore deserving of unequal treatment.[10]

Yet certain types of foreignness have always been considered more threatening than others. Non-Protestant religions—namely Judaism, Catholicism, and Islam—have been seen as foreign religions and their practitioners scripted as foreigners. Anti-Catholicism, anti-Semitism, and Islamophobia have focused not only on theological debates over faith but also on the alleged foreign influence of these religions in the United States—and fears that each group was connected to a foreign entity or power (global Jewry, the Vatican, or radical Islamic clerics abroad) that was controlling adherents in the United States and interfering with US sovereignty.

Gender and sexuality have also impacted who is targeted by xenophobia. Poor immigrant women have been labeled economic threats on the assumption that they were more likely to become dependent on the state, and immigration laws that allow for the exclusion of immigrants "likely to become a public charge" have overwhelmingly been applied to women and children. Women who were charged with immoral behavior such as premarital sex were almost always excluded, while men were never even questioned about or judged by their sexual histories before, during, or outside of marriage. Immigrants who were or were perceived to be homosexual, or who practiced what was considered to be non-normative sexual behavior or expression, have also been treated as threats to America and its people.[11]

As bias based on gender, class, religion, and sexual orientation have intersected with racism, it has created particularly virulent forms of xenophobia. In the nineteenth century, all Chinese women were believed to be prostitutes who threatened Americans with disease and interracial sex. In the next century, poor Mexican women were vilified for having too many so-called anchor babies and taxing welfare agencies. And today, hijab-wearing Muslim immigrant women are condemned for their alleged lack of assimilation and their religiosity.

Race is the single most important factor in determining which foreigners are targeted for xenophobic discrimination and which ones are not. This is because xenophobia is a form of racism. It defines certain groups as racial and religious others who are inherently inferior or dangerous—or both—and demonizes them as a group based on these presumptions. Xenophobia has also been an inextricable part of race making in America; it has shaped how Americans classify people by race and rank them in America's racial hierarchy. Lastly, xenophobia has become an institutionalized form of racial discrimination and racial domination.[12]

There are many examples of how xenophobia as racism has worked in American history. One of the most important is from the early twentieth century when xenophobes turned to eugenics and "science" to classify humans into distinct races and to "prove" the inherent superiority of white northern and western Europeans. They then used that science to lobby for immigration restrictions based on race. Northern and western Europeans were favored above all other groups through an immigration quota system that was implemented in the 1920s and remained in place until 1965.

Not all efforts to limit or regulate immigration are xenophobic or racist. But many have been primarily driven by racism and an irrational fear and hatred of foreigners rather than by rational economic, political, or foreign policy considerations. They demonize immigrants as the "problems" while ignoring larger global factors (such as US policies and intervention) that drive migration, including undocumented migration. As a result, many legitimate immigration debates have been turned into full-blown immigration panics, and lawmakers have targeted specific populations instead of implementing nondiscriminatory solutions. Moreover, many contemporary policies have been built on the foundation of earlier xenophobic laws. The US government's current border security efforts, for example, have been rooted in a century-long history of defining all Mexican immigrants as "illegals" or as dangerous criminals. A direct line can be drawn from this history to current racial profiling practices and "show me your papers" laws that empower local officials to ask (mostly Mexican-appearing) individuals about their immigration status during lawful stops or arrests far into the country's interior. Xenophobia also impacts how even neutral policies can be enforced in discriminatory ways. In the early twentieth century, immigration officials on Ellis Island used the law barring immigrants who were "likely to become public charges" as an effective means of denying entry to Jewish immigrants. Across the country on Angel Island, officials weaponized it to bar South Asians.[13]

As a form of racial discrimination, xenophobia has not distinguished between immigrants who have entered with authorization and those who have not, or between immigrants and US citizens. Instead, it has ensnared entire populations, regardless of immigration or citizenship status, and the strain and violence of xenophobia has had generational consequences.[14] Take, for example, the 1882 Chinese Exclusion Act, initially passed as a temporary measure to bar Chinese laborers; it made it harder for all Chinese, including American citizens of Chinese descent, to enter and reenter the country for generations, until the law was repealed in 1943. Or consider the mass deportation of Mexicans during the Great Depression. Initially designed to target those in the country without authorization, the xenophobic campaign ultimately involved the removal of legal residents and US-born Mexican American citizens. Such episodes continued: during World War II, two-thirds of the Japanese Americans who were forced out of their homes and into incarceration camps were US citizens. And today, many of the people impacted by the United States' growing deportation regime are US citizens in mixed-status families, typically undocumented immigrant parents and their citizen children.

Xenophobia is not only about immigration; it is about who has the power to define what it means to be American, who gets to enjoy the privileges of American citizenship, and who does not. The nation's founding documents outlined the basic rights to be bestowed on Americans (equality; the fundamental rights to life, liberty, and the pursuit of happiness; and the right of the people to govern themselves democratically). But the question of who actually counts as an American has been a source of constant debate. Xenophobia has been instrumental in creating the terms of permission.[15] Immigrants who were deemed capable and worthy of American citizenship were admitted and allowed to become naturalized citizens; those who were not were increasingly restricted, excluded, barred from naturalized citizenship, or expelled. Race has always been the determining factor in distinguishing "good" immigrants and future Americans from "bad" ones.

Xenophobia has also driven *nativism*, the naming of white Anglo-Saxon Protestant settlers and their descendants as "natives" to the United States and the granting of special privileges and protections to them. Although nativism is often used interchangeably with *xenophobia* as a shorthand for antiforeign sentiment, it is related but distinct. Its roots are in the early and mid-nineteenth century when white Protestant settlers began using and claiming the term *native American* for themselves. They sought to assert dominance over new immigrants from Europe—especially Catholic Europe—who were, through their numbers and political participation, changing the balance of power in the United States. As so-called native Americans, white Protestants believed they should be recognized as "true" Americans who alone knew what was best for the country. They also insisted that they deserved preferential treatment and rights—such as the ability to hold public office—while claiming that foreigners did not. A deep-rooted fear of displacement drove these early expressions of nativism (and white supremacy) and continues to drive them today.[16]

Asserting native American status was clearly about immigration, but it was also about real Native Americans, a crucial fact that has long been ignored by writers and scholars. The nineteenth century was not just being changed through immigration; it was also being transformed by continuing territorial expansion, Native American wars, and the forced removal of Native Americans from their homelands. When white Americans claimed native status, they were not claiming indigenous roots. What they were asserting was a native claim to the land, in order to legitimize their territorial gains and the continuing campaigns against Native Americans. It was used to justify both past and ongoing white settlement (and the attendant broken treaties and racial terror that made this possible). These were simultaneously acts of physical, legal, political, and rhetorical dispossession that worked hand in hand with xenophobia, slavery, and white supremacy to create a distinct and racist American national identity. Into the twentieth and twenty-first centuries, nativism continued to drive ongoing inequality and discrimination against Native Americans and others while advocating for "America First" policies that opposed US involvement in both world wars, supported immigration restriction, and fueled the white nationalism that helped elect Donald Trump to the presidency in 2016.[17]

ACROSS THE CENTURIES, xenophobia has endured in the United States. Generations of anti-immigrant leaders, politicians, and citizens have adapted xenophobia to identify new threats and enact new solutions to the "problem" of immigration. Just a few decades after Irish Catholics had been demonized as the greatest threat to America, for example, they were grudgingly accepted as "good immigrants" and even "good Americans" as the nation began to grapple with the arrival of new immigrant threats from China and southern and eastern Europe. America's history of xenophobia has also helped it persist across the centuries. Past campaigns have provided powerful images, discourses, and legal precedents that have been constantly adapted to suit new needs and contexts. In this way, xenophobia has become normalized and has succeeded through repetition, expanding on an established anti-immigrant playbook to mo-bilize public opinion and policy against the latest immigrant threats.[18] During and after the successful exclusion of Chinese immigrants, for in-stance, groups considered to be "just like" the Chinese (such as Japanese, Koreans, South Asians, and Filipinos) were similarly condemned to im-migration restriction and exclusion. The characterization of all Mexican immigrants and Mexican Americans as "illegal aliens" or foreigners in their own land in the early twentieth century has also helped justify mass deportation drives targeting them in the twenty-first.

Xenophobia has even persevered alongside civil rights. After the civil rights movement delegitimized explicit racism, xenophobes learned to rely on color-blind racism to achieve their anti-immigrant agendas. In-stead of justifying immigration policies that explicitly singled out im-migrants on the basis of their religion or race, for example, xenophobes have used code words like *national security* or *law and order* as the basis for discriminatory treatment. Through this form of *color-blind xenophobia*, anti-immigrant campaigns still disproportionately impact nonwhite im-migrants and those perceived to be nonwhite, but do so under the guise of nondiscrimination.[19]

Xenophobia has also endured because it has helped some of the country's most important institutions to function and thrive: American capitalism, democracy, and foreign relations.

Xenophobia is profitable. The US economy has flourished by exploit-ing workers, especially those whom American society has already defined as dangerous, "illegal," and unworthy of protection or equal rights. These workers become a permanent class of deportable immigrants who remain socially marginal and economically exploitable even as they continue to serve American economic interests. At the same time that xenophobia has regulated the movement of certain immigrants, US capitalism has ensured that cash and goods continue to flow freely across borders.[20]

Xenophobia also translates into big business. As the United States has arrested, detained, and deported growing numbers of immigrants since the late twentieth century—and relied on privately run immigrant detention centers to do so—many American corporations have profited handsomely. Corrections Corporation of America (CCA) is a prime example. CCA won its first government contract in 1984 to run an immigrant detention center in Houston. Its annual revenue rose from $50 million in the early 1990s to $462 million in 1997. By 2008, 13 percent of its $1.5 billion annual revenue came directly from immigration enforcement contracts with the federal government. In 2016, that share was 28 percent.[21]

And xenophobia sells. Demonizing immigrants has sold books and attracted TV viewers, radio listeners, and online visitors. In the 1840s, lurid anti-Catholic tales of sex and depravity inside convents turned many books into best sellers. In the 1880s, San Francisco's *Wasp* magazine beat out all of its competitors with its richly illustrated anti-Chinese diatribes. In the 1920s, Madison Grant's *The Passing of the Great Race* became a best seller and helped justify further immigration restrictions. Patrick Buchanan's books blaming immigration for the "decline" of the United States and the West have continued to sell xenophobia in the twenty-first century.

Xenophobia and American capitalism work together in one more way. Xenophobia has helped siphon working-class resentment away from corporate greed and economic inequality and direct it toward immigrants. Scapegoating foreigners has also helped undermine interracial labor movements that challenge the worst corporate abuses. At the same time, promoting and celebrating the "good immigrant"—that is, the "capitalist immigrant" who embodies the American work ethic—has sustained public confidence in a meritocratic economy. Immigrant entrepreneurs and empire builders from Scottish immigrant Andrew Carnegie to the Ukrainian-born WhatsApp founder Jan Koum have been lionized as capitalism's heroes.[22]

Just as xenophobia has helped American capitalism thrive, so has it been part of American democracy. As part of the nation's founding, xenophobia worked alongside slavery and settler colonialism to limit who could become American citizens. The Declaration of Independence proclaimed that "all men are created equal," but it was inequality rather than equality that characterized the United States' actual laws. Under the 1790

Naturalization Act, for example, only "free white persons" were allowed to become naturalized citizens, excluding Native Americans, African Americans, and nonwhite immigrants and refugees who would come in later centuries. In this way, American citizenship and the power to vote was tied to whiteness.

Xenophobia has also driven the democratic process. Across the centuries, Americans of all backgrounds have supported and fully participated in *political xenophobia*, the demonization of immigrants to secure votes, elect anti-immigrant lawmakers, make anti-immigrant policy, and gain political power. In turn, xenophobia has also been a major function of American state building. It has increased budgets for certain government agencies and helped expand the reach and power of democratically elected and controlled governments.[23]

Xenophobia has also been part of this country's foreign relations, through US imperialism and international relations. The United States built its empire of territory, trade, and power by disparaging foreign countries and their peoples as racially inferior, backward, and conquerable. Viewing Mexico, for example, or Hawai'i, or Puerto Rico, or the Philippines in these ways justified not only war and territorial expansion but also unequal status for these imperial subjects within the United States. Meanwhile, US intervention abroad has created instability and forced people from their homes. Some of these refugees have made it to the United States only to become targets of xenophobes who fail to understand America's role in causing global migration.[24]

Our treatment of specific immigrants in the United States has also been determined by our nation's relationships with foreign countries. This pattern has repeated itself time and time again, in the anti-German hysteria that accompanied US involvement in World War I, the incarceration of Japanese Americans during World War II, and the rise of Islamophobia during the war on terror. American xenophobia has been one of our exports, too. In the early twentieth century, American labor leaders traveled to Canada to help establish branches of anti-Asian organizations already active in the United States and incite anti-Asian riots in Vancouver in 1907. Eugenicist Harry H. Laughlin, whose congressional testimony helped shape the United States' national origins quota system during the 1920s, later teamed up with Cuban colleagues to advance similar immigration policies in Latin America in the 1930s.[25]

Over the course of the twentieth and twenty-first centuries, the US government has sought (and pressured) cooperation from other countries to achieve its own immigration priorities. Beginning in the early twentieth century, American officials negotiated with both Canada and Mexico to police the northern and southern borders and prevent the entry of undocumented Chinese immigrants. During the next century, the United States helped shape (and fund) the Southern Border Program, which pressured various Central American governments, as well as the government of Mexico, to regulate migration from Central America into Mexico and stop migrants from reaching the US-Mexico border. These measures have included increased border patrols and detention and deportation procedures that, according to critics, violated migrants' human rights.[26]

By the twenty-first century, American xenophobia had, in effect, expanded the defense of "America for Americans" far beyond the actual borders of the United States.

IT TURNS STORMY as I leave Ellis Island. I look out the rain-splattered windows of the tour boat and see clouds close in on the Statue of Liberty. The weather matches my mood. The historical narration celebrating the United States as a nation of immigrants is still playing through the ship's speakers, and as it does, it glosses over, yet again, our long history of xenophobia. This history is not well known. It has been forgotten and erased, or taught to us as a series of mistakes. I am becoming convinced that this historical amnesia has left Americans ill-equipped to make sense of xenophobia today. Confronting the truth of this history is not enough to defeat xenophobia. But it is a start.

ONE

"STRANGERS TO OUR LANGUAGE AND CONSTITUTIONS"

Benjamin Franklin was alarmed. It was 1755, and huge numbers of "swarthy" foreigners were flooding the colonies. They threatened to overwhelm the British with their numbers, strange ways, and "Disagreeableness and dissonant Manners," he claimed. Instead of assimilating, they were "herding together [and] establish[ing] their languages and manners to the exclusion of ours." Franklin in fact doubted whether the new arrivals were even capable of assimilating. They could "never adopt our Language or Customs, any more than they can acquire our Complexion," he decided.[1]

He did not mind small numbers of these foreigners coming into the country. After all, they had a few virtues. They worked hard. They were frugal. And, he conceded, they contributed "greatly to the improvement of a Country." However, the best and brightest of their group were not coming to America. According to Franklin, the ones who did travel across the ocean were "the most ignorant stupid . . . of their own nation." They were also a political risk. They were not "used to Liberty" and thus did not know how to use it, he explained. They were completely different from the English settlers who founded the colonies.[2]

Franklin argued that if future immigration was not checked, the very well-being of the colonies was at stake. The foreigners would soon "outnumber us." The English would "not be able to preserve our language, and even our government will become precarious," he predicted. The end of English "laws, manners, liberties, and religion" in the colonies would soon follow. Something must be done, he urged. Franklin suggested that the colonies exclude "all blacks and tawneys," and instead increase "the lovely white," whom he defined as English. "Why should *Pennsylvania*, founded by the *English*, become a colony of *Aliens*?" he asked. German immigration, he passionately concluded, was a danger that must be checked.[3]

Germans were not the only foreign "outsiders" in colonial America. Many colonies opposed the migration of foreign convicts and paupers, and so-called poor laws were regularly used to expel individuals from other countries, colonies, and even towns. Catholics were largely prevented from landing in some colonies, and Jews also faced discrimination in many places. But it is Franklin's—and his colony's—antipathy toward German immigrants that marks an important starting point in America's long history of xenophobia.[4]

Derided as "strangers to our laws and constitutions" by Pennsylvania governor William Keith, German immigrants became the subject of much debate and fear in the British colonies. Some even viewed them as "constitutionally" (i.e., physically and biologically) alien to the English. The arguments used against Germans established a template of anti-immigrant attitudes, prejudice, and rhetoric that would be repeated and refashioned for later immigrant groups. These would harden into a core ideology of xenophobia that would endure across the centuries: there were too many foreigners; they were too strange and different; they were not assimilating; they threatened peace and security. Pennsylvania's anxiety about German immigration also resulted in some of the first immigration regulations enacted in the colonies, policies that would be expanded for other immigrants in later years.

The story of German immigrants in Pennsylvania also highlights the complexity of xenophobia as well as the different contexts in which it flourishes. This was not just a story of fear and hatred of immigrants; it was also a story of slavery, dispossession of native peoples and their sovereignty, and the white supremacy on which the United States was founded. Germans came, many by invitation, as part of three major movements of people transforming the Americas in the seventeenth and eighteenth centuries: the voluntary migration of white settlers participating in European colonial expansion, the forced migration of enslaved Africans, and the coerced movement of native peoples off their lands by white settlers. Pennsylvania played an important role in all three movements.

Bordering the Atlantic Seaboard in the east and Native American lands in the west, Pennsylvania was a "middle" colony in many ways. Though English, Pennsylvania was linguistically and culturally diverse. It was home to the largest migration of non-English foreigners in all the British colonies. It had a long-established history of slavery and Black Codes that regulated the lives and freedom of slaves. And it was the site of fast-paced white settler westward expansion, growing anti–Native American violence, and all-out war involving Pennsylvanians, the British, the French, and Native Americans.

Set against this backdrop, Pennsylvania lawmakers vilified Germans as "strangers" and targeted them for special scrutiny. But Germans provided much needed labor and bodies to settle and develop the colony. Moreover, they were neither slave nor Native American, but white. And in the lead-up to both the Seven Years' War and the American Revolution, the line between whites and African Americans and whites and Native Americans became increasingly important. Pennsylvania embraced Germans as white settlers, a category that carried growing privilege and power in colonial America. European immigration was thus only loosely regulated, and Germans were granted almost automatic naturalization rights, which also came with the power to vote.

Xenophobia became an American tradition. But this fear had limited impact in a colonial society that depended on white settlers to build and expand what would become the United States.

CAPTAIN JOSEPH WASEY'S aptly named ship *America* sailed into Philadelphia on August 20, 1683. On board were several German men and families, including Francis Daniel Pastorius, the leader of a colony of

German Mennonites searching for religious freedom in America. They had been at sea since May 4. Thirteen more Mennonite families reached Philadelphia in early October. By the end of the month, Pastorius had founded Germantown, where forty-two people settled in twelve homes. Most were weavers. Others were pig farmers and tradesmen.[5]

These early German settlers joined nearly one million people who migrated to the lands that would become the United States before 1787. They were a diverse group. Six hundred thousand were Europeans, mostly from England. The rest came from German-speaking lands, Northern Ireland, Scotland, the Netherlands, France, and Spain. Three hundred thousand African slaves arrived in the British colonies in chains. Germans made up the colonies' largest non-British white community. They outnumbered the English and were second only to the Scots. Indeed, in British America, the word *foreigner* almost certainly meant "German." And Pennsylvania, home to nearly one hundred thousand ethnically German residents before the Revolutionary War, was their main area of settlement.[6]

They came from the Rhenish Palatinate of what is now southwestern Germany, where crop failures and social and religious conflict had caused economic ruin for decades. Villages emptied out as more and more people sought their fortunes abroad. Most went east to Hungary, Romania, and Russia, but a growing number took the much longer journey to North America. In the early 1700s, another group of Mennonites followed Pastorius and settled in Newburgh, New York.[7]

Letters and reports sent back home by these "newlanders" were filled with endless praise. Pennsylvania was "like an earthly paradise," one wrote. There was abundant land, and the average farm was 125 acres, about six times the size of what the typical farmer in southwestern Germany held. The soil yielded three times as much wheat per acre as in Germany. Skilled laborers were in demand and were paid well. The woods, valleys, and rivers were rich with wildlife, and food was inexpensive. There were almost no taxes. There was no mandatory military service. But there was freedom. "One could live there as a good Christian in solitude, as one pleased," one settler told his family. Read over and over and passed along to relatives, neighbors, and friends, these letters helped spark a chain migration. In 1725, Charles Hector wrote in his diary of the emigration fever that took hold of his hometown of Berleburg, Wittgenstein. The letters that one young tailor sent inspired more than one hundred people to follow him abroad. First his mother, a widow, went. Then his mother-in-law. Other families soon followed. Over the course of the eighteenth century, even more fled.[8]

This was not just a one-sided migration; recruiters in Pennsylvania directly encouraged and facilitated migration with promises of free land, economic opportunity, religious toleration, and political liberty. Pennsylvania, like other British colonies, depended on large numbers of European settlers to expand England's presence and power. A steadily growing white population increased land values and provided much needed labor and capital, which in turn helped fuel territorial expansion and economic development. England alone could not supply the vast numbers of settlers needed, and so English authorities began to promote the American colonies as both a refuge and a land of opportunity for all of Europe's oppressed and downtrodden. As a largely Protestant population that could serve as a "security measure" against an expanding Catholic France, Germans were heavily recruited by both colonial officials and ship masters.[9]

William Penn, founder of the province of Pennsylvania, actively encouraged settlement among Quakers and non-Quakers from throughout the British Isles and beyond. He promised equal rights and opportunities to all as part of his "holy experiment." He recruited settlers through pamphlets and promotional writings and through agents posted in London, Dublin, Edinburgh, and Rotterdam. He enthusiastically described nature's great bounty of "lovely Flowers," plentiful fruit, and game in what he called "Penn's Wood." In 1677, he visited Germany to officially establish the Frankfurt Emigration Society, which organized the departure of fifty ships bound for Pennsylvania between 1682 and 1684. Penn was not alone. Many American landlords and speculators used their transatlantic networks to recruit potential emigrants. Enterprising merchants on both sides of the Atlantic then turned the business of transporting passengers into profitable ventures.[10]

Combining slave trade shipping technology with ethnic-based recruitment, the transatlantic migration business became established, profitable, and commonplace by the 1730s. These technological and entrepreneurial innovations would be important not only for the establishment and growth of German immigration during the colonial era but also for the mass migrations from Europe during the nineteenth and twentieth centuries. Tasked with filling the ships' holds with paying passengers, recruiters sold prospective migrants on the idea and promise of America.[11]

The typical German immigrant was a husband and father who came to Pennsylvania with his wife and two or three children. He was a farmer, or a tradesman—a shoemaker, tailor, cooper, carpenter, or blacksmith. He was typically Protestant (Lutheran or Reformed), but early settlers also included a minority of Catholics, Quakers, Mennonites, and Moravians. Some families paid their own way. Others agreed to become indentured servants in America in exchange for passage fare (which often exceeded a year's income) before leaving home. About half of all Europeans who settled in colonial America came indentured, and Philadelphia was home to the largest and most active servant market. Regardless of how they arrived, early German immigrants benefited from good timing. They were able to acquire large tracts of land (often a hundred or more acres) and were relatively prosperous within two decades of settlement. Pennsylvania was indeed, for many Germans, the "best poor man's country."[12] First, though, they had to survive the journey.

"In the month of May 1750 I left my birthplace Enzweihingen in the district of Vahingen," wrote Gottlieb Mittelberger, a schoolmaster and organist destined for Philadelphia. Including delays, inspections, and travel time, it took Mittelberger six months to travel from Enzweihingen to Philadelphia. First was a seven-week journey to Rotterdam. After waiting for six weeks, he then headed to the English port of Cowes. There, Mittelberger joined five hundred other passengers "packed in almost like herring" onboard the *Osgood* for the ten-week journey to Philadelphia.

The ship quickly became a cesspool of human misery. As Mittelberger recorded in his diary, the journey was plagued with poor food ("so dirty as to be hardly palatable at all") and filthy water ("black, thick with dirt, and full of worms"), and that was when such luxuries were available at all. Crowded and unsanitary conditions all resulted in "vomiting, various kinds of sea sickness, fever, dysentery, headaches, heat, constipation, boils, scurvy, cancer, mouth rot, and similar inflictions." The "smells, fumes, [and] horrors" on board were inescapable. Some days there was frost. Other days there was stifling heat. Every day was accompanied by fear, misery, and an abundance of lice (so much so that "they have to be scraped off the bodies"). During calm days at sea, the conditions were barely tolerable, Mittelberger explained. But during stormy weather "all this misery reaches its climax." Even healthy and optimistic passengers began to "curse the other, or himself and the day of his birth." The six-month journey involved "such hardships that it is really impossible for any description to do justice to them," Mittelberger wrote with resignation.

Once in Pennsylvania, Mittelberger expected the worst of his travails to be over. Instead, he was shocked by the misery that he and his fellow Germans encountered in the colony. Many arrived extremely ill. Some families were so impoverished that parents were forced to send their children into servitude, selling their children "like so many head of cattle." The newlanders, recruiters, and ship agents, Mittelberger believed, had all misled Germans with their unrealistic promises. He published an account of his four-year sojourn in America in 1756 in an attempt to set the record straight. But *Journey to Pennsylvania*—a "description of the country in its present condition, but also a detailed account of the sad and unfortunate circumstances of most of the Germans who have moved to that country or are about to do so"—was in many ways too late. Mass migration from Europe was increasing.[13]

With transatlantic migration profitable on both sides of the ocean, non-English immigration multiplied throughout the eighteenth century. In 1717, three ships carrying 363 German passengers arrived in Philadelphia. Between 1727 and 1740, eighty more ships brought Germans to Philadelphia, New York, Baltimore, and Charleston, South Carolina. Peak German immigration to colonial America was in the mid-1750s, when 113 shiploads of Germans sailed into Philadelphia between 1749 and 1754. During that decade, they made up 35 percent of all immigrants arriving in the colonies. In total, an estimated 85,000 Germans settled in the British colonies. Over 86 percent entered through Philadelphia.[14]

BY THE 1710s, Pennsylvania authorities began to question whether so much immigration was good for the colony. Admittedly, immigrants brought much needed labor and prosperity to Pennsylvania, but some leaders were concerned that so many non-English foreigners were dangerous. Germans were especially considered problematic. They caused land disputes and increased tensions with Native Americans, it was said. They kept to themselves, clinging to their foreign tongues and strange ways. Their loyalty to the British Crown was suspect. Prominent colonial leaders expressed these anxieties in both public and private.

In 1717, James Logan, an elite businessman and friend of the powerful Penn family, wrote with concern about the increased "Number of these Strangers" and "their Swarms." He claimed that "Our Countrey [sic] People are inflamed against" the Germans and suggested that the colony be "resolved to receive no more of them." Governor William Keith publicly sounded the alarm in the fall of 1717 when he warned that "great numbers of fforeigners [sic] from Germany, strangers to our Language & Constitutions," had arrived in the colony. They came without any documentation about who they were and "whence they came." They brought crime and poverty. But most importantly, their mere foreignness—their non-Englishness—made them suspect. Were they "Enemys" [sic] or friends (i.e., loyal to the Crown)? Governor Keith called on the Provincial Assembly to limit immigration to ensure "Publick [sic] Welfare" and for the good of "your own People." Do not "lose any Time in securing yourselves, and all the People of this colony," he instructed.[15]

Public outcry gradually grew louder over the years. In 1727, Governor Patrick Gordon informed the provincial council that four hundred German immigrants had recently arrived in Philadelphia and that several more ships were soon expected. That fall, five ships from Rotterdam brought 1,300 people to Philadelphia in a single month. Rumors spread that 5,000 to 6,000 more would be arriving the next year. Public reaction was swift and strong. Gordon called on the government to act. The Germans, "strangers daily pour[ing] in," he reported, were transporting themselves "without any leave obtained from the Crown of Great Britain." He warned that the "vast number of armed fforeigners [*sic*] crowding in upon us" would soon turn the "English Plantation" that was Pennsylvania into "a Colony of Aliens." He urged the British Parliament to monitor the newcomers.[16]

Other politicians added their own condemnations. Philadelphia mayor Isaac Norris charged that the Germans "seem[ed] to be the very scum of mankind." He worried that their "Disproportionate increase" was damaging the colony's prospects. Germans' alleged inability to assimilate to English customs and allegiances continued to be a main topic of concern. Governor Gordon insisted that the Germans were "ignorant of our Language & Laws." They settled "in a body together," making, as it were, "a distinct people from his Majesties Subjects." Benjamin Franklin believed that the "Palatine Boors" were so different from the English that they even had different standards of beauty. "The German Women are generally so disagreeable to an English Eye," Franklin bluntly explained, "that it wou'd require great Portions [money] to induce Englishmen to marry them. Nor would the German Ideas of Beauty generally agree with our Women."[17]

Others worried that if the Germans could not become English, they might become "savages" in the backcountry, where the gulf between Native Americans and Europeans was not always as wide or as fixed as many provincial elites would have liked. In fact, authorities often viewed Native Americans and poor whites as similarly uncontrollable threats to the social order. Pennsylvania officials often feared that the "lower sort" of new European immigrants might form alliances with Native Americans. Or they might even assimilate into Native American–ness. Using labels often reserved for indigenous peoples, James Logan warned that the Germans were a "warlike and morose People" who could be disruptive and difficult to control.[18]

Another (contradictory) worry was that Germans were too good at being white settlers. Colonial governments did not hesitate to break Native American treaties and use fraud and intimidation to wrest more and more territory and resources from native peoples. This included the infamous "Walking Purchase" of 1737, in which Thomas Penn cheated the Lenni Lenape (called Delawares by the English) out of twelve hundred square miles instead of the forty they expected to cede. Choosing profits from land speculation over treaties and agreements with Native Americans, colonial authorities often looked the other way while land-hungry settlers steadily encroached on native land. And when settlers, German and non-German alike, set out for the backcountry and took up land without knowledge or consent of either the proprietors or Native Americans, authorities also hoped that they could act as a buffer between the English in the east and Native Americans in the west. But when Germans participated in the common practice of land grabbing, they were frequently vilified for it. The Germans, Logan explained, were "troublesome settlers to the government [and] hard neighbors to the Indians."[19]

With public opposition to German immigration on the rise, Pennsylvania's Provincial Assembly began an official investigation in 1727. Although it found that a good number of the German immigrants were "very sober and honest People," it also confirmed and repeated many of the charges made against them. They were squatters whose actions created "great Prejudice and Disquiet" when they refused to pay quitrents (land tax) to the proprietors or quarreled with the Native Americans. Lawmakers also chastised the Germans for their failure to "yield Obedience" to the government or to assimilate by speaking English and adopting English ways. The assembly officially concluded that continued immigration "might be of dangerous Consequence to the Peace" of the colony.[20]

Growing xenophobia led to action. Beginning in 1717, Pennsylvania authorities started to regulate German immigration. The assembly ordered shipmasters to provide lists of the number and the "Characters" of passengers arriving on their vessels. A law resulting from the 1727 investigation expanded on these requirements and ordered the lists to contain passenger names, occupations, and previous residences. Notation of their "intentions in coming hither" were also to be included. Public health was a concern too. In 1718, a health officer was appointed to visit and report on all vessels coming into Philadelphia. If any person with an infectious disease was discovered onboard, the ship was ordered to anchor one mile from the city. When an epidemic broke out in Philadelphia in 1743, the governor approved the purchase of an island at the junction of the Schuylkill and Delaware Rivers. A hospital for sick passengers was built in 1750, and laws passed in 1750 and 1756 tried to ensure the safe arrival of healthy immigrants.[21]

The provincial government also required an immigrant registry. As early as 1718, Governor Keith suggested that all immigrants "take such Oaths appointed by Law as are necessary to give assurances of their being well affected to his Majesty and his Government." Put into effect in 1729, the Pennsylvania law required every white male over sixteen years old to register and sign oaths of allegiance and abjuration within forty-eight hours of his arrival. Another law attempted to discourage the importation of "lewd, idle and ill-affected persons" by imposing a forty-shilling-per-capita tax on all alien immigrants. The taxes were eventually rescinded and replaced with a law that required shipmasters to return all "poor and impotent" immigrants or post a bond against their becoming public charges. Ship masters convicted of importing criminals were also fined five pounds per immigrant.[22]

The registration requirement remained in place in Pennsylvania throughout the colonial era. This law predates the 1740 Plantation Act passed by the British Parliament to regularize the naturalization process and to encourage immigration to the American colonies, and it became the model for the US Naturalization Act of 1790. Tellingly, although the statute applied to "every white male," historians note that only Germans were registered with regularity.[23]

German newcomer John Meurer registered and gave his oath of loyalty when he arrived in Philadelphia in 1742. The registration included clear instructions for all signatories to pledge allegiance to the king and his successors, to conduct themselves as good and faithful subjects, not revolt against his Majesty, and not settle on lands not their own. All arrivals were also required to renounce allegiance to the pope, a clear indication of the law's anti-Catholic position. Two copies of the oaths were signed; one for the Crown and the other for the government of Pennsylvania. And then the newcomers were dismissed. "This done, they wished us good success," Meurer remembered.[24]

These early regulations of German immigration were important for what they did and for what they did not do. By legislating that all adult white males register with the authorities but applying it mostly to German immigrants, they targeted Germans for special scrutiny, thereby treating Germans unequally from other foreigners arriving in the colony. The new policies also operated on the belief that German immigrant men, as a group, were either disloyal or indifferent to the British Crown and posed a specific danger to the colony. Although this may have been true of some Germans, it was likely true of other non-English settlers as well. But only Germans were subjected to special scrutiny for their alleged disloyalty. Moreover, they were not measured as individuals; all German men were treated as a group. This separate and unequal group-based discrimination became one of the hallmarks of xenophobia in the United States, and in this way, the registry can be viewed as one of the earliest examples of state-sanctioned xenophobia in American history.

But significantly, the laws did not restrict immigration or change the terms of naturalization. In fact, they provided an important mechanism to *facilitate* naturalization and to incorporate "strangers and foreigners" into the colony. The act of registering German immigrant men was not part of a larger surveillance network designed to keep track of suspicious foreigners. That would come later. Instead, immigrant registration was paired with whiteness, an oath of loyalty, and the right of naturalization: all that was needed was an oath of allegiance to the king and the proprietor within three months of arrival and the paying of a small fee of twenty shillings. Typically sworn within three days of arrival, the oath provided an important mechanism to quickly naturalize German immigrants; grant them important legal rights and protections under provincial law, such as the right to acquire, hold, and sell property and pass it to their heirs; and assimilate them into English culture.[25] European immigrants were also granted full access to the provincial courts, a right that was denied to all Native Americans and African Americans. Registration thus became the first step toward full integration and equal rights.

In essence, while colonial authorities expressed their doubts and anxieties about German immigrants, they still believed that Germans could be assimilated and were desirable colonial subjects. White settlers supported and enhanced the colonies' military security, economic prosperity, and rapid and sustained growth. Even the registration requirement did not slow German immigration or restrict the rights of Germans in the colony. This is because Germans were not just immigrants; they were necessary white settlers who participated in and helped expand England's colonial project—and became, in effect, colonizers themselves. Making these foreigners full members of the society served the colonies' interests. Between 1740 and 1773, Pennsylvania registered and naturalized more than six thousand people.[26]

The need to attract white settlers thus served as a counterpoint to xenophobia, and this need produced both liberal immigration policies that brought growing numbers of European settlers to the colonies and generous naturalization policies that promised these aliens virtually the same rights as English subjects. As early as 1710, King George I himself had explained how state-sponsored Protestant German immigration and naturalization facilitated England's territorial expansion of the colonies. All Germans and Swiss who were not Catholics, he declared, were to receive a transportation subsidy and granted fifty acres of land west of the Allegheny Mountains, "usually considered a part of Pennsylvania, but not yet belonging to it." There was enough land for one hundred thousand families, he predicted, and Germans would have express permission to live there, "not as foreigners, but . . . [with] the same rights as [the king's] natural-born subjects."[27]

Colonial authorities followed the king's mandate, and in 1723, Governor Keith expressly invited the first German families to come to Pennsylvania to further the colonization of Native American lands. In 1723, sixteen German families traveled from the large and established German community in New York's Schoharie Valley to south-central Pennsylvania near Tulpehocken Creek. At that time, the area was held by the Lenni Lenapes, whose land was being steadily crowded by a growing number of white settlers as well as displaced Native Americans like the Conestogas, Tutelos, Nanticokes, and Conoys, who had already been forced west. In 1741, the Lenapes complained to the governor about the hundred or so German families who had settled on their land; these Germans did not recognize the Lenapes' ownership of the land, they protested, and in fact caused an "Uprore" in an effort to "sceare us." The Lenapes were concerned that if the settlers were not removed, they would be free to engage in their "wicked Ways to take our Land and never give us any thing for it." They asked Thomas Penn to "take these people off from our Land . . . that we may not be at the trouble to Drive them off."[28]

Despite tense relations between Germans and the Lenapes, the Tulpehocken settlement remained. And as the numbers of German immigrants entering the colony increased over the decades, they expanded the Tulpehocken settlement, connected it to the large German community in Philadelphia, and made it part of Pennsylvania's large German settlements that eventually extended throughout Philadelphia, Berks, Northampton, York, and Lancaster Counties.[29]

SOON, OTHER FORCES began to impact Germans' place in colonial Pennsylvania. Competition for land and resources among European settlers and Native Americans increased midcentury. Germans typically settled in frontier regions with large tracts of land suitable for farming. Often, these lands had only been recently wrested from Native Americans or were in regions that Native Americans still possessed. By the time the first German families settled in Pennsylvania in the 1710s, the Pennsylvania frontier had already been pushed thirty miles west. Caught between France and England as well as the growing white frontier population, Native Americans were forced to move farther and farther away from their ancestral territory. By midcentury, they had become refugees in their own land.[30]

During the Seven Years' War, which lasted from 1756 to 1763, the British military presence on the frontier further threatened the fragile alliances between Native Americans and white settlers. Aiming to seize control of the American frontier from the French and conquer New France, the British sent unprecedented numbers of troops to America. British and colonial forces established controls on Native American travel, migration, and contact with whites and fortified white settlements against both French and Native American aggression.[31]

When the English suffered a stunning defeat at Fort Duquesne (near Pittsburgh) in 1755, the French and their Native American allies went on the offensive. Emboldened by early British defeats, the Lenapes and Shawnees, who had been supplied with French arms, began to attack colonial settlements in Virginia, Maryland, and Pennsylvania. They hoped to strike back at those who had forced them out of their homes and stop new white settlement on the frontier. Men and women were murdered in their homes and on their farms. In 1755, the Delaware leader Pisquetomen led a deadly raid against a Pennsylvania German settlement. Fifteen were killed and multiple homes and barns were burned.[32]

The Germans were forced to flee eastward. By March 1756, an estimated seven hundred settlers had been killed in Native American raids in Pennsylvania, Virginia, and North Carolina. Thousands more had abandoned their farms and livelihoods and headed out into the backcountry. These moves threatened older areas of white settlement and pushed the colony into wider war between whites and Native Americans and between England and France. Fear and terror gripped the region.[33]

As fighting intensified on Pennsylvania's frontier, Germans became more directly involved in military action. They affirmed their loyalty to the British Crown and publicly pledged to assist the king, the governor, and the Pennsylvania Assembly against French encroachment. Conrad Weiser, a lieutenant colonel in the Pennsylvania army, organized German-speaking settlers into a military force and directed their action against the Lenapes. Germans contributed to the British defense of Pennsylvania with wagons, horses, feed, and tools. German missionary Christian Frederick Post was credited with encouraging the Lenapes, Ottawas, and Shawnees to end their alliances with the French. As a result, French troops were promptly forced to abandon their fortress at the forks of the Ohio and Allegheny Rivers. Pennsylvania Germans thus played a critical role in vanquishing both the French and the Native Americans in the colony, all while proving their loyalty to the British Crown.[34]

By the 1760s, war had hardened the territorial, political, and racial boundaries in Pennsylvania. It brought diverse Europeans and colonists together, both in terms of a shared and increasing dissatisfaction with the British empire and in forging new definitions of race in America. But the conflict had also further separated whites from Native Americans. Differences among colonial peoples in the colony—whether political, economic, religious, or ethnic—became increasingly characterized by race: Native American, black, or white. In turn, race was then used to further control people by categorizing them as separate and distinct.[35]

In 1763, numerous Native American raids on settlements in western Pennsylvania, Maryland, and Virginia killed or captured two thousand white settlers during what the English called Pontiac's Rebellion. Militias were reorganized and anti–Native American sentiment expanded. United in their outrage, fear, and thirst for revenge, settlers began to treat all Native Americans, regardless of allegiance, indiscriminately as enemies who needed to be rounded up, driven off, or exterminated. *Savage* quickly came to be applied to Native Americans only. Germans became something different: white.[36]

Soon, anti–Native American terror swept the countryside. Provincial authorities and publicists played off and profited from the growing fear among whites with anti–Native American pamphlets, sermons, petitions, newspaper accounts, poems, and plays that recounted Native American attacks in gruesome detail. Survivors told grisly horror stories of their neighbors' murders. It became harder and harder to think about Native Americans as allies or as sovereign peoples to negotiate with. Now, all Native Americans threatened the region's peace and security. And, similarly, all those who had suffered at the hands of these "savages" were considered "white people," including non-English immigrants. The label became a unifying identity and racial category that pitted all Europeans in the middle colonies against all Native Americans.[37]

Thus, despite occasional attempts to regulate immigration, anti-German xenophobia in colonial America had a limited impact. Only a few anti-immigration laws were passed in the colonies, and they were not thoroughly enforced. Most laws were designed to encourage migration. Some even offered inducements to those willing to come and settle, including tax exemptions and services to survey, plot, and title land. Local governments tried to make it as easy as possible for European foreigners to be admitted and to enjoy equal rights and benefits. All things considered, colonial America was pro-(white) immigration and pro-(white) settler.[38]

Even Benjamin Franklin never called for ending German immigration altogether. "I am not for refusing entirely to admit them into our Colonies," he explained. He understood their "fondness for their own Language & Manners." This was "natural," he conceded. "It is not a Crime." But he did recommend that actions be taken "to distribute [the Germans] more equally" throughout British America. And for those already in the colonies, Franklin had a clear and ready answer: assimilate them. "Mix them with the English, establish English Schools where they are now too thick settled."[39]

THE GERMAN COMMUNITY in Pennsylvania emerged from the Seven Years' War with a new political voice, and they were not afraid to use it. They did not hold provincial offices in Pennsylvania until the late colonial period, but they did vote ("in droves," as Benjamin Franklin complained), and their large numbers gave them a political clout that was often decisive in important matters governing the colony. In 1765, Franklin would be one of their first casualties when his blunt opinions about German settlers were used against him.[40]

For Pennsylvania, 1765 marked an important election year. At stake was the question of whether Pennsylvania should remain a proprietary colony ruled by the Penn family or become a royal colony ruled by the Crown. Franklin advocated for the latter position. Germans supported the former. Hoping to secure the German vote, members of the Proprietary Party emphasized to Pennsylvania Germans how well the current system worked. They also gleefully reprinted Franklin's anti-German remarks and emphasized some of Franklin's most damaging remarks, like his complaint that German immigrants were "Palatine Boors" who "herded" together. Although Franklin had used the term *boor* to refer to low-class, uneducated farmers, his political opponents claimed that he had referred to Germans as pigs.[41]

Public reaction to Franklin's anti-German remarks was strong and unforgiving. Three days before the election, Germantown printer Christoph Saur published a sixteen-page attack on both royalization and Franklin's anti-German bigotry. He repeatedly used Franklin's words—especially the insulting "Palatine Boors"—against him. Other publications printed parallel columns of Franklin's words alongside a German translation so that readers could study both. The German Freeholders of Philadelphia published a particularly damaging broadside against Franklin in 1764. It pointedly raised the question of whether Franklin could be trusted to protect German interests and rights. "Does Mr. Franklin merit a vote on the coming election day from a single German?" the Freeholders asked their members. The answer was an unqualified "no." The Freeholders exhorted readers to withhold their votes for Franklin "since he has not deserved it of us."[42]

Franklin laughed off these political shenanigans. But German voters did not get the joke. Voter turnout for the election skyrocketed. In the past, only about 10 percent of eligible voters had participated in elections. That year, more than 40 percent of eligible voters went to the polls. German immigrant voters were especially well represented. "Never before in the history of Pennsylvania . . . have so many people assembled for an election," Frederick Muhlenberg, son of the prominent Lutheran minister and future member of the Continental Congress, observed.[43]

Franklin lost his bid for reelection. It was a stunning defeat. Since his first run for office in 1751, the voters of Philadelphia had always elected him to the assembly. Surely, some voters simply did not agree with Franklin's political position. But it was also clear that German voters had made a decisive difference in the result. They used the power of the vote to challenge Franklin's xenophobia. An election-day cartoon made the connection clear. It portrayed crowds of Germantown residents lining up to vote, cheered on by onlookers. One member of the crowd asks, "Who dares defame The German name?" An angel soars above heralding a trumpet and a message: "THE *Germans* are Victorious." Meanwhile, the cartoon figure of Franklin morosely observes the procession and laments, "See how these Palatine *Boors* herd together."[44]

Pennsylvanians' fears that German immigrants would forever remain "strangers" who threatened the colony were unfounded. The "German problem" disappeared by the 1760s. But it wasn't just because German immigrants adapted; what mattered more was that the colony accepted them. By the American Revolution, the Germans had been included as members of the same "common stock" as other white settlers.[45] The recruitment, free migration, and generous naturalization of white settlers remained an American priority through the eighteenth century. Indeed, King George's attempts to limit immigration and intervene in the naturalization of foreigners in the colonies became one of the strongest grievances against the Crown leading up to the revolution.[46]

The treatment of German immigrants contrasted sharply with how Native Americans and African Americans were treated in colonial America. While German and other European immigrants were incorporated into colonial America as whites with full and equal membership, Native Americans were increasingly attacked. They were deemed "foreign" in their own land, peoples to be controlled, pushed aside, and exterminated. They were decidedly outsiders in colonial America, denied any genuine or stable sovereignty. Americans' increasing claims of "nativity" in the colonies as "native Americans" in the late colonial and early national period was yet another way in which white settlers continued to disinherit indigenous peoples from their own lands.[47]

At the same time that Germans were migrating to colonial Pennsylvania, ten to fifteen million Africans were forcibly transported to the Americas (three hundred thousand to the British colonies that would become the United States) and enslaved. From 1700 to 1750, slaves made up 75 percent of all transatlantic migrants who arrived in the Americas. Slave codes denied blacks citizenship and prohibited them from owning or carrying arms, trading goods, possessing land, receiving an education, and leaving their master's property without permission. The codes governed whom they could socialize with and with whom they could form families. Marriages between two slaves were not recognized. Wives and husbands, children and parents could all be separated from each other. Free blacks also saw their rights eroded in the eighteenth century. The right to vote was withheld from all blacks in the Southern colonies, free or not.[48]

Racial inequality became further embedded in American law after the Revolution. The 1790 Naturalization Act was the first statute to codify naturalization in the United States and represented the founders' intention to foster the transformation of the colonies into a politically integrated white republic. In an act of inclusion that demonstrated faith in the as-similability of European immigrants, it declared that "any alien, being a free white person" who had resided in the United States for as little as two years, could become an American citizen after taking an oath of allegiance to the US Constitution. Neither religion nor national origin was a bar to naturalization. Such an expansive and inclusive provision, of course, also served the needs of the new nation. By allowing all whites to be-come citizens, it facilitated the demographic and military expansion of the country.[49]

But its exclusionary design was obvious as well. Indentured servants, slaves, and women were not eligible. Free blacks, Native Americans, and, later, any other immigrant group deemed to be nonwhite could not be-come naturalized citizens. The lack of citizenship for all of these groups would have lasting, generational consequences. Without citizenship, they lacked political power. At the same time, tying citizenship to whiteness also made future European immigrants both white and American, while nonwhite immigrants were not. The racial barriers to naturalization would not be completely lifted until 1952.

BENJAMIN FRANKLIN'S PREDICTION that "swarthy" German immigrants would "overwhelm" the United States turned out to be right in a sense. Over the course of US history, America's gates always remained open to German immigrants, and indeed, they had privileged access into the country compared to many other groups. As a result, more have come from Germany than from any other country. From 1820 to 1920, nearly 7.2 million Germans immigrated to the United States, making up around 11 percent of the total immigration for those years. From the 1830s through the 1950s, Germans were either the largest or second largest immigrant group in the United States. Today, more Americans claim German heritage than any other ancestry. Many American presidents, including Dwight Eisenhower and Donald Trump, are of German descent. In many ways, America is German America.[50]

Yet anti-German xenophobia during the colonial era established important precedents for later anti-immigrant campaigns, in terms of both what it did and what it did not do. Repeated charges that there were too many German foreigners, that they did not assimilate, that they were somehow inherently different, and that they threatened the peace and security of the colonies helped establish the tradition of xenophobia in the United States. And despite the large number of German Americans in the country, anti-German xenophobia resurfaced during times of high immigration in the 1850s and again during World War I. Sometimes, it was violent.

Nevertheless, Germans, especially Protestant Germans, were never targeted in the same ways as other nonwhite, Catholic, and Jewish immigrants were. Both their whiteness and their faith protected them from harsher forms of xenophobia that aimed to limit or expel certain immigrants. By the mid-nineteenth century, Americans had identified another much greater immigrant threat to America—from Catholic Europe, especially Ireland. And the grave danger that this so-called invasion of poor Irish Catholics posed to the United States helped transform xenophobia in the United States. No longer just a set of anti-immigrant attitudes that led to a loose set of poorly enforced regulations, mid-nineteenth-century xenophobia used both anti-Catholicism and racism to spur the creation of America's first anti-immigrant political party as well as new policies directed at immigrants already in the United States. Xenophobia moved to the center of American politics, and with it came a new definition of what it meant to be an American.

TWO

"AMERICANS MUST RULE AMERICA"

On the morning of election day on August 6, 1855, James Speed looked out his office window in Louisville, Kentucky, and witnessed a mob attack. Groups of men were falling on Irish and German Catholic Americans who were attempting to cast their ballots at the courthouse. Bloody skirmishes followed as the would-be voters were beaten with sticks or short clubs. All across the city, members of the anti-immigrant and anti-Catholic American Party, also known as the Order of the Star-Spangled Banner and the Know Nothing Party, took control of polling places and chased naturalized citizens and foreign-looking voters away. Any immigrant "unlucky enough to be caught," Speed recalled, was beaten or shot.

The Know Nothings were convinced that Catholic immigrants posed a serious threat to the country and to American institutions. They objected to the large numbers arriving into the country and into Louisville, where foreigners made up 36 percent of the city's population. They believed that foreigners were prone to drunkenness and crime and found their drinking and carousing on Sundays to be particularly offensive. And they feared immigrants' growing political power and the increasing presence of the Catholic Church in the country. In particular, the Know Nothings were convinced that Catholic immigrants were part of a foreign papal conspiracy to infiltrate America.

Local Protestant leader Reverend Robert J. Breckinridge and *Louisville Journal* editor George D. Prentice expertly stoked the flames of prejudice in the months and weeks leading up to the riots. The *Journal* claimed that Irish and German immigrants were stocking up on firearms and hiding them in the city's Catholic churches as part of a secret plot to take over the United States. Prentice exhorted citizens to prepare themselves to defend American democracy.

On election day, armed members of the Know Nothing Party gathered at the city's polling places before dawn with a plan to prevent immigrants from voting. They handed out yellow tickets to Know Nothings and Know Nothing–approved voters that allowed them to freely proceed to the polls. Meanwhile, some naturalized immigrants and people who looked and sounded foreign were required to produce their naturalization papers by Know Nothings standing outside the polling places. Others were simply chased from the polls and beaten. This widespread (and illegal) voter intimidation greatly decreased the rate of voting and caused significant delays in the election. Naturalized citizens and self-proclaimed Know Nothings also started fighting near the corner of Shelby and Green Streets.

Soon, five hundred Know Nothing rioters tore through the city looking for foreigners. When they arrived in the German and Irish sections of town, they set houses on fire and destroyed German-owned businesses. Believing that Catholics were arming themselves with a secret cache of weapons hidden in the city's two Catholic churches, the mob set out to burn down the Cathedral of the Assumption and St. Martin's Church. Only after the mayor searched the premises and found no stashed weapons did the mob turn away, but not before a Catholic priest was stoned to death.

Around three or four o'clock in the afternoon, a mob armed with muskets and bayonets pulled a cannon up Main Street. They raided Armbruster's Brewery, helping themselves to apple and peach brandy, then set it aflame and killed ten people. Residents who tried to escape the Irish tenements on Quinn's Row (owned by Irish American Patrick Quinn) were shot. Quinn himself was beaten and shot while the mob set homes on fire. As the sun set, the skies in Louisville glowed red from the flames of burning buildings, and the city's streets were stained with blood. In total, an estimated five hundred rioters tore through the city. The number of people who died during the riots is unknown, but estimates range from twenty-two to a hundred, most of them Irish and German Catholics; many more were injured. After the riot, hundreds of Catholics fled Louisville and never returned.

Bloody Monday, as the Louisville violence came to be called, was one of the worst anti-immigrant riots in American history. It was not the first time that anti-Catholic xenophobia had turned vicious; riots had ripped through Philadelphia, New York, and Boston a decade before. In May and July 1844, Catholics and Protestants violently battled each other in Philadelphia in clashes that left a dozen dead, many more wounded, dozens of Irish homes burned to the ground. Thousands of Irish families fled their homes in panic. Nor would it be the last: within a year after Bloody

Irish and German Catholic immigrants steal the ballot box while their coconspirators cause a riot at an American polling place. Although this political cartoon from the 1850s blames immigrants for the violence, the xenophobic American Party, or Know Nothing Party, were in fact the main instigators of destructive and deadly riots in many American cities during the 1840s and 1850s. Courtesy Everett Collection.

Monday, anti-Catholic and anti-immigrant violence erupted in Chicago, St. Louis, Cincinnati, and New Orleans.[1]

Just as immigration had sparked debate and controversy during the colonial era, so did it become one of the most divisive political issues in the United States in the decades before the Civil War. Foreigners were certainly still needed, especially to work in the country's new industries and factories. European immigrants were also crucial assets in the continued expansion of the United States. As the federal government took Native American lands by cheating or by force, the US-born and foreign-born white settlers who rushed in to lay claim to the property were essential to the government's ability to retain control over its widening territory.

Nevertheless, as the Bloody Monday riots reveal, an increasing number of Americans were convinced that immigration, especially Catholic immigration, was a threat to the country. Just as large numbers of Germans had been considered threats to English dominance in the British colonies, nineteenth-century Catholic immigrants were considered dangerous to Protestant America. What spurred rioters to take to the streets in Louisville, Philadelphia, New York, and other American cities in the mid-nineteenth century was not just a general disdain for foreigners, their numbers, and their "strange" ways, however. It was a heightened and almost hysterical fear that Catholic outsiders were intent on taking over the United States.

Drawing on a long tradition of anti-Catholicism in the British Empire and in colonial America, preachers like Lyman Beecher and groups like the Know Nothings argued that Catholicism and Catholics were dangerous to American values and institutions, which were distinctly and unalterably *Protestant*, they insisted. Catholicism was, they declared, antithetical to America, and Catholic immigration was a plot orchestrated by foreign governments in an effort to wrest control of the country away from Americans and into the hands of the pope. A "Protestant Crusade" connected America's anti-Catholic and xenophobic traditions together for the first time to frame opposition to these immigrants in military terms—as a necessary defense of the nation.[2]

But anti-Catholic xenophobia was not only about religion. It was also about immigrants' foreignness, as well as their class, national origin, and perceived race. As the largest group of immigrants coming to the United States before the Civil War, Irish Catholics fleeing mass starvation and destruction in famine-era Ireland bore the brunt of xenophobes' wrath. The racialization of Irish Catholics as biologically inferior to white Anglo-Saxon Protestants helped establish a pattern of racial xenophobia that would become dominant in the late nineteenth and twentieth centuries. Through Irish immigration to the United States, *race* came to mean more than just white versus black. Scientists started categorizing humanity into different "racial" groups by ascribing inherited and immutable characteristics to them. Naming and treating all Irish peoples as members of the distinct and distinctly inferior "Celtic" race in the mid-nineteenth century was an important facet of race making and xenophobia in the United States. Both a religious problem and a racial problem, Irish Catholic immigrants were singled out as scapegoats for America's social, political, and economic ills. Actively promoted in pulpits, newspapers, and books, xenophobia flourished across the country.

Groups like the Know Nothings transformed xenophobia into an organized political movement. They demonized foreigners. They formed a political party devoted to curbing the rights and influence of immigrants and naturalized citizens. They mobilized voters to elect anti-immigrant lawmakers, make anti-immigrant policy, and gain political power. In short, they spearheaded the birth of *political xenophobia* in the United States.

Know Nothings also promoted a new definition of Americanness and *nativism*, the naming of white Anglo-Saxon Protestant (WASP) settlers and their descendants as "natives" to the United States and the granting of special privileges and protections to them. With its roots in both settler colonialism and the ongoing dispossession of indigenous peoples, Know Nothing nativism continued to exclude indigenous people from the American nation and explicitly denied their claims to land and sovereignty. In applying the rhetoric and politics of nativism to immigration, Know Nothings fueled xenophobic legislation that attacked the civil and political rights of Catholic immigrants and Catholic Americans. The Know Nothing Party was short-lived, but its brand of nativism and political xenophobia continued to reshape America and American politics long after its demise.

"FARE YOU WELL, poor Erin's Isle!" the popular Irish emigrant ballad began. "I now must leave you for a while." The song, titled "The Irish Refugee, or Poor Pat Must Emigrate," reflected the forced nature of Irish migration during and after the Great Potato Famine. Unable to pay rent, Irish tenants were evicted onto the streets to "beg and starve for meat," the song described. Between 1.1 and 1.5 million people (over 15 percent of the total Irish population) died of starvation and famine-related diseases from 1846 to 1855; 2.1 million fled during those same years. A third of the Irish population was gone—dead, or abroad. If only Ireland "had its own, her noble sons might stay at home, but since fortune has it otherwise, Poor Pat must emigrate," the anonymous songwriter lamented.[3]

A million and a half came to the United States alone. They were the largest immigrant group in the United States in the 1840s, accounting for 45 percent of the total number of new arrivals. In the next decade, they made up 35 percent of all new immigrants.[4]

The Irish had already known their share of hardship before the potato blight attacked their crops in the mid-nineteenth century. Catholic Ireland had been under the oppressive rule of Protestant Britain since the sixteenth century. Protestant landlords, many of them absentee, were installed and eventually owned most of the land in Ireland. Harsh penal laws stripped Irish Catholics of many rights, including the ability to vote, hold office, or own land. Increasing farm mechanization and massive population growth put even more pressure on rural farming families. Those who remained on their farms were able to survive thanks to the hardy potato, a nutritious crop that grew well even in Ireland's rocky soil. By the 1840s, almost half of the country's population was dependent on the food, income, and rent money that potatoes provided. Then, disaster struck in the form of *Phytophthora infestans*, or potato blight.[5]

In 1845, farmers started reporting that a strange disease was turning the leaves and stems of potato plants dark green to purplish black. Underground, potato tubers were becoming a foul-smelling mush. Much of the year's potato crop rotted in the fields, and the mold spread rapidly across the country. By October, the *London Illustrated News* reported that there was hardly a district in Ireland in which the potato crops at present were uninfected, "perhaps we might say, *hardly a field*." In 1846, the blight returned and again destroyed almost the entire potato crop in the country. With no potatoes to eat or sell, families faced starvation.[6]

The British government's response was completely inadequate, to the point of being cruel. It continued to export Irish grain away from the starving millions in the country and brought it to England instead. The government's primary form of relief was to send the poor to the workhouses. Required to provide financial relief to a growing number of homeless, destitute, and sick, landlords passed on their costs to the already struggling peasants. When their tenants were unable to pay their rents, landlords evicted them en masse. Between 1849 and 1854, 50,000 families—totaling 250,000 people—were permanently evicted from their homes.[7]

Men, women, and children began dying of starvation and famine-related diseases. Newspapers, travelers' journals, and official agencies reported mass graves throughout the country. "Death by Starvation" read a December 1846 headline in the *Cork Examiner*. Disease and death were in every quarter, with fever, dropsy, diarrhea, and famine eradicating whole families. Some areas had turned into ghost towns; only the dead and dying remained.[8]

By 1848, when the blight struck down the potato crop once again, the Irish were fleeing in the hundreds and then the thousands. The *Cork Examiner* reported "hundreds frantically rushing from their home and country, not with the idea of making fortunes in other lands, but to fly from a scene of suffering and death." Many fled to the United States. By 1860, one in four New Yorkers was Irish, including many women, who made up the majority of domestic servants in the city. In Boston, immigrants and their children outnumbered non-immigrants, leading Unitarian minister Theodore Parker to call Boston the "Dublin of America."

Lyman Beecher, the famous Presbyterian preacher and pastor of Boston's Hanover Church, took a more openly hostile approach. He sounded an alarm that would be heard across the country.[9]

IN THE FALL of October 1832, Lyman Beecher was heading west. He was giving up his comfortable position preaching to Boston's business and political elite for the backwaters of Ohio in order to serve as president of Lane Seminary in Cincinnati. He wanted to bring evangelical Protestantism to the wild West.

The journey was marked with hardships and delays. The Beechers lost their luggage and were caught in a rainstorm without any dry, clean clothes. It would be several days before they were reunited with their trunks. Their mountainous crossing from Harrisburg to Wheeling, West Virginia, was excruciatingly slow. Then, when they were about to board the steamboat to Cincinnati, news of a deadly cholera epidemic in the city forced them to delay for over a week. Once in Cincinnati, Beecher continued to be tested. Within a year, most of his seminary students, all of whom were passionate antislavery crusaders, had become disgusted with Beecher's lukewarm support of abolitionism and had gone to study with a rival. The rigors of frontier life also claimed the life of Beecher's wife.[10]

Still, the preacher persisted. He believed that he was doing God's work. He was convinced that the West was where "the religious and political destiny" of the United States was to be decided. There was plentiful land for white families to farm, and the region, with its multitudes of Catholic Mexicans and heathen natives, was in dire need of Protestantism. The West would become the seat of America's growing empire, and, in the minds of Northerners, a place where slavery would no longer compromise the nation. The West was also where the coming battle between Protestantism and Catholicism was to be fought. A Protestant West would serve as a bulwark against the Catholic North in Canada and the Catholic South in Mexico. Beecher felt destined to help guide the United States toward this triumphant moment in its history and in the history of humankind.[11]

Beecher was a leading commander in the nineteenth-century Prot-estant Crusade that connected America's anti-Catholic and xenophobic traditions for the first time. Anti-Catholicism had long been part of Brit-ish and colonial American life. Despite the fact that Catholics were a small minority in the British colonies, American colonists had enacted a series of anti-Catholic laws that limited their rights and freedoms. In Massachusetts, the Puritans attempted to bar all Catholics by adminis-tering oaths of allegiance that specifically denounced the pope. A 1647 Massachusetts law also decreed that any Jesuit or priest coming within the colony was to be banished, and, if he should return, executed. Con-necticut had a similar law that allowed anyone without a warrant to seize any priest found within the dominion. Although these laws were rarely enforced and were eventually changed or repealed by the early nineteenth century, anti-Catholic prejudice endured.[12]

Up through the mid-1830s, American anti-Catholicism focused its condemnation on Catholicism as a religion and the Catholic Church in general. But as the numbers of immigrants from Catholic Europe began to grow, the Catholic menace and the foreign menace merged into one great threat that, as xenophobes argued, imperiled the very future of the United States. The message was a new one: Catholicism was not just a distant threat that resided largely outside the United States. Now, it was destroying the country from within.

The battle would be fought in the West, a region that was supposed to be destined for the use and prosperity of white Protestant American settlers. Under the 1803 Louisiana Purchase, the United States laid claim to 530 million acres, and after President Thomas Jefferson sent forth ex-ploratory missions to survey and map the land, Congress invested in and encouraged the building of roads, canals, and railroads. Six new states were admitted into the Union between 1816 and 1821 alone. By 1830, more than four million of the nearly thirteen million inhabitants of the United States (not including Native Americans) lived between the Appa-lachian Mountains and the Mississippi River.

Simultaneously, the federal government forced Native Americans from their homelands. In 1830, President Andrew Jackson signed the

Indian Removal Act, which voided existing treaties with Native Americans and led to the forced mass migration and displacement of thousands. Despite fierce Cherokee opposition and a US Supreme Court ruling in favor of the Cherokee, the US government entered Cherokee lands. Assisted by thousands of white settler "volunteers," government agents hunted, imprisoned, raped, and murdered Native Americans, then forced the survivors on a thousand-mile march to the newly established Indian Territory, now in Oklahoma. Approximately four thousand Cherokees died on this forced march, known as the Trail of Tears, and Native American removal became part of a much larger policy aimed at cleansing Native Americans from all lands east of the Mississippi.

As Native Americans were forced out of their homelands, European immigrants were moving in. By 1850, more than 270,000 Germans lived in the Midwest. A decade later, there were over one million. In Wisconsin, foreign-born residents were almost as numerous as US-born residents, and foreigners outnumbered American-born people in many cities, like St. Louis.[13] Anti-Catholic leaders worried that the growing numbers of foreigners would allow them to dominate the region. They would then rise in armed revolt and establish Catholic rule in the country. America's "manifest destiny" to expand the United States' territorial boundaries all the way to the Pacific Ocean would be threatened.

Samuel F. B. Morse, better known as the inventor of the telegraph, helped spread this new message of anti-Catholic xenophobia in a series of writings published in the 1830s that effectively identified immigration, something that had previously been considered beneficial to the United States, as a dangerous threat. In his book *Foreign Conspiracy Against the Liberties of the United States*, Morse accused the Catholic Church of populating the American West with Catholic immigrants for the express purpose of undermining American democracy. He argued that the Catholic Church, in league with European monarchs, was intent on both political and religious domination of the United States. An invading force of Catholic immigrants was the key factor in this strategy of domination. Once they became naturalized US citizens, their votes were "easily purchased" by demagogues and unprincipled politicians. Catholics were already interfering in elections in Michigan, South Carolina, and New York, Morse insisted. And Americans were woefully unprepared for the coming battle. Lulled into complacency, they were "unsuspicious of [the] hostile attack" that was inevitable. Morse called for all Americans to prepare themselves for immediate action.[14]

New technology like Morse's telegraph expedited the spread of these ideas and, thanks to the enormous growth and distribution of print media like newspapers, magazines, and books like Morse's, anti-Catholic xenophobia spread. Traveling ministers delivered fire-breathing anti-Catholic sermons across the country. *The Protestant*, the first openly anti-Catholic weekly newspaper, debuted in New York in 1830. It joined hundreds of anti-Catholic novels, plays, histories, travel books, children's books, almanacs, and even gift books that American publishers were printing in the early nineteenth century.[15]

Readers bought these hate-filled publications in record-breaking numbers. In 1834, rumors that a young woman was being held against her will at the Ursuline convent in Charlestown, Massachusetts, inspired the publication of a best-selling book about the Catholic church's alleged abuses—but not before it also inspired a violent mob to burn the convent and school to the ground. In 1836, another tell-all anti-Catholic book broke sales records. Allegedly written by a former nun who had escaped from the Hotel Dieu nunnery in Montreal, *The Awful Disclosures of Maria Monk* falsely claimed that nuns were forced to have sex with priests and that the infants born of these unions were baptized and then strangled to death. Although completely fabricated by a group of anti-Catholic leaders in Montreal, *The Awful Disclosures* became a popular best seller, selling three hundred thousand copies prior to the Civil War.[16]

But it was Lyman Beecher's 1835 book *A Plea for the West* that best connected America's older tradition of anti-Catholicism with the newer one of xenophobia. Beecher warned that a "tremendous tide of European emigration" was rushing into the West "like the waters of the flood." Like Morse, Beecher believed that these settlers were under the control of European powers. The "potentates of Europe" were attacking "our liberties," Beecher claimed, by organizing and paying for the mass migration of

Catholic foreigners onto America's shores. The immigrants were poor. They were criminals. And once in the United States, they were crowding American prisons and poorhouses, leaving hardworking Americans to foot the bill. With the power to vote, the "mass of alien voters" was easily controlled by unscrupulous demagogues or manipulated by priests and Catholic monarchs. They would then "decide our elections, perplex our policy, inflame and divide the nation, break the bond of our union, and throw down our free institutions."[17]

Catholic foreigners, Beecher concluded, should thus be viewed as a military threat; as a hostile "army of soldiers, enlisted and officered, and spreading over the land." He called on his colleagues to join him in the struggle for God and country. "Blow the trumpet around you!" he instructed. Lay Protestants could join the fight by building and supporting Protestant schools, churches, colleges, and seminaries. Beecher additionally insisted that the federal government immediately and energetically "control both the number and the 'general character of immigrants.'" For his part, Beecher vowed to continue his efforts. As he wrote to a friend in 1842, "I am on the field. The battle is begun."[18]

As Lyman Beecher was fighting his battle against Catholicism in the West, a number of organizations were forming political parties and legislative agendas to combat the threat allegedly posed by foreign Catholic immigration. The Native American Democratic Association formed in New York City in 1835 on a platform of bringing "American Born Citizens" together to protest the growing influence of "aliens" in the city. They warned that poor and criminal foreigners, especially the "low Irish," were sweeping into the country, and that immigrants were gaining unprecedented (and dangerous) political power. That November, they shocked the local political world with their platform of keeping "America in American hands" and won 39 percent of the vote in city elections. In Philadelphia, the Native American Association was formed with similar goals. Although it claimed that it remained open to immigrants, it emphatically denied their right "to have a voice in legislative halls" or to hold office "under any circumstances." It called for a repeal of the naturalization laws, which it stated had "now become an evil." In New York, the anti-immigrant

American Republican Party briefly attracted support in 1843 and 1844 with its message that immigrants were responsible for bankrupting the city government. Almost identical to its predecessor, called the Democratic Association, the American Republicans lobbied against foreign-born Catholic influence within the Whig and Democratic Parties and promised to restore what they called the Protestant Ascendancy of New York City government and politics.[19]

Xenophobes were particularly concerned over the perceived Catholic threat to public schools. In 1843, tensions between Catholics and Protestants turned into a full-fledged controversy. Catholic parents strenuously objected to the use of the Protestant King James Bible (which was deeply offensive to Roman Catholics because of its roots in the Protestant Reformation) in public schools, while anti-Catholic leaders insisted that the King James Bible was necessary to turn Catholic children into good American citizens rather than pawns of the Catholic Church. Controversy erupted when Archbishop John Hughes of New York City demanded that Catholics be given public money to set up their own schools. When their appeals were rebuffed, Catholics later established an independent Catholic school system that spread across the country. Meanwhile, the anti-Catholic American Republicans used the controversy to mobilize voters, surprised the New York City political establishment with their healthy share of the vote, elected their mayoral candidate to office, and founded a party newspaper they titled the *American Citizen.*[20]

In 1845, the Order of United American Mechanics was founded in Philadelphia following the great anti-Catholic riots that ravaged that city. They vowed to wage a fight against labor competition from immigrants, the prominence of naturalized foreigners in politics, and what they believed to be the growing threat from Catholicism in the United States, especially in the public school system. The order pledged to turn its campaign against immigrants into a campaign to renew America. Its message had a broad appeal. In 1853, a junior branch of the organization was established—the Junior Order of United American Mechanics, drawing members who were white men between ages sixteen and fifty, of "good moral character" who believed in God, favored the separation of church and state, and supported public education. The order also provided mutual aid benefits for its members and at its height claimed two hundred thousand members.[21]

Another organization, the American Protestant Society, established in 1847, was extremely successful at drawing the churchgoing middle classes into an organized anti-Catholic movement. It established chapters around most eastern cities and raised substantial sums of money every year. These self-proclaimed patriotic and benevolent societies became masters at self-promotion and propaganda. They sent out speakers who warned against the twin dangers of Catholicism and immigration. They created and circulated publications like the monthly magazine *Order of United Americans* and *The Republic, A Monthly Magazine of American Literature, Politics, and Art*, which were popular among its mostly working-class membership.[22]

In 1849, the Order of the Star-Spangled Banner was formed in New York. Like its predecessors, this fraternal organization similarly vowed to reduce the political influence of Catholic immigrants. It attracted members with its anti-Catholic, anti-party, anti-liquor, and, in the North, antislavery agenda. By the end of 1853, chapters had been established in New Jersey, Maryland, Connecticut, Massachusetts, and Ohio. Order members, who were required to be US-born citizens, Protestant, and not married to a Catholic, promised to protect American citizens and their institutions and challenge the policies of the Roman Catholic Church and other "foreign" influences. They had to be willing to obey the order's rules without question and pledge to uphold the secrecy of the organization, which included an elaborate system of passwords, phrases of recognition, and signals of distress. Members routinely responded that they "knew nothing" if asked about the organization, and thus, the nickname *Know Nothings* was earned.[23]

ON THE EVENING of Wednesday, October 12, 1853, a number of concerned white male citizens secretly gathered in East Boston to form a local Know Nothings chapter. Recording secretary Solomon Bradford

Morse Jr. (no relation to Samuel) diligently took notes but was careful to maintain the cloak of secrecy that was central to the party's culture and practice. No meeting locations or officers' names were recorded. Nor were there lengthy descriptions of what was discussed and resolved. Instead, Morse only noted that the meeting took place at the "known place" and vaguely reported every week that "the regular business of the order was transacted." The order's records did include the organization's pledge to support and protect the "rights of the American Born against every form of foreign influence upon our Free government." Over the next few years, Secretary Morse would dutifully log the names of 761 new members.[24]

The American Party's pledge did not elaborate further on what kind of "foreign influence" these East Boston residents were protecting the "American Born" from, but other documents made clear that Catholic immigrants were considered the primary menace. Among the resolutions that members unanimously adopted in 1855 was one that stated that "no foreign criminal or pauper" should be permitted to remain within the territory of the United States and another declaring that no person of foreign birth should be naturalized unless he had resided within the United States for twenty-one consecutive years. Others prohibited any "person who is not a protestant and a native born citizen of the United States" to be sent to any foreign power as the representative of the United States or to hold office in the federal government. In 1855, the Know Nothings decided to build an independent political party and run their own slate of candidates who would turn their values into a political and legislative agenda. The American Party was born, and with it, political xenophobia became an American tradition.[25]

Know Nothing ideology focused on a number of core beliefs. First, Catholicism, the party leaders argued, was dangerous and un-American. Know Nothings echoed Protestant religious leaders like Lyman Beecher and insisted that Protestantism defined American society. Everything that was great about America—its freedom, liberty, and support for civil, religious, social, and personal rights and progress—could be traced back to Protestantism, they insisted. In contrast, they claimed, Catholicism was the direct opposite of Protestantism. The Catholic Church represented monarchy, aristocracy, and other forces that were in direct conflict with American ideals and virtues of republican democracy. To the Know Nothings, Catholicism and foreignness were one and the same. "Its organization is foreign, its agents, guides and directors, are in great part foreign; its paramount attachments are foreign; its moral if not its political allegiance is foreign," they stated. And Catholicism's "ambition" in America was to essentially occupy and usurp, as a foreign country would. The Know Nothings pointed out that Catholic immigrants who formed their own militia units, mostly as a means of social interaction and recreation, could already be part of a military force preparing for a takeover.[26]

Immigrants, a Know Nothing paper also declared, were the chief source of crime in the country. Their love of alcohol led to public drunkenness, liquor trafficking, and crime. As a result, immigrants were much more likely to be arrested than native-born citizens, the publication claimed, and violent crime, including labor conflicts, was reaching epidemic proportions in many major US cities. The group criticized national policy that allowed a "flood of ignorance, vice and crime . . . into the heart of our country." Know Nothings additionally blamed immigrants for low wages and the weak status of American workingmen. "Why are you poor?" the Know Nothing *Almanac* asked in an 1856 appeal to workingmen and -women. The answer was clear: "competition of foreign cheap labor in the American labor market." The immigrants were used to "starvation wages" and living in squalid poverty in Europe. But Americans should not be degraded into accepting the same. Immigrant labor reduced the wages of American workers and left them vulnerable "to a condition worse than that of Negro slavery," the propagandistic publication argued.[27]

The *Almanac* had identified a popular message. Technological innovation and industrialization had brought telegraphs, railroads, and factories to antebellum America. But not all residents benefited from these changes. Bankers and industrialists were getting wealthier and wealthier while working conditions and the status of workers eroded. Factory work—with its emphasis on efficiency and profits—meant long hours, deplorable working conditions, and few rights for workers. Women and children, who made up a majority of workers in some textile mills, often worked up to seventy hours a week for sometimes just pennies a day. The gulf between rich and poor widened, and as worker dissatisfaction and labor protests increased, many blamed immigrants for their hardship.[28]

There was little truth to these charges, though. Immigrant workers were typically taking over the most unskilled and menial work, thereby elevating US-born workers to more skilled, supervisory, and higher-paying positions. Wages remained constant up through 1855, and in industries that employed both immigrant and American-born workers, the wages in these industries were often higher than those that employed only US-born workers. Nevertheless, within the context of a rapidly changing economy, increasing inflation, and higher prices for goods, the message that immigrants were causing these economic changes had great appeal and perhaps felt like an emotional truth.[29]

While economic competition, crime, and pauperism were major issues, the Know Nothings' chief concern was that Catholic immigrants were highly active politically and were making large political gains. "We find that in some of our States," the party reported in 1855, "the alien, stranger equally to our tongues, our laws, and even our homes," had the power to decide the outcomes of critical elections. But immigrant votes were not the result of a healthy democratic process, the Know Nothings declared. Rather, immigrant political activity was organized in neighborhood saloons and the profits from the sale of alcohol financed the careers of immigrant politicians. Together with Catholic priests (ruled by the pope in Rome), they determined how Catholics voted. Unscrupulous immigrants also sold their votes to the highest bidder and practiced extensive fraudulent voting. Professional politicians and demagogues who cared only for political power rather than the public good were only too happy to benefit from these ill-gotten votes. Such practices posed a major threat to the American political system, the Know Nothings insisted, additional proof that Romanism stood in direct antagonism with American liberty.[30]

The Know Nothings were generally anti-Catholic and anti-immigrant. But they also specifically identified Irish Catholic immigrants as a particularly dangerous threat to the United States. Drawing on deep-rooted prejudices already entrenched in British and American popular culture and thought, the Know Nothings consistently dehumanized the Irish as being racially inferior, grouping them with Native Americans and African Americans. They promoted a racial stereotype of "Paddy," the archetypical Irish Catholic male who spoke with an atrocious Irish brogue; often uttered high-pitched screeches; sported fiery red hair and rosy, liquored cheeks; and was temperamental and violent. Cartoons of Paddy depicted him as dirty, ragged, and dark-skinned. He had a low brow, a "lantern" (thick, square) jaw, and "simian" or apelike features.[31]

The stereotype of "Bridget," the archetypical Irish Catholic woman, was similarly unflattering. She was uncivilized and lacked refinement. As a domestic servant, she was a necessary fixture in any middle-class white household, but she was also a force of disruption and destruction. Coming from a rough peasant background, Bridget was unused to fine furniture and belongings. And she could not be counted on to cook fine cuisine. She was either breaking her mistress's fine china and glassware or attempting to steal them. She had a temper and would bristle at even the slightest criticisms. She terrorized her mistress with her "strong arm and voluble tongue." The well-circulated stereotypes of Bridget or "Biddy" served many purposes. By contrasting rough, masculine Bridget with her refined, educated, and genteel Protestant American mistress, American magazines pointed out the alleged differences between both Irish and American women and, more broadly, the Irish and American "races."[32]

It was also commonly believed that Irish Catholics were unfit to become Americans. In 1840, for example, the *North American Review* explained that the Irish people had been "worn down"; they were "servile victims of licentiousness and poverty" resulting from their Catholic faith and harsh British rule. Unaccustomed to self-government, Irish Catholics could be a danger to a self-governing republic like the United States that welcomed all whites to citizenship. Some American reformers believed that the Irish could be rehabilitated into proper American citizens once they were freed from the yoke of British tyranny and Catholic domination and exposed to proper Protestant American values and public education.[33]

But as the migration of Irish Catholics increased during the famine years and as anti-Catholic xenophobia spread, these stereotypes about the Irish were no longer attributed to their poor upbringing and Ireland's oppressive conditions. Instead, such stereotypes were believed to be qualities, characteristics, and deficiencies that were part of their blood, endemic to the Celtic race. Faith in America's ability to change the Irish began to fade. As Unitarian minister Theodore Parker proclaimed in 1849, "It is not surprising . . . that the Irish are ignorant, and, as a consequence thereof, are idle, thriftless, poor, intemperate, and barbarian." It would be ludicrous, Parker continued, that the "mere repeal of bad laws" would make this "vicious population . . . industrious, provident, moral and intelligent."[34]

Increasingly, the Irish were considered biologically distinct from Anglo-Saxons altogether—an inferior race. These ideas were promoted and circulated not only through popular culture, the media, and social commentary but also through the new racial "sciences" of phrenology and physiognomy. Practitioners of what would later be called scientific racism claimed that humans were divided into several distinct races that all possessed different hereditary physical characteristics as well as different intellectual capabilities, moral values, behavioral traits, and more. Moreover, they placed races into a strict hierarchy. At the top was the Anglo-Saxon race. At the bottom was the Negroid. Although the Irish were near the top, they were still considered far inferior to the ideal Anglo-Saxon. They were intellectually inferior, morally suspect, and prone to manipulation. They were biologically incapable of intelligent and independent participation in the governance of the nation. In some scientific illustrations, the difference between Celts and Anglo-Saxons was even starker—the Irish were ranked just a level or two above the animal kingdom and dehumanized just like African Americans.[35]

Irish immigrants were linked to both Native Americans (the Puritans commonly gave the derogatory label of *Wild Irish* to the Irish community in Boston) and African Americans (as similarly dark-skinned, apelike,

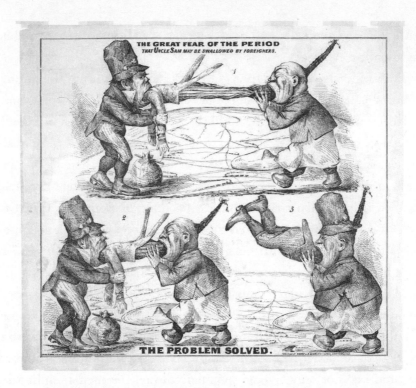

A central feature of xenophobia in the United States has been to promote the idea that immigrants—especially those considered to be racially inferior—will displace white Anglo-Saxon Protestant Americans. "The Great Fear of the Period That Uncle Sam May Be Swallowed by Foreigners." San Francisco: White and Bauer, between 1860 and 1869. Courtesy of the Library of Congress.

savage, rapacious, and violent) as a way of demonstrating Irish racial inferiority. Because they often worked and lived alongside African Americans, the Irish came to be known as "niggers turned inside out," while African Americans came to be known as "smoked Irish." The Irish were also likened to the Chinese, the other great immigrant menace of the nineteenth century. As New York politician George Templeton Strong claimed, "our Celtic fellow citizens are almost as remote from us in temperament and constitution as the Chinese."[36]

Significantly, the Irish were certainly still "white," and membership in the so-called Celtic race never translated into the same systemic discrimination and segregation that African Americans, Native Americans, Asian Americans, and Latinx peoples faced. Irish immigrants were

...igible for citizenship after a five-year waiting period, for example. And, after they became citizens, Irish men could and did exercise their power to vote. Still, in antebellum America, Irish Catholics were subjected to a hardening xenophobia and racialization that marked them as substantially different (and racially inferior) to other European immigrants and white Americans. Under the Know Nothings, they would also face new infringements upon their political, civil, and legal rights.

Nineteenth-century xenophobia also focused on the extreme poverty of famine-era immigrants. Fleeing mass starvation and destruction in Ireland, the Irish were the "most impoverished immigrants" ever to arrive in the United States. Only a small percentage were skilled workers; the rest were forced into the hardest and lowest-paying jobs. Last hired, they were often the first fired and were more likely to become public charges than other groups like Germans. But xenophobes did not view immigrant poverty as a consequence of the miserable conditions that immigrants had fled or of the xenophobia and segregation that limited their opportunities in the United States. Instead, anti-Catholic leaders depicted Irish immigrants as naturally lazy and indolent, as part of their racial character. The new immigrants were "too lazy to work" and ended up in the poorhouse at the public's expense, the Know Nothings complained.[37]

These were old and effective arguments. British colonists had enacted so-called poor laws that established each town's financial obligation to support its local poor *and* its right to support and expel poor people. Massachusetts and New York had laws authorizing local officials to "dispose" or "send" transient poor from their cities. Towns in New England regularly practiced the "warning out" of outsiders as a means of financial and social control. After the revolution, Massachusetts passed a comprehensive poor law that targeted foreigners: all non-naturalized foreigners were ineligible for settlement and subject to removal.[38]

Building on these attitudes and laws, the Know Nothings argued that immigrant pauperism was not just a financial burden; it was also a menace to America's free republican society. Economic self-sufficiency and upward social mobility, they believed, were cornerstones of American greatness. Poor Irish men flouted the way that America was supposed to work, with men supporting their dependent wives and children. The failure of the Irish to support their own families, it was believed, unfairly taxed the rest of America's hardworking citizens.[39]

By the early 1850s, the Irish had been racialized to such a degree that references to the Anglo-Saxon (or Anglo-American) race versus the Celtic race permeated the media, political discussions, religious sermons, literary publications, and even government publications. Riots involving the two groups were even interpreted as evidence of the "race war" brewing between Saxon and Celt.[40]

But another war over slavery was also casting a long shadow on antebellum American politics and contributed to the Know Nothings' political organizing and appeal. Know Nothings were divided—as other political parties and Americans in general were—over the issue of slavery. Southern Know Nothings favored the expansion of slavery, but most Northern Know Nothings were vehemently opposed to it. These Northerners particularly condemned the 1854 Kansas-Nebraska Act, which allowed for voters in these two territories to vote on whether slavery would be permitted within their borders. Based on the idea of popular sovereignty, the bill included a clause repealing the Missouri Compromise of 1820 that prohibited slavery in these northern territories.[41]

The Know Nothings' antislavery position also attracted voters who believed that Catholics supported the institution of slavery and its expansion in the United States. As the *Chicago Tribune* explained in 1852, the Catholic Church and slavery were based on the same "ignorance and abasement of human kind." The paper also claimed, without proof, that "ninety-nine one hundredths" of all Catholics supported slavery. Preacher Theodore Parker went even further. "I am told there is not in all America a single Catholic newspaper hostile to Slavery; not one opposed to tyranny in general; not one that takes sides with the oppressed in Europe," he claimed.[42]

Many Irish immigrants and Irish Americans did in fact support slavery and were known to be antiblack as well. Vulnerable themselves to charges that they were racially inferior, Irish Americans often used antiblack racism as a way to prove their whiteness. As abolitionist Frederick

Douglass explained, the Irish had been taught "to hate and despise the colored people" and to believe that African American adversity was "essential to their own prosperity." Know Nothings in turn used the general pro-slavery position of Irish Americans to validate their own antislavery and anti-Catholic xenophobic positions.[43]

In Boston, a controversial fugitive slave case involving the government's capture of runaway slave Anthony Burns also contributed to anti-Irish sentiment. As the government prepared to arrest Burns and return him to slavery in the South, opposition grew so intense that officials feared a riot and called on the militia to enforce public safety. Most Massachusetts militia units refused to comply, but a number of Irish units did. Their participation was cited as evidence that all Irish supported slavery, and the Burns case proved to be a powerful recruitment tool for the local Know Nothing Party.[44]

Anti-party sentiment and distrust of professional politicians also contributed to the Know Nothings' rise. Voters complained of rotten politicians who were more interested in staying in power than they were in heeding the will of the people. Both the Whig and Democratic parties were corrupt, many claimed, and were willing to court the immigrant vote for political gain. Unable to withstand the divisions over slavery, the already weak Whig Party collapsed, and with it came an end to the two-party system.

Into this political chaos stepped the Know Nothings. A growing movement against "politics as usual" channeled support over to them, as an alternative to what many believed was a corrupt and unresponsive party system. A national emergency, they claimed, had brought about the necessity for a Great American Party. The Know Nothings promised to change the status quo and curb the influences of demagogues and professional politicians. Its candidates would be "new men" who only sought to bring morality and fairness to politics. It pledged to reform politics with fresh faces and establish a government that delivered fair wages and improved public services and benefits for the people. In Massachusetts, the Know Nothings issued a call to all citizens to participate in the new political movement they were spearheading. A record number of laborers, clerks, schoolteachers, and ministers responded by running for office under the Know Nothing banner.[45]

The last core feature of Know Nothing ideology was its assertion of an exclusive "American" or "native American" identity that appealed to many US-born whites. To the Know Nothings, Americanness was defined through whiteness, Protestantism, and so-called native status. "Americans must rule America" became the Know Nothings' favorite slogan.[46]

How the Know Nothings defined what it meant to be American was significant. The United States and its people, economy, government, and culture were all undergoing rapid and massive change—and the nativism and "native American" identity the Know Nothings promoted offered a stay of collective identity and legitimacy amid the chaos. The actual territorial boundaries of the United States had expanded greatly in the fifty years leading up to the Know Nothings' political rise. Most recently, the United States had just laid claim to huge tracts of land stretching from Texas to the Pacific Ocean at the end of the Mexican-American War. The US government continued to wrest land from Native Americans while encouraging the ongoing migration of white and European settlers. The nation was on the verge of a civil war over slavery and the place of African Americans in American life. Immigration was bringing record numbers of foreigners into the country while many Americans were migrating themselves, leaving their family homes and communities in the East for new opportunities in the cities or out West. Just what it meant to be "American" amid all of this change was unclear.

The Know Nothings' narrow definition of *American* as white Anglo-Saxon Protestants had deep roots. What was new was the use of *native* American to define a new type of citizen who was allegedly superior to both Native Americans and foreign immigrants. In this way, the Know Nothings were not only anti-immigrant; they were pro-"native." The emphasis on native status in the Know Nothings' definition of *American* had nothing to do with indigenous roots. Rather, the Know Nothings and other self-proclaimed "native Americans" seized the *native* label from indigenous peoples and claimed it for themselves. They were not the first to do so. "Playing Indian," or expropriating what was believed to be native symbols, names, rituals, and dress, had a long history in the United States. When crucial distinctions between an *us* and a *them* had to be drawn, white Americans had always relied on the imagery of Native Americans to represent identities that were supposed to be unquestionably American. In colonial America, revolutionaries performed Indianness to highlight their own American (rather than European) roots and identity. Most famously, the American patriots of the 1773 Boston Tea Party donned costumes and yelled out what they believed to be Native American war cries as they dumped British tea into the Boston Harbor. The Improved Order of Red Men, the fraternal organization begun by white men during the War of 1812, pioneered the use of Native American imagery and symbols as a form of American patriotism by forming local "lodges" and "wigwams" and bestowing on their leaders such titles as *Grand Sachem*, *Chief*, *Squaw*, and *Warrior*.[47]

The Know Nothings drew on these same symbols and ceremonial language. Know Nothing chapters were called *wigwams* and leaders were called *Grand Sachems*. Know Nothing popular culture also used native symbols as an expression of their claimed native status. An 1854 illustrated advertisement for Know Nothing Soap sold by a Boston-based company, for example, prominently features two Native Americans beside an American flag. This expropriation served many purposes. First, it aided white American efforts to both literally and figuratively replace indigenous peoples in the United States in the "founding" of the country, and it reaffirmed their own status in a changing country.[48]

One of the places where this was most effective was in Massachusetts. The state was in the midst of tremendous demographic change in the early nineteenth century, and not coincidentally, both claims of "native Americanism" and xenophobia flourished there. In 1830, nearly all residents in the state had been Protestants living in the same rural or coastal areas where their families had lived for generations. They were rooted in their local communities, institutions, and cultures. A generation later, most had migrated to cities, and Massachusetts had become the nation's most densely populated, industrialized, and urbanized state.[49]

The Know Nothings sought to profit from both xenophobia and nativism. Advertisement for Know Nothing Soap, Geo. A. Hill & Co., 1854. Courtesy of the Library of Congress.

Even more sons and daughters of Massachusetts were migrating west to Michigan, Indiana, Illinois, Wisconsin, and Minnesota in search of new economic opportunities. At the same time, Boston, the state of Massachusetts, and the New England region in general were declining in importance on the national stage. Meanwhile, foreigners arrived daily. Twenty-two percent of residents in 1855 were foreign-born, and four-fifths of those were Irish Catholic. The sense of cultural displacement and resentment was palpable. In 1855, Dr. Josiah Curtis predicted that it would be "very difficult to name a day in the future, when the number of American citizens . . . will again constitute a majority of those who shall inhabit the present limits of Boston."[50]

In the midst of all of these changes remaking their world, New Englanders turned to reclaiming (and rewriting) the past. They fostered a new and sometimes passionate interest in genealogy and local history in order to lay claim to a "native" identity that placed them as the "first" peoples of consequence in North America, historians have shown. Their published family histories and local histories became an important means of establishing just who they thought belonged in New England, as well as who should have positions of power and privilege in a changing America. Native Americans were especially important in these works— through their absence. By completely ignoring and deliberately "writing Indians out of existence" in local histories, white settlers, leaders, and statesmen promoted the idea that Native Americans had "disappeared" or "vanished" from the region. New Englanders then claimed that they had "replaced" Native Americans as the indigenous or real "native sons and daughters" in the United States. These acts served the necessary purpose of establishing New England as the undisputed site where America was "founded" as a "cradle of national liberty" and where modern American culture continued to flourish under these self-proclaimed "native" Americans.[51]

Erasing indigenous peoples, the real natives, from history and obscuring their ongoing presence and active participation in contemporary society also served the purpose of refuting Native American sovereignty and ongoing claims to land and rights. Happening amid forced Native American removals across the country at midcentury and growing conflicts between Native Americans and whites in the Midwest and Far West, the use and abuse of Native American histories and culture was not inconsequential. It worked hand in hand with nineteenth-century settler colonialism.

Claiming native status also helped white Anglo-Saxon Americans define themselves in opposition to growing numbers of foreign immigrants. On the one hand, white Americans retold the myth of the vanishing Indian to legitimize their claim to native territory. On the other hand, they emphasized immigrants' dangerous foreignness in order to delegitimize immigrants' claim to America. One result was *nativism*, the naming of white Anglo-Saxon Protestant settlers and their descendants as the true natives to the United States who deserved special privileges and protections. Another was the creation of the *native* American: an American national identity based on the dispossession of indigenous peoples, the promotion of xenophobia, and the strengthening of white supremacy.

These connections between settler colonialism, xenophobia, and nativism are readily apparent in the records of the East Boston chapter (known as Wigwam 5 of the State of Massachusetts) of the American Party. Diligently managed by recording secretary Solomon Bradford Morse Jr., most of the official party's bound volumes are meticulous notes of chapter business. But Morse devoted other pages to his own family's genealogical research. The two projects—waging a war against dangerous foreigners who were displacing old, established families like his, and confirming just how old and established his family was and the role that it had played in founding the nation—were directly linked in Morse's mind. This Know Nothing chapter closed in 1856, but two years later, Morse repurposed volume three of the chapter's official records for his own Morse family history research. That his own son, Solomon B. Morse III, had recently gone out west to California like so many of New England's children was likely resting heavily in his mind at the same time. Entries include a steady list of names and biographical details dating the family tree back to Joseph Morse, who was born in England and emigrated to New England in 1646, and Alice Carpenter Southworth, who sailed to Plymouth in 1623 and shortly after her arrival married Plymouth governor William Bradford. Morse was also careful to include histories of the Bradford family in England and America, passenger lists for the *Mayflower*, and some of the other ships carrying Pilgrims to New England.[52]

With this family history, Morse established a Puritan pedigree that was beyond dispute. That he found it necessary to become so involved in the country's leading anti-immigrant organization made clear how threatened people like Morse felt by immigration. When the mass migration of foreigners seemingly challenged their demographic dominance and status, nativism was deployed against immigrants in order to establish authority over the newcomers, affirm their continued identification as the true founders of the nation, and maintain their political leadership. Know Nothing Henry Gardner—who was elected governor of Massachusetts in 1854—made this exact point to the Boston *Bee* when he explained in 1856 that Know Nothings were simply following the wishes of the revolutionary generation to beware of "foreign influence." When "governed EXCLUSIVELY BY AMERICANS—by those who have been born and reared upon its soil," he explained, Americans could "confidently expect a return to the pure and thoroughly American Policy of our early Presidents."[53]

This position helped justify the Know Nothings' attempts to limit the political power of immigrants by changing existing naturalization laws allowing the foreign-born to apply for naturalization after five years' residence. This was much too short, the Know Nothings argued. Foreigners were made American citizens "altogether too rapidly," the Boston *Know Nothing* paper declared. Know Nothings proposed a waiting period of twenty-one years. It took that long for a native-born American to gain the full rights of citizenship, they reasoned. It should take that long for the foreign-born. (Significantly, though, even the Know Nothings never proposed to deny Catholic immigrants the right to become naturalized citizens, as was the case with Chinese immigrants, nor ignore this right, as was the case with Mexican Americans and African Americans.)

They also insisted on granting special privileges to US-born (and white Protestant) Americans by electing only members of this rarefied group to political office. The official examiner's questions for admission into the American Party asked prospective members to agree to use their influence to elect only native-born citizens of America "to the exclusion of all foreigners, and to all Roman Catholics, whether they be of native or foreign birth." In this way, the Know Nothings successfully spearheaded efforts to institutionalize distinctions (and inequality) between so-called natives and foreigners in law.[54]

With their unique blend of populism, grassroots organizing, and secret members-only culture, the Know Nothings expanded their influence and their ranks across regions and states. They politicized and popularized xenophobia through a broad network of councils, state and national meetings, and newspapers. And they promised to save the country from ruin, offer a "remedy which shall restore peace," and "inaugurate a new era" based on "native American" identity and superiority. But first, they had to govern.[55]

DURING THE 1854 elections, Know Nothing victories stunned the nation. They were successful in California, Indiana, Maine, and Ohio, as well as in their traditional strongholds of Massachusetts, Rhode Island, New

Hampshire, Connecticut, Pennsylvania, and New York. By the end of 1855, the Know Nothings had captured eight governorships, controlled nine state legislatures, and had elected more than a hundred congressmen as well as the mayors of Boston, Philadelphia, and Chicago.[56]

No state was more successful in turning the Know Nothing movement into a political reality than its bastion of Massachusetts, which by this time was rife with nativist anxieties. On the eve of the November 1854 elections, the Massachusetts Know Nothings had established 410 councils with seventy-three thousand members, a number that represented well over half the number of votes usually cast in state elections. Both the Whigs and the Democrats had failed to mount a significant response to voter concerns. These included not only a backlash against immigration but also national issues like slavery and local ones like explosive urban and industrial growth. Massachusetts Know Nothings promised to protect the state from immigration and out-of-touch political leaders.[57]

Two out of three voters in the state supported a Know Nothing candidate during the 1854 election. Know Nothing candidates were chosen for all of the state offices, every one of the state senators, and all but three of the 378 seats in the state house of representatives. They swept municipal elections in Boston, Roxbury, and Cambridge. In Boston, Know Nothing mayoral candidate Jerome Van Crowninshield Smith was elected with the largest vote in the history of mayoral elections in the city. In the span of a single election, the Know Nothings unceremoniously drove the state's political elite from power and took control of its government.[58]

The Know Nothings entered office with a clear political mandate, but hopes for their government quickly dissipated as rivalries erupted among lawmakers. Former Democrats and Whigs wanted to address rapid urbanization and industrial growth. Antislavery advocates (also known as *free-soil Americans*) wanted to focus on combating slavery. Die-hard xenophobes had their own anti-Catholic and anti-immigrant agenda. The new Know Nothing lawmakers were also woefully inexperienced. Placing political newcomers into office had been part of the Know Nothing appeal. But inexperienced lawmakers hampered the business of actual governing. The new legislature, for example, had twenty-four clergymen and numerous doctors, clerks, skilled workers, teachers, and a large number of laborers who all were committed to governing but had little actual experience doing so.[59]

The Know Nothing government did have some legislative achievements regarding slavery and women's rights. These included a resolution urging Congress to restore the Missouri Compromise and repeal the Fugitive Slave Law; the passage of state laws that gave single women the same rights as married women to make business transactions, make a will, and go to work without the consent of a husband were also significant advances for women. But where the Know Nothing government was most effective was in turning their vision of extreme xenophobia into what historians have called a "state-sponsored attack on the civil and political rights of the foreign-born and Roman Catholics" that went far beyond any anti-immigrant measures in the United States.[60]

In control of nearly the entire Massachusetts state government, the Know Nothings were free to target the Irish Catholic minority with little or no opposition. They took over the power from the courts to pass judgment on applications for naturalization. They required a daily reading of the King James Bible in the public schools, disbanded the Irish militia units, dismissed Irish state workers, banned the teaching of foreign languages in the public schools, called on the federal government to extend the residency requirement for naturalization from five to twenty-one years, established a Nunnery Committee tasked with inspecting nunneries and convents for suspected abuses, and limited public office to US-born citizens only. They also strengthened the restriction of poor immigrants entering the state by railroad and effectively brought immigration enforcement into the country's interior. Massachusetts officials turned away 499 immigrants in 1855 and 363 in 1856. Even after the Know Nothings were kicked out of office, rejections continued under the Republican officials who replaced them. Two hundred sixty-three immigrants were denied entry in 1857.[61]

But perhaps the most consequential law that the Know Nothings implemented was a new deportation policy that expanded the state government's authority to deport foreign paupers and at the same time broadened the category of people who could be deported. Like their policies on immigration restriction, these would continue long after the party collapsed. State officials working under the auspices of the State Board of Commissioners of Alien Passengers and Paupers, an agency tasked with controlling immigration and poor relief first established in 1851, regularly visited almshouses, immigrant hospitals, state lunatic hospitals, and local charitable institutions to identify deportable immigrants. As precursors to the immigration raids that federal immigration officials would later use as part of federal deportation policy, these annual visits provided authorities with the opportunity to examine and interrogate poor immigrants and remove them under Massachusetts law to any place "where he belongs." Historians have shown that with these laws, Massachusetts—before, during, and after the Know Nothing reign— forcibly removed more than fifteen thousand immigrants from the state between 1850 and 1863. In 1858, a new state legislature reorganized the Commissioners of Alien Passengers and Foreign Paupers but continued the Know Nothings' policies of aggressive deportation. That year alone, 3,369 paupers were expelled from the state, not much less than the 4,028 during the two-year Know Nothing reign.[62]

Deportation was often cruelly enforced. Some deportees were elderly and had been in the United States for nearly forty years. Poor Irish women and children who were widowed, unemployed, or abandoned (in other words, among society's most needy) found themselves at the mercy of immigration officials. Deportees' physical and mental health were often ignored before sending them on strenuous overseas journeys. Some perished along the way, while others died on arrival in Europe. Many Irish deportees were sent to New York, Canada, England, or Ireland without regard for their own wishes; they were often cast aside on arrival, without any basic provisions such as food, shelter, clothing, or money. And officials often forcefully and sometimes illegally removed people without the required court warrants. They also unlawfully expelled American citizens of Irish descent despite the fact that state law explicitly allowed only noncitizens to be sent overseas.

The Know Nothings' approach to immigration would also influence an emerging body of immigration policy at the national level. The specter of poor immigrants flooding into the United States remained an issue of public concern for decades and led to the passage of the Immigration Act of 1882. Passed three months after the Chinese Exclusion Act, the 1882 law was the country's first general immigration law that applied to all immigrants and prohibited the landing of paupers and criminals; it also provided for the deportation of criminals who escaped exclusion at the time of arrival.[63]

Massachusetts, where the Know Nothings had been able to turn their extreme political xenophobia into a state-sanctioned assault on immigrants, represented the party at its most successful. But as party leaders proved helpless to enact a broad or significant legislative agenda nationally, criticism of the Know Nothings increased, and the party began to lose momentum after that peak of 1854. Detractors ridiculed the party's secrecy and condemned some of the anti-immigrant violence that occurred in the name of Know Nothingism. Internal dissension further weakened the party from within.

Yet the reopening of the slavery question dealt the final blow to the American Party—and its decline was stunningly swift. As the United States headed toward a bloody war over slavery, the Know Nothings held their national convention in 1855. Party leadership appeared to equivocate on the issue of extending slavery by adopting platforms that accepted the Kansas-Nebraska Act. In response, most Northerners abandoned the Know Nothings and joined the emerging Republican Party in droves, helping to transform the Republicans (whose standard-bearer, Abraham Lincoln, denounced the Know Nothings) into the nation's dominant political party. Pro-slavery members fractured off from the Know Nothings and sided with the Democrats.[64]

In 1856, the Know Nothings nominated former president Millard Fillmore as their presidential candidate. Fillmore succeeded in winning the electoral votes of only one state. This embarrassing performance further weakened the party. Moreover, the federal government never acted on the Know Nothing's signature issue of a twenty-one-year wait for immigrant naturalization. By 1860, when many of its former members carried Abraham Lincoln to victory, the American Party was no more.

MUCH CHANGED OVER the years—secession, war, reconstruction. By the late nineteenth century, Irish and German Catholics had even become grudgingly accepted. One hundred fifty thousand Irish and Irish Americans fought for the Union during the Civil War, and although their service and sacrifice did not erase all prejudice against them, they did quiet critics who had questioned their loyalty to the country. Significantly, Irish Americans also retained and used their power to vote—becoming central political actors whom many politicians could not afford to offend. Signs of this appeared even prior to the war; when Stephen A. Douglas debated Abraham Lincoln in 1858, for example, he stressed that pure white Americans came from "every branch of the Caucasian race," including the "Irish one."[65]

As early as 1862, there was no more talk of a race war between Anglos and Celts. Instead, the Irish were quietly included as the same kind of "white" as Anglo-Saxons and Scandinavians when a US congressional committee unproblematically included all three groups in the "white race" that was the "natural" population of the nation. In 1864, President Abraham Lincoln insisted that the Republican Party officially add a pro-immigration plank to its platform. "Foreign immigration, which in the past has added so much to the wealth, development of resources, and increase of nations," it stated, "should be fostered and encouraged by a liberal and just policy." That same year, Congress passed a bill to encourage immigration, in recognition of the country's continued need for more laborers. Other government policies, like the 1862 Homestead Act, which encouraged westward migration and white settlement, were promoted in Europe and led to increased European immigration.[66]

Following emancipation at the end of the Civil War, new and existing problems of race, citizenship, and immigration grew larger in the popular imagination. African Americans were now free, and former slaves were now citizens. But equality would prove to be elusive; in fact,

African Americans were considered an even greater racial threat after the Civil War than before. Southern states passed a series of Black Codes designed to maintain the same racial and economic inequality that had existed under slavery. They also codified white supremacy by depriving African Americans the right to vote, serve on juries, or own or carry weapons. In some states, they were even prohibited from renting or leasing land. The United States also continued to wage a military war against Native Americans up through the end of the nineteenth century, and a new immigrant threat from China began to eclipse the one from Catholic Ireland.

For their part, Irish Americans continued to exercise their political power and their whiteness in ways that protected them from further stigmatization. They even became leaders of other anti-immigrant movements, most notably the campaign to exclude the Chinese. Indeed, their efforts to expel Chinese immigrants earned them a reputation as "Irish Know Nothings." In this way, xenophobia shifted shape; it found a new target. Now, the enemy was on the West Coast.[67]

THREE

"THE CHINESE ARE NO MORE"

On April 5, 1876, twenty-five thousand people gathered in San Francisco's Union Hall for a statewide meeting on Chinese immigration. Five thousand crowded into the vast auditorium. The rest assembled outside on specially built platforms and crowded the blocks surrounding the hall. It was the largest gathering the Pacific Coast had ever seen. No one, it seemed, wanted to miss the opportunity to voice their opinion on "*the* question of the day," the "Chinese question."[1]

San Francisco mayor Andrew Jackson Bryant set the tone with his opening speech. Chinese immigration, he gravely declared, was an issue that involved "every man, woman, and child, not only of the Pacific Coast, but also of the entire United States." Following Bryant was a parade of the state's leading politicians, who spelled out in great detail the evils of Chinese immigration and the damage it was inflicting on the state. California governor William Irwin even blamed the Chinese for subverting "everything that goes to make up American civilization." After some additional speeches, several anti-Chinese resolutions were read aloud.[2]

The case made against Chinese immigration recycled many of the same arguments used against Irish Catholics: Chinese immigrants undercut American workers. They were criminals who filled the state's prisons and asylums. They operated in secret through their own societies;

they followed their own laws. The diseases they carried were "infectious and horrible."[3]

Other arguments were specifically tailored to the Chinese. One was about sex and gender. Anti-Chinese activists claimed that Chinese immigrants posed a sexual danger to the country and its citizens. Chinese female prostitutes caused "moral and racial pollution" through their interracial liaisons, while Chinese men lured pure and innocent white women into their dens of vice and depravity. With many of their wives and children remaining in China, they also lived in so-called bachelor societies that many Americans considered deviant. Moreover, Chinese men were depicted as effeminate because they engaged in "women's work" of cleaning and cooking.[4]

The greatest condemnation, however, was about race. Although the Know Nothings had claimed that the Irish belonged to the so-called Celtic race, the Irish had always remained white. The Chinese were different. They were unquestionably not white and would never be able to become "American," anti-Chinese activists argued. Instead, the Chinese "are of a distinct race, of a different and peculiar civilization," one anti-Chinese resolution proclaimed at the San Francisco meeting. "They do not speak our language, do not adopt our manners, customs or habits, are Pagan in belief." Chinese immigration, the organizing committee concluded, was "an evil of great present magnitude."[5]

Speakers at the San Francisco rally agreed that immediate action was needed. The anti-Chinese organizing committee urged a delegation to go forth to Washington, DC, and lobby for restrictive legislation at the federal level. So enthusiastic was the response to this suggestion that thousands stayed at Union Hall and strategized until eleven o'clock at night. Nearly twenty thousand people signed an anti-Chinese petition bound for Washington, DC. Just a few blocks north, Chinatown was shuttered. No one was on the street. Businesses were closed and protected by iron bars. Inside, anxious Chinese gathered together to wait out the night. They sat on chairs, benches, and counters and watched for angry crowds to descend on their homes and businesses. That night, they were safe. But the anti-Chinese movement was just gaining momentum, and with it, racism and xenophobia became more tightly connected.[6]

Later that same week, San Francisco lawyer H. N. Clement stood before a California state senate committee and sounded the alarm: "The Chinese are upon us. How can we get rid of them? The Chinese are coming. How can we stop them?" Clement's panicked cries and portrayals of Chinese immigration as an evil, "unarmed invasion" were being shared by several witnesses before the committee, which was charged with investigating the "social, moral, and political effects" of Chinese immigration. From April 11 to June 3, five state senators held fifteen sessions and interviewed sixty individuals in the state capital of Sacramento. All 165 pages of the completed testimony were dutifully recorded and printed in a report that was part of a calculated attempt to politicize anti-Chinese xenophobia and launch a national campaign to restrict Chinese immigration. Multiple state efforts had failed to achieve this goal, and Californians were now setting their sights on the US Congress. As the committee's "Address to the People of the United States upon the Evils of Chinese Immigration" made clear, the people of California had "but one disposition upon this grave subject . . . and that is an open and pronounced demand upon the Federal Government for relief."[7]

The California state senate suggested a plan of action. If Chinese immigration continued unrestricted, the committee members warned, the country would be subjected to a "dangerous unarmed invasion" of foreigners who were completely unassimilable. In twenty years, Chinese would occupy the entire Pacific Coast "to the exclusion of the white population," and the whole seaboard would become but a "mere colony of China," it hysterically claimed. "The people of this State have been more than patient," the committee members insisted. But their patience had worn out. In an attached memorial directed to members of the US Congress, the committee urged national lawmakers to repeal the 1868 Burlingame Treaty, which permitted the free emigration of Chinese to the United States, and restrict Chinese immigration. In an effort to promote its anti-Chinese platform across the country, the state government also sent the report to all "leading newspapers of the United States," as well as to every member of the US Congress and the governor of each state. Another two thousand copies were printed up for general distribution.[8]

Anti-Chinese xenophobia relied on many of the political tactics first used by the anti-Catholic Know Nothing Party. Anti-Chinese groups were highly organized, specialized in appealing to the masses, and were politically astute. Like the Know Nothings, anti-Chinese leaders also promoted a new kind of American national identity that further distinguished "Americans" from new and dangerous immigrants invading the United States. This nativist identity similarly rested on the erasure of indigenous peoples begun by the Know Nothings.

But what was significantly different in anti-Chinese rhetoric was the explicit grouping of *all* European immigrants as full Americans. Immigrants from across the Atlantic were no longer the "scum of Europe" sent by the pope to control the United States, as the Know Nothings had claimed a generation before. As California lawmakers and anti-Chinese spokespeople—many of whom were Irish or Irish American themselves— argued, Chinese were a threat to "our own people," whom they defined as the "original settlers of California, along with their children" and "recent immigrants from the East and Europe."[9]

By using this definition, anti-Chinese politicians conveniently ignored African Americans, Mexican Americans, and the hundreds of indigenous nations who were already present in California before white settlement, just as the Know Nothings had done on the East Coast decades before. But they also unambiguously included all European immigrants as "our own people." To some extent, these sentiments reflected the racial dynamics in the West, where claims to and privileges of whiteness were central to sustaining the West as a "white man's frontier." The anti-Chinese and later anti-Japanese movements would consistently distinguish between the need to welcome all European immigrants and to close the doors to all Asians. "We want *all good people from all parts of Europe*," Italian American A. Sbarboro passionately claimed at a California anti-Asian meeting in 1901. Arguing that distinctions should be made *between* European and Asian immigrants rather than *among* European immigrants, xenophobes like Sbarboro continued to expand the boundaries of whiteness while advocating for Asian exclusion.[10]

This emphasis on whiteness also revealed how American xenophobia came to focus more on race rather than on religion during the anti-Chinese movement. European immigrants, especially Catholics and Jews from southern and eastern Europe, would still be targeted by xenophobia, religious intolerance, and immigration restriction, but Asian and Mexican immigrants would face even more discriminatory policies in the twentieth century.

The anti-Chinese campaign also went much further than what even the most extreme Know Nothing politicians had envisioned. Anti-Chinese leaders not only successfully politicized the issue of Chinese immigration; they garnered the support of both major political parties and the full weight of the US government. The US Congress eventually heeded the call of Californians and other Westerners to protect them from the so-called Chinese invasion with the passage of the 1882 Chinese Exclusion Act. The first law to establish significant federal control over immigration, the Chinese Exclusion Act legalized xenophobia on an unprecedented scale. It not only singled out a specific group for exclusion; it also helped shape the modern system of immigration regulation that would be used around the world.

THE WOMEN SANG songs of loss, grief, and anger. So many of their husbands, fathers, and brothers had left their villages in South China's Pearl River Delta for Gum Saan ("Gold Mountain") and had never returned. "I beg of you, after you depart, to come back soon," they sang. "Also, I beg of you that your heart won't change / That you keep your heart and mind on taking care of your family." Known as *gam saan haak*, or Gold Mountain men, Chinese had first gone to the United States in search of gold during the California gold rush. Only a few struck it rich, but most stayed to work in the mines or in the booming gold rush economy. There were plenty of jobs. American labor recruiters began heading to China and bombarded prospective immigrants with the message that, as one advertisement proclaimed, "Americans are very rich people. They want the Chinaman to come. . . . Money is in great plenty and to spare in America." By 1870, there were sixty-three thousand Chinese in the United States, over three-quarters of them in California.[11]

Over the decades, the demand for Chinese labor increased. In 1865, the first Chinese were hired by the Central Pacific Railroad to clear trees, blast through mountains, and lay tracks on the great transcontinental railroad heading east from Sacramento. Making up 90 percent of the workforce, they worked long hours in the heat and snow but were paid less than white workers. Company president Leland Stanford praised the Chinese as "quiet, peaceable, industrious, [and] economical" and admitted that the railroad could not have been built without them. But when Stanford and the other railroad barons gathered at Promontory Point, Utah, to celebrate the completion of the railroad on May 10, 1869, Chinese workers were excluded from all official photographs commemorating the occasion.[12]

Despite the mistreatment and discrimination they faced in the United States, Chinese immigrants kept coming. There were few reasons to remain in China. War, foreign imperialism, high taxes, and population growth all made it harder and harder for rural families to support themselves, especially in the southeastern province of Guangdong. A seemingly endless stream of natural disasters, plagues, and famines battered the countryside while the Qing Empire faltered and China underwent a revolution in 1911. The Chinese increasingly began to leave their home villages and head to larger cities in search of work. Soon, they began leaving China altogether for new homes around the world. Migrant letters, newspapers, and folk songs fueled migration. "Try to leave the village," Wong Sing Look's brother (already in the United States) advised him in a letter. "You can never make a living there."[13] Chinese immigrants also kept coming to the United States, because they had become indispensable in the mines, factories, and fields of the West. They were hired again and again for jobs that were believed to be too dirty, dangerous, or degrading for white men and were paid on a separate and lower wage scale from whites.

The nearly 139,000 Chinese who entered the United States between 1870 and 1880 were only a small fraction of the total number of immigrants (nearly 3.2 million, mostly from Europe) who also arrived in the country during the same decade. Nevertheless, their presence sparked some of the most violent and racist campaigns in US history.[14]

At first seen as exotic curiosities from the Orient, Chinese immigrants came to be viewed as threats, especially as their numbers grew throughout the Gold Rush period and as the United States grappled with issues of slavery and freedom, conquest and colonization. These were all racial issues: Native American wars, struggles over African slavery, and the conquest of the West were tied to race-based ideas of who belonged in the United States and where they fit in the country's racial hierarchy. The Chinese were the largest group of nonwhite immigrants to come to the United States and were not considered immigrants like those from Europe. Instead, Chinese immigrants and Chinese Americans were treated more like African Americans and Native Americans as race problems to be stringently controlled (as in Jim Crow segregation) or expelled and driven off (as in the ongoing war against Native Americans.) As a result, they were denied similar rights and freedoms, such as the right to become naturalized citizens.[15]

An economic recession in the 1870s added some materiality to these debates. With California's economy devastated, demagogues such as California Workingmen's Party leader Denis Kearney (an Irish immigrant himself) capitalized on the deep sense of economic insecurity among the working classes in San Francisco and blamed Chinese workers for unfavorable wages and the scarcity of jobs. Other labor leaders joined the debate and charged that Chinese were imported slaves, or *coolies*, engaged in a new system of slavery that degraded US labor. Samuel Gompers, president of the American Federation of Labor, framed this issue explicitly by asking the question: "Meat vs. Rice—American Manhood vs. Asiatic Coolieism. Which Shall Survive?"[16]

Promoted by labor leaders like Kearney and Gompers, anti-Chinese sentiment proved to be popular. It also turned out to be profitable. Just as anti-Catholic xenophobia inspired the publication of numerous best-selling books, the anti-Chinese movement also helped sell many newspapers, journals, and magazines. One illustrated magazine dominated the American public's understanding of the Chinese "immigration problem." First printed in 1876, the *San Francisco Illustrated Wasp* became a successful weekly magazine focusing on social and political satire. San Francisco had a dozen or so weekly magazines, but the *Wasp* rose above its competitors with its vibrant and politically astute illustrations that were the first mass-produced large-scale colored cartoons in the United States. A political dissident forced to flee from his home in Czechoslovakia, *Wasp* owner Francis Korbel relished in exposing political corruption and growing government and corporate power. But it was his devotion to the anti-Chinese movement—and his realization that the anti-Chinese cartoons he published would attract readers and maximize profits—that motivated the *Wasp* to take a leading role in animating anti-Chinese racist hysteria. The publication consistently depicted Chinese immigration as an infestation destroying the United States, Chinese laborers as ruthless competitors, and the Chinese "way of life" as inherently immoral. In many illustrations, Chinese were completely dehumanized and portrayed as vermin.

George Frederick Keller, another immigrant from Prussia who began his career by creating cigar labels for Korbel, was the talented artist behind many of the *Wasp*'s high-quality political cartoons. Combining attention to detail with new color printing technology, Keller masterfully captured white Californians' fears about Chinese immigration in the 1881 illustration "A Statue for *Our* Harbor." A statue of a grotesque Chinese male coolie in San Francisco Bay mocks New York's Statue of Liberty, then under construction. Instead of wearing graceful flowing robes like his New York counterpart, he wears disheveled rags. Instead of a torch, he holds an opium pipe. His slanted eyes, gaunt features, and rat-tail-like braid mark him as menacing and racially inferior. He stands as a triumphant victor over a defeated California, represented by the skull under his foot, the rats scurrying around the pedestal, capsized ships, and crumbling foundation. A slant-eyed moon looks on in approval as the statue spreads filth, immorality, diseases, and ruin to white labor across the land.

"A Statue for Our Harbor." By George Frederick Keller, *The Wasp*, November 11, 1881. San Francisco History Center, San Francisco Public Library.

A STATUE FOR *OUR* HARBOR.

The *Wasp*'s racist campaign against the Chinese paid off handsomely. While many of its rivals were forced to shut down operations within a few years, the *Wasp*'s circulation grew to five thousand within months of its first issue, reaching seven thousand by 1879. It quickly became the most widely read magazine on the West Coast.[17]

By the time the anti-Chinese citizens' committee gathered supporters together in San Francisco in 1876, Chinese immigrants had already been singled out for discriminatory treatment in California for over two decades. As early as 1852, California's Foreign Miners' License Tax targeted Chinese immigrants with expensive monthly license fees. Although the law was aimed at all foreigners, it was primarily enforced against the Chinese, and over the years, the state collected millions of dollars from them. In 1854, the California Supreme Court ruled that Chinese immigrants, along with African Americans and Native Americans, were prohibited from giving testimony in cases involving a white person. In support of its decision, the court argued that Chinese immigrants were a "distinct people . . . whom nature has marked as inferior." Animosity and state-sanctioned discrimination against the Chinese reached a new level by the 1860s and 1870s. A Chinese Police Tax was levied on all Chinese people living in the state in 1862, and over the next decade, various laws barred Chinese people from testifying in criminal or civil cases, attending public school, working on county irrigation projects, and owning property.[18]

San Francisco inaugurated its own special campaign against the Chinese through a series of municipal ordinances designed to single out Chinese people for harassment. There was the Lodging House Ordinance, or Cubic Air Ordinance, which required every lodging house to provide at least five hundred cubic feet of air space for each lodger—a direct shot at the Chinese who, out of necessity, tended to live in crowded rooming houses. There was also the Queue Ordinance, which required every male prisoner sentenced to jail to have his hair cut to within one inch of his scalp. As the name suggests, this bill targeted Chinese men who wore their hair in a queue, a long braid down their back with the forehead shaved, as required by the Chinese empire.

In 1870, the state legislature passed a law forbidding the landing of any "Mongolian, Chinese, or Japanese female for criminal or demoralizing purposes," a law that the state commission of immigration used to deny entry to all Chinese women. Many of these laws were found unconstitutional or rarely enforced. The 1870 law, for example, was declared unconstitutional by the US Supreme Court on the grounds that it exceeded the police power of the state, violated the United States' Burlingame Treaty with China, the Fourteenth Amendment, and the 1866 Civil Rights Act.[19]

But far from deterring California's anti-Chinese leaders, these defeats convinced them that the only course of action was to take their case to Washington, DC. Some limited federal restrictions were already in place. The Coolie Trade Act of 1862 outlawed "coolie labor" and US involvement in the so-called coolie trade that brought over 250,000 Chinese and

420,000 South Asian immigrants to the Caribbean and Latin America as indentured laborers. The 1875 Page Act barred Asian women suspected of prostitution, as well as Asian laborers transported to the country as contract laborers. This law was broadly used to deny entry to all Chinese immigrants, especially women. Both the 1862 and 1875 laws would become important blueprints in the eventual exclusion of all Chinese laborers in 1882, especially in how they identified Chinese immigrants as unfree (and racially inferior) peoples like African Americans. But they fell far short of the goal of total exclusion that many anti-Chinese leaders pushed for.[20]

Although Chinese immigration was a central issue for California, it was not yet a national one. Beyond the Rockies, opinions varied. Some people believed the problem was just a West Coast problem—a regional one that didn't concern them. Or they dismissed the idea that Chinese immigrants were dangerous. Some Americans were even in favor of it, seeing their own financial benefit. Southern plantation owners and northeastern shoe factory owners, for example, tried to recruit Chinese laborers. And many were unfazed when the United States and China signed the 1868 Burlingame Treaty, which recognized the "inherent and inalienable right of man to change his home and allegiance" and underscored the principle that both the United States and China benefited from unrestricted migration between the two countries.

California politicians, joined by others up and down the Pacific Coast, grew increasingly frustrated. Beginning in 1875, they vowed to bring their message to the rest of the country. Their timing was excellent.[21]

The year 1876 became a major turning point in the anti-Chinese movement, pushing it out past the Rockies to make it an American issue. Rising Chinese immigration was one factor. More Chinese immigrants (60,505) had come through San Francisco's Custom House in the preceding three years than at any other time since 1852. Labor unions and anti-Chinese organizations also mobilized xenophobia, turning it into a mass movement. Membership in anti-Chinese organizations grew across the state throughout the 1870s, and all of the anti-Chinese clubs in the state unified under the umbrella of the Anti-Chinese Union in order to advance their twin goals of Chinese exclusion and Chinese expulsion. They vowed to "discourage and stop any further Chinese immigration" and to "compel the Chinese living in the United States to withdraw from the country." With labor leaders as well as US senators, congressmen, and almost every prominent politician in the state active in the organization, the union's membership marked how anti-Chinese xenophobia had become a mainstream political issue.[22]

And, most crucially, 1876 was an important presidential election year; both the Republican and the Democratic parties were locked in a highly competitive race for the White House. For the first time, the electoral votes from the West Coast could tip the balance of power in Washington. Both parties were eager to demonstrate to Western voters that they understood their issues and would protect their interests. What voters in California and other Pacific Coast states unequivocally wanted—what was their issue, what they thought would protect their interests—was an end to Chinese immigration.

California's anti-Chinese leaders played their cards well. In March 1876, San Francisco mayor Andrew Jackson Bryant called for a committee to be sent to Washington, DC, to lobby for exclusion. "This is the best time to go to Washington," he told the San Francisco Board of Supervisors. "We are on the eve of a presidential election and both parties are looking toward the coast for aid." In return, they demanded action on Chinese immigration. Their efforts were strategically timed to impact the national nominating conventions that summer. Both parties responded by seriously examining the Chinese immigration issue on a national level. In July, the US Congress tasked a joint commission to travel to the Pacific Coast to "investigate" Chinese immigration. Hearings began in October in San Francisco's Palace Hotel.[23]

ENCOMPASSING AN ENTIRE city block on the corner of Market and New Montgomery Streets in downtown San Francisco, the Palace Hotel was considered America's first luxury hotel and was marketed as "the world's grandest" when it opened in 1875. At seven stories high, the hotel was the largest built in the West and was an architectural and technological marvel. It was made with the finest materials available and built by artisans imported for their talent and skill. Five state-of-the-art hydraulic elevators whisked guests to their destinations in luxurious comfort. The grand court had seven tiers of galleries that rose to a beautiful leaded-glass dome. There was a marble-flagged office, a ballroom, separate ladies' and men's reception rooms, a billiard room, a barbershop, a bar, and a 150-foot-long dining room. The huge public rooms were adorned with gracious woven rugs commissioned in France, two grand pianos, and landscape paintings celebrating the beauty of California: Lake Tahoe, Yosemite, and the Golden Gate.[24]

On Wednesday, October 18, 1876, the US senators and congressmen of the Joint Special Committee to Investigate Chinese Immigration gathered in rooms A and B of the Palace Hotel to begin their work. The chair of the committee, Senator Oliver Hazard Perry Throckmorton, had traveled from Indiana. Representative Edwin R. Meade came from New York. Senator Aaron A. Sargent from Nevada City, California, and Representative William A. Piper from San Francisco probably had the shortest journeys. Two other committee members, Senator Henry Cooper from Tennessee and Representative Benjamin Wilson from West Virginia were absent the first few days but joined the committee's work in later meetings. A stenographer was also present.

The committee got to work right away. What was billed as a fair-minded "investigation," however, was, in reality, stacked against the Chinese from the beginning. It called several witnesses to the hotel on Thursday, October 19. Over the next thirty days, the committee met seventeen times and heard testimony from 130 witnesses, almost all of whom gave testimony against the Chinese. Among the first to do so were Frank M. Pixley, "representing the people of San Francisco"; former San Francisco mayor Frank McCoppin, and Cameron H. King, president of the Anti-Chinese Union.

The three were eminently qualified witnesses. McCoppin had served as San Francisco's mayor from 1867 to 1869 and was the first Irish-born American mayor in the entire United States. Pixley was a former

California forty-niner who had arrived during the Gold Rush. He served one term as the state attorney general in 1862 and was the founder of the influential publication *Argonaut*. His opposition to Chinese immigration stemmed from a general brand of racism (before the Civil War, he stated his opposition to the spread of slavery, but not to slavery itself; he also opposed the migration of African Americans into the West) as well as a distinct racism directed at the Chinese. The Chinese were, he told Senator Charles Sumner in 1870, "thoroughly antagonistic in every particular, in race, color, language, religion, civilization, and habits of life altogether from our people." Should Chinese immigration continue unchecked, he dramatically claimed, they would simply "overrun our land." Cameron King, originally from New York, was a lawyer with political connections and a leader of the influential anti-Chinese organization.[25]

McCoppin, Pixley, and King established the main arguments against Chinese immigration that would be elaborated on by most other witnesses appearing before the special committee. McCoppin described Chinese immigration as an invasion. China had an enormous population of four hundred million, he explained, making up one-third of the world's population. And it was increasing rapidly. As a result, the pressure to emigrate from that "crowded hive" was great. The introduction and improvement of steamship travel made passage around the globe easier, faster, and cheaper. Already, the Chinese could be found "in every part of the civilized world," he pointed out. The Pacific Coast of North America was particularly vulnerable; a mere forty-dollar ticket put the Chinese just four weeks' sail from San Francisco. He also declared that the Chinese as a race were unassimilable, that no amount of time or schooling could ever change the Chinese into Americans. Unlike other immigrants who came to the United States, McCoppin explained, "the Chinaman, though *in* this country, *is not of it.*"[26]

Pixley picked up on these points during his turn before the committee. The Chinese, as a race, were "as immoral to the very last degree," he explained. They were not Christian, but were atheists, heathens, and polygamists. They totally disregarded oaths. Some of that immorality was evidenced in the frightful prevalence of prostitution in the Chinese quarter, he continued. The Chinese were also considered a massive public health menace. Leprosy was common among them, Pixley argued, and some of the "most fearsome, loathsome, and terrible diseases with which civilization has been infected" thrived and spread in Chinatown.[27]

All three emphasized how the Chinese competed unfairly with white labor, preying on white men. "Many of them are most excellent and good laborers," Pixley conceded. They could perform light labor but were far inferior to white workers and were "not as strong or as brave" as them. Their willingness to work for lower wages also allowed them to monopolize significant parts of the labor force: cigar making, wool manufacturing, domestic service, agriculture, mining, and railroad building. This competition drove the white worker, the "true American hero," Pixley argued, to starvation.[28]

Anti-Chinese Union president Cameron King added his own staunch prediction: if Chinese immigration continued, white labor, through no fault of its own, would be "driven from our State." The Chinese—the people who would replace white laborers—were "filthy, vicious, ignorant, depraved, and criminal." They were a "standing menace to our free institutions, and an ever-threatening danger to our republican form of government." Pixley and King spent little to no time considering the fact that it was the white factory owners, railroad barons, and farmers who set the wage scale—not the Chinese. Instead, anti-Chinese witnesses pounded away at their argument that the low wages paid to and accepted by Chinese immigrants was evidence of Chinese racial inferiority, not of capitalistic competition. The only solution, the witnesses argued, was federal legislation targeting Chinese immigration and a modification of existing international treaties. After the joint congressional committee concluded its work at the Palace Hotel, Senator Aaron A. Sargent wrote the final committee report.[29]

AARON SARGENT HAD a "punishing hatred of the Chinese." A former cabinetmaker, printer, and California forty-niner, Sargent became the nation's foremost leader of the anti-Chinese movement in the 1870s. A

Radical Republican who entered Congress in 1861, he supported the use of federal military force in the South and voting rights for African Americans. But beyond that, he showed little tolerance for any group that was not white, of English descent, and Protestant: Sargent supported the segregation of African Americans. He had a "low regard" for Mexicans. He tried to cut federal appropriations to Native Americans and declared the need to remove them by "whiskey or by war or by emigration" in order to secure their land for the transcontinental railroad. He also didn't like Catholics. But Sargent reserved a special hatred for Chinese immigrants. He was an honorary vice president of the Anti-Chinese Union of San Francisco, and when he became a US congressman, Chinese immigration became a special area of his expertise and influence. As his biographer explained, Sargent had a simple solution for the problem of the Chinese in the United States: "He wanted them out of California, and out of the United States." Sargent would work tirelessly toward the goals of Chinese exclusion and expulsion throughout his long career.[30]

As early as 1862, Sargent declared on the floor of Congress that Chinese immigrants were a great menace to the state of California. They were "slaves and criminals of strange tongue, vile habits, impossible of assimilation, and with customs difficult to penetrate [who] swarm by the thousands to our shores like the frogs of Egypt." When Congress debated a naturalization bill in 1870, Sargent enthusiastically backed a measure that would prevent any person of Chinese or Japanese origin from being naturalized. In his remarks to Congress, Sargent explained that the "Chinaman, as a race" was in every sense of the word the opposite of an American citizen. They lived "upon a lower plane, entirely different from that occupied by our thriving, healthy, prosperous, happy population. . . . They live as Americans cannot."[31]

Sargent would continue to rail against the Chinese on the floor of the House and the Senate over the next several years. A few weeks after the April 1876 anti-Chinese meeting in San Francisco, Sargent called on the president to renegotiate the US treaty with the Chinese government to restrict "the great influx" of Chinese into the United States. He then dramatically presented two large bound volumes containing the signatures of twenty thousand citizens supporting the anti-Chinese resolution. Having captured the attention of his colleagues, he gave one of the most virulent anti-Chinese speeches the Senate had ever heard. Months later, when it came time to summarize the findings of the joint

WHERE BOTH PLATFORMS AGREE.—NO VOTE—NO USE TO EITHER PARTY.

In this July 14, 1880, cover illustration of *Puck* magazine, Republican presidential candidate James Garfield (left) and Democratic presidential candidate Winfield Hancock (right) nail a Chinese man in between the anti-Chinese platforms of both parties. Illustrator J. A. Wales bluntly identified one of the reasons why the anti-Chinese movement enjoyed bipartisan support in the illustration's title: "Where Both Platforms Agree—No Vote—No Use to Either Party." *Puck*, July 14, 1880. Courtesy of the Library of Congress.

congressional commission, Sargent did not mince words. The Pacific Coast was in the midst of a crisis, he argued. Chinese immigration was a terrible evil and the country was at a crossroads. In time, it "must become either American or Mongolian," he insisted. California and the other Pacific Coast states could remain states of the Union, or, if "given over to a race alien in all its tendencies," become "provinces of China." It was up to Congress to decide.[32]

On February 28, 1882, Senator John F. Miller of California introduced a bill in the US Congress to exclude Chinese immigrant laborers from the country. The California Republican spelled out the imminent danger that Chinese immigration posed. There were too many in the country, not to mention the untold millions who could take a boat to American shores, like a naval invasion—they were a "degraded and inferior race" and a threat to national security. With their "machine-like" ways and their "muscles of iron," they stole jobs from white workers in every field of industry: the farm, the shoe bench, and the factory. Miller proclaimed that a vote for Chinese exclusion was thus a vote both for labor and for the "public good" of the country.[33]

A few members of Congress opposed the bill. Former Radical Republicans, such as Massachusetts senator George Frisbie Hoar, called the discriminatory Chinese Exclusion Act "old race prejudice," a crime committed against the Declaration of Independence. But on the whole, politicians in both the Senate and House, from both political parties, and from across the United States, quickly agreed with Senator Miller. "The gate . . . must be closed," Representative Edward Valentine of Nebraska implored.[34]

The Chinese Exclusion Act marked one of the most important turning points in America's long history of xenophobia. First, it established the United States' sovereign right to regulate foreigners into and within the nation and legalized the restriction, exclusion, and deportation of immigrants considered to be threats to the United States. In 1889, the US Supreme Court upheld the constitutionality of the Chinese Exclusion Act, and more broadly, the right of the United States to exclude foreign immigrants, stating that the power to exclude foreigners was one of the sovereign rights of the US government as delegated by the Constitution.

This right also included barring returning American residents of Chinese descent who had previously been legally admitted in order to protect US "peace and security." In doing so, Chinese exclusion set in motion the transformation of the United States into a "gatekeeping nation," one that began using federal immigration laws to exclude, restrict, and control allegedly dangerous foreigners, often on the basis of race, national origin, ethnicity, class, and sexuality. In the 1880s, the United States was the first gatekeeping nation. Today, of course, every nation is.[35]

The Chinese Exclusion Act also justified immigration restriction in the name of national security, a rationale that would later be used to close the gate to more immigrants, especially in times of war. The first lines of the law specifically stated that it was the "opinion of the Government of the United States [that] the coming of Chinese laborers to this country endangers the *good order* of certain localities within the territory thereof."[36]

And the act also established Chinese immigrants—categorized by their race, class, and gender relations as the ultimate example of the dangerous, degraded alien—as the yardstick by which to measure the desirability (and "whiteness") of other immigrant groups. No other group had been officially singled out for immigration exclusion or banned from naturalized citizenship based on their race and national origin before. Moreover, the only other immigrants to be similarly banned from the country in 1882 were convicts, lunatics, idiots, or any people considered to be public charges. Because it specifically barred Chinese laborers, the Exclusion Act also discriminated on the basis of class. Laborers were barred for a period of ten years, but certain professional and elite classes were exempt from exclusion: students, teachers, travelers, merchants, and diplomats. These migrants benefited cross-national interests, maintaining friendly and profitable economic, diplomatic, cultural, and educational ties between the United States and China. By creating a two-tiered system of exclusion (laborers) and entry (elites) among Chinese immigrants, the Exclusion Act thus also created a hierarchy and paradigm of "good" versus "bad" immigrants that would shape both xenophobia and immigration policy in later decades.[37]

Xenophobia sells. In 1886, the Geo. Dee Dixon company used the Chinese Exclusion Act to sell its laundry detergent. Uncle Sam, holding a proclamation and a can of detergent, forcibly kicks Chinese immigrants out of the United States. "We have no use for them since we got this WONDERFUL WASHER," he proclaims. Shober & Carqueville Lithograph Company, c. 1886. Courtesy of the Library of Congress.

With Chinese exclusion, the United States also became a global leader in the enactment of racist immigration restriction laws. Its Chinese exclusion regime became a template or reference point for immigration policy around the world—and an American export. Canada, for example, shared not only a border with the United States but also a growing Chinese immigrant population in the nineteenth century. Many Canadians believed that Americans' problems with Chinese immigration mirrored their own. As one Canadian labor journal explained, "change the word American to Canadian and it applies to this side of the line as well as the other." Eastern Canadian labor organizations even adopted San Francisco labor leader Denis Kearney's war cry of "The Chinese Must Go."[38]

Canada also followed the US method of establishing government commissions to investigate the "problem" of Chinese immigration and relied on US intelligence to do so. In 1879, the Canadian Select Committee on Chinese Labor and Immigration began its work in the Dominion by first familiarizing itself with the significant evidence gathered by the US government in San Francisco. The committee noted that the American investigations had already demonstrated the "undesirableness of encouraging Chinese labor and immigration" and implied that the need to come to their own independent conclusion was unnecessary. Five years later, another Canadian commission began its investigation by also starting in the United States. Commissioners from Canada's 1884 Royal Commission on Chinese Immigration were instructed to go to San Francisco, where they interviewed many of the witnesses who had participated in the US joint congressional investigation in 1876. When the Canadian commission completed its work, it offered a sobering conclusion: "The Chinaman seems to be the same everywhere." Chinese immigration was not just a local or even national threat, the commissioners implied. It was a global one.[39]

The response to this perceived threat would have global implications. But the US style of Chinese exclusion was not always followed directly. Canada, for example, chose to impose hefty head taxes on all Chinese laborers as a way to deter immigration in 1885. The hope was to achieve exclusion without offending China, a British (and therefore Canadian) ally. When the initial $50 head tax was not enough of a deterrent (and the Chinese kept on coming), Canada raised it to $100 and then $500. From 1885 to 1923, Chinese immigrants paid $22.5 million to the Canadian government for the privilege of entering and leaving the country. In 1923, Canada abandoned the head tax system altogether in favor of its own American-style Exclusion Act, which prohibited all people of Chinese origin or descent from entering the country. Consular officials, children born in Canada, merchants, and students were the only exemptions.[40]

In Mexico, where Chinese immigration was described in catastrophic terms as *peste amarilla* and *invasión mongólica* ("yellow wave" and "Mongol invasion"), local harassment and racial violence were the most common responses to Chinese immigration. There was an anti-Chinese riot in Mazatlán in 1886, and several unprovoked attacks on Chinese occurred in Mexico City beginning in the same year. Then came the massacre of Chinese in Torreón on May 5, 1911. The "two-day orgy of unbeliev-able brutality" resulted in the deaths of 303 Chinese (out of an estimated 600 to 700) and $850,000 worth of property damage to Chinese busi-nesses and homes. In 1927, the treaty between Mexico and China was canceled.[41]

By the 1930s, most countries in Latin America had restricted Chi-nese immigration in one way or another, varying from total exclusion to various regulations that limited the number of Chinese immigrants allowed in each year. The global debates over Chinese immigration had far-reaching consequences for the regulation of immigration around the world and led to what historians have called the first "restrictive interna-tional migration regime."[42] As other Asian immigrants followed in the footsteps of the Chinese, they would feel the aftershocks.

The Chinese Exclusion Act also transformed how immigration re-strictions were enforced in the United States. Written into the act itself were several major changes. All would become standard means of in-specting, processing, admitting, tracking, punishing, and deporting immigrants in the United States. First, the Exclusion Act laid the foun-dation for the establishment of the country's first federal immigrant in-spectors. Although the Bureau of Immigration was not established until 1894 and did not gain jurisdiction over the Chinese exclusion laws until 1903, the inspectors for Chinese immigrants (under the auspices of the US Customs Service) were the first to be authorized to act as immigra-tion officials on behalf of the federal government under the terms of the Exclusion Act.[43]

Second, the enforcement of the Chinese exclusion laws set in mo-tion the federal government's first attempts to establish a system of sur-veillance and control over a specific immigrant population in the United States. Because the Chinese were considered such a threat, a population that required massive amounts of regulation, US officials painstakingly identified and recorded all of the movements, occupations, and familial relationships of Chinese immigrants, returning residents, and US-born citizens of Chinese descent. Government officials on both sides of the Pacific Ocean achieved this through registration documents, records of entry and reentry, certificates of identity, and voluminous interviews with individuals and their families. Section 4 of the Exclusion Act, for example, required that all departing Chinese laborers apply for and possess "certificates of registration" that contained their name, age, occupation, last place of residence, and personal description. This information was recorded in Chinese registry books kept in the customs house. The certificate entitled the holder to "return and reenter the United States upon producing and delivering the [document] to the collector of customs." This laborer's return certificate was the first reentry document issued to an immigrant group by the federal government, and it served as an equivalent passport facilitating reentry into the country. The Chinese remained the only immigrant group required to hold such reentry permits (or passports) until 1924, when the new Immigration Act of that year issued—but did not require—reentry permits for other aliens.[44]

In 1893, all Chinese people in the United States were also required to register with the federal government to obtain "certificates of residence" and "certificates of identity" that served as proof of their legal entry and lawful right to remain in the country. These documents contained the name, age, local residence, and occupation of the applicant (or "Chinaman," as the law noted), as well as a photograph. Any Chinese laborer found within the jurisdiction of the United States without a certificate of residence was to be "deemed and adjudged to be unlawfully in the United States" and vulnerable to arrest and deportation. No other immigrants were required to hold documents proving their lawful residence or be subjected to what would later be called "show me your papers" practices, until 1928, when immigrant identification cards were first issued to new immigrants arriving for permanent residence. These were eventually replaced by "alien registration receipt cards" (i.e., green cards) after 1940.[45]

The Chinese Exclusion Act set another precedent by defining "illegal immigration" as a crime. With no federal restrictions on immigration prior to the Chinese Exclusion Act, there were no "illegal immigrants"; after the law, there were. Chinese immigrants became the first to be classified as illegal and the first to be charged with the new crime of illegal immigration. The act declared that any person who secured certificates

The Chinese exclusion laws required all Chinese immigrants to register with the US government and initiated an extensive system of surveillance that involved both local and federal officials. John T. Mason, a justice of the peace in Downieville, California, carefully recorded the personal details of local Chinese in an 1894 album he used to identify them and track their movements in and out of the United States. On these pages, the mug shots of three women and one man appear next to Mason's careful cursive notes indicating names, occupations, ages, places of residence, height, and physical characteristics. A fifty-five-year-old woman identified as housekeeper Ung Gook, or "China Susie," appears in the upper right-hand page. Mason found "no marks" on her face. An additional note was added in 1900 noting that she had "Gone to China for good." Photographs of Chinese men and women in Sierra County, 1894 (pp. 26–27), Vault 184, California Historical Society.

of identity fraudulently or through impersonation to be guilty of a misdemeanor, fined them $1,000, and imprisoned them for up to five years. Any person who knowingly aided and abetted the landing of "any Chinese person not lawfully entitled to enter the United States" could also be charged with a misdemeanor, fined, and imprisoned for up to one year. Defining and punishing undocumented immigration directly led to the establishment of the country's first federal deportation system, and one of the final sections of the act declared that "any Chinese person found unlawfully within the United States shall be caused to be removed therefrom to the country from whence he came." These initial forays into federal immigration regulation would be further codified for all immigrants in the Immigration Act of 1891, helping to turn the United States into a "deportation nation."[46]

As HARSH AS the actual exclusion act was, it represented only one aspect of the larger anti-Chinese campaign. Xenophobia directed against the Chinese was not only about preventing new Chinese immigrants from entering the country; it was also about getting rid of the ones who were already here. Cities and states passed a range of laws that discriminated against the Chinese, barred them from certain jobs and neighborhoods, and curtailed their freedoms and rights in the United States. These were the so-called legal means of harassing the Chinese into leaving the country. When that didn't work, xenophobes tried physical harassment and removal. Entire Chinese communities were forcibly expelled from their homes, and deportation and violent expulsion became another new tool in America's war against immigrants.[47]

Some of the worst anti-Chinese violence took place in the Pacific Northwest. In 1870, there were only 234 Chinese people in Washington territory, just 1.0 percent of the population—not exactly a threat overrunning the territory or a significant enough number to legislate against. But they had already been banned from voting as early as 1853. In 1863, they were barred from testifying in court cases involving whites. The next year, a poll tax was enacted for Chinese people under the title "An Act to Protect Free White Labor Against Competition with Chinese Coolie Labor and to Discourage the Immigration of Chinese in the Territory."[48] To marshal the resources and energy to disenfranchise less than 1 percent of a population can only be attributed, we might assume, to deep-rooted malice and to racial resentment.

A devastating national economic recession left scores of white and Chinese laborers unemployed in the 1880s. Anger toward Chinese immigrants reached a peak. The exclusion of new Chinese immigrants under the Chinese Exclusion Act, many felt, was not enough. The white citizens of Seattle did not want *any* Chinese people in the city at all. It was not a question of *whether* the Chinese should go, it was a matter of *how*, and *how soon*.

In the fall of 1885, the Knights of Labor and white vigilante groups began shouting that "the Chinese must go." White workers made up a core part of the movement, but a broad range of citizens (including lawyers, judges, politicians, businessmen, and property owners—in other words, people who had less to fear, in terms of job security, from Chinese labor) were also involved. The Liberal League, an organization whose sole mission was to purge Washington Territory of its Chinese people, was formed. Although they all agreed on the pressing need to expel the Chinese from the city, Seattle residents could not agree on a single course of action. Proposals to extend a "general invitation . . . to the Chinamen to leave" were floated at first. Others put forward a boycott. "Let us not give them employment; let us not give them our washing to do; let us not allow them in our kitchen, in our mills, mines, or workshops," suggested Judge Cann to an overcrowded anti-Chinese meeting in Seattle on September 21. "If they do not earn anything, they will leave," he reasoned. A special women's committee was established to "visite [*sic*] the women of Seattle and induce them to discharge their Chinese" cooks and servants.[49]

These supposedly mild proposals were met with angry and passionate calls for direct and immediate action. The anti-Chinese feeling was so intense in the city in late September 1885 that Washington territorial governor Watson C. Squire made a special trip to Seattle to push for calm and peaceful adherence to the law.[50]

Seattle was not the only city organizing against the Chinese. In the years since the Exclusion Act was passed in 1882, many cities and towns throughout the West had expelled Chinese residents from their jurisdictions. In February 1885, the Chinese in Eureka, California, had been given a mere twenty-four hours to leave the city before they were forced onto two steamships and Chinatown was destroyed. More than one hundred Chinese families lost their belongings in Tulare, California, when the Chinese quarter was burned down. On September 2, twenty-eight Chinese people were massacred at Rock Springs, Wyoming, and the homes and bunkhouses of seventy-nine Chinese workers were torched. The bodies of the dead were thrown into the fire; the wounded, unable to run, were also tossed onto the pyre.[51]

By the fall of 1885, expulsion fever spread to Washington territory. In September, Chinese people had been murdered in Squak Valley (Issaquah) and driven out of Coal Creek and Black Diamond. The Port Townsend Mill Company bowed to threats from the Knights of Labor and fired every one of its Chinese workers. Amid all this violence, anti-Chinese meetings continued. Governor Squire reported to the US secretary of the interior that "violent and incendiary" threats to "rid the country of the Chinese" were being made at numerous meetings organized by the Knights of Labor.[52]

The governor was particularly concerned about the cities of Tacoma and Seattle, where both city politicians and labor leaders were encouraging the use of force to rid their localities of the hated Chinese. In late September, Seattle Knights of Labor leader Daniel Cronin objected to "taffy" plans like economic boycotts. He also dismissed the work of diplomats and lawyers who were taking too long to solve the problem, he argued. Instead, he advocated for bold action. "If the Chinamen are not removed," he ominously warned, "there will be riot and bloodshed this winter."[53]

At the September 28 Anti-Chinese Congress, delegations from across Washington Territory gathered to advocate for expulsion. One speaker shouted out to the crowd: "This Chinese question has been debated for a long time. The question is, shall they go or stay?" "Go! Go! Go!" the audience shouted back enthusiastically. "How?" the speaker asked. "By force!" the crowd responded. A resolution to expel all Chinese by November 1 was unanimously approved. Couched in the language of self-protection and civic duty, the congress declared that citizens must organize themselves "for the expulsion of, and protection against the invasion and the presence of elements foreign to the principles of the laws of existence, of self-protection, of mutual good government." A committee was to report on the progress of Chinese expulsion on November 6. At the conclusion of the meeting, labor leader Cronin ominously stated, "If the Chinamen are here on the 6th of November, I would not like to be in this town."[54]

The supporters of Chinese expulsion were deadly serious in accomplishing their mission. Seattle mayor Henry L. Yesler received an anonymous letter promising destruction of the city if he interfered with the expulsion. "I Got 25# OF Dinemite [sic] within ONE Mile OFF SEATTLE to Dispose of ANEY [sic] time AFTER Nov 1st," the letter writer informed the mayor. Governor Squire took the threats seriously enough to warn the city's Chinese residents to "quietly withdraw." He pledged that he would do all he could to prevent acts of violence toward the Chinese residents in Washington Territory, but he conceded that given the "excited state of public feeling," an "outrage might be committed before the authorities could prevent it." It was "best . . . to scatter," the governor suggested.[55]

Two October incidents added to Chinese immigrants' anxiety. On Saturday, October 10, anti-Chinese leaders descended into Chinatown—near Washington Street, between Second and Third Avenues—to notify Chinese residents that the majority of the people of Seattle wanted them to leave the city. They also left printed materials with the same message throughout the quarter. Two weeks later, a "monster [anti-Chinese] demonstration and parade" of nearly 2,500 people took place in the city. Three bands played during the march and participants carried banners that read: "White laundries are good enough," "Down with the Mongolian Slave," "Discharge your Chinaman," and "John, Go." Later that night, several buildings in Chinatown were torched.[56]

Fear was palpable among the Chinese residents in Washington. Chinese residents were expelled from Bellingham on November 1; five hundred fled their homes and businesses in Tacoma during the first week of November. The forced expulsion of the rest of the city's Chinese residents (around two hundred) began on the morning of November 3. At nine o'clock, a mob of five hundred armed white men, brandishing their weapons, descended into the Chinese quarters downtown and along the wharf. Going from house to house, they shouted that the Chinese had four hours to leave.[57]

By midday, the Tacoma mob was restless; they wanted the roundup to be finished. Men began to kick down doors, drag Chinese from their homes, pillage their businesses and laundries, and throw furniture into the streets. Women were forcibly pulled out of doors. Pistols were aimed at the Chinese. Two hundred Chinese were marched through the pouring rain to a railroad station located miles from town. Two died from exposure. Those who had enough cash bought tickets on an overnight passenger train out of town. Others climbed onto freight trains. Some were even forced to walk a hundred miles to Portland.

On Thursday, November 6, the white residents of Tacoma set fire to the houses and businesses that the Chinese had just vacated. A large crowd gathered to watch Chinatown burn to the ground. Throughout this entire ordeal, Governor Squire failed to fulfill his promise to use the power of the law to protect Chinese residents. The city's police and political leaders were no help to the Chinese either. The police stood by, and Mayor Robert Jacob Weisbach reportedly participated in forcing Chinese residents out of their homes and businesses. He later proudly posed for a photograph with a group of leaders responsible for "causing the Chinese exodus."[58]

THE
Chinese Must Go!
Mayor Weisbach
Has called a **MASS MEETING** for this (Saturday) evening at 7:30 o'clock
AT ALPHA OPERA HOUSE.
To consider the Chinese question.
TURN OUT.

Many public officials actively promoted and participated in anti-Chinese violence during the 1880s. In 1885, Mayor Robert Jacob Weisbach helped organize the expulsion of Chinese residents from Tacoma. WSHS 1903.1.4, Washington State Historical Society, Tacoma.

By November 4, the whites in Tacoma were giddy with their success. John Arthur wrote to Governor Squire the day after the expulsion. "The Chinese are no more in Tacoma," he began. There were a few Chinese residents still packing up their stores, but they were to be gone by the next day, and then Tacoma would be "*sans* Chinese, *sans* pigtails, *sans* moon-eye, *sans* wash-house, *sans* joss-house, *sans* everything Mongolian," he gleefully reported. Twenty-seven whites were arrested for their part in the expulsion and charged with conspiring to insurrection and riot, depriving Chinese subjects of equal protection under the law, and breaking into houses and driving out Chinese occupants. But all charges were later dropped, and Tacoma's strategy of dealing with the Chinese became later known as the Tacoma Method and was used to round up and purge Chinese people from throughout the West during the 1880s.[59]

The same week that Tacoma was expelling its Chinese, labor leaders and anti-Chinese activists in Seattle organized in advance of their November 1 deadline to rid the city of "Chinese slave labor." One hundred fifty distressed and terrified Chinese decided to follow the governor's advice to "scatter themselves" and fled Seattle by boat and train before the deadline. The governor instructed Sheriff John H. McGraw to organize protection for the city against mob violence. McGraw assembled a force of about four hundred citizens, many of whom had advocated for legal, diplomatic, and peaceful removal of the Chinese (as opposed to violent and unlawful removal), and swore them in as deputies. Calling themselves the Home Guard, they trained and developed plans to defend the city in case of an emergency. Federal troops descended on Seattle to quell any rioting or expulsion.[60]

November, December, and January passed, and the Chinese remained in Seattle. But anti-Chinese meetings continued through January 1886. Both the Seattle city council and the territorial legislature attempted to legislate against the Chinese. The city council passed a so-called cubic air ordinance, modeled after the San Francisco law. This required each resident of Seattle to sleep in an area that was at least eight by eight by eight feet, specifically targeting Seattle's crowded rooming houses where the Chinese often lived. It went into effect in December. In February 1886, the city council passed additional ordinances intended to harass the Chinese into leaving. One banned the operation of wash houses in wooden buildings; another prohibited the sale of goods in the streets. The council also began to require a license fee for fruit vendors. The territorial legislature added its own anti-Chinese legislation and introduced a series of petitions and bills to bar aliens incapable of becoming citizens (a status that applied only to Asian immigrants at the time—drawn out in this way because of their supposed inassimilability) from owning land, gaining licenses to operate laundries (again, a specific shot at Chinese businesses), and working on public works. Another measure made it illegal for any private industry or quasi-public corporation to employ Chinese workers.[61]

On February 6, 1886, the Knights of Labor met at the Bijou Theatre. Speaker after speaker argued that the time for peaceful measures had passed. The group passed new resolutions. One denounced "Chinese slave labor" and proposed naming those who employed Chinese as "enemies of the public." Another appointed a committee to patrol Chinatown to determine whether the city's new cubic air ordinance was being enforced and to take a census of the Chinese still remaining in Seattle and the names of their employers, a list that the committee threatened to publish. Lastly, the group promised a boycott of the Seattle residents they determined were pro-Chinese.[62]

The next morning at daybreak on February 7, anti-Chinese "committees" got to work. The gangs entered Chinatown and began ordering the Chinese to leave the city or "take the consequence." They forced open doors to homes and businesses and ordered the Chinese to report to the wharf to board a steamship that would take them out of town. Enforcers stayed behind to make sure the orders were followed, while others marched on to the next house or business. Other "committees" visited private homes that employed Chinese servants and rounded them up as well. By late morning, wagons appeared in Chinese neighborhoods. With the aid of a growing crowd of around 1,500 supporters, the "Chinese were piled in and hauled" to the dock at the foot of Main Street, where some 350 were placed under guard. The scene was pitiable, according to Ida Remington Squire, the governor's wife, who was sequestered in a downtown hotel.

The Chinese prisoners were "trembling and crying," while the crowd of whites were "running, yelling, and hooting at their heels."[63]

The sheriff's Home Guard assembled to face off the mob. A scuffle ensued, and five rioters were shot, one fatally. Only the arrival of federal troops and the establishment of martial law calmed the city. But it was too late for the Chinese. Those who had not already been forced out by the mob left on their own by February 14, 1886. Like Tacoma, the Chinese were "no more" in Seattle.

CHINESE IMMIGRATION PLUMMETED as a result of the Exclusion Act and the violent expulsion campaigns that followed. In 1882, before the Chinese Exclusion Act went into effect, 39,579 Chinese people had entered the United States. Thereafter, the numbers fell to an all-time low in 1887—the year immediately after the Seattle expulsions—when immigration officials admitted only ten Chinese immigrants into the United States. The Chinese in America referred to the Chinese exclusion laws as a "hundred kinds of oppressive laws." They affected every aspect of Chinese immigration to the United States, determining who would be able to immigrate and casting a long shadow on Chinese immigrant lives in the United States.[64]

But the Chinese did not passively accept injustice. They protested and engaged in fierce battles to challenge the legality of the laws and the ways they were enforced. "Why do they not legislate against Swedes, Germans, Italians, Turks, and others?" Yung Hen, a Chinese poultry dealer in San Francisco, asked a newspaper in 1892. "There are no strings on those people. . . . For some reason, you people persist in pestering the Chinamen."[65] When the constitutionality of Chinese exclusion was upheld, attention turned to opening up additional immigration categories within the confines of the laws. The Chinese in America hired lawyers and used the courts to affirm the rights of merchant families, returning laborers, US citizens of Chinese descent, and their families to enter and reenter the country. The efforts centered in San Francisco, the main port of entry for Asians entering the United States.

The Exclusion Act required all Chinese passengers to be inspected and approved for admission. At first, these inspections took place on arriving steamships, but as inspections became lengthier and more complex, they required some maneuvering. Chinese passengers were kept on board the boat they had arrived on, and then transferred to another vessel docked in the harbor when that ship had to return across the ocean. Steamship detention continued like this for almost twenty years, causing immigration officials to complain of the "large floating Chinese alien population in the Bay."[66]

To help solve this problem, the Pacific Mail Steamship Company, one of the largest shipping lines on the Pacific Ocean, built a detention facility for Chinese passengers near its offices on Pier 40 in San Francisco. The "detention shed" provided a place to hold Chinese, but it was crowded, unsanitary, and dangerous. Immigrants complained that it was an "iron cage" or a "Chinese jail." Inspectors admitted that it was a "fire trap" and did not provide proper security. What was needed, immigration officials insisted, was an isolated and secure facility where Chinese (and other immigrant) detainees could be separated from US citizens while they were examined for contagious diseases, interrogated to ensure that they were eligible to enter the country, and detained until they were either admitted into the country or denied entry and returned to their country of origin. Angel Island—the largest island in the San Francisco Bay—seemed to offer the perfect solution.

On January 22, 1910, the Angel Island Immigration Station opened its doors. Over the next thirty years, it processed, admitted, detained, and rejected immigrants from Europe, Asia, Australasia, and Latin America—and was one of the most important immigrant gateways to America. From 1910 to 1940, one million people were processed through the port of San Francisco on their way into or out of the country.[67]

Some 178,000 Chinese men and women were admitted into the country through Angel Island. Both new immigrants and returning residents and citizens faced ever-tightening exclusion laws and strict enforcement procedures at the immigration station. They filled out form after form, arranged for witnesses to testify on their behalf (if they were entering as merchants, these witnesses had to be white), and subjected themselves to humiliating and invasive medical examinations and hostile interrogations. Most were forced to hire attorneys who guided them through the growing complexity of government rules regulating Chinese immigration. Over the years, it became harder and harder for Chinese immigrants to enter the United States.

As a result, some resorted to evading or circumventing the laws. "We didn't want to come in illegally, but we were forced to because of the immigration laws," explained immigrant Ted Chan. "They particularly picked on the Chinese. If we told the truth, it didn't work. So we had to take the crooked path." Some falsely claimed membership in one of the classes that were exempt from the exclusion laws, such as Chinese merchants or native-born citizens of the United States. The 1906 earthquake and fire in San Francisco destroyed all of the city's birth records, and the number of Chinese people claiming to have been born in the United States (most likely fraudulently) significantly increased in the years afterward. If they were successful in their gambit, they could make it official, and their immigration status allowed them to enter and reenter the United States and to bring in their wives and children.[68]

A multinational business in immigration documents and papers documenting fraudulent relationships, or "paper sons," sprang up to help people get to America. Chinese immigrants or returning residents started by exaggerating the number of children they had when they first testified before immigration officials. Some claimed to have three or four children, when in fact they had only one or two. These family members would be recorded in the individual's record with the government, and because centralized birth records in China did not exist and thus could not be used to corroborate such claims, these lists opened up legal pathways for immigrants to enter the United States. Often, Chinese immigrant men sponsored their own children. But they also commonly sold an immigration slot to a relative, a neighbor—or a complete stranger. Because there was no other way for a working-class Chinese immigrant to come into the country, buying fake papers was an extremely common and often effective way of circumventing the exclusion laws.

Once US immigration officials caught on to the "paper son" system, though, they responded with harsher enforcement measures designed to uncover any fraud or deception. Sometimes their own biases as well as the institutionalized discrimination built into the laws made enforcement practices overly harsh. Immigrant inspectors were known to have "extreme anti-Chinese prejudices" that resulted in "a sort of reign of terror" against the Chinese. As a result, Chinese applicants for admission—including those who had a legal right to enter and those who were trying to enter under false pretenses—were subjected to longer and longer interrogations, cross-examinations, detentions, and legal bills.[69]

Arriving Chinese immigrants were first subjected to invasive and humiliating medical examinations. Doctors and nurses pored over applicants' bodies searching for physical defects and even measured body parts to determine age. They also looked for parasitic "Oriental" diseases that were not contagious but were grounds for exclusion if untreated after arrival. Chinese immigrants then had to make their case for admission into the country. They were questioned for hours and days about their status, family relationships, and home villages. Typical questions included the following: What are the marriage and birth dates of all of your family members? Where are your paternal grandparents buried? How many steps lead up to your house? How many rows of houses are in your village? Who lives in the third row? Name all occupants, ages, and whereabouts of the family in the third row, fourth house. When did you last see your alleged father? What did you do together? Some applicants were even required to draw extensive maps of their villages, compete with the location of major landmarks, houses, and detailed notes on the residents of each dwelling.

The same questions were then asked of the applicants' relatives and witnesses. If there were major discrepancies, immigrant inspectors concluded that the claimed relationship did not exist and that the basis for admission was in jeopardy.

These intensive interrogations led to lengthy detentions. One hundred thousand Chinese were detained on Angel Island. They made up 70 percent of all detainees, and their average stay was for two to three weeks—the longest of all the immigrant groups coming through Angel Island. The lengthiest recorded detention was that of Kong Din Quong, who spent 756 days imprisoned on the island in 1938. (Across the country, only 20 percent of immigrant arrivals to Ellis Island were detained. Detentions typically lasted one to two days, and 98 percent of immigrants were admitted.)[70]

Chinese immigrants bitterly resented their long detentions on Angel Island. Many expressed their frustration, anger, and despair by writing poems on the wooden walls of the immigration station. More than two hundred poems, most of them written anonymously, can still be found in almost every corner of the men's detention barracks on Angel Island (now preserved as a National Historic Landmark). They bear witness to the trauma of xenophobia.

> *I clasped my hands in parting with my brothers and classmates.*
> *Because of the mouth, I hastened to cross the American ocean.*
> *How was I to know that the western barbarians*
> *had lost their hearts and reason?*
> *With a hundred kinds of oppressive laws, they mistreat us Chinese.*[71]

THE CHINESE EXCLUSION Act was supposed to be a temporary measure, but it ended up lasting for sixty-one years. In 1888, a second law, known as the Scott Act, placed further restrictions on Chinese laborers and affirmed the principle of immigration exclusion for the Chinese. Laborers who had returned to China were forbidden to reenter the United States unless they had wives, children, parents, or property or debts in excess of $1,000 there. In 1892, the exclusion laws were extended for another ten years under the Geary Act. The Chinese Exclusion Act was renewed again in 1902 and made permanent in 1904. It would not be repealed until 1943, and generations of Chinese Americans would wear the scars inflicted by its violence and inequality.[72]

But anti-Chinese xenophobia and its campaign to both exclude new Chinese immigrants and expel resident Chinese Americans from the United States would ripple far beyond Chinese America. The anti-Chinese movement and its effective use of racism and xenophobia was weaponized to further racialize other threatening, excludable, and undesirable aliens. Following the exclusion of Chinese immigrants, for example, xenophobes became increasingly alarmed about new immigration from Asia, particularly from Japan, Korea, South Asia, and the Philippines—all condemned as more "Oriental invasions." San Francisco newspapers urged citizens to "step to the front once more and battle to hold the Pacific Coast for the white race," and by the 1930s, these groups were barred as well.[73]

Claims that the growing numbers of southern and eastern European immigrants similarly threatened the United States grew increasingly common by the late nineteenth and early twentieth centuries. Because distinctive physical differences between "native" white Americans and European immigrants were not readily apparent, xenophobes became adept at manufacturing racial difference. Intellectuals, lawmakers, and scientists promoted an elaborate set of racial ideas that identified southern and eastern Europeans as racially inferior and dangerous. In 1894, they formed a new anti-immigrant organization in Boston. It was called the Immigration Restriction League.

• FOUR •

THE "INFERIOR RACES" OF EUROPE

At 4:31 p.m. on Thursday, May 31, 1894, a small group of Boston's political, academic, and literary elite gathered in a State Street law office. Among those present were Robert DeCourcy Ward, an American climatologist and future Harvard professor whose family dated back to the *Mayflower*; lawyer Charles Warren, another *Mayflower* descendant and future Pulitzer Prize winner; and lawyer Prescott Farnsworth Hall, a legal expert whose English ancestors had also settled in America in the 1600s. In addition to their Harvard educations (all had been members of Harvard's Class of 1889), the three men were convinced that Anglo-Saxon traditions, peoples, and culture were being drowned in a flood of racially inferior foreigners from southern and eastern Europe. Together, in that law office, they formed the Immigration Restriction League (IRL).[1]

Over the course of its twenty-seven-year history, the IRL crafted and perfected a new xenophobic message designed to influence policy. It built on previous xenophobic campaigns—most notably, the Know Nothings' reaction to a changing America. The mid-nineteenth century of the Know Nothings had been shaped by high immigration, debates over slavery, and westward expansion. The close of the century brought similarly massive transformations: more immigration, Jim Crow segregation, and the closing of the frontier.

But some things distinguished the IRL's xenophobia from the Know Nothings'. Although religion continued to influence the xenophobic leaders' definition of which immigrants were dangerous (Catholics and Jews) and which ones were not, race played a much larger role in shaping their beliefs about the looming threat of immigration. In this way, the successful race-based campaign against Chinese immigration and the passage of federal laws like the Chinese Exclusion Act helped pave the way for the IRL, its message, and its work. But for the IRL, racial difference and superiority was not just a matter of whites versus nonwhites. It was also a matter of different *kinds* of whiteness.

Undergirding their xenophobia were advances in scientific racism that expanded the number and types of racial classifications, as well as a new embrace of eugenics, the biological engineering of the nation's population through direct state intervention. Using head size and shape, physiognomy, hair and eye color, and physique, scientists classified humanity into distinct "races" and argued that each was endowed with certain immutable characteristics, advantages, and disadvantages. They also ranked them. At the top of this racial taxonomy were whites and Europeans, particularly Anglo-Saxons and so-called Nordics. The Irish, or Celtic race, were still somewhat suspect, and anti-Catholicism resurfaced at the turn of the century through groups like the American Protective Association. But the Irish had proven that they could assimilate; more to the point, they had also become politically powerful. Even if they were Catholic, their Irish "race" was now more important than their faith. They, along with Germans, Scandinavians, and others from northern and western Europe, were accepted as part of the white race. At the same time, xenophobes claimed that there were now newcomers who were from even poorer racial stock—a far greater threat to white America. This evolution in race making, a process historians have called "how the Irish became white," revealed the ways in which xenophobia swept up certain immigrants into the American nation as it barred and swept out others.[2]

African Americans, Native Americans, and Asians dominated the lowest rungs of America's racial hierarchy, with southern and eastern Europeans just above them. They were white, but not white enough. Indeed, "science" affirmed that instead of one white race, there were many; in comparison to those of northern and western European descent, the so-called Slavs, Hebrews, Mediterraneans, and Alpines constituted classes of inferior whites. These "new" immigrants, the IRL claimed, were innately inferior to their own Anglo-Saxon stock and to the "old" immigrants from northwestern Europe. With inferior mental capacities and "natural" inclinations toward dependence and passivity, they could never fully participate in and contribute to American democracy. They were constitutionally incapable of imbibing essential American values. Many of these immigrants from the farther-flung corners of Europe were also Catholic or Jewish, poor, and engaged in what were considered politically radical causes such as labor activism, socialism, and anarchism. All of this—perceived racial inferiority, religion, poverty, and radicalization—swirled in a potent brew to fuel a powerful xenophobia.

By the 1910s, the IRL also fully embraced—and helped promote—eugenics to justify immigration restriction and to engineer the racial composition of the country. The IRL was convinced that if immigration were left unregulated, these foreigners would overrun the nation and bring harmful and contagious diseases. They would erode American institutions and values, and leave the United States to perish. The most dangerous classes of immigrants had already been excluded by law (Chinese, lunatics, polygamists, anarchists, etc.), but the IRL believed that the United States was defenseless against the growing numbers of racially inferior European immigrants swarming to its shores.[3]

Xenophobes like the three IRL founders not only helped promote white supremacy, racism, and eugenics; they also invented a new way of spreading and legislating xenophobia. Publicizing its xenophobic positions with statistics and junk science in the nation's most respected academic and nonacademic journals, the IRL became the nation's first anti-immigrant think tank and lobbying firm. Active IRL members included some of the nation's most prominent and powerful figures—their prestige lending an air of respectability, intellectualism, and scientific and political pedigree to the association. These included, to name just a few, publisher Henry Holt, novelist Owen Wister (a personal friend of

Theodore Roosevelt), and the presidents of Harvard and Stanford Universities. The involvement of noted academics across the country was particularly effective—not only were these members able to burnish the credentials of the IRL, but their positions allowed them to sponsor social research.

Under the auspices of its well-respected members, the IRL methodically amassed data. It promoted its positions through editorials and speeches and distributed its reports and articles to journalists, politicians, businessmen, and community leaders—to influence opinion and to recruit new members. In its first three years alone, the IRL printed 140,000 copies of its pamphlets. It bragged that its publications were making their way to over five hundred newspapers nationwide. And within a year of its founding, there were chapters in New York, Philadelphia, Albany, San Francisco, Chicago, Milwaukee, and Brooklyn. Beyond the dissemination of its propaganda, the IRL also directly lobbied lawmakers to adopt immigration restriction in order to manage the racial makeup of America.[4]

Yet there were many defenders of immigrants. Social scientists like Horace Kallen and Randolph Bourne promoted cultural pluralism and immigrant integration. Immigrant-led organizations, lawyers like Max Kohler, and settlement house workers like Jane Addams also worked tirelessly on behalf of immigrants and their rights. But by the 1920s, the IRL's brand of xenophobia had become widely accepted; it was promoted by Americans from across the political spectrum, conservatives and progressives. Workers, bosses, academics, social workers, and housewives considered immigration a problem. Anti-immigration sentiment was steeped into the same progressive-era movements to ban child labor, regulate railroads and monopolies, clean up urban slums, combat political corruption, and advocate for temperance. IRL members also thought of themselves as reformers who had the best interests of the country in mind. But the IRL's recommended immigration "reforms" only legitimized racial discrimination in immigration policy and ended up eroding the very ideals and American values its members were purportedly acting to preserve.

The IRL lobbied for and helped pass new immigration laws, such as a literacy test and an "Asiatic Barred Zone" that eventually became part of the 1917 Immigration Act, as well as a new system of discriminatory national origins quotas that were enshrined in the 1921 and 1924 Immigration Acts. In the end, the xenophobia promoted by the IRL went mainstream and succeeded in slowing immigration to a mere trickle after 1924.

"I AM GOING to America because in that direction lies hope," the man explained. He was uneducated, Jewish, and poor. America was a long way away from where he was in Kovno, Russia. But he felt he had no other choice. "Here I have only fears to confront me," he told an American visitor in 1891. "The hope may prove delusive, but here the fears are certainty."[5] For decades, Jews living in Tsar Alexander II's Russia had been subjected to a growing list of anti-Semitic laws and actions that threatened their livelihoods, freedom of movement, and lives. Jews were prohibited from owning or renting land outside towns and cities. They were barred from most professions, and students were excluded from secondary schools and universities. The *pogroms*, terror campaigns full of violence, looting, and massacres, were especially horrific. Eyewitnesses described how Russian peasants and soldiers viciously attacked Jews and destroyed Jewish homes and villages. In 1891, Jews were forced out of Moscow, St. Petersburg, and Kharkov. By 1897, 97 percent of Russia's Jewish population—4.5 million people—was forced into segregated shtetels in the Pale of Settlement, a region stretching from the Baltic states through Poland and western Russia to Ukraine and the Black Sea. Seeking freedom from persecution, one-third of all eastern European Jews left the region—68 percent of them fled from Russia alone.

Their migration was part of a dramatic shift in immigration patterns to the United States—away from northern and western Europe and toward southern and eastern Europe. Over 17.7 million immigrants arrived in the United States between 1880 and 1910. The largest number came in 1907, when 1.2 million entered. That year, four out of five newcomers were from southern and eastern Europe. In the 1870s, for example, 55,789 Italians entered the United States. During the 1890s, 651,893 arrived. The migration only grew from there; over the first decade of the twentieth century, more than two million Italians were admitted into the United States. The 1910 census also recorded over one million Yiddish-speaking foreign-born residents. These immigrants were exactly the grave "problem" that the IRL was committed to stopping.[6]

AT JUST TWENTY-FIVE years old, Prescott Farnsworth Hall was an unlikely activist. He had grown up sickly, and his overprotective parents had raised him in a cocoon, dreadfully afraid that harm would come to their fragile child. As a result, Hall grew up "a frail little hothouse plant," as his wife later described. He had lifelong insomnia, anxiety, and depression and found solace in his library during his many sleepless nights. Enveloped by the dark quiet and surrounded by his books, he would read or write until just before dawn and then fall into an exhausted sleep for a few hours. His gaunt frame, pale complexion, and sunken eyes belied the passion and energy he committed to the cause of race-based immigration restriction. He wielded his pen as a weapon against the masses arriving in the country and "did the work of ten men," according to a fellow member of the league.[7]

Over the next twenty-five years, Hall made it his mission to help white Anglo-Saxon America reclaim its former glory. Living and working in Boston as his ancestors before him, he would have been struck by the dramatic changes transforming his city. The 1880 census revealed that 63 percent of Bostonians were immigrants or the children of immigrants. In the next decade, Irish Catholics, who had been targeted by Massachusetts Know Nothings just a few decades before, were now running the city's police and fire departments and were increasingly elected to office in towns and cities across the state. Powerful and assimilated, they were grudgingly accepted as "honorary Anglo-Saxons"—"good" immigrants, in other words. In 1884, Bostonians elected Hugh O'Brien, the city's first Irish Catholic mayor.

Still, old New Englanders were acutely aware of being displaced—or perhaps they were even more aware than ever. Harvard historian Francis Parkman warned his fellow New England Protestants that they would "do well to remember that the Catholic population gains on them every year" through immigration and growing birth rates. And new alien menaces were threatening the United States. Prescott Hall was one of the most effective in sounding the alarm through his many articles and reports published in the nation's leading journals and IRL publications.[8]

Following in the footsteps of the Know Nothings who had begun to identify the quintessential "native American" in relation to immigration— white, Anglo, Protestant, and male—Hall explained that before the Civil War, there was "a fairly definite American type" that had formed from common "racial origin" (mainly "Teutonic"), and a shared set of "American" ideals and practices. This "American," Hall continued, relied "upon self-help rather than the paternalism of the State." He was "firm in his allegiance" to common religious and social standards, such as education and participatory democracy. Unlike the Know Nothings, however, Hall broadened the "American" type to include Irish and German Catholics. He deftly (and unproblematically) discounted earlier portrayals of Irish Catholics as racially inferior, unassimilable, and dangerous. Instead, he described them as members of "the most intelligent . . . and desirable races of Europe." The Irish, Germans, and Scandinavians, Hall explained, were "kindred" to the descendants of the "original stock" of English settlers and Americans already here. All peoples from northern and western Europe shared "a common heritage of institutions," if not of language. They were "thrifty immigrants" who had "built up our country." Time had proven that they in fact were easily assimilated into American society, and they had become "patriotic American citizens."[9]

To Hall's great panic, however, recent immigrants from Austria-Hungary, Russia, Poland, and Italy were, without question, "the most illiterate and the most depraved people" from Europe. They were "of entirely different races—of Alpine, Mediterranean, Asiatic, and African stocks." These races were uniformly and dangerously different from "Americans." They had "an entirely different mental make-up." They had widely different political and social values. They were unfamiliar with America's democratic institutions. They brought crime, illiteracy, and dangerous political and labor radicalism. Writing in 1897, Hall posed a question that would shape the immigration debate for the next thirty years: "Do we want this country to be peopled by British, German, and Scandinavian stock, historically free, energetic, progressive, or by Slavic, Latin, and Asiatic races, historically downtrodden, atavistic, and stagnant?"[10]

Under Hall's leadership, the IRL boldly declared that the United States had a serious "immigration problem." They found support from many like-minded Americans. Protestant Clergyman Josiah Strong, for example, had already proclaimed that America was in crisis from the evil of immigration in his 1885 book, *Our Country*. Writer Thomas Bailey Aldrich expressed the fears of many when he published his 1895 poem that warned of the "wild motley throng" surging through America's "wide open and unguarded" gates.[11]

Francis Walker, former Civil War general, lawyer, economist, and president of the Massachusetts Institute of Technology (MIT), added his respected voice to the growing xenophobic drumbeat when he announced that the United States was heading toward a demographic catastrophe. At the close of the nineteenth century, he explained, the United States was at a tipping point. Millions of Hungarians, Bohemians, Poles, south Italians, and Russian Jews, whom Walker referred to as "beaten men from beaten races," were swarming into the United States. Not only were they racially inferior to previous generations of immigrants, they were also crowding into the cities in an indigestible mass. The United States had been firmly settled—the frontier was "closed," and there were no more "free public lands," he explained. Where would this foreign element go to be transformed from European peasant into American independent farmer? Moreover, the arrival of these "vast numbers" of aliens, with their poor standards of living and repellent habits, was causing what sociologist Edward Ross would later term "race suicide." Americans shrank from social contact and economic competition with these foreigners in their midst, Walker claimed. They were becoming increasingly "unwilling to bring forth sons and daughters" who would be forced to compete against these inferior peoples for the prosperity, peace, and security that was their birthright. If the trend continued, he predicted, Americans would eventually die out—extinct in their own homeland.[12]

Walker and others pointed to immigration as the source of all unwanted social, economic, and political change. In reality, immigration was just as much a symptom as a cause of America's transformation in the early twentieth century. Scandals erupted throughout the era, giving the appearance that government was hopelessly corrupt and that democracy no longer worked in America. Industrialization was turning the United States into an economic powerhouse, but the new economy did not benefit everyone equally. A few were made enormously wealthy while growing numbers were left in wretched poverty. Industrial capitalism brought many material benefits, but it also turned workers into a mass of unskilled disposable labor, easily replaced. This stark divide in wealth and opportunity was exacerbating chasms between the very poor and the very rich.

Class tensions erupted in the mines, on the factory floor, and in the streets and often merged with xenophobia, as they did in Chicago's Haymarket Square in May 1886. On the evening of May 4, police closed in on a peaceful group of workers, many of them immigrant, who had gathered to protest the killing of two workers by police the previous day. A bomb went off, killing seven police officers. Calls to catch and severely punish lawless foreigners echoed from coast to coast. Unable to discover the bomb thrower's identity, Chicago authorities sentenced six immigrants (five of them German) and one American-born protester to death and another German-born protester to a long prison term. After Haymarket, the charge that violent immigrants were behind most of the current "labor troubles" persisted and led to increased calls for immigration restriction. The great economic recession that had begun in 1893 added to Americans' sense of economic upheaval and social chaos and immigrant scapegoating.[13]

Politically and territorially, the United States was being remade and expanded. In 1890, the last of America's long history of Native American wars ended with the massacre of 146 Sioux at Wounded Knee on

the Pine Ridge reservation in South Dakota. Centuries of forced removals and exile to reservations, brutal massacres, and coercive assimilation
practices had seemingly ended the "Indian problem." The "Negro problem" had been similarly brought under control with the establishment of
Jim Crow segregation, keeping African Americans separate and unequal.
That same year, the US census declared the frontier "closed." But, of
course, the United States was emerging as a powerful empire overseas after the Spanish-American War—with new territories in Hawai'i, Cuba,
Puerto Rico, and the Philippines. The United States was also changing
from a nation of farmers working the land to a nation of workers in cities.
Among the rural to urban migrants were two million African Americans
fleeing the South for new lives and economic opportunities in the urban
North. The growing women's suffrage movement and women's demand
for political rights, legal equality, and economic opportunity additionally
challenged long-established notions of gender and the place of women
(and men) in the United States.

These decades of upheaval forced many Americans to reconsider what
was working in their country and what was not, as well as what it meant
to be "American." Immigration was, along with a number of "isms"—
feminism, radicalism, and pan-Africanism—increasingly considered
inherently dangerous to the country. A growing number of American organizations relied on xenophobia to quell these reactionary forces. The
emergent labor movement viewed opposition to immigration as a natural
and necessary form of "self-protection," as American Federation of Labor
(AFL) president Samuel Gompers argued at a 1905 immigration conference. The KKK, which experienced a nationwide resurgence in the early
twentieth century, viewed immigration (especially Catholic and Jewish
immigration) as an additional "degenerative" force destroying the American way of life, as hazardous as African American equality and miscegenation. Dedicated to preserving an "America for Americans," the Klan
became key supporters of race-based immigration restriction, and the
Klansman's Creed was explicitly xenophobic and nativistic: "I believe in the
limitation of foreign immigration. I am a native-born American citizen
and I believe my rights in this country are superior to those of foreigners."[14]

One of the first activities undertaken by the IRL was to investigate the arrival and processing of immigrants firsthand at the Ellis Island immigration station in 1895. During its visit, the IRL group would have likely seen young Scandinavian, German, Swiss, and Irish women coming to work as domestic servants; Syrian mothers carrying heavy bundles; Dutch families; and Italian, Hungarian, and Polish men in rough jackets and work boots, all making their way through the station, waiting to be inspected. There might have even been some Italian stowaways. One British journalist visiting Ellis Island the same year as the IRL delegation admirably described the multitudes of people arriving in the United States as "home-seekers." Hall did not agree; he was greatly troubled by the "general undesirability" he saw in the large numbers of foreigners at the immigration station in April 1895.[15]

The IRL visit had been arranged by special invitation from immigration officials, and members were granted extraordinary access to witness and participate in the immigrant screenings at the station over the course of several days. Hall and Ward concluded that the government officials were very efficient in carrying out their work, but they also found that the current law was "radically defective and ineffective" in keeping out a "large class of undesirable immigrants."[16]

In December 1895, Charles Warren and Robert Treat Paine Jr. spent an additional three days at the immigration station. Armed with pamphlets in English and other languages, the two men proceeded to examine six shiploads of immigrants and administer a reading and writing test. Altogether they examined 1,000 Germans, Bohemians, Finns, Russians, Hungarians, Croats, and Ruthenians. The Germans and Bohemians, they found, could read and write. But nearly half of the Russians and Croatians and over a third of the Hungarians could not. After this data-gathering expedition, the two men left the immigration station convinced that a literacy test would be an effective way of restricting immigrants from southern and eastern Europe. In 1896, Hall returned to Ellis Island with two other IRL leaders. This time, they spent several days examining 3,174 Italian immigrants. They found that just 68 percent were illiterate, but only 197 were excluded from entry. The IRL members left Ellis Island appalled at the limits of existing laws to keep out unfit immigrants.[17]

These visits to Ellis Island had a lasting impression on the founders. In witnessing the thousands of immigrants disembarking from the steamships, crowding through the processing center, and then heading out into America, they could literally see America transforming before their very eyes. Anglo Americans, like themselves, were being quickly displaced by what they considered to be highly undesirable immigrants. And with this demographic change, should it go unchecked, would come the destruction of the country that their Anglo-Saxon forebears had built.

In publication after publication, the IRL sounded the alarm. In "Various Facts and Opinion Concerning the Necessity of Restricting Immigration" (1894), they reprinted statements from a wide range of politicians, religious leaders, academics, businessmen, and social reformers expressing grave concern over immigration, the resulting "alien degradation of American character," and the need for more regulation. In "Twenty Reasons Why Immigration Should Be Further Restricted Now" (1894) the IRL explained that the present laws were not keeping out foreign criminals and paupers—that immigration was damaging both the interests of the workingmen and the stability of American society. The IRL weaponized statistics—no matter how untrustworthy the source or method of calculation—to claim that foreigners committed more than half of all crime and made up one-third of the entire mentally ill population and nearly 60 percent of all who lived in poverty.[18]

Hall and the rest of the IRL were especially concerned about the "influx" of Italians, whom they considered one of the "more ignorant races of Europe." In a special report on the group, the IRL noted that not only was there an alarming number of Italians entering the United States, but a great majority of both the men and the women were illiterate. The IRL was not alone in identifying Italians as particularly undesirable foreigners. Italians, especially southern Italians, were racialized as primitive, prone to violence, anarchy, criminality, poverty, and rebellion. The largest group to arrive in the United States from 1880 to 1920, Italians faced a powerful xenophobia that identified them as a dangerous racial menace to the United States. Commonly described as "savage," "swarthy," or "dark-skinned," Italians were yoked to Native Americans and African Americans, also labeled inferior races. Prescott Hall went so far as to categorize the southern Italians as "partly African, owing to the negroid migration from Carthage to Italy." To many whites, Italians were both "like Negroes" and also "as bad as Negroes." In some areas of the Jim Crow South, some Italians also crossed racial lines by working alongside, fraternizing with, and even marrying African Americans. They were consistently maligned as "guineas," an old slur for African Americans that referred to their origins on the West African slaving coast, or "greasers," an insult typically hurled at Mexican Americans, which allegedly referred to both groups' allegedly poor hygiene and sloppy appearance.[19]

Stereotypes about Italians' innate criminality were widely promoted in the news media and by writers and academics. In the aftermath of the infamous murder of the New Orleans police chief in 1891 by "dagoes" (and the subsequent anti-Italian riot and lynching of eleven Italian American men by the KKK-like White League), the *New York Times* condemned the "sneaking and cowardly Sicilians" who brought their "lawless passions, cut-throat practices, [and] the oath-bound societies of their native country." They were "a pest without mitigation," the newspaper declared. The 1911 US Immigration Commission offered the government's official indictment on Italians when it declared that "certain kinds of criminality" were inherent in the Italian race. And sociologist Edward Ross offered his scientific opinion that no other group matched the Italians "in propensity for personal violence." They led the foreign-born, Ross claimed, in all sorts of heinous and particularly violent crimes: murder, rape, blackmail, and kidnapping. It was, Ross explained, an inextricable part of their makeup.[20]

Italians were also given the dubious honor of being called the "Chinese of Europe," and both groups were seen as in-between, or "yellow," "olive," or "swarthy." Their shared use as cheap labor also linked the two. Italians were often called "European coolies" or "padrone coolies." Hall and the IRL effectively used the tactic of linking the new "Italian problem" with the old "Chinese problem" to expand the organization's influence and secure support from white workers—they drew on fears that were already activated in Americans to animate new ones. In a 1908 letter to labor unions, for example, the IRL affirmed that Chinese immigration was the ultimate evil but warned that growing Italian immigration could "swell, as did the coolie labor," until it overwhelmed American workers.[21]

The IRL was convinced that unrestricted immigration of groups like Italians must end. Existing laws were doing little to nothing to protect the United States. The paltry head tax of fifty cents required of all immigrants, for example, was insufficient in keeping out larger numbers of undesirable immigrants, they believed. One of the IRL's first recommendations was to increase the head tax to $25 or $50 in order to weed

THE HIGH TIDE OF IMMIGRATION—A NATIONAL MENACE.

Immigration statistics for the past year show that the influx of foreigners was the greatest in our history, and also that the hard-working peasants are now being supplanted by the criminals and outlaws of all Europe.

Xenophobia has often used the language of natural disasters to define immigration as a threat. In this 1903 illustration published in *Judge Magazine*, Uncle Sam clings to the shore, defending the United States, while the "high tide" of "riff raff" immigration threatens to flood the country. Several different immigrant threats are represented among the invasion: paupers, illiterates, anarchists, outlaws, degenerates, criminals, and members of the mafia, all male and all drawn in stereotypical fashion to represent southern and eastern Europeans, Mexicans, and Chinese immigrants. Louis Dalrymple, *Judge Magazine*, August 22, 1903. The Ohio State University, Billy Ireland Cartoon Library and Museum.

out all but the most "industrious and frugal." The IRL also recommended a literacy test, an idea that came from efforts to disenfranchise African Americans in the South and which it had tested on Ellis Island. There was a close connection between illiteracy and "other undesirable qualities" such as crime, Hall explained in an article. A simple reading and writing test would thus "exclude the dangerous and unassimilable elements by a certain and uniform method" while still allowing in the remaining "desirable" immigrants.[22] Hall and the IRL promoted the passage of a literacy test in multiple speeches and publications. They found a ready ally in Congress in Henry Cabot Lodge, senator from Massachusetts.

The son of a rich China trade merchant who came from the oldest white New England families, Lodge had been elected to the US House of Representatives in 1886. Seven years later, he moved to the Senate. Like Hall and other founders of the IRL, Lodge was convinced that immigration was the primary cause of the many social, economic, and political problems plaguing the United States. He identified immigrants with poverty, crime, disease, anarchism, and polygamy. As early as 1891, he called for restrictions on immigrants "from races most alien to the body of the American people" and recommended a literacy test to separate this supposed wheat from the chaff. His proposed measure still allowed in "every honest immigrant who really desired to come to the United States and become an American citizen," he maintained. But it excluded all those "whose presence no one desires," who endangered American workingmen and institutions, and whose exclusion was "demanded by our duty to our own citizens."[23]

In 1897, both houses of Congress approved the literacy test bill, which proposed to bar all immigrants over age sixteen who were unable to read a twenty-five-word passage of the US Constitution that had been translated into their native language. Much to Lodge's disappointment, the bill was vetoed by President Grover Cleveland, who soundly dismissed Lodge's position. "The same thing was said of immigrants who, with their descendants, are now numbered among our best citizens," the president told Congress in his veto message. Many of Lodge's colleagues also remained reluctant to support a measure aimed at restricting any immigration from Europe, because European immigrants became naturalized citizens, voted, and had the power to remove them from office. Lodge tirelessly introduced the literacy measure again in 1902, 1903, 1904, and 1906 without success, but he remained undeterred. He pledged to the IRL that he would advance toward their common cause from his lofty position in the highest ranks of government.[24]

ANOTHER NEWCOMER TO the IRL brought even greater change to the organization. Famed eugenicist Madison Grant, a vocal racist who railed against the "great mass of worthless Jews and Syrians who are flooding into our cities," joined the group as its vice president in 1909. Grant would be the first to admit—and with relish—that he came from good stock. He was tall and strikingly handsome. He was an impeccably smart dresser and was known for his "upright carriage" and his perfectly trimmed mustache. He made his rounds among the other lordly patricians in Manhattan society. He was a wealthy sportsman and hunter, a passionate conservationist, a charter member of the Society of Colonial Wars, and founder and later chairman of the New York Zoological Society. He counted President Theodore Roosevelt and many other leading politicians, thinkers, and scientists among his closest friends and colleagues. He was a published author whose early works included a series on North American animals like the moose, caribou, and Rocky Mountain goat. But his most influential publication would come in 1916.[25]

During and after World War I, many writers condemned immigration, and a growing number of books kept up a constant trade in xenophobia, including Frank Julian Warne's *The Immigrant Invasion* (1913), Edward Alsworth Ross's *The Old World in the New* (1914), Lothrop Stoddard's *The Rising Tide of Color Against White World-Supremacy*, Clinton Stoddard Burr's *America's Race Heritage* (1922), and Henry Pratt Fairchild's *The Melting Pot Mistake* (1926). But Grant's *The Passing of the Great Race* was the most popular and influential. First published in 1916, it went through several later editions in quick succession.

Grant spent his life honing the ideas he would put forward in this magnum opus. Like his fellow members of the IRL, he set out to "rouse his fellow Americans to the overwhelming importance of race." He was convinced that race was the central determinant in the history of humankind. How certain civilizations produced leaders and conquerors while others stagnated, for example, was not a result of economic or political factors but of race; it was all down to the inevitable "existence of superiority in one race and of inferiority in another."[26]

Grant's understanding of race was drawn from decades of work by European and American scientists like Arthur de Gobineau, Houston Stewart Chamberlain, Henry Pratt Fairchild, and William A. Ripley, who all argued that race was an immutable "biological reality" that determined a human being's disposition, behavior, and physical and intellectual abilities. Environment, culture, and education could only do so much to change a person's innate abilities and characteristics, they explained. Grant and other racialists used this "science" to categorize humanity into different racial groups and place them into a strict hierarchical order based on intellect, ability, and morality.

In *The Passing of the Great Race*, Grant argued that Europe was divided into three races: Nordics, Alpines, and Mediterraneans. He argued that each group was a distinctive race and thus possessed (and inherited) distinct moral, social, and intellectual characteristics that made some more fit to lead than others. The Nordic race from northern and western Europe, for example, was "long skulled, very tall, fair skinned with blond or brown hair and light colored eyes." These "blue eyed Nordic giants," were, by far, the superior race. Grant explained the signs and meaning of Nordic superiority through the language of race (white), religion (Protestantism), and gender (masculinity). The Nordic race was "domineering, individualistic, self-reliant," he explained. They were "jealous of their personal freedom both in political and religious systems" and as a result were usually Protestants. Chivalry and knighthood, he suggested, were "particularly Nordic traits." And because of their natural superiority, Grant surmised, the Nordics were "all over the world, a race of soldiers, sailors, adventurers, and explorers, but above all, of rulers, organizers, and aristocrats." These masculine abilities contrasted sharply with all other European races, who were feminized, physically smaller, and purportedly less capable of ruling and exploration.[27]

The Mediterranean race from southern Europe was also long skulled, but "the absolute size of the skull" was less. They had "very dark or black" eyes and hair and "the skin [was] more or less swarthy." They were shorter than the Nordic race and their "musculature and bony framework [was] weak." While the Mediterranean race was "inferior in bodily stamina" to the Nordic race, Grant found that they were superior in the (feminine) fields of art. The Alpine race from central and eastern Europe was a race of peasants: "round skulled, of medium height and sturdy build." They, too, lacked the masculinist abilities of the Nordic race. Moreover, they did not even seem to excel at the "feminine" arts like the Mediterraneans. They were consigned to the lowest rank of the European races.[28]

Using this theory of Nordic racial and male superiority, Grant went on to argue against the twin evils of interracial mixing and immigration. African Americans, he contended, had become a "serious drag on civilization" from the moment they had been given the rights of citizenship. Keeping them separate was necessary for the health of the country. Under no circumstances could they (or any other "inferior" race) be allowed to mix with the superior white races. This mixing, he explained, would inevitably lead to the dilution of greatness of the original superior stock. When a white man and a Native American mixed, Grant further claimed, the result was a Native American. The "cross between a white man and a Negro [was] a Negro," he continued. And "a cross between any of the three European races and a Jew is a Jew." From Grant's perspective, Jim Crow segregation had proven to be an effective tool to thwart the potential black-white mixing that was endemic to the "Negro Problem." Grant would continue to demonstrate his commitment to maintaining racial inequality and segregation by helping to pass Virginia's Racial Integrity Law of 1925, which defined anyone with any nonwhite blood as nonwhite.[29]

As long as African Americans remained separate and unequal in the south, Grant reasoned, the alien menace of immigration remained by far the greatest threat. The advent of steam-powered transportation reduced the transatlantic journey to a matter of days. Speed, coupled with the prevalence of prepaid tickets, made the United States more accessible than ever. Between 1905 and 1914, almost 9.9 million immigrants entered the United States. This was the highest recorded ten-year period of immigration in US history.[30]

Grant witnessed this transformation firsthand in his hometown of New York City. During his lifetime, the city's population had increased by 250 percent, mostly from immigration. By 1894, 1.4 million out of New York City's total population of 1.8 million had been born abroad or had at least one parent born abroad. Put another way, foreigners and their children outnumbered "native" Americans by a ratio of three to one. Grant's city was becoming unrecognizable—with overcrowded and tenement houses, foreign peoples, languages, and customs.[31]

According to Grant, unlimited immigration coupled with Americans' naïve belief in the melting pot theory of assimilation were destroying the nation. America had been brimming over with greatness when the population was mostly Nordic. "But now swarms of Alpine, Mediterranean, and Jewish hybrids threaten to extinguish the old stock unless it reasserts its class and racial pride by shutting them out," he argued. It was a matter of numbers and race. Eugenicists warned that white Anglo-Saxon Protestant civilization could not withstand an onslaught of racially inferior immigrants, who brought harmful diseases to the United States. Grant put it more starkly: "We Americans must realize," he explained, "that the altruistic ideals . . . and the maudlin sentimentalism" that had allowed millions of immigrants to enter the country were now "sweeping the nation toward a racial abyss." If the melting pot was allowed to "boil without control," he warned, the "native American of Colonial descent" would become extinct.[32]

Grant and others also infused an important gender-based rationale into their race-suicide argument. Women of the inferior races were, paradoxically, excellent breeders; they were contributing to the increase of these undesirable populations in the United States. But many eugenicists also laid the blame for white Anglo-Saxon race suicide on white college-educated women. Suffragists advocating for equal rights and the masculine privilege of voting, and others like birth control advocates who desired control over their fertility, were having fewer children, degrading the virtues of motherhood—and allowing these "excellent breeders" to populate the country. US-born white women, eugenicists argued, had a patriotic duty to prevent race suicide by increasing their fertility. In a 1905 speech before the National Congress of Mothers, President Theodore Roosevelt elaborated on these messages of "race suicide" to exhort white women to maintain their "proper" female roles as "helpmate, housewife, and mother" by having multiple children. He labeled families with only two children "selfish" because they shrank from "the most elemental duties of manhood and womanhood." If all true Americans abandoned their obligations to robustly procreate, they would help bring about the suicide of their race. "In two or three generations," he predicted, "it would very deservedly be on the point of extinction."[33]

Of all of the so-called inferior races coming to the United States, Grant expressed a special animosity toward Jews. In 1920, he confided to Prescott Hall that the "exodus of Polish Jews" to the United States was by far "the most serious immigration matter that now confronts us." A growing number of Americans agreed. Not only were Jews non-Christian, but they were also viewed as a greedy and dishonest people who were determined to take over the economic and political institutions of the United States. They had not always been labeled as such. Up through the mid-nineteenth century, Jews had been subjected to prejudice and anti-Semitism, but they had generally fared better in comparison to other immigrant groups like Irish Catholics and Chinese and racial minorities like Native Americans and African Americans. Beginning in the late nineteenth century, however, anti-Semitism became entrenched in American society as part of the new scientific racism and xenophobia. America's hatred of Jews extended into every corner of society. Manhattan's upper-class elite barred Jews from the most exclusive gentlemen's clubs, resorts, and private schools. Discontented farmers in the Midwest and South who formed a new political party known as the Populists blamed Jews, whom they believed controlled the nation's banks, for their economic suffering. Both Protestant and Catholic religious leaders promoted anti-Semitic stereotypes of Jews as Christ killers and as dishonest and greedy businessmen. Eugenicists argued that Jews were irredeemable and biologically inassimilable. The KKK actively promoted Jewish conspiracy theories and charged that they were congenitally incapable of virtue or patriotism.[34]

By the turn of the century, Jews were identified as one of the most racially inferior European immigrant groups coming to the United States. William Ripley, the MIT economist whose work Grant greatly admired, promoted the theory that Jews were a particularly "deficient" race of immigrants. Claiming that they had an inherent distaste for outdoor and physical labor, Ripley suggested that Jews were among the "most stunted peoples in Europe" with "narrow chests, "defective stature," and "deficient lung capacity." Prescott Hall linked Jews to other allegedly racially unassimilable and inferior races like Asians when he claimed that the Hebrews were "still, as it always has been, an Asiatic race." Edward Ross accused eastern European Jews of being immoral and unethical criminals because of their "inborn love of money-making." Others described all Jews as "moral cripples" with warped souls and claimed that criminality was an inherent Jewish trait. And Protestant religious reformers' claims that Jews led an international criminal ring to bring prostitutes (sold into what was known as "white slavery") into the United States were tinged with anti-Semitism.[35]

Anti-Semitism became part of mainstream media and culture. Henry Ford's *Dearborn Independent* published a long-running series of articles claiming that a vast Jewish conspiracy was infecting and controlling America. He then published the articles in a four-volume publication titled *The International Jew* that was distributed nationally to his car dealerships. The popular *McClure's Magazine* printed articles by future Pulitzer Prize–winning author Burton J. Hendrick on "The Jewish Invasion of America," which described Jews as inassimilable aliens who were taking control of New York City's businesses, real estate, and city government. "No people have had a more inadequate preparation, educational and economic, for American citizenship," he concluded.[36]

Subjected to a dangerous onslaught of "swarms" of Jews and other inferior races into the country, Grant predicted the "passing of the great race" that had made America so great. Americans of "Colonial stock," he lamented, would be crowded out from the country that they had "conquered and developed." They would choose not to reproduce in order to save potential sons and daughters from the degradation of competing with racially inferior peoples. And gradually, the "native American" would be displaced and withdraw from the scene altogether.[37]

All was not completely lost, he insisted. If the Nordic race fulfilled its destiny and led the country during these troubled times, salvation could be at hand. Nordics, no matter how burdensome the responsibility, needed to answer the call. As Henry Fairfield Osborn, a leading eugenicist and president of the American Museum of Natural History, explained in the preface to *The Passing of the Great Race*, the United States must depend on the Anglo-Saxon branch of the Nordic race for "leadership, for courage, for loyalty, for unity and harmony of action, for self-sacrifice and devotion to an ideal." This was not a matter of either "racial pride" or "racial prejudice," he insisted, but was, rather, "a matter of love of country."[38]

Grant's book had become a seminal text of American life by the 1920s. The fourth edition, published in 1921, included a documentary supplement and a new introduction. By now, Grant's ideas had worked their way into politics, science, the humanities, culture, and the law. Scholars in biology, sociology, anthropology, history, psychology, geography, and zoology at the nation's best colleges and universities referenced his work and assigned his book to their students. Excerpts were reprinted in newspapers, ladies' magazines, and even KKK pamphlets. Religious leaders quoted him in sermons. Lawmakers read passages from Grant's book aloud during congressional debates.[39]

The timing of this new edition was fortuitous. For the past decade, Congress had been slowly turning toward endorsing large-scale immigration restriction. In 1911, the US government was concerned enough with the issue to commission a massive study on immigration led by US senator William P. Dillingham, two other US senators—including sympathetic Henry Cabot Lodge—three representatives, and three other citizens appointed by President William Howard Taft. The resulting forty-one-volume congressional report, known as the Dillingham Commission reports (1911), confirmed that mass immigration was indeed a "problem" and that it was the federal government's job to solve it. More-over, its *Dictionary of Races or Peoples* endorsed the IRL's paradigm of "old immigrants" versus "new immigrants" that dominated the contemporary debate over immigration. It included the government's definitive list of races and ethnic groups and their general characteristics and physiogno-mies. It also ranked them according to desirability. The commission of-fered helpful generalizations about the immigrants coming to the United States that made it clear which ones were good, such as Scandinavians, "the purest type," and which ones were bad, such as Slavs, who exhibited "fanaticism in religion, carelessness as to the business virtues of punc-tuality and often honesty," and Italians, who were allegedly "excitable, impulsive, highly imaginative, impracticable." It recommended major transformations in immigration policy that would ensure that both the "quality and quantity" of immigration be managed "as not to make too difficult the process of assimilation."[40]

In the years leading up to World War I, xenophobia also worked hand in hand with a vigilant American nationalism and nativism. Au-thor James Murphy Ward warned of the economic, political, and national security "menace" that aliens posed to the United States and advocated for a total suspension of immigration and the protection of American citizens in his 1917 book titled *The Immigration Problem, or America First*. Moreover, the 100 percent Americanism that was being promoted as part of the US war effort demanded universal conformity and total na-tional loyalty. So-called hyphenated Americans who did not offer com-plete allegiance to the United States were denounced in 1916 by President Roosevelt, who called for a "nationalized and unified America" and an "AMERICA FOR AMERICANS."[41]

During the war, a wave of virulent and violent anti-German hyste-ria swept across many communities, surprising German Americans who enjoyed their reputation as one of the most assimilable and reputable of immigrant groups by the early twentieth century. Suspected as poten-tial "enemies within" the United States whose German heritage allegedly made them loyal to Germany, foreign-born Germans were brutally at-tacked and humiliated. The Committee on Public Information, the

American agency tasked with promoting support for the war, popularized images of the Germans as "Huns," a reference to the barbaric tribe that laid waste to Europe in the fifth century. Like these "beasts," modern-day Germans were portrayed as ruthless and violent. German-language newspapers were shut down and German-language instruction was attacked. The state of Louisiana made it unlawful to teach German at all levels of education. Lists of "disloyal" German Americans were published in newspapers, and "pro-German" books were publicly burned.[42]

In Minnesota, the state Commission of Public Safety was granted sweeping powers to censor the German-language press, register aliens, and pressure immigrants into purchasing Liberty Bonds. In South Dakota, suffragists tapped into deep-rooted xenophobia to cast German immigrants—even those who were naturalized Americans—as ignorant, lawless, and undeserving of the vote in order to push through a woman suffrage amendment to the state's constitution in 1918. That same year, German American farmer John Meints was tarred and feathered by a group of men in Luverne, Minnesota, and German-born Robert Prager was lynched in Collinsville, Illinois. Anti-German fever even extended to the renaming of certain foods. Sauerkraut, for example, became known as "liberty cabbage." German Americans were pressured to assimilate and Americanize their names.[43]

These movements validated Grant's cause. The Great War, Grant explained, had forced Americans to realize that their country, "instead of being a homogeneous whole, was a jumbled mass of undigested racial material."[44] Soon, the popular xenophobia playing out in the press and in communities across the nation was becoming legitimized in law and policy. Much to the delight of the IRL, Congress overrode a presidential veto and passed the Immigration Act of 1917. The law increased the government's emphasis on immigration *restriction* and not just immigrant regulation. This meant passing laws that actively tried to reduce the number and types of immigrants coming into the United States rather than merely keeping records of new arrivals.

It started with an increase on the required head tax, raising it to $8 in order to deter poorer immigrants from coming. It also expanded the list of prohibited "undesirable" immigrants to include people considered mentally deficient (so-called idiots, imbeciles, the feeble-minded, and "persons of constitutional psychopathic inferiority"); people who were considered physically unfit or who posed a public health risk (people with epilepsy, the insane, people with chronic alcoholism, people with tuberculosis or a loathsome or contagious disease); people who were believed to have suspect morals (prostitutes, polygamists, draft evaders, and people convicted of "crimes of moral turpitude"); and others such as anarchists, contract laborers, and unaccompanied minors.

This greatly expanded list of excludable immigrants reflected the ways in which eugenicists used the tool of immigration law to preserve the allegedly superior breeding stock of the Anglo-Saxon race and exclude the defective and unfit. The different categories of unfitness all worked together, they reasoned. Members of the inferior and inassimilable races were more likely to lack the moral and physical fitness to be productive citizens. They were thus more likely to commit crimes, engage in perverse activity, and become indigent, thereby sapping both the moral, political, and economic strength and resources of the country. Unsurprisingly, the definitions of just who was considered unfit were disproportionately applied to any "genetically inferior" or "defective" group, including African Americans, Native Americans, Asians, southern and eastern Europeans, poor women, and those suspected of homosexuality or gender nonconformity. Women, for example, were far more likely than men to be barred for "crimes of moral turpitude," such as adultery and premarital sex. In addition, women suspected of prostitution or of being "likely to become a public charge" continued to come under the scrutiny of immigration officials.

The 1917 act's naming of "persons of constitutional psychopathic inferiority" as an excludable class reflected the US government's newfound interest in a "new species" of undesirable immigrants, those engaged in allegedly perverse or degenerate sexual activity or behavior. This category, which included "persons with abnormal sexual instincts" as well as "the moral imbeciles, the pathological liars and swindlers, the defective delinquents, [and] many of the vagrants and cranks," was used to measure and exclude immigrants "afflicted with homosexuality," as well as immigrants who did not conform to binary gender norms. In doing so, the 1917 law legitimized the government's systematic and institutionalized discrimination against homosexual immigrants and others to the United States.[45]

The act also expanded the racial exclusion of Asian immigrants by creating a geographic region called the Asiatic Barred Zone and prohibiting all immigrants from almost the entire Asian continent from entering the United States. A solution pushed for by a growing number of xenophobes who wanted to extend the Chinese exclusion laws to other Asians, the 1917 Immigration Act served as a centerpiece in a series of exclusion laws that gradually closed America's gates to nearly all Asians in the early twentieth century. Under the act, an estimated population of five hundred million people from modern-day India, Pakistan, Afghanistan, Iran, Saudi Arabia, Russia, and Indonesia were officially barred. (The

THE AMERICANESE WALL, AS CONGRESSMAN
BURNETT WOULD BUILD IT.
UNCLE SAM: You're welcome in—if you can climb it!

The literacy test that the Immigration Restriction League had long championed as a means of restricting immigration from southern and eastern Europe was finally passed as part of the 1917 Immigration Act, sponsored by Congressman John Lawson Burnett. In this 1903 cartoon, Uncle Sam peers over the "Americanese Wall" built with books and armed with ink pens. Raymond O. Evans, *Puck*, March 25, 1916. Courtesy of the Library of Congress.

Philippines was not included in the ban because it was a US territory at the time. Immigration from Japan had also already been curtailed.)[46]

A last component of the law was a new literacy test that had been the IRL's signature issue for years. It barred all foreigners who lacked basic reading ability in their native language and served as the first serious effort to restrict European immigrants. The night the law was passed, members of the IRL jubilantly celebrated over dinner at the Union Club on Boston's Beacon Hill.[47]

The war ended, but xenophobia did not. World War I had transformed xenophobia into a mainstream political issue, and support for immigration restriction based on race increased. Immigrants were blamed for rising unemployment as the country transitioned from war to peace. After the 1917 Bolshevik Revolution in Russia, foreign communists and anarchists (typically Italians, Russians, and Jews) supplanted the German "Hun" as perceived threats to the peace and security of the United States. In the United States, a string of mail bombs sent to well-known capitalists like John D. Rockefeller Jr. and government officials such as attorney general A. Mitchell Palmer confirmed suspicions that immigrants were dangerous after an investigation identified the Palmer bomber as an Italian immigrant from Philadelphia. Independent organizations like the National Security League and the American Defense Society, together with the government-sponsored American Protective League, helped promote the message that foreign radicalism was being brought to the United States by hordes of unassimilable foreigners. What became known as the Red Scare of 1919–1920 involved a period of national hysteria that used a defense of Americanism to identify and punish the anarchist bombers. But it was also used to discredit the political left and support conservative economic and political policies.

In the view of so-called super patriots like attorney general A. Mitchell Palmer, workers' strikes were not just considered labor action, but anti-American immigrant rebellions. Fourteen states made it a crime to belong to a radical organization, and in 1918, Congress authorized the deportation of aliens simply on the grounds that they belonged to an organization that advocated revolt or sabotage. Palmer ordered the

arrest of four thousand suspects in thirty-three cities. Only forty actually admitted that they had any anarchist goals. By the summer of 1920,
the Red Scare was mostly over, and Palmer's overzealous approach was
largely discredited. Still, the effects of the raids and arrests decimated the
communist left and greatly affected the Socialist Party and the Industrial
Workers of the World. It also justified the actions of federal authorities to
target entire groups of "new immigrants" as foreign radicals and political
subversives. These political affiliations soon became part of the alleged
"racial" characters of specific immigrant groups like Jews and Italians.[48]

By the 1920s, Congress was moved to act. In 1921, it passed an
Emergency Quota Act to cut immigration from southern and eastern
Europe. The act established numerical limitations (355,000 per year)
on immigration for the first time in US history. It also restricted the
number of aliens admitted annually to 3 percent of the foreign-born population of each nationality already residing in the United States in 1910.
These "national origin quotas" were designed to limit the immigration of
southern and eastern European immigrants, whose populations had been
much smaller in 1910. By the same token, the act was designed to favor
the immigration of northern and western European immigrants who had
as a group already been a large presence in the United States in 1910.[49]

Madison Grant could not help but gloat. It was the year that *The
Passing of the Great Race* was in its fourth edition; he could claim that
his book's purpose to "rouse his fellow-Americans to the overwhelming
importance of race and to the folly of the 'Melting Pot' theory" had been
thoroughly accomplished. The "immigration of undesirable races and
peoples," he wrote in 1921, had been stopped.[50]

But Grant's work was not yet over. He served as the key advisor to
Representative Albert Johnson (a Republican from Washington) who
chaired the House Committee on Immigration and Naturalization and
pushed for ever greater immigration restrictions. Grant's longtime friend
Prescott Hall was, by 1920, gravely ill. He turned instead to eugenicist
Harry H. Laughlin, who emphasized the importance of basing immigration policy on racial rather than on economic considerations. And lawyer John B. Trevor, another Grant friend and founder of the American

Coalition of Patriotic Societies, helped draft a quota plan designed to reduce the number of southern and eastern European immigrants coming into the United States even further.

When congressional hearings got under way, there were only a few dissenters. One was Emanuel Celler, a first-term congressman from Brooklyn. The grandson of German immigrants, Celler had put himself through college and law school at Columbia University after his parents died when he was eighteen. He paid his tuition bills by selling wine (mostly to Italian immigrants) and was known for his firebrand style of politics. He arrived in Congress in March 1923 as debates about immigration were under way. He was just thirty-four.

At first, Celler felt adrift in his new position. He spent his weeks in Washington listening to his colleagues condemn immigrants and African Americans. Then he would return home to Brooklyn, his "district of aliens," and think over the gap between what his congressional colleagues claimed about immigrants and the reality of immigrant life that Celler knew firsthand. "I knew the Irish and the Jews and the Italians and the Greeks," he wrote in his memoir years later. "I knew the women in the Brooklyn tenements who scrubbed their floors again and again in the helpless fight against squalor." To Celler, his immigrant neighbors and constituents were real people who strove to fulfill their American dreams amid the "disappointing heartbreak" and struggle that was their American reality. Celler reminded his colleagues that the condemnation they were hurling at the Italians, Jews, Slavs, and Poles had once been applied to the Germans, Irish, and Scandinavians. He argued that new restrictions would set "race against race, class against class" and suggested that it was not based on logic but rather on irrational hysteria brought about by the world war. His colleagues "listened, but did not hear," he remembered sadly. A new immigration law passed in 1924 with a wide majority.[51]

The Immigration Act of 1924 built on the 1921 law and inaugurated a comprehensive new "regime of immigration restriction" that unquestionably legitimized immigrant exclusion and restriction on the basis of race as an acceptable policy—even a respected tradition—in the United

States. It reaffirmed numerical limits on immigration and reduced the annual cap to 155,000. It also explicitly put in place various policies of restriction, exclusion, and border policing that corresponded to a hierarchy of immigrant (and racial) desirability. European immigrants (still desirable, but not in such great numbers, especially from southern and eastern Europe), were restricted. The formula used to calculate the national origins quotas for each country was changed to 2 percent of the foreign-born population of each nationality already residing in the United States in 1890, when southern and eastern European immigrants had yet to arrive in large numbers.[52]

The law thus froze the ethnic composition of the United States population and tried to reset it back to what it was prior to 1890. Countries like Great Britain, Germany, Ireland, Sweden, and others in northwestern Europe received nearly 87 percent of the visas, while countries like Poland, Italy, Czechoslovakia, and Russia received just over 11 percent. Italy, which had sent 222,260 immigrants to the United States in 1921, now struggled with a quota of 3,845. Still, the Immigration Act drew a new line around all of Europe and preserved the right of migration and naturalized citizenship for all Europeans. It constructed, as historians tell us, a "white American race" that included all people of European descent in a common whiteness. At the same time, it hardened the line between whites and nonwhites.[53]

Asian immigrants (still emphatically undesirable) were excluded by the act's provision denying admission to all aliens who were "ineligible for citizenship" (i.e., those to whom naturalization was denied). In this way, the law reaffirmed Asians' racial unfitness to US citizenship and justified their continued exclusion from the country. The 1924 immigration act also discriminated against immigrants from Africa. Like Americans whose ancestors had come from northern and western Europe, African Americans could also trace their roots back to the country's founding; they could have argued that they qualified as "colonial stock." Under the new system, the African continent (mostly colonies controlled by European powers) might have also received generous quotas, given the proportion of the American population that was African American at the time.

However, Africa's quotas were set at a hundred visas—the minimum. Lawmakers justified this discrimination by explaining that it was impossible to determine the exact locations African Americans had originally come from.

After the law passed, its supporters celebrated. Representative Johnson labeled the law "America's Second Declaration of Independence." President Calvin Coolidge was a fan. He had long expressed his support for immigration restriction based on race and had used Grant's ideas to declare that "America must be kept American" in his first annual address to Congress in 1923. He signed the Immigration Act into law on May 26, 1924.[54]

Congressman Emanuel Celler did not celebrate. He viewed the law as the legitimization of xenophobia, plain and simple. It embodied the "distrust of aliens enacted into Immigration Law. . . . We were afraid of foreigners; we distrusted them; we didn't like them."[55]

The 1924 Immigration Act had Madison Grant's fingerprints all over it. It represented the culmination of decades of work by him, Hall, and other xenophobes in pushing the country toward a policy of race-based immigration restriction. Under the new law, migration to the United States fell drastically. In 1925, annual immigration dropped by 50 percent. But perhaps Grant's greatest influence would tragically be found in Germany, where the Nazis frequently praised the United States for standing "at the forefront of race-based lawmaking." They admired not only America's system of Jim Crow segregation but also its immigration and naturalization laws and the creation of de jure and de facto second-class citizenship for African Americans, Mexican Americans, Asian Americans, and the subjects of American colonies like Filipinos. Adolf Hitler routinely quoted Grant in his speeches and even wrote Grant a letter describing *The Passing of the Great Race* as "my bible." In his unpublished sequel to *Mein Kampf,* drafted in 1928, Hitler applauded the 1924 Immigration Act as an effort to exclude the "foreign body" of "strangers to the blood" of the ruling race. The United States' recommitment to being a "Nordic-German" state was to be commended. America became, in Hitler's view, a racial model for Europe.[56]

As Nazi racism put into action Hitler's beliefs in racial "purity" and the superiority of the "Germanic race," German Jews were made into second-class citizens and stripped of their political rights. On November 9, 1938, Nazi followers led a night of mass violence against Jews, killing ninety-one and arresting up to 30,000 more in what would be known as Kristallnacht, the Night of Broken Glass. By that year, about 150,000 German Jews, or about one-fourth of the population, had already fled the country.

Most countries, including the United States, were unwilling to grant them refuge, however. Many of the same organizations and leaders who had led the charge against southern and eastern European immigration now claimed that Jewish refugees would take jobs away from worthy Americans, an argument that resonated widely with an American public suffering through the country's greatest economic depression. Father Charles E. Coughlin's fiery tirades helped anti-Semitism reach new heights during the 1930s, as did other forms of organized anti-Semitic movements and actions. In 1939, 60 percent of Americans polled opposed a bill that would have allowed twenty thousand German Jewish children to come to the United States. The bill's opponents, who preached an "America first" nativism and racism, included the American Coalition of Patriotic Societies, the American Legion, and the IRL. Laura Delano Houghteling, wife of the US immigration commissioner and cousin to President Franklin Roosevelt, famously testified that "20,000 charming children would all too soon grow into 20,000 ugly adults."[57]

The Roosevelt administration made no attempt to bypass existing laws to rescue Jewish refugees. The president did open the immigration quotas up to its full use for a short time, but this action resulted in such sharp criticism that he made no further substantial effort to resettle refugees again. The State Department discouraged or actively opposed almost all efforts to establish a more generous refugee policy, and Congress made no adjustment to the immigration laws or the strict quotas. As hundreds of thousands of Jews tried to flee Europe, they found long and oversubscribed waiting lists for US immigrant visas, even as the quota for immigrants from Germany remained unfilled. Approximately 125,000

Germans, mostly Jewish, immigrated to the United States between 1933 and 1945, but because of government inaction, hundreds of thousands of people—again, most of them Jewish—never made it off of the visa waiting list. In 1940, the list was three hundred thousand people long. In 1941, the State Department canceled the waiting list altogether as the United States entered the war.[58]

Nazi racism and American racism and xenophobia converged over the tragic voyage of the *St. Louis*, a German ocean liner carrying 937 passengers, most of them Jewish refugees, to Cuba in May 1939. Although most had proper landing certificates entitling them to enter Cuba, the ship was turned away in Havana after the Cuban president, acting on the country's own xenophobia and anti-Semitism, refused to let all but twenty-six of the refugees land. The *St. Louis* tried to seek refuge in the United States instead. They sailed so close to Miami that the passengers could see the city lights twinkling, but with the US Coast Guard tailing the ship to prevent anyone from swimming ashore, US officials refused to let them dock. The *St. Louis* was forced to return to Europe. Some passengers were sent to Great Britain, where all but one survived the war. The rest went to Belgium, the Netherlands, and France—all countries that would eventually be invaded by the Nazis. By the end of the war, 254 of the *St. Louis* passengers had been murdered in the Holocaust.[59]

MADISON GRANT WAS able to see and enjoy the impact of his work before his death in 1937. Following the passage of the 1924 Immigration Act, total immigration fell sharply, helped along by the global economic depression, which hampered international migration in general. Thanks to his efforts and those of other xenophobes, the immigrants who continued to come to the United States were the "right" kind. Immigration from northwestern Europe rose from under 20 percent of total migration during 1910–1920 to nearly 40 percent during the 1930s. In contrast, immigration from southern and eastern Europe fell from nearly 71 percent during 1910–1920 to just under 30 percent during the 1930s. Just as Madison Grant had designed, the immigration of inferior races of

Europe had been halted or stopped altogether. Even refugees fleeing Nazi Europe could not find a way into the United States.

But xenophobes pointed to another crisis brewing along the US-Mexico border. While the 1924 act had perfected the exclusion of Asians and greatly restricted immigration from southern and eastern Europe, immigrants coming from the Western Hemisphere were not included in either the numerical restrictions or the national origins quotas. Congress believed that an open immigration policy with its neighbors like Canada and Mexico was important to maintain for both economic and diplomatic reasons. Immigration increased, especially from Mexico, to fill jobs left vacant by dwindling numbers of immigrant laborers entering the United States. But as businesses failed, banks closed, and Americans suffered, Mexicans became xenophobia's next target, and calls to "get rid of the Mexicans" sounded loudly throughout the Great Depression.

• FIVE •

"GETTING RID OF THE MEXICANS"

Several hundred people, mostly men, were enjoying the afternoon sun in Los Angeles's La Placita Olvera on February 26, 1931, when federal agents and local police suddenly swept into the park and launched a massive immigration raid. Over two dozen plainclothes Los Angeles policemen blocked the exits while a half dozen federal immigration agents ordered everyone in the plaza to sit down. Panic swept through the crowd as the officers interrogated everyone and demanded identification papers, documents, or passports. After an hour, seventeen men—including eleven Mexicans, five Chinese, and one Japanese—were taken into custody.

Moisés González was one of them. He had just joined a crowd of spectators at the plaza when officials demanded his documentation. He was able to produce the papers given to him when he had entered the country at El Paso in 1923. But the immigration agents confiscated his documents and detained him in the city jail anyway. He was released only after his brother, an official with the local Federation of Mexican Societies, vouched for him. Mexican vice consul Ricardo Hill was also stopped by immigration officials near the plaza. Only after he produced his consular credentials was he let go. Across the country, dozens of raids followed as part of the federal government's new mass deportation campaign targeting Mexicans during the Great Depression.[1]

Once heavily recruited by many US employers, Mexicans had become America's latest "immigration problem" by the 1930s. The charges made against them were numerous and familiar: they were too many; they were an inferior race; they were cheap laborers who took jobs away from deserving American citizens; they were poor and taxed local welfare offices; they were criminals. And they flooded the country in defiance of increasingly stringent immigration policies and procedures at the border. This made them not only undesirable but a new kind of immigrant: "illegal."

During the Depression, Mexicans were targeted for mass deportation like no other group. Violence and what one local government official called *scareheading*, using a campaign of fear to drive immigrants out of the country, were specifically deployed against them as more and more Americans called on their government to "get rid of the Mexicans." From 1929 to 1935, the federal government deported 82,400 Mexicans—46 percent of all deportees, even though they made up less than 1 percent of the total US population.[2]

Federal deportation drives were also accompanied by local efforts to remove destitute Mexican American families. Social workers and local relief officials pressured, coerced, and deceived thirty thousand to forty thousand Mexican and Mexican American families to go to Mexico and never return. Although officials used the term *repatriation* to convey a voluntary movement, *coerced emigration* more appropriately described the involuntary—and in many cases, permanent—relocation of Mexicans and American citizens of Mexican descent to Mexico. Some Mexicans did voluntarily return to Mexico, but local and federal policies that one government commission labeled "unconstitutional, tyrannic, and oppressive" also drove this movement. Because these efforts did not distinguish between longtime residents, undocumented immigrants, and American citizens of Mexican descent, this was not just a xenophobic campaign to get rid of foreigners—it was a race-based expulsion of Mexicans. Altogether, nearly 20 percent of the entire Mexican and Mexican American population in the United States was pushed out of the country. Sixty percent were American citizens by birth. For most, expulsion was final.[3]

The mass deportation and repatriation of Mexicans and Mexican Americans revealed how racism, nativism, and xenophobia became more intertwined during the Great Depression. Anti-Mexican racism that classified Mexicans as an inferior and hybrid (Spanish, indigenous, and black) race had long been part of US imperialism and expansion into the Southwest—it had specifically been used to justify the Mexican-American War. Now, under new economic pressures during the 1930s, it worked with xenophobia and nativism to categorize Mexicans as both a racially inferior and, crucially, a *foreign* population. The anti-Mexican campaign was built on earlier efforts. Laws like the 1882 Chinese Exclusion Act and the 1924 Immigration Act had already given the federal government much greater power to regulate immigration, and during the Great Depression, deportation and repatriation became the government's weapons of choice. The United States was turned into a "deportation nation."

IN 1946, WRITER and activist Carey McWilliams mused that Mexicans in the United States were "not really immigrants; they belong to the Southwest." After all, McWilliams explained, much of the American West, including the states of California, Texas, Colorado, Arizona, New Mexico, Utah, and Nevada, had belonged to Mexico until the Mexican-American War redrew the international boundaries for both nations. After the US victory in 1848, the Treaty of Guadalupe Hidalgo promised that the seventy-five thousand to one hundred thousand Mexicans already in the Southwest would receive "all the rights of citizens of the United States," including citizenship. But although Mexicans had been granted these privileges of whiteness by law, they were far from equal.

In spite of "belonging" to the Southwest, Mexicans became "foreigners in their native land" after Americans annexed the region following the United States' victory. Constitutional guarantees offered by the Treaty of Guadalupe Hidalgo were not honored, and many Mexicans lost their lands through legal and illegal means. Their whiteness was questioned, and a new system of "Juan Crow" racial segregation became institutionalized in the Southwest. By the early twentieth century, there were separate Mexican neighborhoods, schools, stores, restaurants, barbershops, and theaters. Some Mexicans were even disenfranchised. Tejanos (Mexican Americans in Texas) were routinely subjected to violence, poll taxes, and intimidation that kept them from voting. In California, a law allowing only whites to vote disenfranchised the majority of Californios (Mexican Americans in California), who were of mixed Indian and Spanish descent. By the early twentieth century, many Mexicans were US citizens in name only, victims of both anti-Mexican racism that classified them as inferior and anti-Mexican xenophobia that foreignized them. Both would help turn Mexicans into "illegal immigrants," a category quickly perceived to be the most threatening type of foreigner.[4]

But territorial expansion and rapid industrial growth in the early twentieth century required a massive number of workers, and Mexico was increasingly the source of that labor. Between 1900 and 1930, one and a half million Mexicans, mostly men, migrated north. In the 1920s, Mexicans accounted for over 11 percent of the total immigration to the country. By 1928, there were two million Mexicans in the United States, with 82 percent residing in Arizona, California, New Mexico, and Texas.[5]

They came at the invitation of American businesses. Southwestern farmers, mine operators, railroad corporations, and large construction firm owners crafted a powerful economic and racial rationale to justify unrestricted Mexican immigration across the border. First, they argued that Mexican men were especially suited, both physically and mentally, for the demanding manual labor required. As W. E. Goodspeed, superintendent of the California Orchard Company, explained, Mexicans were not only "well versed in agricultural pursuits," they were "fitted by natural environment to withstand our climatic conditions" and perform physically demanding work. Others even argued that Mexicans were better suited to this work than whites. George P. Clements, a Canadian-born physician who moved to Southern California and became a landowner, grower, and head of the Los Angeles County Agricultural Department, considered himself an expert on Mexican immigration and explained that Mexicans possessed unique "crouching and bending habits" that whites did not.[6]

Others pointed out that the fact that Mexican men commonly migrated back and forth across the border (instead of settling in the United States) was another advantage. They did not pose a permanent economic or social threat to American citizens. R. G. Risser, manager of the crop production department of the California Vegetable Union, explained that the Mexican male immigrant "goes from one locality to the other as the season's activities requires his service." He performed heavy fieldwork and picked perishable crops efficiently. He then returned home. Mexican men, as "transit and mobile" workers, were ideal immigrants.[7]

Some, like S. Parker Frisselle, a spokesman for the California Farm Bureau Federation, even explained that Mexican immigrants naturally wished to return to Mexico. "My experience of the Mexican," he explained in congressional hearings in 1926, "is that he is a 'homer.' Like a pigeon, he goes back to roost." As a result, there was "no established Mexican population" in the United States and would likely never be. Clements offered a similar analogy. Mexicans were like "swallows." Like migrating birds, Mexicans returned to Mexico every year and had "no intention of becoming citizens within the United States." He thus concluded that Mexicans *should be in no way considered an immigrant.*" And if they did decide to settle permanently in America, Clements helpfully pointed out, they could always be deported.[8]

Moreover, these self-proclaimed experts added that the Mexican male worker (in comparison to the stereotypically violent African American or the unionizing, rabble-rousing European immigrant) was docile and easily managed. His Mexican heritage and culture made him willing to perform hard work for low pay and ask for little in return. Clements offered a typical example of this rationale when he praised Mexican workers for performing the most difficult work without complaint. A Mexican worker "filled every requirement for agriculture and rough industry even to the loss of his health, his morals, his earnings, and his attitude toward life," he claimed.[9]

Such descriptions of alleged Mexican characteristics and behavior became part of the accepted wisdom and knowledge about Mexican men and peoples in general, part of what made them a distinctive "race."

They were useful laborers but not particularly good potential American citizens, given how passive and uncivilized they were. These traits were given further credibility by government officials. Economist Victor S. Clark argued in 1908 that despite some racial and cultural shortcomings, Mexican workers were "docile, patient, usually orderly in camp, fairly intelligent under competent supervision, obedient and cheap." The 1911 Dillingham Commission also found Mexican immigrants to be a "fairly acceptable supply of labor" and unproblematic "as long as most of them return to their native land after a short time."[10]

To further shore up their interests, employers emphasized Mexican immigrants' crucial role in supporting the American economy. The California Development Association insisted that the sheer absence of white laborers in the state had created "a vacuum" that only Mexican labor could fill. Clements argued that white workers were, of course, employers' first choice, but they were "growing scarcer every day." European immigrants did not venture west in great numbers, he explained, and "the Asiatic has been legislated out of the country." Mexican laborers were the only choice, both in industry and in agriculture.[11]

George H. Mosher of the Holmes Supply Company succinctly summed up the dominant view held by businessmen in the Southwest. As he explained to a gathering of businessmen and government officials assembled by the Los Angeles Chamber of Commerce in 1927, "nothing but Mexican labor" filled the needs of his employer, the Santa Fe Railway. The company had experimented with other kinds of laborers including Japanese from California, African Americans from Texas, and Greeks from Chicago. Some lasted only a few days, a few weeks, or one season, he claimed. But the Mexican worker—he came back year after year. In twenty-five years working for the railroad, he had not found "a class of labor that has been as satisfactory as the Mexican," he stated. Mosher made sure to point out that his experience on one railroad was not an exception but the rule. "Nearly all the railroads in the country are using Mexican labor," from the Pennsylvania line in the east to the Santa Fe line in the west and the Chicago, Milwaukee, and St. Paul line in the north, he said. If Mexican immigration was curtailed, Mosher predicted, "it will deprive the whole country of labor we have to have."[12]

With the help of such spokespeople, the economic argument in favor of Mexican immigration muted any opposition. Mexican immigration increased in the first three decades of the twentieth century, especially after the passage of the 1924 Immigration Act. Most immigrants were male workers, but Mexican women were often favored for work in canneries, laundries, and packinghouses. Railroad and other labor contractors ran a highly organized and large-scale labor recruiting business that brought Mexican laborers to railroad construction sites, mines, farms, and factories. In California, Mexicans filled a serious, chronic labor shortage caused by a ban on Japanese laborers in 1908 and the Immigration Acts of 1917, 1921, and 1924. During the 1920s, Mexicans were the largest ethnic group of farmworkers in California, helping the state become the biggest producer of fruits and vegetables in the West by 1929. That same year, Mexicans made up nearly 60 percent of the region's workforce building and maintaining railroads. Mexicans were second only to Germans in terms of the numbers of new immigrants coming into the country by 1927. They were also moving farther east, into the interior in search of work. Mexican workers could be found in the sugar beet fields in Colorado and Minnesota as well as the factories of Chicago and the steel mills of Pittsburgh.[13]

"GOOD-BYE, MY BELOVED country," the workers sang. "Now I am going away; to the United States, where I intend to work. . . . I go sad and heavy-hearted to suffer and endure; My Mother Guadalupe, grant my safe return." The *corrido*, or Mexican ballad, "An Emigrant's Farewell," told of the anguish of one young man as he departed his home for the United States. But it also expressed the homesickness and suffering of many Mexican immigrants in the United States.[14]

There were many good reasons to leave Mexico, including unstable and perilous conditions under the reign of President Porfirio Díaz (1876–1911) through the Mexican revolutionary period (1910–1920). Porfirian economic policy focused on modernization and Westernization and explicitly favored foreign (especially US) investment, at the expense of Mexican farmers and workers. The country experienced rapid but very unequal growth, fueled by agricultural and mineral exports to the United States and European countries. Uncertain economic conditions became much more pronounced at the end of Díaz's era. Widespread drought and hunger also ravaged the land from 1905 to 1907, and poverty and landlessness increased.[15]

Although Díaz was reelected to a seventh term in 1910 at age eighty and with thirty-five years as president behind him, growing social and economic inequality in the country gave rise to an anti-reelectionist movement led by Francisco I. Madero, who declared the Díaz election null and void. An armed revolt kicked off, and Díaz resigned in May 1911 after federal troops were defeated. As Mexico entered a decade-long struggle for military and political control, the revolution shook the foundations of Mexican society. One-tenth of the country's population died in just ten years. Warring factions swept through towns and destroyed farmland and railroads. Much of the countryside was ruined by continuous armed rebellion. The violence greatly disrupted the Mexican economy, and inflation and unemployment rose, sending even greater numbers of Mexicans abroad in search of survival. Many continued to come long after the war as an increase in commercial agriculture in both the United States and Mexico drove more Mexicans from their own farms and into those in the United States.[16]

The US government facilitated this mass movement throughout the early twentieth century with a deliberate policy of "benign neglect" at the US-Mexico border. In the early 1900s, only sixty Bureau of Immigration agents were regularly stationed along the entire two thousand-mile length of the US-Mexico border stretching from the Pacific Ocean to the Gulf of Mexico. Even after the government increased its border surveillance to apprehend immigrants attempting to enter the United States without inspection, agents were mostly concerned with stopping Asians and Europeans. Mexicans faced long lines and rude immigration officials, but many federal immigration policies, such as the law barring migrants who were "likely to become a public charge," the literacy test, and the head tax provisions of the 1917 Immigration Act, were often ignored for Mexican migrants. Border Patrol agents were instructed to literally look the other way when Mexican workers were needed to harvest crops, build railroads, or work in the mines or factories. Until the 1920s, Mexicans routinely crossed the border to work during the agricultural season, returned south for a few months or longer, and then remigrated north again. The "northern pass," in effect an unregulated or unevenly regulated border crossing into the United States, was traversable for generations of Mexicans.[17]

At the same time that Southwestern employers, corporate spokesmen, and their political allies were making the case for Mexican immigration, others were wondering at what cost. Mexicans had proven to be efficient laborers and provided a "cheap and elastic labor supply" for the Southwest, conceded writer Samuel Bryan in 1912. Nevertheless, he wondered whether "the evils to the community at large" were worth it. According to Bryan, the "evils" included Mexicans' low standard of living and even lower morals, their illiteracy, their "utter lack of proper political interest," their impact on wages for "the more progressive races," and finally, their "tendency to colonize in urban centers, with evil results." Added together, these qualities stamped them as "a rather undesirable class of residents."[18]

A growing number of leading spokesmen and politicians went further than Bryan to explicitly identify Mexican immigration as a threat to America's racial, cultural, and social integrity. Some of these attitudes were rooted in the racism first popularized during the Mexican-American War. In the midst of ongoing westward expansion, many white Americans felt that Mexican people were racially mixed, inferior, lazy, and ignorant—and that white racial superiority justified them in taking over Mexican lands, annexing Mexicans into the country, and redrawing borders. By the 1920s, Mexicans had been made into foreigners, their historic ties to the lands that were now part of the United States erased. Many Americans questioned why Mexicans—now just another threatening group of foreigners—should be allowed to keep coming, especially since the United States was moving toward successfully excluding Asians and restricting southern and eastern Europeans. "What is the use," Congressman Albert H. Vestal of Indiana asked with frustration in 1924, "of closing the front door to keep out undesirables from Europe [while] permit[ting] Mexicans to come in here by the back door by the thousands?"

Economist Roy Garis elaborated on this point. "We barred the gate to Europe and closed the door to Asia but the entrance to the South has remained open," he explained. "The restrictive program is thereby virtually nullified . . . it destroys the biological, social and economic advantages to be secured from the restriction of immigration."[19]

Closing the back door to Mexicans, however, proved to be more difficult than closing the front door to Europeans and Asians. Unlike other groups, Mexicans had deep and historic ties in the United States, especially in the Southwest. They were not *foreign*, nor were they *strangers*. They were also legally white. Thus, one of the first tasks xenophobes faced in mounting the campaign against Mexican immigrants was to make them nonwhite, alien, and "illegal." But how to accomplish this swiftly to bar the gate and lock the door on another immigrant group?

One of the most effective spokespersons in the anti-Mexican campaign was Congressman John C. Box of Texas. A lawyer and Methodist minister, Box began his career as a small-town Texas mayor before being elected to serve in the House of Representatives in 1918. Box's roots in the cotton and grazing country of Texas's second district made him believe that he was an expert on the growing Mexican immigration problem. He argued that Mexican "peon labor" was a major threat to the white farmers of his district, and he vowed to protect them in the face of this increasing economic danger.[20]

But Box was most passionate when discussing the racial threat of Mexican immigration. Drawing from a now familiar xenophobic playbook, Box denigrated Mexicans by likening them to Native Americans and African Americans. Recycling language first used to justify US conquest of Mexican land and peoples prior to the Mexican-American War, Box used Mexicans' mixed-race heritage as a sign of their racial inferiority. They were, he claimed, a dangerous cocktail of the "low-grade Spaniard, peonized Indian, and negro slave mixe[d] with negroes, mulattoes, and other mongrels, and some sorry whites." Weighed down by centuries of Catholicism and feudalism, Box and others argued that the Mexican people as a whole were backward and lazy and had little experience (or interest) in self-governance. Look in any "huddle of Mexican shacks," he explained before Congress, and one found "apathetic peons and lazy squaws" along with filth, disease, "promiscuous fornication, bastardy, lounging, beans and dried chili, liquor, general squalor, and envy and hatred for the gringo." Box argued that only immigration restriction could protect the United States.[21]

Other xenophobes drew on anti-Chinese xenophobia to emphasize both the racial and immigration threat posed by Mexicans and likened them to a foreign invasion of cheap, unassimilable laborers. Major Frederick Russell Burnham warned that "the whole Pacific Coast would have been Asiatic in blood today except for the Exclusion Acts. Our whole Southwest will be racially Mexican in three generations unless some similar restriction is placed upon them." (Burnham, of course, conveniently ignored the fact that the Southwest—as well as most of the American West—had already been "racially Mexican" long before he himself had migrated west.) Increased Mexican migration to Texas was an especially contested issue, and xenophobes there pointed to the example of California and Chinese immigration to allude to their state's future. "To Mexicanize Texas or Orientalize California is a crime," raged one commentator. Progressive politician Chester H. Rowell argued that the Mexican invasion was even more detrimental than the Chinese one, because at least the "Chinese coolie" would not "plague us with his progeny." His wife and children remained in China, and he returned there himself "when we no longer need him." Mexicans, he argued, might not be so easy to send back. Other xenophobes extended the racial unassimilability argument to Mexicans by claiming that they "can no more blend into our race than can the Chinaman or the Negro."[22]

While Box and others elaborated on the racial threat that Mexicans allegedly posed in Congress, other anti-immigrant groups like the American Legion, the American Federation of Labor, the Native Sons of the Golden West, and the California Joint Immigration Commission tried to bar Mexicans from naturalization. Xenophobes argued that Mexicans were racially inferior and "unfit to be citizens," especially because of their indigenous roots. Thus, both continued Mexican immigration and Mexican Americans' growing political power, they argued, would only add to the United States' existing race problems. Mexicans, many argued, were the "Negro problem" of the Southwest: a nonwhite, problematic population that was diseased, mentally inferior, and unfit for citizenship. In 1928, the American Eugenics Society made this point explicitly when it warned that "our great Southwest is rapidly creating for itself a new racial problem, as our old South did when it imported slave labor from Africa."[23]

Xenophobes also carefully crafted a narrative about Mexicans that erased their historic presence in and claims to the US Southwest and instead remade them as foreign invaders. Roy Garis focused on this characterization. Testifying before a congressional committee on immigration in 1930, the economist described the Southwest as under siege, enduring a "Mexicanization" that jeopardized maintaining it as the "future home for millions of the white race." The full impact of this conquest would be disastrous, according to Garis: property values would decrease as would America's morals and political and social values; a new and dangerous race problem that would "dwarf the negro problem of the South" would be created; and lastly, the United States and "all that is worthwhile in our white civilization" would be destroyed.[24]

Others elaborated on the idea of Mexican immigration as a dangerous "infiltration" or an "invasion." According to these critics, the problem was twofold: new and unrestricted immigration from Mexico, including women, and the high birth rates within the Mexican community already in the United States. No longer was Mexican immigration composed of only migrating male laborers. Now it included a growing population of Mexican women and Mexican Americans born in the United States who stayed. A California government report found that births of Mexicans in the state represented nearly 18 percent of all births in 1929. In some cities near the border, the figure was as high as 60 to 70 percent. Both far outstripped the birth rate among whites.[25]

Supporters of restricting immigration from Mexico weaponized these statistics. Writing in *Current History*, Remsen Crawford argued that the Mexican birth rate would "eclipse . . . native American [white] workers" and that whites were already being "driven out of areas of the Southwest." Roy Garis was even more blunt. "Mexican immigration is now a national problem rather than a problem of the Southwest," he declared. "We cannot postpone the erection of an adequate barrier any longer, for it is an invasion, even more serious than if it were military." Garis went on to describe Mexican immigration as a "reconquest" of the United States, a theme that would become popular among xenophobes again at the end of the twentieth century.[26]

A near hysterical campaign depicting Mexicans as dirty and diseased also stoked the fires of growing xenophobia. Mexican immigrants were regularly charged with being responsible for outbreaks of contagious diseases, such as typhus, plague, and smallpox. Border officials considered Mexicans as a group to be "likely . . . vermin infested," and Mexicans were subjected to intrusive, humiliating, and harmful disinfecting baths and physical examinations by US Public Health Service officers upon entering the country.[27]

Even more common was the charge that Mexicans, especially men, were innate criminals who brought border violence and crime into the United States. The Mexican "bandit," typically a poor, working-class immigrant male who engaged in both small and large crimes, had long been a stock character in American popular culture, and the trope was extrapolated to apply to all working-class Mexicans. During the violent Mexican revolutionary period, Mexican immigrants were even more likely to be linked with unrest and violence as well as with the smuggling or trafficking of illicit goods across the border. During the Great Depression, Mexicans would be charged with another kind of criminal activity: the newly recognized crime of illegal entry.[28]

The campaign to restrict Mexican immigration gained momentum throughout the 1920s. In Congress, Representative Box introduced a succession of bills to restrict Mexican immigration under the national origins quota system established through the 1924 Immigration Act. He had the support of small farmers, labor unions, eugenicists, and restrictionists. But representatives of big agriculture in California, Arizona, Texas, New Mexico, Idaho, Wyoming, and Colorado and lobbyists in the railroad, cattle, and mining industries organized a stiff opposition. The bills failed.

Lawmakers in Congress did manage to bring about other changes in immigration regulation that greatly impacted Mexican immigration, however. Beginning in August 1928, consular officers began to deny visas to most Mexicans seeking entry into the United States who were illiterate, likely to become public charges, or contract laborers. The impact of these new regulations was great. Between 1923 and 1929, an average of 62,000 Mexicans a year entered the United States. After the changes went into effect, only 2,457 Mexicans were admitted into the country in 1930. After March 1930, all Mexican laborers, with the exception of those who had previously resided in the United States, were also unilaterally denied visas.[29]

At the same time that lawmakers were restricting Mexican immigration at the border, they were also beginning to classify certain acts of migration as "illegal." For most of its history, there was no "illegal immigration" in the United States, because there were no laws that placed restrictions on immigration or that labeled some forms of entry legal and others illegal. But after the United States began restricting and excluding more and more classes of immigrants—Asians, southern and eastern Europeans, poor people, people with diseases, and so on—many immigrants began to find loopholes in the laws, enter without inspection, or otherwise come into the country without authorization. They evaded immigrant inspectors, stowed away on ships, bribed officials, and used fraudulent papers to enter the country. What would become known as illegal immigration was commonplace, even routine, in some ports of entry and border crossings. Even undocumented immigration, which could include failure to possess a head tax receipt (begun in 1917), failure to pay the visa fee (begun in 1924), or failing the literacy test (begun in 1917) was not considered a criminal act. After 1929, it was.

The Immigration Act of March 4, 1929, subjected all immigrants who entered the United States without documentation to criminal charges, fines, imprisonment, and deportation. Undocumented immigration was now officially classified as a punishable crime. Congress approved another law, Public Law 1018, which made crossing into the United States without a visa a misdemeanor with a penalty of up to one year in prison.

The law also made the reentry of a previously deported individual punishable by up to two years in prison. The laws applied to all immigrants, but they were designed to impact Mexican immigrants specifically. For decades, Mexicans had been encouraged by labor agents to enter informally without an inspection, head taxes, or a record of their entry. The new laws suddenly made these typically Mexican ways of entering the country a crime; it disproportionately impacted them. Common laborers were now "innocent victims of a situation they are not guilty of creating," sociologist Emory Bogardus observed. Mexicans became the quintessential "illegal alien" and the "illegal alien criminal."[30]

Deportation was another tool wielded against Mexicans and with much greater force and impact than it was applied to other immigrants. Deportation had a long history as an immigration policy in the United States. It was used to remove Chinese people who were "unlawfully within the United States" as part of the 1882 Chinese Exclusion Act. Criminals and aliens who had become public charges within one year of landing were also deportable under the 1891 immigration law. Two years later, the Supreme Court affirmed that the federal government's right to expel foreigners was "absolute" and unqualified. This ruling (*Fong Yue Ting v. United States*) in a Chinese immigration case allowed the state to deport *all* immigrants, even lawful permanent residents, at any time and for any reason. The 1917 Immigration Act extended the period of deportability to five years, and the federal government's enforcement capabilities were expanded with congressional funding.

Even with these new laws, however, deportation was not widely used before the 1920s. The expense of transporting European and Asian immigrants across the Atlantic and Pacific coupled with a lack of immigration agents to carry out the arrests, detention, and deportation hampered large-scale deportation efforts. Moreover, there was a consensus that expelling immigrants after they had settled in the country was cruel. As a result, only a few hundred aliens were deported by the US Immigration Service each year between 1892 and 1907. That number increased to two or three thousand a year between 1908 and 1920. But in 1924, the US Border Patrol was created to regulate immigration at the border, prohibit unauthorized immigration, and guard against what some believed to be a potential invasion of aliens.[31]

Not all immigrants were treated equally under the emerging deportation regime, however. Just as American xenophobia treated European, Asian, and Mexican immigrants distinctly in the 1924 Immigration Act, so did US deportation policy. European and Canadian immigrants who entered without authorization were not targeted for mass deportation; they were also able to take advantage of policies that regularized their status. In particular, they were routinely allowed to leave the country, reenter as legal immigrants (typically through Canada) and avoid deportation. In these ways, European immigrants were "made legal," a status that reinforced their privilege as white immigrants.[32]

Mexicans, though, remained "illegal," a status that reinforced their nonwhiteness. The Border Patrol thus focused the nation's immigration enforcement efforts on Mexicans and often used them as instruments of racial terror and control. The patrol's first recruits came from organizations, such as the Texas Rangers and the KKK, that had their own traditions of racial brutality, and in the first decades of its existence, the agency often relied on raw violence to restrict Mexican immigration. Moreover, because the Mexican immigrant threat was considered a racial problem, not just a legal problem, the construction of Mexicans as "illegal aliens" applied not only to recent arrivals but to naturalized US citizens and American-born citizens as well; in other words, it was a label assigned to all Mexicans, as a perceived race. Throughout the 1930s, Mexicans made up at least 85 percent of all immigration prisoners, and in some years, they were 99 percent.[33]

A new chapter in the history of Mexican migration into the United States had begun.

ON THURSDAY, OCTOBER 24, 1929, the US stock market crashed. Less than a month later, it had lost a third of its precrash value. By 1932, the market hit bottom. The effects of the Depression were soon felt nationwide, across all economic sectors. In 1930, 4.3 million people were unemployed. The next year, that number had almost doubled to 8 million. By 1933, one-third of American workers, or around 15 million people, were unemployed, and America's banking industry was near collapse. More than five thousand banks failed, taking with them the life savings of thousands of Americans.

Historians now point to a number of factors that caused the Depression, including a weak banking system, industrial overproduction, financial speculation, and shrinking international trade caused by a misguided US law that raised tariffs on international goods. In the 1930s, however, journalists, politicians, and members of the public increasingly blamed immigrants for the mounting economic crisis. Calls for action increased based on the assumption that immigrants were taking away jobs from deserving Americans. In June 1930, the *Saturday Evening Post* blamed immigrants for "forc[ing] American citizens . . . out of employment" and called on Congress to register aliens and place a quota on the Western Hemisphere, a policy change clearly directed at Mexican immigrants. "Mexican exclusion" was the American worker's "only salvation," an economist writing in the *Post* concluded.[34]

Organizations and politicians also echoed these sentiments and advocated for nativist policies that would grant "Americans" certain employment benefits over immigrants. During the depression, the San Diego–based National Club of America for Americans, Inc., for example, wrote to the Los Angeles County Board of Supervisors to propose an ordinance that would prevent "any unnaturalized alien [from working] in Los Angeles County unless no American citizen is available for work." Its membership pledge included a promise to oppose any attempt by Congress to use taxpayer funds to employ aliens or provide them with welfare relief. In Texas, a member of the state chamber of commerce argued that Mexican workers were driving hardworking Americans from good-paying jobs. "The competition of Mexican labor in every walk of life," the lawmaker argued, "is so intense that no room or opportunity exists for the American who wants to work for sufficient wages to support himself and his family."[35] Soon, these attitudes were molded into public policies that directly and disproportionately targeted Mexicans.

BORN IN LOS ANGELES in 1926, Emilia Castañeda remembered a happy childhood in the multiracial neighborhood where she grew up on Folsom Street in Los Angeles's Boyle Heights neighborhood. Her father had migrated north from Ciudad Lerdo in Durango, Mexico, years before and was working steadily as a stonemason and bricklayer. Her mother worked in the household of a wealthy family in west Los Angeles. The family owned a duplex that housed her godparents on one side and her family on the other. There was an RCA Victrola, leather furniture, and brass beds inside and fruit trees, turkeys, and chickens outside. "It was a United Nations" of a neighborhood, she recalled. "There were Mexican people there, and Americans like us who had been born in the United States to Mexican parents. There were Chinese people with Chinese children who, of course, were American Chinese. There were Japanese parents with American Japanese children. Also there were Negro people, Filipino people, Jewish people, and Greeks. There was a mixture and we got along fine," she remembered years later.

But like many American communities, the families on Folsom Street were hit hard by the Depression. "We lost it, since my dad had no employment," explained Castañeda. "A lot of the Mexicans weren't hired because the Anglos came first when there were no jobs." Emilia's godparents could no longer pay rent. The bank foreclosed, and the family lost the house. The family was forced to move multiple times and then was soon forced to go on welfare. Emilia's mother died of tuberculosis. An unemployed widower with hungry children to feed, Castañeda's father became heartbroken and desperate. Meanwhile, social workers and relief officials kept on pushing Mexicans to return to Mexico and even offered free train tickets. Feeling like he had no other choice, Castañeda's father signed up.[36]

For Mexicans in the United States, the Depression was uniquely devastating. As the economy worsened, state and local governments with large foreign populations scurried to pass nativist laws restricting employment to US-born or naturalized citizens. Colorado governor Edwin C. Johnson led the crusade in limiting the possibilities of employment to only "native sons." Other states followed suit. In Arizona, a new law required all public employees to be American citizens. Employers who violated the law faced a $500 fine or a prison term of six months. The federal government also required that all firms supplying it with goods and services hire only US citizens. Major employers and contractors complied. By the time that the New Deal was put into effect, aliens were also prohibited from working on Works Progress Administration (WPA) projects.[37]

Nativist laws such as these made it difficult for any Mexican, including American citizens, to get hired. In 1937, the *New York Times* reported that two million out of two and a half million Mexicans in the United States were out of work. The unemployment rate among Mexicans ranged from 15 to 85 percent depending on the season, location, type of employment, and any local laws prohibiting the hiring of noncitizens. In many parts of the country, anti-Mexican xenophobia also turned violent. In Terre Haute, Indiana, a mob of one hundred men and women marched on a Mexican railroad worker camp and demanded that the laborers quit their jobs immediately. In Malakoff, Texas, the Society of Mexican Laborers was firebombed, and signs warning Mexican residents to leave town were placed throughout the area.[38]

Mexicans living in the United States began to voluntarily cross the border to Mexico beginning during the winter of 1929–1930. Most had been in the United States for several years and were settled into homes and communities but were returning to Mexico as a last resort. In February 1930, the US State Department reported that over five thousand Mexicans were gathered around San Antonio, Texas, preparing to return to Mexico. The next year, growing numbers of Mexicans were crossing through border stations. On January 9, 1931, alone, eight hundred were counted entering Mexico through Nogales and Nuevo Laredo.[39]

In the spring, the trickle had turned into a torrent. At the international bridge crossing near Nuevo Laredo, the American consul reported that every day there was "a line of cars with licenses from nearly half the United States filled with household effects of Mexicans returning." They were forced into Mexico, because "they see no indication of better conditions in the near future." Reverend Robert N. McLean noted that the families traveled in battered Fords with all of the worldly possessions they had accumulated after decades in the United States. "There were beds, bed springs, mattresses, washtubs, cooking utensils, washboards, trunks, cots, tents, tent poles, bedding; and a top one of the loads was a crate of live chickens," he reported. The scene, according to McLean, was pitiable. Only sheer desperation was driving them to abandon their lives in the United States, he believed.[40] For other Americans, the exodus of Mexicans could not happen soon enough. US government officials started hatching a plan to push them out by force.

The man responsible for the government's deportation campaign was secretary of labor William N. Doak, who oversaw the Bureau of Immigration. Doak had three "cardinal goals" that shaped his tenure as secretary: full employment at high wages, good industrial relations, and protecting the nation against socialists. One group threatened all of these goals: immigrants. They were "the foe within our doors," Doak explained, and they were taking away jobs from unemployed Americans. They also threatened both labor relations and national security by advocating "the overthrow of the Government of the United States."[41]

Doak called on the federal government to enact deeper cuts to immigration and deportation. In 1931, Doak estimated that there were four hundred thousand aliens "illegally residing in the United States" and that one hundred thousand of them could be easily deported. But stopping at one hundred thousand was not good enough, he believed. "I'm going after every evader of our alien laws," Doak declared on April 11, 1931, in order to "give their places to Americans." Doak's xenophobia was not restricted to undocumented immigrants. He supported a 90 percent reduction of all immigration, even on top of the restrictive national origins quotas already in place. In an address before Congress in April 1932, Doak denounced all "alien enemies boring from within to undermine American institutions."[42]

Doak had the full support of his boss, President Herbert Hoover. In his 1930 State of the Union address, the president had urged Congress to increase funding for the government's "vigorous alien deportation drive" and to strengthen "our deportation laws so as to more fully rid ourselves of criminal aliens." Using a rhetorical strategy that would become increasingly popular among later generations of xenophobes, Hoover linked the method of undocumented entry with innate criminal tendencies. "The very method of their entry," he explained, "indicates their objectionable character." And the victims of their future crimes would be both US citizens and "our law-abiding foreign born residents."[43]

With the backing of the president, Doak's immigration agents raided a 1931 Valentine's Day dance at the Finnish Workers' Education Association in New York City. Twenty Department of Labor agents and ten New York City police officers surrounded the building at 10:30 p.m., blocked the doors, and demanded that all one thousand dancers show their credentials or offer other evidence that they were in the country legally. Sixteen men and two women were seized and taken to Ellis Island. The *New York Times* noted that they were just some of the nearly five hundred individuals rounded up in Greater New York and "deported as rapidly as immigration officers could arrange their transportation."[44]

Doak's methods, labeled a "Drag-Net Policy" in the press, were denounced by many politicians. Democratic senator Robert F. Wagner of New York warned that they would, "without question, inflict injury and annoyance upon citizens and aliens alike." But Doak was undeterred. He pledged to identify every immigrant in the country without authorization and expel them "regardless of nationality, creed, or color." The deportation campaign he set in motion, however, targeted Mexicans most of all. Doak's goal was not only to rid the country of Mexicans who had entered the country without proper documentation but to also intimidate residents and even US citizens of Mexican descent to leave the country voluntarily. He was not the only government official to subscribe to such logic. Congressman Martin Dies of Texas blamed immigrants for the unemployment crisis and sponsored a half dozen bills that called for more effective deportation proceedings. In one, he proposed deporting all six million aliens living in the United States.[45]

Doak's immigration agents began carrying out his deportation orders with zeal. They raided dance halls, private homes, and public places across the country from New York to Los Angeles. Despite the fact that Doak claimed that his targets were employed immigrants (in order to give those jobs to "Americans"), the main immigrants caught in the dragnet were jobless and on relief. Doak's campaign yielded immediate results. In the first nine months of 1931, more people were deported from the United States than were allowed to enter. Between 1930 and 1932, fifty-four thousand individuals were deported. Forty-four percent were Mexican.[46]

This deportation effort was national, but the most ambitious deportation campaign took place in Los Angeles County. L.A. was home to both the country's largest concentration of Mexican-born people and broad public support for Mexican deportation. The Los Angeles city council and the county board of supervisors, along with the Independent Order of Veterans of Los Angeles, called for the deportation of undocumented immigrants as a means of aiding (white) unemployed Americans. L.A. supervisor John R. Quinn, for example, was convinced that mass deportation would solve not only the unemployment problem but also the problems of crime and political unrest in the United States. Like President Hoover, he linked undocumented entry to innate criminal behavior, saying that by "ridding ourselves of the criminally undesirable alien," the country would solve a "large part of our crime and law enforcement problem" and save "many good American lives at the same time."[47]

Another champion of the deportation campaign was Charles P. Visel, coordinator of the Los Angeles Citizens Committee on Coordination of Unemployment Relief, a group tasked with connecting job seekers to employers. "We need their jobs for needy citizens," he explained to Colonel Arthur Woods, national coordinator of the President's Emergency Committee for Employment. The problem was that the existing corps of immigration agents in Southern California was not large enough to launch the massive deportation effort that Visel imagined. He wired Secretary of Labor Doak with a request to send federal agents to Los Angeles. Such a show of force, he explained, would create a "psychological gesture" that would "scare many thousand alien deportables out of this district which is the result desired."[48]

With Doak's support, Visel outlined his plan. The first step was to release public statements announcing the deportation campaign in all of the L.A.-area newspapers, especially the foreign-language press. Then agents would initiate the first arrests and publicize the actions widely with photographs; announcements of public support from federal officials in Washington, DC; and follow-up stories. These efforts, Visel explained, would "have the effect of scareheading many thousand deportable aliens." Immigration Service District director Walter E. Carr agreed. "With a little deportation publicity," he told Visel, "a large number of these aliens, actuated by guilty self-consciousness, would move south and over the line of their own accord."[49]

On January 26, 1931, Visel issued his first publicity release announcing the deportation campaign. "Incident to the present unemployment conditions," the release began, "official Washington is deeply concerned over the number of aliens now in the United States, illegally, who are holding jobs that rightfully should be available to those having a legal status here." Visel made it clear that the United States was also sending a message to prospective immigrants to stay at home. Unless some "additional barriers" were put in place, large numbers of aliens would "no doubt seek entry to the country." In ten days, Visel continued, "trained members of the Immigration Department's Deportation Squads" from Nogales, San Francisco, and San Diego would arrive to assist local officers "in rounding up the deportable aliens as fast as the Immigration Department calls for them." Visel pointed out that "deportable aliens" included "Chinese, Japanese, Europeans, Canadians, Mexicans, and in fact people of every nation in the world." But he added additional details that referred to the Mexican population specifically. "It so happens that many of the deportable aliens in this district are Mexican." And he continued to add that the Mexican government was assisting the situation. "They want their people to come home and stay there. They welcome them and are glad to get them back. The Mexican Government offers to pay railroad fare from the Mexican border to their homes for any returning Mexicans who apply."[50]

Newspapers around the Los Angeles area published Visel's release. Some, like the Los Angeles *Illustrated Daily News*, politely recommended that "aliens who are deportable will save themselves trouble and expense by arranging their departure at once." Others specifically named Mexicans and Asians as the primary targets of the deportation campaign despite the government's claim that it was aimed at all deportable aliens. The Hearst-owned *Examiner*, for example, helpfully named "Mexicans, Japanese, Chinese, and others" as deportable.[51]

On Saturday, January 31, 1931, Supervisor William F. Watkins of the Bureau of Immigration arrived in Los Angeles with eighteen immigration agents. Three days later, the arrests began, on Tuesday, February 3. By the following Saturday, thirty-five immigrants had been arrested and eight were immediately returned to Mexico after opting for "voluntary departure." Five additional immigration agents then arrived in the city. On February 13, the agents staged a raid in the El Monte area of the city with the help of the local sheriff's office. Three hundred people were stopped and questioned. Thirteen were jailed, twelve of them Mexicans. The *Examiner* published their names, ages, occupations, birth places, years in the United States, and years or months in Los Angeles County. One had been in the United States for thirteen years. Another was classified as an "American-born Mexican."[52]

The Mexican community in Los Angeles went into an immediate panic. Both Spanish- and English-language newspapers had printed the Visel press release and warned that Mexicans were the primary targets. Some even claimed that *all* Mexicans were to be deported. Throughout the nation's major cities, people who "looked Mexican" found themselves at risk of being picked up and taken into custody. Despite assurances by the immigration authorities that no specific ethnic group was being singled out, others with close ties to the Mexican community lamented that the "Mexican baiters" were increasing the suffering of Mexicans in the area. Streets in East Los Angeles were deserted. Entire families disappeared. Children were taken out of school. "Los Deportados," a famous *corrido* of the period, captured the fear and injustice that many Mexicans felt. "The Anglos are very bad fellows," it began. "Today they bring great disturbance, and without consideration women, children, and old ones they take us to the border. They eject us from this country."[53]

Three weeks into the campaign, immigration agents had interrogated several thousand people throughout Los Angeles county. Two hundred twenty-five were arrested and sixty-four departed voluntarily. Visel could not contain his satisfaction as he reported to Colonel Woods on February 21 on what he called the "deportation alien problem." The campaign was functioning "100% efficiently, quietly." The deported aliens had already "released many hundreds of jobs, which of course will automatically go to those legally in the country and help our situation," he stated.[54]

On February 21, 1931, Bureau of Immigration supervisor William F. Watkins reported to assistant labor secretary Robe Carl White that 230 aliens had been deported, including 110 Mexicans. Another 159 Mexican immigrants had chosen voluntary departure and returned to Mexico. In other words, seven out of ten people deported from the deportation campaign in Southern California were Mexican. At the end of March, Visel wrote to Secretary Doak and gave the immigration officers of the Bureau of Immigration his highest praise. They had completed their work with "efficiency, aggressiveness, [and] resourcefulness." The "exodus of aliens deportable and otherwise" who had been scared out of the community, he claimed, had undoubtedly opened up many jobs for citizens of the United States. "The exodus still continues," he vowed.[55]

Many protested the scale and brutality of the deportation campaign. Locally, James H. Batten, professor at Claremont Men's College and executive director of the Inter-American Foundation, criticized the "epidemic of hysteria against aliens which finds expression in rigid enforcement of the law governing deportations." He warned that such actions would lead to a shortage of Mexican labor and damage the United States' foreign relations with Latin America. The constitutional rights committee of the Los Angeles Bar Association formed a group to investigate the illegal deportation practices targeting the entire Mexican-origin community in the region. This group included several distinguished lawyers who studied fifty-five cases and confirmed that extralegal methods were used. They recommended that all illegal practices be discontinued by the bureau of immigration.

Clarence H. Matson, manager of the foreign commerce and shipping department of the Los Angeles Chamber of Commerce, also criticized the "terrible crusade against the Mexican professional and commercial men, in spite of their many years' residents in United States." He also wondered how the deportation campaign would impact Los Angeles's international image. In particular, he was concerned with how the government's actions would affect the goodwill that the city hoped to foster during the upcoming 1932 Olympic Games. National liberal publications also criticized the campaign. In August 1931, *The Nation* called out the lack of due process in the deportations. "It is an outrage that the immigration bureau officials should be investigators, prosecutors, judges, and a final Court of Appeals in deportation cases, and take their orders from men of the type of William N. Doak." Mexican Americans protested, resisted deportation efforts, and advocated for their civil rights as full-time workers and residents of the United States.[56]

Still, the deportation raids continued. Although the largest raids occurred in California, Mexican communities across the country were subjected to what the Los Angeles *Record* called a "terror reign" and "deportation mania." From August 1933 to May 1934, Mexican nationals were deported from all over the country, as far away as New York, Boston, Detroit, Chicago, Pittsburgh, St. Louis, New Orleans, Kansas City, Denver, Oklahoma City, and Salt Lake City. The worst of the federal government's deportation terror campaign was over by 1934. Immigration levels had decreased dramatically, and under President Franklin Delano Roosevelt, the immigration service grew more reluctant to deport a family member, such as a breadwinner, if their removal would cause an entire family to suffer. After 1934, the number of Mexicans being deported fell by approximately 50 percent.[57]

BUT DEPORTATION WAS not the only tool of the anti-Mexican campaign. For many localities, deportation failed to achieve desired results. It required a lot of personnel and coordination with the federal government. It was costly and time-consuming. Moreover, aliens who became public charges could not be deported simply because they were on relief. And many of the families included American-born citizens, who were nondeportable. Local governments, officials, and the American public demanded what writer and social reformer Carey McWilliams described as "a better scheme."[58]

That "better scheme" was repatriation, the voluntary removal of aliens to their native country. As conditions worsened in the United States, some Mexicans did indeed want to return to Mexico and were swayed by the Mexican government's promises to aid returnees once they arrived across the border.[59] In the United States during the 1930s, however, *repatriation* became less and less of a voluntary migration and more of a form of coercive emigration achieved through deception and control. Much of it was organized by local governments with the assistance of social workers and private charitable agencies. Like the deportation campaign, this movement was specifically aimed at reducing the number of Mexicans in the United States, including those who were legal residents and American-born US citizens.

The goal of the repatriation program was to return indigent Mexicans to Mexico, save welfare agencies money, and create jobs for "real" Americans. Officials and others promoted the idea that the program was justified by the prevailing belief that Mexicans "would be better off" in Mexico among their "own kind." Repatriation was framed as a humanitarian gesture when in actuality it was a tool that continued and perfected the scareheading tactics to oust all Mexicans from the United States. In effect, it veiled xenophobia under the guise of aid.[60]

Working simultaneously and in concert with the deportation campaign, repatriation focused on the perceived problem of welfare dependency in the Mexican immigrant and Mexican American community. Social workers and government officials blamed both Mexican men and women for this problem. Men were not able to support their families and had become dependent on the state, thereby failing at one of the most central responsibilities of American men. Mexican women, on the other hand, were blamed for being hyperbreeders who birthed too many children.[61]

Social workers tried hard to assimilate Mexicans into the "American way of life" in the early twentieth century. These efforts included teaching Mexican women to transform their rural, preindustrial lifestyles into modern American ones by teaching them cooking, cleanliness, English, and the "fundamental principles of the American system of government and the rights and duties of citizenship," as the California state legislature described in 1915. But by the 1920s, social workers had become convinced that Mexicans were an unchangeable population. They were dependent and lacked thrift and ambition. They showed little interest in naturalizing. And because there were so many of them, assimilation efforts were difficult. Social workers collected data on the "problems" Mexicans caused, selectively citing statistics that exaggerated Mexican reliance on relief. They shared their findings at annual social work conferences and lobbied for immigration restriction. By 1928, California state officials were concerned enough about the "Mexican problem" that Governor Clement C. Young called for a fact-finding committee. The results, published in a report two years later, confirmed what officials and the public suspected—and replicated the biases of the social workers. Mexicans made up 11 percent of the population in the United States. But they comprised between a quarter and a third of all welfare cases supported by the Los Angeles Outdoor Relief Department.[62]

Eugenicists built on the already robust stereotype of Mexicans as oversexed hyperbreeders and argued that these deficient racial characteristics posed a huge financial and demographic threat to the country. Los Angeles businessman and eugenicist Charles Goethe explained that "the Mexican, with his low living standards, is a tremendous burden to our relief agencies." Cities were being run down with "Mexican slum belts," and relief costs were mounting because "the peon requires relief out of all proportion to his numbers." Goethe also relayed a powerful, if dubious, anecdote about a Mexican father who applied for charity so that he could pay for the haircuts of his thirty-three children. Invoking eugenic themes of white "race suicide," he calculated that should this man's progeny reproduce at the same rate, he would become the "progenitor of 1,185,921 descendants in but four generations."[63]

Once the nation plunged into the economic depression and Mexicans turned to social welfare agencies to feed and house their families, they faced mounting criticism that they were draining public welfare resources that should be reserved for "Americans." California faced an especially difficult situation when the arrival of hundreds of thousands of Dust Bowl migrants from the Midwest, combined with the worsening economic depression, led to a dramatic increase in the number of individuals requesting welfare assistance. In 1931, Los Angeles County welfare rolls grew from 3,500 individuals to 35,000 families. The numbers on relief were unprecedented for the state and left the L.A. County Department of Charities searching for answers. By 1933 to 1934, the worst years of the depression, 126,000 families totaling 600,000 people were on the welfare rolls in the county. Mexicans made up 10 percent of the welfare population, but less than 40 percent of that number were immigrants. The rest were Americans of Mexican descent.[64]

As the cost of providing assistance to a growing number of needy families and individuals increased, taxpayers started protesting the use of public funds to assist immigrants. They were joined by a number of labor unions, veterans' organizations, and patriotic groups in calling for action, including the repatriation of indigent aliens. But not all immigrants were equally the focus of American xenophobia and nativism. European immigrants were generally treated with greater sympathy, and repatriation was a last resort. In contrast, Mexican families were coerced into repatriation en masse.

Social workers and local relief officials responsible for assisting the needy targeted the most vulnerable for permanent expulsion and found creative ways to expel Mexicans and Mexican Americans. By 1932, local and state officials were energetically and publicly implementing a program of mass removal. They helped promote the idea that Mexicans' use of relief was an illegitimate burden on "American taxpayers." They became powerful voices in support of immigration restriction and worked cooperatively with immigration officials to deport those who sought assistance.[65]

This was achieved in a number of ways. In Los Angeles, the county repatriation program was the brainchild of Frank L. Shaw, the chairman of the board of supervisors' charities and public welfare committee. Shaw estimated that ten thousand Mexican immigrant relief cases cost around

$200,000 a month or $2.4 million a year. If these individuals were re-patriated, he reasoned, county taxpayers could presumably benefit. The county hired a special group of recruiters tasked with educating Mexican immigrants about the repatriation program. County charitable offices of-fered a number of inducements, such as free transportation, food, cloth-ing, and medical aid and the assurance of cooperation by the Mexican government and railroads. They deceived, pressured, and coerced Mexi-cans and Mexican Americans out of Los Angeles to Mexico.[66]

Relief officials, for example, told families that all aid would be cut off unless they accepted the offer to return to Mexico. John Anson Ford, a member of the Los Angeles County Board of Supervisors during the depression, recalled that welfare officials managed the repatriation pro-gram "without necessarily having all the *legal* authority to do so." In talking to Mexican clients, he explained, they "made them think that they had to go back to Mexico." As a result, repatriation was "arbitrarily handled," resulting in "grave economic injustice" to Mexicans and their families. Clements of the Los Angeles Chamber of Commerce confirmed that Mexicans were being persuaded to leave Southern California "either through coercion or actual starvation." As a result, many Mexican immi-grants returned to Mexico under pressure. They felt they had no choice.[67]

Families that included naturalized US citizens and US-born citi-zens faced just as much pressure to repatriate as noncitizen families. As Los Angeles superintendent of charities W. H. Holland explained, the number of indigent Mexicans and Mexican Americans receiving public benefits numbered around sixty-three thousand in February 1934. About one-third, or twenty-three thousand, were American born. Although Holland conceded that the US-born children "must be considered as any other American citizen," he did not count them as citizens when it came to providing relief and routinely lumped them together as "alien Mexican indigent cases." They were a grave "financial burden that the *citizens* of this County can ill afford to carry during the stress of existing economic conditions," he explained in a statement that revealed how his definition of "citizen" did not in fact include Mexican Americans. Acting on these beliefs, social workers pressured all Mexicans and Mexican-descended peoples in the United States to repatriate, often to the point of abuse, because as Holland explained, it was "both an economic and social necessity . . . to the profit of this community." As a result of these policies, American-born children were explicitly deprived of their rights to citizenship in their native land.[68]

H. A. Payne, the Los Angeles County auditor, requested funds and authorization to "move the first load" of Mexicans and Mexican families from Los Angeles to El Paso and then on to Mexico on February 10, 1931. It took some time for officials from the county, the American and Mexican railroad companies, and the Mexican consulate to agree to all of the arrangements. But soon, an agreement was made for Los Angeles County to pay $14.70 per adult to transport them across the border, half that amount for children under twelve. Holland noted that a "lower rate" would be possible if the county "transport[ed] Mexicans in numbers of two hundred or more at a time."[69]

The first trainload of repatriates left Los Angeles on March 23, 1931. Three hundred fifty Mexicans left for El Paso and then for Ciudad Juárez. Another train carried 1,150 Mexican repatriates, including a majority whose fares had been paid by the county and others who made their own arrangements. By the end of April, the trains were regularly leaving the central train station in downtown Los Angeles. Holland reported that 1,600 Mexicans had been repatriated during the month of April 1931 alone. The repatriation train that left Los Angeles on August 17, 1931, carried the largest number of passengers to date in the program, including 899 county-sponsored repatriates and another 400 voluntary repatriates.[70]

On January 12, 1932, a photographer from the *Los Angeles Evening Herald and Express* captured the chaotic scene of 1,400 Mexicans waiting at the city's Central Station to board three special Southern Pacific trains bound for Mexico. Passengers, young and old, male and female, dressed smartly in overcoats, suits, dresses, and hats, crowd both floors of the station's waiting areas. Like most repatriates, they were probably longtime residents of the United States who were being forced from their homes in Los Angeles. Nevertheless, the photograph caption reinforced

Original caption from the *Los Angeles Evening Herald and Express*, January 12, 1932: "Photo shows a crowd of 1,400 Mexicans at Central Station when they departed today for their old homes in Mexico. The families, with their babies, guitars, blankets, shawls and bundles, left on three special Southern Pacific trains chartered by Los Angeles county, which set aside about $15,000 to aid them in their repatriation. Officials estimated that this sum spent on transportation would have recovered within six weeks in savings on charity." Herald Examiner Collection/Los Angeles Public Library.

stereotypes of Mexicans as foreign and uneducated peasants who were returning to their true homes in Mexico. Repatriation was also couched in benevolent and nativistic terms.

Clements and other officials from the county charities department traveled to the Southern Pacific depot on August 17, 1931, to witness the mass exodus. They found a broad cross-section of the Mexican community of Southern California on board the two trains heading to Mexico. Most passengers were young children, most of them American-born. The second largest group were young women (likely their mothers), and then able-bodied men and some elderly. Most of the men had been in the United States for over a decade and spoke English. Clements found that most of the repatriates had been told that "they could come back whenever they wanted to." But this was a lie.[71]

Clements could not help but regret the misinformation deliberately being passed to the repatriates. "I think this is a grave mistake, because it is not the truth," he wrote to an associate. The repatriates were each issued a departure card clearly marked by the Los Angeles Department of Charities and Welfare Department signifying that they had been repatriated at county expense and were thus barred from reentering the United States. No children could return, even if they were born in America, Clements further explained, unless they had documentary evidence and a birth certificate. This was an exceedingly difficult burden of proof to bear on a mobile and young population with little knowledge about the legal conditions and requirements of their departure and possible reentry. The repatriation program's effective de-Americanization of an entire generation was not lost on Clements. "This means that something like sixty percent of these children are American citizens without very much hope of ever coming back into the United States."[72]

Indeed, when repatriates tried to return to the United States after struggling in Mexico, they found themselves unable to do so. According to one federal relief official, hundreds of American-born children who were repatriated with their Mexican parents were living under the "most wretched conditions" a stone's throw from the border. In 1932, the *New York Times* reported on a cable received from Mexico City stating that repatriates from the United States were "almost starving." In May 1934, Pablo and Refugio Guerrero wrote to Los Angeles officials requesting that they and their five citizen children born in the United States be allowed to return to the "country in which they are entitled to live." The family of seven had been deported in December 1932. But the children "do not like the Mexican customs and wish to return to the U.S." Worse, the Mexican government did not grant protections to American-born children. Pablo begged officials to allow them to return to the land of their birth. There is no record of a reply.[73]

One family in particular caught the attention of US officials. A repatriated widow with seven American-born children had "found her way back as far as Nogales, Mexico and then was not permitted to come into the country again. She lives in the most wretched hut with a dirt floor," an official reported. Two of her children had died recently, and "all of the children show marks of malnutrition." The official was moved to act and appealed to his superiors in Washington. "I certainly think that if anyone with a heart were to visit as I did, these children existing and some of them dying, just a few hundred feet across our border, they would agree that the United States should take care of her citizens," he wrote. It is unclear whether these appeals made any difference.[74]

By the fall of 1931, the repatriation trains had become routine. Two trains left Los Angeles on October 29 with approximately 1,200 Mexican repatriates. By the end of 1933, fifteen trains had sent 12,668 individuals to Mexico. Los Angeles's repatriation program—the single largest in the country—would last for four years. Statistics vary on how many left. The *Los Angeles Times* estimated that the "Southern California exodus" numbered 75,000. But hundreds of thousands more were scared into leaving on their own as well. Historians estimate that a third of the Mexican-origin community left Los Angeles for Mexico during the Depression.[75]

Los Angeles County's repatriation program was the most ambitious and organized in the country. But across the nation, other cities, counties, and states also engaged in the systematic removal of Mexicans. Some were even more successful than Los Angeles in terms of numbers. Texas led the country, for example, with 132,639 people of Mexican heritage departing the state between 1930 and 1932. Another 18,520 left Arizona during the same period. And although only 3.6 percent of the Mexican population in the United States lived in Michigan, Illinois, and Indiana, more than 10 percent of the repatriates (32,000) across the United States came from these three states alone.[76]

BY THE END of the Great Depression, the United States had been turned into a "deportation nation" that made no distinction between foreign-born Mexican aliens who had entered the United States without documentation, lawful residents, naturalized citizens, and American-born citizens of Mexican descent. All were targeted and swept up as xenophobia hardened into both an anti-immigrant campaign and a race-based anti-Mexican campaign. An entire generation of American citizens of Mexican descent were de-Americanized and exiled to the country of their parents' birth.

During the next decade, another community of immigrants and American-born citizens would be similarly impacted by xenophobia, racism, and de-Americanization. After the bombing of Pearl Harbor and the United States' entry into World War II, Japanese Americans on the West Coast would be forced to leave their homes, businesses, and farms and were incarcerated in remote prison camps. The official justification was national security, but in reality, racism and xenophobia led the US government to commit this grave injustice.

SIX

"MILITARY NECESSITY"

Betty May Chieko Morita was born on May 30, 1933, in the small town of Odell, Oregon, near Hood River. The eighth child of Mototsugu and Masano Morita, immigrants from Okayama, Japan, Betty was in the third grade when the Japanese attacked Pearl Harbor on December 7, 1941. Although the Moritas had lived peacefully in Hood River for years and counted many white neighbors and classmates among their closest friends, some residents turned against them in retaliation for the attack. Decades of anti-Japanese xenophobia combined with new fears about national security led many Americans to believe that Japanese immigrants and their American-born children were not, and never could be, American—that they were instead loyal to Japan. After Pearl Harbor, anti-Japanese sentiment turned violent. The Morita family's dog was shot on December 7. The Hood River police chief warned Japanese American residents to "stay home," "use the English language if possible," and "do not congregate in one place." These warnings, though well-intentioned, only affirmed the fact that all Japanese Americans were considered enemies of the United States by virtue of their ancestry.

By May 13, 1942, the Moritas were forced out of their home by Executive Order 9066, which authorized the mass removal and incarceration of all Japanese Americans on the West Coast on the basis of what the government called "military necessity." They were first imprisoned in the

War Relocation Camp at Tule Lake in Northern California, just south of the Oregon border. They were later transferred to the Minidoka camp in Idaho and remained confined there until the end of the war.[1]

Isamu Shibayama was born in Lima, Peru, on June 6, 1930, to Yuzo and Tatsue Shibayama, immigrants from Fukuoka, Japan. Baptized Carlos Arturo and known as Art, Shibayama was thirteen years old and living comfortably in Lima when the Japanese attacked Pearl Harbor. Although the attack occurred in the United States and Peru was a noncombatant during the war, Japanese Peruvians were frightened. Anti-Japanese xenophobia had been spreading for decades throughout Latin America, often influenced by US attitudes and actions. As rumors began circulating in Japanese Peruvian communities, the Shibayamas stayed glued to the radio at home and waited for news. But they were still unprepared for what happened next. Along with 1,800 Japanese Peruvians, the Shibayamas were rounded up by Peruvian police, turned over to American troops, forcibly removed from their homes and country, and sent to American prison camps in Crystal City, Texas. They would remain incarcerated as "enemy aliens" in the US until 1944.[2]

Long before Pearl Harbor, Japanese immigrants had been treated as undesirable and dangerous foreigners in the United States and throughout the Americas. Considered racially inassimilable like other Asians, Japanese were confronted with immigration restrictions and laws that curbed their rights in the United States. They were feared for their supposed loyalty to Japan during the war, and the US government treated them as both a racial problem and a national security one. The US response was harsh: the forced relocation and mass incarceration of 120,000 Japanese Americans, two-thirds of whom were American-born citizens, from their homes and into prison camps as "prisoners without trial" for the duration of the war.[3] Like Mexican Americans, an entire generation of Japanese Americans was de-Americanized.

Xenophobia also became an integral part of America's foreign relations during World War II. At the same time that it was incarcerating its own residents and citizens, the US government was also orchestrating and financing the mass roundup of innocent men, women, and children of Japanese descent in twelve Latin American countries, citing "hemi-spheric security." The officially stated goal was to make the nation's southern border safe from infiltration or attack by the Japanese enemy, including Japanese-descended people in the Americas. The unofficial goal was to acquire a supply of people of Japanese ethnicity, an action some have called *hostage shopping*, who could be traded for American ci-vilians stranded in Japan after Pearl Harbor. Unwilling to send Japanese Americans, the United States targeted Japanese Latin Americans. What resulted was a "wartime triangle trade" in Japanese-descended peoples taken from Latin America and brought to the United States for exchange of American civilians and nationals in Japan.[4]

The fact that Japanese Latin Americans were innocent noncomba-tants who had not been accused of, charged with, or indicted for any crime made no difference. Few, if any, received any sort of legal hearing at the time of their deportation. Most did not know why they were being forced from their homes in Latin America. None of this seemed to matter to either the US officials orchestrating the campaign or the Latin American governments cooperating with the United States. By the time the program ended in 1944, 2,264 men, women, and children of Japanese ancestry, in-cluding citizens and permanent residents of twelve Latin American coun-tries, had been apprehended, deported, and incarcerated in the United States. Most Japanese Latin Americans, 1,800, were from Peru. Nearly 900 Japanese Latin Americans were exchanged for American civilians in Japan. One thousand were deported to devastated postwar Japan, a coun-try that many had never been to, at the end of the war. Three hundred sixty-five Japanese Peruvians, like Art Shibayama, stayed in the United States to fight for the right to remain in the country. Erroneously justified as matters of national and hemispheric security, the removal and incarcer-ation of Japanese Americans and Japanese Latin Americans resulted in the wholesale abuse of civil and human rights at home and abroad.[5]

KASHICHI MORITA'S FAMILY were farmers in Okayama, Japan, when his father lost all of their money on a risky sake venture. As the creditors came to the house to cart away the family's worldly possessions, Kashichi's sister sobbed inconsolably. Kashichi had a different reaction. He had been spoiled as a child, but the family's financial crisis forced him to grow up fast. He signed a contract with one of the labor recruiters traveling the Japanese countryside and boarded a ship. Most were heading to the Hawaiian plantations. Kashichi's was headed to Mexico. When the ship first stopped in Seattle, however, he jumped overboard and entered the United States. He soon found work on the railroads and then in Hood River, Oregon, as a farmer. The year was 1910. He was seventeen years old.

Yuzo Shibayama was fifteen when he left his home in Fukuoka, Japan, in 1920 and migrated with his brother to Peru. An uncle had already settled in the Latin American country and was delivering coal in Lima. After one year, Yuzo's brother returned to Japan, but Yuzo stayed on. He eventually saved enough money to open a small coffee shop and then a small imported textile company. By the 1940s, Yuzo and his wife, Tatsue, had seven children and were thriving along with twenty-six thousand Japanese Peruvians in Lima and Callao.

Japanese immigrants, or *issei*, like Kashichi Morita and Yuzo Shibayama, were the second largest group of Asian immigrants (after the Chinese) to come to the United States and to other countries in North and South America during the late nineteenth and early twentieth centuries. Just like the Chinese, Japanese immigrants were heavily recruited to work in the United States. Labor contractors flooded the Japanese countryside targeting young men from farming families who were struggling to pay the high taxes imposed by the Meiji government. The agricultural prefectures of Hiroshima, Yamaguchi, Kumamoto, and Fukuoka in southwest Japan were among the hardest hit. Farmers were required to pay fixed taxes every year regardless of the success of their crops or the market prices for their products. When they could not afford to pay, they were forced to sell their land. Eventually, many family farms were left with plots that were too small to support the entire family. In the early twentieth century many men chose migration abroad instead of compulsory military service as well.[6]

Emigration was not cheap, but a common plantation laborer in Hawai'i could earn four to six times as much in the islands as in Hiroshima. Labor contractors and emigration companies fed the emigration *netsu*, fever, and between 1885 and 1924, 200,000 Japanese went to Hawai'i and 180,000 more went to the continental United States. By 1930, the US census recorded 138,834 Japanese immigrants and US-citizen children in the United States. Of these, 97,456 resided in California alone.[7]

Working as agricultural workers on Hawaiian sugar plantations and on farms up and down the West Coast, Japanese men and women endured backbreaking work from sunup to sundown. Many others worked on railroads and in mines, lumber mills, and fish canneries. Or they were domestic servants in the large cities. In Western states, they became an essential part of the region's agricultural revolution. On the eve of World War II, Japanese Americans grew 95 percent of California's fresh snap beans and peas, 67 percent of the state's fresh tomatoes, and 44 percent of its onions.[8]

With newfound economic security in the United States, many Japanese immigrant men focused on settling down. "It's time you get a wife," Kashichi Morita told his son Mototsugu in the 1920s. Although many young men asked relatives and matchmakers back home to introduce them to suitable spouses, Mototsugu already had a woman in mind. He remembered the three beautiful Sakakiyama sisters in his hometown and had always intended to return to Japan one day and marry the eldest. But time passed, and she married a doctor. He then turned his attention to the second sister, but she also married before he could return to Japan. Finally, he enlisted his father to return to Japan and ask for the hand of the third sister before she too slipped out of his grasp. In Okayama, Masano Sakakiyama agreed and embarked on a ship to the United States.

She joined twenty thousand Japanese women, many of them "picture brides" who were destined to marry men whom they knew only through pictures and descriptions sent through go-betweens and relatives. When ships docked in Seattle or San Francisco, the women crowded at the ships' railings searching for the men to whom they were betrothed. Dockside, their grooms similarly clamored to catch a glimpse of their brides. Mototsugu had rushed from the apple orchards in Hood River to Seattle, and when he and Masano finally met, his clothes were wrinkled and his face sunburned. Masano stared at him in disbelief. She may have been picturing the young seventeen-year-old from her childhood. Or perhaps she was looking for someone who resembled the polished portrait that Mototsugu might have had taken in a fancy studio. In any case, her look of shock and disappointment must have been obvious, because Mototsugu told her, "If you're unhappy by my appearance, it's okay if you want to go back to Japan." But Masano was undeterred. "I know what you look like," she answered. She experienced another shock when she walked into the wooden shack that was to become her new home on the farm in Hood River. Her home in Japan had polished furniture and electricity. This one had furniture made out of orange crates and kerosene lamps. Despite the drastic change in her economic circumstances, Masano stuck it out. She had made her choice, her daughter Betty recalls, and she was determined to stay. Together Mototsugu and Masano had eight children, including Betty May Chieko, who was born at home in 1933.

Most Japanese immigrants headed to the United States and Canada. But when those two countries banned Japanese laborers in 1908, Japanese immigrants headed to Latin America instead. In Peru, Japanese laborers were recruited to work in the guano pits or on sugar plantations. Only a small number remained working in these unforgiving industries. Many soon fled to the cities to work as domestic servants and day laborers. In 1934, there were over twenty thousand Japanese in Peru, mostly in the Lima-Callao area where they ran restaurants, cafés, and grocery shops. Japanese Peruvians were just starting to enjoy a period of economic and community stability when World War II began. This is the Peru in which Art Shibayama grew up.[9]

Art's father was successful enough to own a large and well-furnished house in the section of town where European immigrants and their children lived. The Shibayamas had a maid; a chauffeur drove the growing Shibayama brood to private school in the morning and then to Japanese school in the afternoon. Art grew up speaking mostly Spanish, playing baseball, and spending idyllic summers at the beach in Callao with his maternal grandparents, who owned a small department store in town. He experienced little prejudice or discrimination. But other Japanese Peruvians did, and by the 1930s and 1940s, anti-Japanese laws and a violent race riot in Lima in 1940 were warning signs of more trouble ahead.

Similarly, in Hood River, Oregon, the Morita children were busy attending school and working on the farm. They spent the summers fishing for crawdads and having weenie roasts. They were well integrated in the farming community and counted many white neighbors as friends. Daughter Flora and son Claude were named after the white couple whose land the Moritas leased at the time of their birth. When the family moved to another farm, Betty was named after one of the owners. Still, some of the anti-Japanese xenophobia that had already succeeded in curtailing immigration and restricting the legal and political rights of Japanese Americans made their way into the children's lives. The Moritas were often called "Japs" on the street and got into fights with some of their white classmates. Mototsugu and Masano were barred from becoming naturalized citizens by federal law, and beginning in 1923, Oregon had banned "aliens ineligible for citizenship" like the Moritas from owning and leasing land. One of the leading politicians pushing these anti-Japanese measures was James D. Phelan.

JAMES PHELAN's 1920 campaign poster sent a clear message to California voters. A yellow-skinned hand, clad in a loose-fitting shirt sleeve with the chrysanthemum symbol of the Japanese empire, claws at the state of California. Another hand, this one milky pink and clad in the stars and stripes of the United States, firmly grasps the wrist of the invader in the act of protecting the state. "HOLD," the caption reads. "RE-ELECT JAMES D. PHELAN U.S. SENATOR and let him finish the work he now has under way to stop the SILENT INVASION." Phelan, in a tight reelection fight for his US Senate seat, made his anti-Japanese message of "Keep California White" the centerpiece of his campaign. The stakes were high. The Republican Party in California was becoming increasingly popular with voters, and Phelan, the undisputed leader of the state's

US senator James Phelan's reelection poster, 1920.
Courtesy of the Library of Congress.

Democratic Party, was vulnerable. But Phelan was not just an opportunistic politician spouting anti-Japanese xenophobia during a tight election fight. He had a long history of anti-Asian activism dating back more than two decades.

Born to an Irish immigrant father who had made his fortune establishing banks and insurance companies in San Francisco, Phelan turned from what he called "the sordid messes of business and trade" and became a politician. Elected as a reformist mayor of San Francisco in 1897 at age thirty-five, Phelan spearheaded the city's beautification campaign by erecting classical-style buildings, fountains, monuments, and statues. He helped create public parks and protected natural spaces throughout the city. He promoted the arts and was active in San Francisco's social scene through his multiple club memberships. Impeccably dressed, he was often seen entertaining guests at the Bohemian, Chit-Chat, University, Olympic, or Pacific Union clubs. Phelan dedicated his career to creating a beautiful San Francisco that was the cultural and commercial jewel of the Pacific Coast. But Phelan's San Francisco was meant only for whites. He considered the United States a "white man's country." He also supported Jim Crow segregation in the south, calling African Americans a "nonassimilable and ignorant population."[10]

But it was his decades-long opposition to Asian immigration that defined both James Phelan the man and the politician. When bubonic plague swept through Chinatown in 1900, Mayor Phelan ordered a blockade of the area and warned the public not to employ any Chinese laborers. The next year, he was a major speaker at the Chinese Exclusion Convention, which brought 2,500 delegates to the city to "prevent the threatened invasion of Mongol hordes to the peril and degradation of American labor." Seeking a more national audience, he also published an article in the *North American Review* explaining that the Chinese had a "non-assimilative character" and made "no contribution by service or citizenship or family life to the permanent interest of the country."[11]

By the early 1900s, anti-Chinese activists like Phelan began to turn their attention to Japanese immigrants. Politicians and labor, religious, and civic leaders all believed that growing numbers of Japanese immigrants represented another invasion of unassimilable foreigners who, like the Chinese before them, were an economic threat to whites and another race problem. In these ways, anti-Japanese xenophobia was similar to and drew from the success of the movement to exclude Chinese immigrants.

But anti-Japanese xenophobia was different in key ways. Whereas anti-Chinese activists did not consider China, believed to be a crumbling and inept empire on the verge of collapse, to be an economic or imperial threat to the United States, Japan was different. It had modern industries and a powerful military that had defeated both China (1894–1895) and Russia (1904–1905). Moreover, Japan had imperial ambitions of its own and had begun to act on them with the forceful annexation of Korea in 1910. Japan was a power to be reckoned with, a "yellow peril" that threatened not just the United States but all of Western civilization and white supremacy worldwide.

First expressed by Kaiser Wilhelm II of Germany in 1895, the "yellow peril" hypothesis popularized long-standing European fears of an "Oriental" invasion of the West. By the early twentieth century, many Americans believed that the Japanese empire posed an external threat to the United States, while Japanese immigrants already in the United States posed an internal one. For example, military strategist and author

Homer Lea raised the alarm about the "Yellow Peril" of an expansionist Japan and its dangers to the West Coast of North America in his 1909 book, *The Valor of Ignorance: The Inevitable Japanese-American War*. With detailed maps and copious statistics, Lea argued that the 149,000 Japanese immigrants already in Hawai'i constituted a Japanese occupation of the islands and that a similar "invasion" of Japanese soldiers was well under way in California and Washington. The alleged threat from Japanese immigration was particularly dangerous, he insisted, because, unlike Chinese immigrant communities, the Japanese population included a substantial number of women and children. The Japanese in America seemed destined to remain in the US. Anti-Japanese leader and publisher of the influential *Sacramento Bee* newspaper V. S. McClatchy also explained that given the high birth rates among Japanese immigrants, they "could easily displace our race." San Francisco newspapers echoed these fears with alarmist headlines like "YELLOW PERIL—HOW JAPANESE CROWD OUT THE WHITE RACE."[12]

In 1905, delegates from sixty-seven local and regional labor, political, and fraternal organizations met to form the Japanese-Korean Exclusion League. Their goal was the total exclusion of Japanese immigrants from the United States, including the territory of Hawai'i. With their slogan, "Absolute Exclusion of the Asiatics," the league concentrated its efforts on spreading its message through legislation, boycotts, and propaganda. It also lobbied the San Francisco School Board to segregate Japanese students from whites in the city's public schools.

On October 11, 1906, the school board responded to public pressure and ordered all Japanese and Korean students to attend the city's Oriental School, which Chinese students already attended. President Theodore Roosevelt and his administration, however, balked at the potential rift such an action would cause with Japan. Intense negotiations between San Francisco officials, the California congressional delegation, and members of Roosevelt's administration followed. On March 13, 1907, the school board rescinded the segregation order. The very next day, Roosevelt issued an executive order that excluded from the continental United States all Japanese or Korean laborers traveling from Hawai'i, Canada, or Mexico.[13]

At the same time, anti-Japanese xenophobia turned violent. In the summer and fall of 1906, nearly three hundred attacks on San Francisco Japanese were documented by the local police. In the spring of 1907, tensions erupted again. Beginning on May 20, white mobs roamed throughout the city's Japanese neighborhoods for several nights. Customers were driven out of the Japanese-owned Horseshoe Restaurant at 1213 Folsom Street, and the restaurant and a nearby Japanese bathhouse were destroyed. The next night, a group attacked Japanese homes, businesses, and restaurants throughout the city. Japanese repeatedly called the police for help, but no one came.[14]

Both the school board crisis and the race riots pushed Roosevelt to begin diplomatic negotiations with Japan over the restriction of Japanese laborers. In the "Gentlemen's Agreement" (so named to reflect that Japan participated voluntarily) signed on January 25, 1908, the Japanese government agreed to stop issuing passports to laborers intending to travel to the continental United States. Passports would still be issued to laborers who were already in America and to their parents, wives, and children, but the door to new Japanese immigration was largely closed.

California voters also passed laws aimed at restricting the rights of Japanese already in the United States. The 1913 Alien Land Law allowed "aliens ineligible to citizenship," a legal category that applied only to Asian immigrants, to lease land for only three years and barred them from further land purchases. Japanese immigrants deftly worked around this law by securing leases and land in their US-born children's names or in jointly owned corporations. Amendments to this law in 1919 and 1920 closed these loopholes. By 1923, Washington, Colorado, Arizona, Texas, Oregon, and Idaho had all adopted similarly restrictive alien land laws as well.[15]

Phelan memorialized these anti-Japanese successes in his voluminous correspondence and scrapbook collection. Begun when he was an adolescent, the scrapbooks reflected Phelan's lifelong habit of saving newspaper clippings. His early scrapbooks were filled with pictures of famous actresses and wrestlers he admired. Then as a teenager, he filled them with poetry. But as he entered adulthood and politics, contemporary issues came to dominate. No topic so ruled Phelan's public life as his vehement opposition to Japanese immigration.[16]

Collected articles included, for example, press coverage of Phelan's March 1919 visit to the Angel Island Immigration Station, where he warned that arriving Japanese picture brides signaled a coming invasion. They, and the children they would bear in the United States, were a "national danger and an immediate menace" who threatened "the hold of the white race upon the soil of California," he told San Francisco newspapers. In a series of speeches in Southern California later that month, Phelan further warned that unless Japanese immigration was completely halted, California would become "a Japanese colony" within forty years. The next year, he issued an even more frightening warning. He told county supervisors that Japanese immigrants were driving white settlers out of every county, taking over farms, and perverting schools. "They will destroy American civilization as surely as Europe exterminated the American Indian. . . . It is an invasion. It is a war." Phelan's hysterical warnings were not matched by actual immigration rates. The 1910 census recorded just 72,157 Japanese in the entire United States.[17]

Phelan also insisted that both the Japanese empire and Japanese Americans posed a serious military threat to the United States. In 1906, Phelan was the first politician to publicly spread the message that the Pacific Coast "would be an easy prey in case of attack" from Japan and that the Japanese already in California were an "enemy within our gates." During World War I, Phelan continued to promote this idea despite the fact that Japan was a US ally and had declared war against Germany in 1914. In a written statement on the "Japanese Menace" that he sent to various publications in 1914, Phelan falsely claimed that "Japan has been striking silently and insidiously to find a point of attack on the Pacific Coast." He also told the National Security League that Japan was seeking to establish a military presence on the Mexican coast.[18]

Phelan's constituents were on board with the senator, and many willingly provided ample examples for him to use in his speeches. In 1919, Los Angeles–based real estate agent Randall Phillips reported that the Japanese were "gobbling up the finest country in the world" and constituted nothing less than a "growing cancer." In 1920, Brayton Horton of the northern California town of Truckee reported similar encroachment and referred to the Japanese presence in the state as "the Japanese occupation of California."[19]

By the 1920s, new anti-Japanese organizations such as the Alien Regulation League, the Americanization League, the California Oriental Exclusion League, and the California Joint Immigration Commission all echoed Phelan's opinions and looked to him for leadership. The California Federation of Labor unanimously passed a five-point resolution at its statewide convention in 1919 that echoed Phelan's positions—such as a cancellation of the Gentlemen's Agreement, the exclusion of picture brides, more rigid immigration enforcement, barring all Asian immigrants from naturalized citizenship forever, and an amendment to the federal Constitution that would deny citizenship to the children of Asian immigrants even if those children were born in the United States.[20]

Phelan was a leader of the California Joint Immigration Commission, which, like the Immigration Restriction League in Boston, counted some of the most important local leaders and politicians as its members. It published statements and articles and lobbied politicians to support Japanese exclusion. Its publications constantly referred to Japanese immigration in menacing racial and sexual terms, such as a foreign "penetration" or the "Japanese colonization" of the United States.[21]

Phelan's "Keep California White" campaign proved to be popular. (His opponent, Republican Samuel Shortridge, also passionately participated in anti-Japanese xenophobia during the campaign.) But Phelan could not overcome the statewide Republican landslide that year and was defeated in his reelection bid for the Senate. Despite his loss, Phelan's "yellow peril" fears were in no way discredited. Indeed, they were part of a larger tradition of American xenophobia and racism that proved to be much more enduring than the senator's political career.

Many other politicians, writers, and leaders, for example, were also convinced that the white race (and by extension, "white" nations like the United States, Canada, Britain, France, and Australia) would become vulnerable as "colored races" (and "colored nations") grew in power and in number. Lothrop Stoddard, protégé of eugenicist Madison Grant, sounded the loudest alarm against what he called the global "rising tide of color" in his highly popular 1920 book, *The Rising Tide of Color Against White World-Supremacy*. This book, like Grant's *The Passing of the Great Race*, reached a broad audience and went through fourteen editions in just three years. *The Rising Tide* hysterically warned that population increases, mass migration, and the rise of anticolonial movements in Asia, Latin America, and Africa constituted a "colored peril" that threatened the hegemony of the white race.[22]

Stoddard identified three dangers coming from Asia in general and from Japan in particular: the peril of arms (military expansion), the peril of markets (economic competition), and the peril of migration. The last peril was the most dangerous, according to Stoddard. He went so far as to boldly proclaim that "the question of Asiatic immigration is incomparably the greatest external problem which faces the white world." The permanent settlement of Japanese in the white world, and especially North and South America, threatened "our very race-existence, the well-springs of being, the sacred heritage of our children." Moreover, he continued ominously, it was "already upon us." Stoddard mapped out the battle lines of the coming race war and called for the white world to take action. He argued that only the "rigorous exclusion of colored immigrants" could save the white race. "The gates must be strictly guarded," Stoddard exhorted his readers.[23]

The United States was the first to act with the 1924 Immigration Act. In addition to establishing a national origins quota system, it also barred entry to all aliens who were "ineligible for citizenship" (i.e., those to whom naturalization was denied). This clause was specifically aimed at Japanese. And it was effective. After decades of work by anti-Japanese activists, the gates to the United States were fully barred to Japanese immigrants. Canada followed with a similar policy four years later. But the struggle for Japanese exclusion in the Americas did not end; it merely shifted south.

IN PERU, ANTI-JAPANESE sentiment came from many sectors of society, from sources domestic and international. Both the country's leading business organizations and its labor unions were passionate critics of Japanese immigration and the economic competition that Japanese immigrants allegedly posed. A wide range of news media, including mainstream daily newspapers like *La Prensa* and *El Comercio*, contributed to the anti-Japanese movement with stories warning of *el peligro amarillo*, the "yellow peril," or the "rising tide of yellow immigrants." During the 1930s, *La Prensa* led the media's anti-Japanese crusade with a long-running column on "The Japanese Infiltration" written by Peruvian politicians and intellectuals. Laws discriminating against Japanese immigrants were passed by three different governments from 1919 to 1939.[24]

As in the United States, racism formed a primary foundation of the anti-Japanese campaign in Peru. The white *criollo* (Spanish-descended) elite dominated the country's government, society, and culture in spite of its minority status in the mostly indigenous and mestizo country. Drawing on the eugenics literature circulating throughout Europe and the Americas, Peruvian intellectuals and political leaders expressed concerns about the supposed racial inferiority of its nonwhite populations and their potential to block the nation's economic and social progress. They agreed that if Peru were to welcome immigrants, they should be "compatible races," such as Europeans, who would help whiten the population and solve Peru's race problems. To the distress of Peruvian lawmakers, however, Europeans preferred to migrate to Argentina, Chile, and Brazil. By the 1920s, the "incompatible" Japanese race was the largest immigrant group in Peru's capital city of Lima.[25]

The charge that Japanese immigrants competed unfairly with Peruvians for jobs and in commerce was another common argument in the anti-Japanese campaign. As in the United States, anti-Japanese xenophobia mobilized workers suffering from rising inflation, stagnant wages, and unemployment. In 1917, Lima's main labor union established the Anti-Asian Association. Its newspaper, *La Hoja Amarilla* (The Yellow Page), urged the Peruvian government to end "yellow immigration." As the number of Japanese-owned general stores, coffee shops, and barbershops grew in Lima, the fascist Unión Revolucionaria also organized an anti-Asian society and called for the expulsion of Japanese immigrants and an economic boycott of all Japanese businesses.[26]

Compounding the racial and economic arguments against Japanese immigrants was the belief that the Japanese immigrant community in Peru represented an advance guard of Japan's colonizing force. Echoing other yellow perilists in the United States, former Peruvian president Francisco García Calderón predicted in 1911 that "the Japanese would invade Western America and convert the Pacific into a vast closed sea . . . peopled by Japanese colonies." By the 1920s, *el peligro amarillo* had become a national concern in Peru that had both domestic and international roots and consequences. Peruvian journalists, politicians, and citizens turned their eyes northward to better understand the danger that faced them. In particular, they paid close attention to the United States' 1924 Immigration Act. Just days after it had been made into law, *El Comercio* praised the actions of the US government to "create an ethnic amalgam" from the "best currents of European blood" through its national origins quotas and its exclusion of Japanese immigrants. "Is there any country who can claim the right to disturb this admirable task?" it asked. "No. The law of exclusion is a given." During the next decade, the suggestion to emulate US immigration restrictions continued to be expressed in Peru's mainstream press. In 1934, *La Prensa* held up the United States as an example of how to "impede successive yellow immigration." "We don't see a reason why Peru doesn't follow such a laudable example," the paper concluded.[27]

Peru proceeded to pass a series of anti-Japanese laws. Its 1936 immigration law was passed in direct reaction to both the United States' 1924 Immigration Act and Brazil's 1934 Immigration Act, both of which restricted Japanese immigration. The Peruvian government feared that with North America and Brazil closed to Japanese immigration, the numbers coming to Peru would increase dramatically. The Peruvian immigration law also included quota amendments and racial restrictions modeled on American laws. As a result, Japanese immigration plummeted, just as it had in the United States.[28]

Like in the United States, another series of Peruvian laws curbed the economic and citizenship rights of Japanese immigrants already in the country, and by 1936, the twin goals of the anti-Japanese movement in

Peru—ending Japanese immigration and imposing restrictions on Japanese commercial activities—had been achieved. However, anti-Japanese agitation did not end completely. The city's newspapers continued to publicize sensational stories linking Japanese immigrants to subversive activities. When false rumors circulated throughout the city that firearms had been found in Japanese haciendas, anti-Japanese sentiment erupted into violence in Lima on May 13, 1940. Roving bands of people assaulted Japanese-owned businesses in the city, breaking down doors and attacking shops with clubs. Rioting led to massive looting, often while police looked on. It took an entire day for Peruvian troops to finally control the situation, but by then, almost all Japanese-owned shops had been destroyed, over six hundred homes damaged, scores of individuals injured, and ten Japanese killed.[29]

Just as Peruvians viewed the "yellow peril" in the context of American xenophobia, the United States viewed Japanese immigration in Latin America as part of the larger question of US leadership in the region. The United States had long acted on its claim of dominance in the Western Hemisphere, as first laid out in the Monroe Doctrine. President Franklin Roosevelt's "good neighbor" policy treated Latin American nations as sovereign entities and equal partners, but the United States continued to exert its hegemony in Latin America, albeit by employing economic strength and diplomatic pressure. It also deployed an ideological argument promoting a "western hemisphere idea" that defined the Americas as a "culturally unified, ideologically unique, and politically superior" realm of the globe that was best protected by the United States. At the Pan-American conference meeting in Panama in 1939, the United States sponsored a resolution that clearly declared the United States' right and intention to fight against extra hemispheric ideologies and threats.[30] This policy would translate into direct US intervention in Peru over the issue of Japanese immigration and hemispheric security during World War II.

AFTER THE JAPANESE bombed Pearl Harbor, Betty Morita's father began hearing rumors that the Federal Bureau of Investigation (FBI) was searching homes throughout Hood River. Issei men, especially those who were prominent in the Japanese American community, were disappearing. Their neighbor, Mr. Nishimoto, who was arrested and taken to jail immediately, would become one of the 1,291 Japanese (367 in Hawai'i and 924 in the continental United States) arrested by FBI agents as dangerous "enemy aliens" within the first forty-eight hours after Pearl Harbor. Eventually, eleven thousand so-called enemy aliens would be interned in US Department of Justice camps. Eight thousand were Japanese and were guilty by association rather than by any hard evidence of subversive activities. In addition, the US Treasury Department froze bank accounts and approximately $27.5 million in business enterprises, and real estate owned by Japanese immigrants was handed over to the government.[31] Japanese and other "enemy aliens" were subjected to a special curfew and ordered to turn in their shortwave radios and cameras. Families scrambled to hide or destroy any possessions that would link them to Japan, including treasured family heirlooms and books, letters, private papers, and business records.

Betty's father, older brother, and grandfather began tearing the house upside down searching for anything that might be considered evidence that the family was disloyal. The dynamite that they and many other farmers used to disintegrate tree stumps was considered taboo. Luckily, there was none on the farm, but Betty's grandfather announced to the family that "we gotta get rid of everything Japanese." He built a fire outside the house and burned all of the Japanese dolls that the children had received for Girl's Day and Boy's Day, as well as records of Japanese children's songs and other personal items. "I just stood there and I just cried because I'd see those dolls that we used to display," Betty recalled. "And I said, I said, 'Why, why do you have to do this?' And he said he has to."

More changes impacted the Morita family. They began talking about what would happen if the family were to be separated. Betty's oldest sister was married in March 1942 and had promised Betty that she could be a flower girl. But because the curfew limited how many people could travel long distances, Betty was left behind when the wedding came, unable to attend. Soon, there were photographs in the local newspaper about Japanese Americans in Portland being forced to leave their homes and head to the incarceration camps that were being hastily built. On May 13, 1942, the Moritas were forced to leave Hood River along with all other Japanese American residents. They assembled at the train station under the watchful eyes of armed soldiers before being sent down to the Pinedale detention center in Fresno, California, one of the fifteen facilities euphemistically called "assembly centers" administered by the Wartime Civil Control Administration.

On the eve of the Japanese attack of Pearl Harbor, 125,000 Japanese lived in the continental United States. More than 80 percent lived in the Pacific Coast states of California, Oregon, and Washington, where they made up just 1.2 percent of the population. They represented less than one-tenth of one percent of the total US population, but they had long been victims of a powerful anti-Japanese xenophobia that portrayed them as a national security threat even before Pearl Harbor. A year and a half before the attack, for example, the US government increased its surveillance of Japanese Americans on the Pacific Coast. In 1940, the US Immigration and Naturalization Service (INS) was transferred out of the Department of Labor and into the Department of Justice to align immigration with homeland security prerogatives. The 1940 Alien Registration Act required all resident aliens over age fourteen to register annually with the federal government and supply their fingerprints. Both the Office of Naval Intelligence and the FBI collected information on Japanese communities and created lists of individuals suspected of potential subversive activities. The definition of "subversive activity" was broad and encompassed most Japanese community organizations and any contact, no matter how minimal, with the Japanese government. Immigrants who had led cultural or assistance organizations, Japanese-language teachers, and members of the Buddhist clergy were all identified in the FBI master list as enemy alien "suspects" to be interned in case of war. By 1941, this list was ready, and designs for internment camps for aliens were prepared.[32]

These plans progressed in spite of findings by US government investigations that confirmed the overwhelming loyalty of Japanese American communities. A 1941 report, for example, stated that "better than ninety percent of the *nisei* and seventy-five percent of the original immigrants were completely loyal to the United States." Another explicitly stated that there was "no Japanese problem." The first-generation immigrants would eagerly become naturalized US citizens if allowed. The second-generation nisei were "pathetically eager to show this loyalty." Despite these reports, a strong contingent within the military had already floated the idea of mass removal of Japanese Americans in the event of war. Decades before the attack on Pearl Harbor, US military planners, including Colonel John DeWitt, who would later oversee the mass removal of Japanese Americans, had drawn up defense plans against a potential Japanese attack in Hawai'i. These plans presumed that both first- and

Theodor Seuss Geisel, aka Dr. Seuss, promoted the idea that Japanese Americans were a national security threat and a fifth column working on behalf of Japan in a wartime cartoon titled "Waiting for the Signal from Home." *PM Magazine*, February 13, 1942. Dr. Seuss Collection, Special Collections and Archives, UC San Diego.

second-generation Japanese Americans would assist Japan—and not the United States—during a war.[33]

After Pearl Harbor, DeWitt, now a lieutenant general and head of the newly created Western Defense Command that was charged with defending the entire West Coast, remained convinced that the Japanese in the United States constituted a major national security threat. "The Japanese race is an enemy race," he explained to US secretary of war Henry L. Stimson. Although many American-born Japanese had become Americanized, DeWitt conceded, "the racial strains are undiluted." They remained "potential enemies . . . at large." A year later, he gave the same message to a congressional committee. "It makes no difference whether he is an American citizen, he is still a Japanese." And as he told reporters the next day at a press conference, "a Jap is a Jap."[34]

The press, the public, politicians, and military officials all added to the chorus of voices calling for some action to deal with the presumed threat of Japanese Americans. West Coast newspapers like the *Los Angeles Times* fanned anti-Japanese sentiment with inflammatory and irrational headlines: "Jap Boat Flashes Message Ashore"; "Caps on Japanese Tomato Plants Point to Air Base"; "Jap and Camera Held in Bay City." As early as mid-December 1941, DeWitt proposed the mass removal and incarceration of people of Japanese ancestry. When asked to explain his rationale in light of the fact that there was no evidence of actual incidents of sabotage by Japanese Americans, DeWitt told a congressional committee that "the very fact that no sabotage has taken place to date is a disturbing and confirming indication that such action *will* be taken."[35]

On February 19, 1942, President Roosevelt signed Executive Order 9066, which directed the secretary of war to prescribe certain "military areas with respect to which the right of any person to enter, remain in, or leave shall be subject to whatever restrictions the Secretary deems necessary." It allowed for the government to round up and expel entire communities without compensation, due process, or proof of wrongdoing. In Hawai'i, which was still under martial law, General Delos Emmons, acting as military governor, saw no "military necessity" to forcibly remove Japanese from the islands. After all, they represented over 90 percent of the workers in vital industries like transportation, agriculture, and carpentry. Mass "evacuation" was unnecessary, dangerous, and impractical, he believed. In the end, only 1,444 Japanese (979 aliens and 535 US citizens) were taken into custody and incarcerated in camps on the US mainland. The Japanese who remained in Hawai'i, however, were subjected to severe and largely unwarranted restrictions under martial law for the next four years. In the continental United States, many alien Italian and German Americans were also forced to move out of supposedly sensitive areas, and thousands would eventually be interned. But unlike Japanese Americans, they were treated as individuals according to due process of law.[36]

The United States' forced removal and incarceration of Japanese Americans had international consequences as the Roosevelt administration focused on not only national security but hemispheric security as well. A Japanese military invasion was a real possibility, officials like US secretary of state Cordell Hull believed. But the "Japanese question" and the loyalty of Japanese residents in North and South America was also a cause for concern in the US government. In 1940, the Canada–United States Permanent Joint Board of Defense was established to prepare for

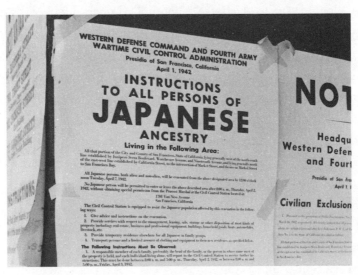

Exclusion Orders posted at First and Front Streets in San Francisco, California, directing the removal of people of Japanese ancestry from the city, April 11, 1942. Photographer Dorothea Lange. National Archives.

the defense of the North American continent and the northern half of the Western Hemisphere. It was here that the "problem" of Japanese residents in Canada and the United States was discussed. At the first meetings of the chiefs of staff of the US and Canadian armies, the United States raised the necessity of imprisoning Japanese Americans immediately after the outbreak of a war in Japan. The board agreed that in the event of war with Japan, the two governments "should follow policies of a similar character" in relation to their resident Japanese."[37]

While the United States was engaging in discussions about North American defense with Canada during the late 1930s, it was also organizing Latin American countries around similar issues. At the 1938 International Conference of American States in Lima, organized by the United States, foreign ministers of all Latin American countries approved a resolution that called for joint action in the case of an outside attack. This resolution, known as the Declaration of Lima, also included a provision that denied rights to certain foreign ethnic groups and another that opposed political activity by foreigners. These prewar discussions and agreements not only established a new phase of Latin American solidarity and collective security with North America; they also laid the groundwork for Latin American cooperation in the US deportation and internment program during the war.

The United States' influence was most strongly felt in Panama, Mexico, and Peru. With its long expanse of coastal areas along the Pacific Ocean, Peru was considered a special security risk for the United States. Conferences between US military officials and Peruvian authorities began in 1940, and soon thereafter, US military advisors were dispatched to Peru to focus on navy, aviation, and army operations in the country. They were joined by FBI agents who had been authorized by Congress to engage in intelligence gathering in Peru—and throughout the Western Hemisphere.[38]

ART SHIBAYAMA WAS heading to an overnight fishing trip with his father and some friends on December 7, 1941. When they heard what had happened at Pearl Harbor, they abandoned their plans and rushed home. Peru would not declare war on the Axis powers until 1945, but it was already a close ally to the United States, and Japanese Peruvians suspected that a US war with Japan might mean trouble. US surveillance of the Japanese in Latin America increased in the days following Pearl Harbor. US embassy officials, FBI agents, and officers in the Office of Strategic Services (the precursor to the Central Intelligence Agency [CIA]) stationed in various Latin American posts sent reports back to America on the activities of local Japanese populations. Four days after the attack, the US Army issued instructions for the "internment of enemy aliens" in Panama, which included the construction of an internment camp at US expense. Japanese aliens in or near the US-controlled Canal Zone were arrested by Panamanian and US agents, and all 171 Japanese residents, including men, women, and children, were rounded up with funds provided by the US War Department and incarcerated.[39]

By the end of December, the Japanese of nearby Ecuador were also removed from their homes and put into a camp. Authorities were ordered to "monitor them closely" for any sabotage activity. Mexico followed. Under pressure from the United States, the Mexican government ordered all Japanese residents to leave Baja California for the interior on January 5, 1942. Some were given just five days' notice to leave their homes. All Japanese and other Axis nationals residing within two hundred kilometers of the Pacific Coast and one hundred kilometers of the US-Mexico border were forcibly relocated to Mexico City or Guadalajara. Over the course of the war, the United States orchestrated and financed the removal of 4,058 Germans, 2,264 Japanese, and 288 Italians from thirteen Latin American countries and imprisoned them in the United States. These numbers were sizable, especially for the German population, but the campaigns directed at European immigrants did not equal the mass expulsion that the forced removal of Japanese, particularly from Peru, eventually became.[40]

Beginning in April 1942, Peruvian and US authorities started to initiate an extensive deportation and incarceration program that sent 1,800 Japanese Peruvians to the United States. Peruvian authorities cooperated eagerly, but it was the United States that masterminded, organized, and paid for the forcible deportation of Japanese Peruvians from their homes, their transportation to the United States on American ships, and their incarceration on American soil.

One individual in particular—a US embassy official named John K. Emmerson—was responsible for shaping the US government's perspective that there was "no doubt" that the Japanese in Peru were "dangerous," "thoroughly organized," and "intensely patriotic" toward Japan. They would "follow implicitly the directions of their leaders," Emmerson claimed. Based at the US embassy in Lima, Emmerson reported to his superiors in Washington, DC, that the Japanese colony in Peru represented a clear "problem of hemisphere defense." They remained unassimilated and "emotionally tied to their homeland." Even the second-generation nisei had "little sympathy for Peru" and "little pride in Peruvian citizenship." Echoing the sentiments of Lieutenant General DeWitt in California, Emmerson concluded that despite the fact that there had been no acts of sabotage by Japanese discovered to date, future acts were likely.

Emmerson's views steadily became the foundation for US opinion and policy. By the summer of 1942, the US State Department reported to the US attorney general that it regarded the "Japanese colony in Peru . . . as a menace to the security of the hemisphere" and stated its desire to "remove these persons from Peru at the earliest opportunity." Only "mass removal of Japanese from Peru" was the "one permanent solution of the problem," US ambassador R. Henry Norweb ominously claimed.[41]

As the United States embarked on its program of forced removal, relocation, and incarceration of Japanese Americans, it urged Latin American governments to conduct surveillance of their own "alien enemy" populations and establish domestic internment programs if necessary. In April 1942, Ambassador Norweb suggested that US treatment of Japanese Americans could prove instructive to the Peruvians. "We may be able to assist the Peruvian Government by making available information and suggestions based upon our own handling of Japanese residents in the United States," he explained. The embassy could emphasize through propaganda how threatening the Japanese population was to national security and then hopefully persuade Peru to deport some two to three hundred "undesirable Japanese" within a matter of weeks.[42]

The United States pressed Latin American countries to join in hemispheric security efforts aimed at "making the Western Hemisphere as watertight as possible for economic and military defense in the face of the Axis attack on the U.S." But American officials did not trust their southern counterparts to do the job effectively on their own. The FBI reported in 1942 that the Peruvian government had "not exercised enough control over the large Japanese colonies." Officials demonstrated both condescension and racism when they questioned whether the government, made up of a "heterogeneous collection of races" who failed to cooperate with each other, was equipped to take on necessary action in the face of sudden danger.[43]

Throughout the war, the United States maintained a desire to "have as free a hand as possible" in the matter of deportation and incarceration in what US State Department officials claimed was "in the interest of hemisphere defense." The United States then used the recently established Inter-American Emergency Advisory Committee for Political Defense to push through policies that had already been decided on in Washington. In May 1943, the committee adopted a resolution that called on American republics to intern and expel dangerous Axis nationals. But the committee later concluded that Latin American nations were not capable of thoroughly completing these actions on their own. Direct US involvement in securing the hemisphere was considered crucial.[44]

Peru was only too happy to cooperate with these US-led efforts. Just two days after the attack on Pearl Harbor, President Manuel Prado offered Peru's support of the United States. The Prado government also proceeded to contribute its part to hemispheric security by targeting its Japanese population. It froze Japanese assets, curbed Japanese commerce, and restricted the freedom of movement of Japanese peoples. Japanese-language schools were closed, and Japanese organizations were disbanded. With the aid of the US government, including the FBI, the Office of Strategic Services, and the State Department, the Peruvian government initiated a joint deportation campaign. Using US intelligence,

Peruvian officials established a blacklist of commercial enterprises owned or operated by people of German, Japanese, or Italian ancestry or nationality. As the US State Department acknowledged in 1945, the primary targets of the blacklist were Japanese business owners in Lima.[45]

Over the next three years, Peru offered to send *all* of its Japanese to the United States, an estimated thirty thousand people. As early as February 11, 1942, Peruvian officials asked the US embassy if it would allow Peru to deport Japanese, including women and children, who were not suspected of any "subversive activities." Five months later, US ambassador Henry Norweb reported that Peru's president Manuel Prado was "very much interested in . . . getting rid of the Japanese in Peru" in the hopes of settling the problem "permanently." Peru, Norweb added, "would like to be sure that these Japanese would not be returned to Peru later on." Ultimately, while officials like Ambassador Norweb believed this solution to be "ideal," the United States ultimately declined Peru's offer—but only because of a lack of available shipping.[46]

On December 24, 1941, a blacklist of "dangerous Axis nationals" provided by the US State Department was published in major Peruvian newspapers. Like the initial roundups of issei in the United States, the individuals targeted included community leaders, such as teachers, journalists, and officers in Japanese immigrant organizations. Beginning in late 1942 and into 1943, Japanese people began to be randomly arrested; there was no apparent "list" anymore. Most Japanese businesses were ordered to close, and many of these businesses were sold without compensation. The Peruvian government prohibited Japanese from freely traveling outside their city or town of residence. Telephones and shortwave radios were prohibited, and Japanese residents were barred from obtaining licenses to hunt, fish, or possess firearms. Japanese Peruvians lived in a constant state of fear and anxiety. As the weeks passed, more and more Japanese people were arrested, often randomly. Indeed, when the first vessel sailed out of Callao on April 5, 1942, less than 5 percent of the Japanese passengers appeared on the official Proclaimed Lists.[47]

Art Shibayama's grandparents were among the first to be seized. Forced from their home and store in Callao, they were transported to the United States and imprisoned in a detention camp for "enemy aliens" in Seagoville, Texas. They were also among the first to be used in the US-Japan civilian exchanges and were sent to Japan. Art never saw them again. Art's father, Yuzo, continued working at his successful textile import and dress shirt business. But as Art remembered, "every time a US transport came into the port of Callao, word got around and . . . [the] father or head of the family went into hiding, including my father." Yuzo managed to escape detection for some time, but after the Peruvian police arrested his wife and eleven-year-old daughter to lure him out of hiding, he turned himself in. The family was given a week to get ready and then they were deported on board the US Army transport *Cuba*. They and the other Japanese prisoners were marched over the gangway surrounded by US soldiers carrying rifles with fixed bayonets.

From April 1942 to October 1944, four ships operated by the US government transported Japanese Peruvians and other Japanese Latin Americans to the United States. Just as with Japanese Americans, Latin American deportees had not been charged with any crimes of espionage, sabotage, or subversive activity, nor had they been given hearings of any kind after their arrest.[48]

Conditions on the transport ships were dismal and crowded. Some families, like the Shibayamas, were separated from each other during the entire three-week voyage. Women and children were put in a small cabin on deck, and adolescent boys and adult men were put down below. The boys and men were allowed to go on deck only twice a day for ten minutes, and during that time, the women and children were forced to stay inside the cabin. Art did not see his mother and sisters for the entire twenty-one-day journey to New Orleans. Moreover, most of the deportees had little idea of where they were going or what their futures held. The deportees were heavily guarded by US military personnel armed with machine guns and rifles who spoke neither Spanish nor Japanese. The ship was also guarded by military destroyers and submarines as it traveled north.

MOST OF WHAT Betty Morita remembered of the Pinedale detention center in Fresno was that it was excruciatingly hot. The sun baked the bare concrete floor. During mealtimes, the inmates were forced to stand in line in the hot sun for hours. With no shade for protection, people would regularly faint from the heat. She also remembered the complete lack of privacy. The communal bathrooms had no toilet or shower stalls or doors, only an open space where everyone was forced to perform their private business in public.

The Moritas' experience was similar to that of most other Japanese Americans. "Evacuees" were sent to sixteen "assembly centers" established by the newly created Wartime Civil Control Administration in California, Oregon, Washington, and Arizona. These new "homes" were often hastily erected on state fairgrounds or horse racetracks, where the inmates were kept in former animal stalls and barracks. Barbed-wire fences and guard towers surrounded the facilities. Entire families were crowded into poorly constructed rooms no bigger than twenty by twenty feet. Mattresses were made out of bags and straw, the food was of poor quality and lacked variety, and the medical facilities and care were inadequate. The Moritas stayed at Pinedale for three months before they boarded a boxcar train that took them to the Tule Lake camp in Southern California. They joined other Japanese Americans who were being transferred to the ten newly constructed War Relocation Authority camps: Amache in Granada, Colorado; Gila River and Poston, Arizona; Heart Mountain, Wyoming; Jerome and Rohrer, Arkansas; Manzanar and Tule Lake, California; Minidoka, Idaho; and Topaz, Utah.

In the midst of the government's forced relocation and incarceration, a young man named Fred Korematsu refused to leave his home in San Leandro, California. When he was discovered in May 1942, he was arrested and sent to prison. Ernest Besig of the American Civil Liberties Union (ACLU) approached Korematsu to test the constitutionality of Executive Order 9066, and the case went to court. As Korematsu later explained, "I felt that . . . you know, that, 'Hey, this is wrong,' and that I was an American . . . I was determined that my rights were violated, and making me an 'enemy alien' was wrong." A federal district court convicted Korematsu of defying military orders in September 1942, and he was forced to move to the Topaz internment camp in Utah. From within the camp, Korematsu appealed the decision and the case went to the US

Supreme Court. In December 1944, the court issued its ruling: three justices found that incarceration had clearly violated Fred Korematsu's constitutional rights and that racial discrimination was a central motivating factor in the overall treatment of Japanese Americans. They were in the dissent. A majority of justices upheld the constitutionality of the order and of incarceration. Justice Hugo Black, a former member of the KKK in Alabama, delivered the court's opinion. The high court accepted the army's position that removal and incarceration of Japanese Americans was a "military necessity" and in essence justified bowing to military demands during a time of war.[49]

While the *Korematsu* case was weaving its way through the courts, forced removal and incarceration remained US policy. At Tule Lake, Betty's grandfather worked as a janitor, her sister was a waitress, and Betty was attending school when conflict rocked the camp. In early 1943, the US government required all Japanese Americans age seventeen and older to take a loyalty questionnaire. It asked a range of questions, but two in particular caused a great deal of confusion and controversy. Question 27 asked all draft-age males: "Are you willing to serve in the armed forces of the United States on combat duty, wherever ordered?" Question 28 asked all others if they would be willing to "swear unqualified allegiance to the United States of America . . . and foreswear any form of allegiance or obedience to the Japanese emperor, or any other foreign government, power or organization?" For some inmates, especially the US-born nisei, answering *yes* to both questions was easy even if they were uneasy with the questions themselves.

Others were suspicious of the US government's motives and resented the entire premise of the loyalty program. For the first-generation issei, the choice was even harder. Question 28 asked them to renounce their Japanese nationality even though they were barred by law from becoming US citizens. Many believed that if they answered *yes* to this question, they would become stateless. However, if they answered *no*, they might be forcibly separated from their families or targeted for further government reprisal. After much discussion, anxiety, and soul searching in the camps, most inmates answered *yes* to the loyalty questions, and over 1,200 men volunteered for the US Army. The US government began to issue draft notices to Japanese Americans in the camps in January 1944. The 10 to 15 percent who answered *no* to the two questions were officially classified as "disloyal" and were transferred to the newly segregated camp at Tule Lake. As the camp received these new inmates, the Moritas were moved from Tule Lake to Minidoka in Idaho in the summer of 1943. While Betty's brother Paul was drafted into the US armed forces, she started fifth grade in camp, where she and her classmates were required to say the Pledge of Allegiance every day. They would remain there until October 1945.[50]

AFTER THREE WEEKS on a US Army transport ship, the Shibayamas arrived in New Orleans in the spring of 1944. They were taken to the INS facility, where they were forced to remove all of their clothing and stand naked in groups while they were sprayed with insecticide. They were also officially processed by US immigration authorities. In what one INS camp commander later acknowledged as legal "skullduggery" made possible only during wartime, the INS classified the new arrivals as "undocumented immigrants" or "illegal aliens" who were entering the country without valid visas and passports.[51]

Japanese Latin Americans were then sent by train to one of six "enemy alien" camps run by the INS. The largest were in Texas at Kenedy, Seagoville, and Crystal City. The others were at Kooskia, Idaho; Missoula, Montana; and Santa Fe, New Mexico. Art Shibayama's family was sent to Crystal City, the largest detention camp located about 120 miles southwest of San Antonio. Known as the family camp, it eventually held 962 families, most of whom were Japanese, who lived in shared temporary housing units with one, two, or three other families. In total, there were three thousand to four thousand people in the camp.

As "interned foreign nationals," internees could claim some protections and minimal standards in treatment and conditions in the camps under the Geneva Convention. Each housing unit had cooking facilities, cold running water, and basic furniture and furnishings. There were

Japanese Latin Americans arriving at Camp Kenedy, Texas, under armed guard, August 1943. National Archives.

stores, schools, a hospital, and churches. A 1943 US government film about the Crystal City camp profiled healthy, active detainees living peaceably in Texas where "the sun shines practically every day of the year with a cool breeze from the Gulf in the evening." With roomy accommodations, bountiful gardens, and healthy and plentiful food, the film's narrator explained, the wartime detainees "lived, worked, and played under traditional American standards of decent and humane treatment." The camera caught children playing in the camp swimming pool, smiling delivery men bringing fresh milk, and an armed guard waving from atop the guardhouse.[52]

Despite these amenities and the US government's media portrayal of Crystal City, there was no mistaking the purpose of the camp. It was surrounded by a ten-foot-tall fence, floodlights, and guard towers that guaranteed that escape was impossible. "We were like bird[s] in a cage," recalled Seiichi Higashide, a Japanese Peruvian imprisoned at Crystal City. The camp was like a "city behind barbed wire."[53] Plus, there was constant frustration, fear, and anxiety about what the future held outside of the camps. Families remained separated across seas and borders, and many did not know whether they would be forced to "return" to Japan, a country that many had never been to or had not seen for years, or whether they would be allowed to return to Peru.

AFTER THE END of the war in 1945, families started leaving the Minidoka camp in droves. The US Supreme Court had ruled that the government had no authority to incarcerate loyal citizens, and the blanket exclusion orders barring Japanese Americans from the West Coast were lifted. As the last camp closed in March 1946, the War Relocation Authority encouraged people to move out of the camps as soon as possible and to seek opportunities in the Midwest and on the East Coast, rather than on the West Coast where officials reported anti-Japanese violence, discrimination, and intimidation.[54] Betty Morita, her parents, and her baby sister remained in camp, unsure of whether to return to Hood River or move somewhere else. The Moritas eventually moved to Chicago, where the two older daughters had already resettled.

In Crystal City, Art Shibayama's family and other Japanese Peruvians remained unsure about their futures long after the war ended. Days and months passed without knowing if they would be allowed to return to Peru, or if they would be forced to go to war-ravaged Japan. Most, like the Shibayamas, wanted to go back to Peru. But the Peruvian government refused to allow any Japanese Peruvians to return. Staying in the United States was not an option either. Three weeks before sending warplanes to bomb Hiroshima and Nagasaki, US president Harry S. Truman had issued an executive order authorizing the removal of enemy aliens who were "within the territory of the United States without admission under the immigration laws" from the *entire* Western Hemisphere. Because Japanese Latin Americans had not been formally admitted into the country as legal immigrants, this order applied to them. The US government, which had masterminded their arrest, forced deportation, and incarceration in the United States, had classified them as illegal aliens. Moreover, delegates who gathered at a 1945 Conference on the Problems of War and Peace in Mexico City agreed that any person whose deportation was considered necessary for reasons of security of the continent should be prevented from "further residing in this hemisphere."[55]

The repatriation of Japanese Peruvians began. Between November 1945 and June 1946, more than nine hundred Japanese Peruvians were sent to Japan. Some of these repatriates went voluntarily. Others returned under duress. With their property confiscated or lost in Peru and with both the Peruvian and US governments refusing to allow Japanese Peruvians to either return to Peru or remain in the United States, most Japanese Peruvians felt that they had no other choice. In Crystal City, the Shibayamas held out hope that they might be allowed to go back to Peru. But on February 20, 1947, the entire family, including Art's parents and his seven siblings, were ordered deported from the United States.[56] Unwilling to go to Japan, the Shibayamas and 364 other Japanese Latin American deportees decided to organize an effort to remain in the United States.

A family of Japanese Peruvians, all wearing identification tags, being cleared by officials before being repatriated to Japan, 1943 or 1944. National Archives.

Attorneys Wayne M. Collins and A. L. Wirin of the California office of the ACLU took up their cases and served as tireless advocates for the deportees. Collins tried to put an end to US deportations of Japanese Peruvians; counseled and assured his clients, including the Shibayama family; and badgered officials in both the United States and Peru for their actions during and after the war. The deportees were "hapless victims of international intrigue, connivance and malice," Collins argued in a 1947 letter to US secretary of state George C. Marshall. They were "guiltless of any wrongdoing," had been "kidnapped" and "abducted," and now faced "pointless and patently absurd" classifications as being unlawfully in the United States. To former secretary of the interior Harold L. Ickes, Collins was even more forthright. "Not one of these persons at anytime whatever was a source of danger to Western Hemisphere security."[57]

In 1946, Collins filed writs of habeas corpus on behalf of the deportees in the federal district court of San Francisco. In his application to the government on behalf of the Shibayamas, Collins asserted that family members were "persons of good moral character . . . and that their deportation would result in serious economic detriment" to the children, including the youngest, George, who had been born in the United States and was a US citizen. As a result of these actions, the Shibayamas were allowed to stay in the United States on a "parole" basis and were sent to work as undocumented immigrants sponsored by Seabrook Farms in New Jersey. In 1954, half of the "illegal entrants" from Latin America were formally given entry visas through an amendment in the Refugee Act of 1953, the first step toward permanent residency in the United States.[58]

After a few years working twelve-hour shifts at Seabrook, the Shibayamas moved to Chicago to rebuild their lives. Classified as illegal aliens, they continued to fight the government's deportation orders and reported to the immigration service every year as required. Then in 1952, Art was drafted into the US Army. "I couldn't believe it because here I am [an] illegal alien," he recalled. But since he was fighting deportation, he thought he'd better comply with the orders. He was stationed in Germany during the war and served honorably, all the while fighting for the right

Art and Betty Shibayama, Fort Sheridan, Illinois, April 1952. Courtesy of the B. Shibayama Family Collection, Densho Digital Repository.

to remain in the United States legally and become a US citizen, a process that would take almost two decades. Around the same time, Art met a young Japanese American woman who had herself recently moved to Chicago after being incarcerated during the war. They fell in love and got engaged before Art was sent overseas. Her name was Betty Morita.

THE SHIBAYAMAS WOULD spend the next decades rebuilding their lives. In their later years, they would become fierce advocates in the Japanese American redress movement, which established a government commission to investigate the government's claim that incarceration had been a "military necessity." The commission issued a scathing rebuke of the government's actions and condemned the "grave injustice" done to Japanese Americans. Along with other Japanese Americans, Betty eventually received an official apology from the US government and a reparation payment. Art's application, however, was denied, because the government had designated him an illegal alien at the time of incarceration. Art continued to fight for a full apology and fair restitution on behalf of all Japanese Latin Americans. But it never came. When he died in 2018, his lifelong quest for equal justice remained unfulfilled.[59]

Meanwhile, the xenophobic immigration laws that had been put into place before the war—Asian exclusion laws, national origins quotas, and a number of others barring immigrants ranging from anarchists to illiterates—kept the United States closed to most immigration. By the

1960s, a new generation of politicians found the explicitly discriminatory policies to be out of step with the growing civil rights movement and hypocritical to America's support for freedom, equality, and democratic values during the Cold War. A campaign to reform the nation's immigration laws began in the 1960s, and while it brought much needed change, xenophobia adapted, flourishing even in the midst of civil rights.

• SEVEN •

XENOPHOBIA AND CIVIL RIGHTS

President Lyndon Baines Johnson was in a good mood. It was a beautiful October day in 1965 and he was on Liberty Island in New York. He stood, poised to give his speech, with the Manhattan skyline behind him and the Statue of Liberty to his left. Joining him were several hundred invited guests, including the first lady, Lady Bird Johnson; their daughter Luci Baines Johnson; Vice President Hubert Humphrey and his wife, Muriel; Senators Robert Kennedy and Ted Kennedy; and several governors and members of Congress. The occasion was a major bill-signing ceremony. After months of backroom negotiations, the president was going to sign a historic immigration bill.

Johnson had been looking forward to celebrating the passage of this bill for several weeks. He had originally wanted the event to take place on Ellis Island, but the former immigration station was in such poor condition that the ceremony was moved to Liberty Island. Still, the president got his other wishes. He wanted veteran lawmaker and bill co-sponsor Representative Emanuel Celler, Democrat from New York, at the ceremony, and he wanted to make sure that pictures of the event made it into the newspaper. Celler and his wife, Stella, had positions of honor right behind Lady Bird Johnson and Muriel Humphrey. Two other notable lawmakers flanked the president's desk. To the president's left was Senator Ted Kennedy of Massachusetts, who had served as acting chair of the

Senate Immigration Subcommittee. Opposite Kennedy was Congressman Michael A. Feighan of Ohio, chair of the immigration committee
in the House.

The placement of the three lawmakers was deliberate. Celler, chairman of the House Judiciary Committee, was a longtime advocate of immigration reform. He had first entered Congress as a thirty-four-year-old
Democrat in 1923 and had represented the Italians, Jews, and African
Americans from his Brooklyn district for over forty years. He was himself
a grandson of Jewish immigrants from Germany, and as a freshman congressman, he had been an outspoken critic of the national origins quota
system established in the 1920s. In one of his first speeches in Congress,
he had called the 1924 Immigration Act "cruel and heartless." In 1965
on Liberty Island, his place directly behind Johnson honored his tireless
work on immigration over the decades.[1]

Ted Kennedy, the young senator from Massachusetts and brother to
the slain president, was also given a place of honor. He had deftly moved
the immigration bill through the Senate, even garnering praise from
Southern Democrats who opposed the bill. For both Celler and Kennedy, the immigration law was a landmark piece of civil rights legislation.
As Kennedy would explain the next year, the act "marked a victory for
the forces of common sense and decency, and for the cumulative efforts
over many years of dedicated individuals in government and throughout
American citizenry." Along with other laws aiming to ensure civil rights,
end poverty, and expand access to education and health services, the law,
Kennedy claimed, reaffirmed "our nation's continuing pursuit of justice,
equality, and freedom."[2]

Feighan, a lawyer from Cleveland with over twenty years in Congress, had no lofty words of support for the law. In fact, he was a hard-
liner on immigration and had never shown much interest in immigration
reform. He was certainly aware of the obstacles that current policies imposed on his constituents from the twentieth district in Ohio, many of
whom were southern and eastern European immigrants and their families. He regularly received requests for help granting or extending visas
or staying deportation orders, and the many letters of gratitude sent to

the congressman reveal that he assisted a great many of them. But he was regularly at odds with the more progressive members of the Democratic Party over immigration. Described by the *New York Times* as an ally of "right wing cranks" and "an intellectual bedfellow with the conservative and patriotic groups who . . . most stoutly defended the status quo in immigration matters," Feighan strongly supported the national origins quota system, counted Emanuel Celler as a longtime political nemesis, and had been a thorn in Johnson's side during the whole process leading up to the bill signing.[3] But in the end, all parties had compromised, and the three lawmakers took up their appropriate places around the president. Feighan was as far away from Celler and Kennedy as possible.

The 1965 Immigration and Nationality Act abolished the discriminatory national origins quotas that had been in place since 1924. It explicitly prohibited discrimination on the basis of race, sex, nationality,

President Lyndon B. Johnson signs the Immigration Act on Liberty Island in New York City on October 3, 1965. Representative Michael Feighan (white hair and glasses) is in the foreground in the far left of the photograph; Representative Emanuel Celler (with glasses) and his wife, Stella, are just over the president's right shoulder. Senators Edward M. and Robert F. Kennedy stand behind the president on the far right. LBJ Library photo by Yoichi Okamoto.

place of birth, or place of residence in the US government's decisions to issue immigrant visas. Instead of setting limits on immigration based on national origins quotas and on an annual cap of 155,000 total immigrants per year, it set limits on immigration through a preference system that granted visas based on family reunification and professional skills, an annual per-country cap of 20,000, and an annual cap of 170,000 entries from the Eastern Hemisphere (defined as Europe, Asia, and Africa) and 120,000 from the Western Hemisphere, defined as the Americas. (In 1978, the hemispheric caps were abandoned and replaced with a global cap of 290,000.) Spouses, minor children, and parents of American citizens were exempt from these numerical ceilings.[4]

At the bill signing, Johnson talked of civil rights and equality. The historic law, Johnson explained, abolished the "un-American" national origins system, repaired "a very deep and painful flaw in the fabric of American justice," and corrected "a cruel and enduring wrong in the conduct of the American Nation." The old system based on "prejudice and privilege" had cast a shadow upon the "gate to the American Nation." Now, alongside the Statue of Liberty, Johnson declared, "America was recommitting herself to honoring its immigrant heritage" and how "our beautiful America was built by a nation of strangers."[5]

The president's pronouncement was fitting. The Immigration Act was a major immigration and civil rights law. It ended the policy of admitting immigrants according to racist ideas of "inferior" and "superior" immigrants and unequal quotas that reinforced that racism. And it established the principle of equality in immigration law. A few weeks after the act's passage, a coalition of dozens of humanitarian, religious, and ethnic organizations praised Congress for passing such important legislation. The United States had finally established an "immigration policy consistent with our national philosophy that all men are entitled to equal opportunity regardless of race or place of both," it grandly declared. Scholars praised the legislation as bringing the "civil rights revolution" to immigration law and for being a symbol of the "new global egalitarianism." It remains the foundation of US immigration policy today and represents the last time Congress passed comprehensive immigration reform on such a large scale. It also ushered in a new era of mass migration, predominantly from Latin America and Asia, that transformed the United States.[6]

But xenophobia did not end with the 1965 Immigration Act. Johnson's moving declaration of an end to discrimination only masked the perseverance of xenophobia and the inauguration of *color-blind xenophobia*, opposition to immigration that is purportedly based on neutral and ostensibly fair factors such as economics, national security, and legal status (rather than race, religion, or national origin) but is still shaped and motivated by racial anxieties and bias.

New restrictions in the 1965 Immigration Act, for example, included the first-ever numerical cap on immigration from the Western Hemisphere and reflected Congress's clear intent to restrict immigration from Latin America, especially Mexico. These restrictions, combined with other measures that ended certain types of Mexican migration or required increased documentation, singled out Mexican immigrants for restriction and scrutiny. What followed was record numbers of immigrants entering the country without authorization, second-class status for undocumented immigrants, and a new regime of immigration enforcement focused on arrests, detention, and deportation. In addition, the law affirmed the decades-old exclusion of gay and lesbian immigrants as "aliens afflicted with . . . sexual deviation" and prohibited them from receiving visas. This ban targeting homosexual immigrants would not be lifted until 1990.[7]

How lawmakers designed and included provisions that discriminated against certain immigrants in a law that was intended to eliminate discrimination reveals much about how durable xenophobia was even in the midst of the civil rights movement, and how it became a dominant and growing aspect of immigration policy in post–civil rights America.

THE SYSTEM THAT was in place before Johnson signed the 1965 bill was highly discriminatory. A century of immigration law had already excluded several categories of people—criminals, prostitutes, paupers, those likely to become public charges, anarchists, illiterates, and aliens convicted of a crime involving "moral turpitude." Immigration decreased after the 1924 Immigration Act, but it did not end altogether. Foreign policy, humanitarian crises, and domestic needs pushed lawmakers to pass immigration legislation on an ad hoc basis. The 1943 Magnuson Act, for example, repealed the Chinese exclusion laws and allowed Chinese immigrants to become naturalized citizens as a symbol of support and solidarity to China, an American ally during World War II. Similarly, legislators also lifted the bans on immigration from India and the Philippines and allowed nationals from those countries to become naturalized citizens. Laws such as the War Brides Acts of 1945 and 1947 facilitated the admission of wives, fiancées, and families of returning US soldiers. The Displaced Persons Act of 1948 authorized the admission of two hundred thousand displaced Europeans. It eventually allowed in over eighty thousand Jewish displaced people with the aid of Jewish agencies. Five thousand Chinese, mostly students who were already in the United States, were allowed to remain in the country after the Communist Revolution in China. As a concession to US employers, the United States and Mexico negotiated a 1942 agreement to bring in temporary workers, known as *braceros*, to address the wartime labor shortage. Lasting until 1964, the program eventually brought 4.6 million Mexican workers to the United States.[8]

These new policies were important and helped pave the way for more comprehensive reform in 1965. Nevertheless, support for the national origins quotas remained popular, and when Congress addressed immigration in 1952 with the McCarran-Walter Act, or the Immigration and Nationality Act of 1952, the discriminatory system remained in place. Eighty percent of visas were still reserved for western and northern Europeans. In addition, more screening measures to bar suspected communists were put in place, as were harsher provisions for deportation. The ban on Asian naturalization was lifted, but Asian immigration remained very low, with most countries allotted minimal quotas of only one hundred people per year. There was also a worldwide quota of two thousand Asian immigrants per year, and Asians remained the only group regulated by race rather than nationality or place of birth. This meant that the entry of a Canadian of Chinese descent, for example, was counted against China's national quota, rather than Canada's. Immigration enforcement targeting undocumented Mexican immigrants also increased during this period. In 1954, the US Border Patrol reported that it had deported over one million Mexican immigrants during the campaign known as Operation Wetback. By the 1960s, immigration to the United States had reached a historic low. According to the 1970 US Census, less than 5 percent of the US population was foreign-born, down from nearly 15 percent in 1910.[9]

But the country was also being transformed by the civil rights movement, immigrant activism, and new political leaders committed to equality and immigration reform. Momentum came from the White House under President John F. Kennedy. Bringing about fair and just immigration laws had long been an interest of the Kennedy family. In 1896, John F. Fitzgerald, the son of Irish immigrants, became outraged during his first term in the House of Representatives when Republican senator Henry Cabot Lodge, also from Massachusetts, introduced a bill that would have barred any illiterate immigrant from entering the country. Fitzgerald lashed out against prejudice in a speech on the House floor. More than half a century later in the House of Representatives, his grandson Jack took a stand against the 1952 Immigration and Nationality Act, which sought to maintain the national origins quotas.

Kennedy was in the minority. Lawmakers like bill co-sponsor Senator Patrick McCarran, a Democrat from Nevada, were driven by the xenophobic belief that a discriminatory immigration system was needed to maintain the mostly northern and western European–descended ethnic and racial makeup of the United States. "The cold, hard truth is that in the United States today there are hard-core, indigestible blocks who have not become integrated into the American way of life," he explained. "Today, as never before, untold millions are storming our gates for admission; and those gates are cracking under the stream." If America, "this last hope of Western civilization" and an "oasis of the world," were to open up its gates, McCarran continued, it would be "overrun, perverted, contaminated, or destroyed." He predicted that any change in the quota system would be a tragedy not only for the United States but also for humanity in general.[10]

Like Kennedy, President Truman also opposed the McCarran-Walter Act and vetoed the bill. The quota system had always been "based upon assumptions at variance with our American ideals," the president declared in his veto message. Its greatest vice was that it "discriminates, deliberately and intentionally, against many of the peoples of the world." It was "false and unworthy" when it was first signed into law in 1924. "It is even worse now," he proclaimed. Congress overrode the president's veto, and the Immigration and Nationality Act became law on June 27, 1952. Truman responded to the veto override by establishing a presidential Commission on Immigration and Naturalization, which bluntly laid out how US immigration policy discriminated against "the non-white people of the world," who constituted between two-thirds and three-fourths of the world's population. Inside Congress, Northern liberals like Emanuel Celler, New Jersey Democrat Peter Rodino, and New York Republican Jacob Javits were joined by Senators Hubert Humphrey of Minnesota, Philip A. Hart of Michigan, Herbert Lehman of New York, and Jack Kennedy, newly elected to the Senate in 1953, to lobby for change. Bipartisan support for immigration reform slowly grew. When Dwight Eisenhower campaigned for the presidency, he distanced himself from the McCarran-Walter Act, stating that it hurt US foreign policy goals. As president, he sent messages to Congress recommending immigration reform.[11]

In 1958, Kennedy outlined a radical new vision for US immigration policy in his book *A Nation of Immigrants*, an unabashed celebration of America's immigrant heritage and a call for immigration reform. "Immigration policy should be generous; it should be fair; it should be flexible," he wrote. He drew attention to the ways in which the United States' discriminatory immigration policy was a foreign relations liability in the ongoing propaganda war with the Soviet Union. With a new policy of nondiscrimination, he explained, "we can turn to the world, and to our own past, with clean hands and a clear conscience."[12] Such sentiments were beginning to resonate with a broader group of lawmakers and their constituents.

In 1960, both the Democratic and Republican platforms attacked "obsolete immigration laws" and the discriminatory national origins system. Some of the most vocal supporters of immigration reform came from immigrant and ethnic advocacy groups. Chief among them were Italian Americans, who at the time comprised the largest population of foreign-born Americans. A prominent group of civic, political, and religious leaders formed the American Committee on Italian Migration (ACIM) and organized Italian Americans across the country to lobby for immigration reform. Focusing on how current immigration laws impacted Italian Americans, leaders pointed out how the national origins quotas unjustly separated European American families and kept worthy and productive future Americans from emigrating. Testifying before the senate in 1965, for example, Joseph Errigo, the national chairman of the Sons of Italy Committee on Immigration, pointed out that Italy had 249,583 people waiting for admission into the United States. He urged Congress to "abolish a system which is gradually becoming unpopular and inoperative."[13]

In addition to criticizing the current system for its unfair treatment of Italians, the ACIM also used both the mantle of civil rights and Cold War US foreign policy objectives to lambast the current system of immigration regulation. ACIM poster boards proclaimed that "A Discriminatory Immigration Law is a Contradiction of the Concept that All Men are Created Equal" and "Consistency in Foreign Relations Demands a Non-Discriminatory US Immigration Law." The national origins quota system, the organization argued, was "un-American," was "hate-filled," and constrained American citizens of southern European ancestry as "second-class" citizens. Tying migration to Cold War anxieties, the ACIM also used the specter of communism to warn that only migration would "remove the danger inherent in masses of restless, hungry and desperate human beings" from succumbing to communism in Europe. Italians and others in southern and eastern Europe "must migrate or burst through the seam of Democracy's boundaries to flood all free Europe with a ravaging tide of Communism," the organization warned.[14]

As president, Kennedy introduced his proposal to revise and modernize the country's immigration laws in July 1963. In a special message to Congress on that day, he called immigration reform, especially the abolition of the national origins system, "urgent and fundamental." His

The American Committee on Italian Migration advocated for immigration reform by calling for nondiscriminatory policies, c. 1963. American Committee on Italian Migration Records, IHRC159, Immigration History Research Center Archives, University of Minnesota.

bill, he claimed, was meant to "serve the national interest and reflect in every detail the principals of equality and human dignity to which our nation subscribes." It proposed to gradually eliminate the allocation of visas based on the national origin quotas. Instead, family reunification and skill and ability would take precedence. Where immigrants came from would no longer be relevant; no one country could receive more than 10 percent of the available slots annually. There would be no limitations on Western Hemisphere immigration, and discrimination against Asian immigration would be abolished. However, the exclusion of gay and lesbian immigrants remained.[15]

The legislation went nowhere. Michael Feighan, the Democratic representative from Cleveland who had just been elected chairman of the House Subcommittee on Immigration and Nationality, refused to schedule any hearings of the legislation. The effort died with the president four months later.[16]

IMMIGRATION REFORM HAD not been one of Lyndon Johnson's primary legislative issues before becoming president. But it had been one of Kennedy's clear domestic priorities, and in pushing for immigration reform,

Johnson exhibited his commitment to follow through on the previous president's agenda. In his first State of the Union address in 1964, President Johnson passionately echoed Kennedy's support for immigration reform and called for an end to the national origins quota system. The system was "incompatible with our basic American tradition," the president declared. He envisioned a world "in which all men, goods, and ideas can freely move across every border and every boundary." For the United States, a "nation that was built by the immigrants of all lands," the essential question was not, "In what country were you born?" but rather, "What can you do for our country?" Attorney general Robert F. Kennedy reintroduced his brother's immigration bill on the one-year anniversary of its first introduction by President Kennedy.[17]

Johnson then got down to the business of politicking. He called members of both the Senate and House immigration subcommittees to the White House. With the television cameras recording, he informed them that a new immigration law was a key priority for his administration and asked if he could count on them for their support. On January 13, 1965, he introduced his immigration bill, one that was largely modeled after President Kennedy's 1963 proposal to end the national origins quotas and give preference to skilled professionals and family unification, to Congress.[18]

The administration's position was clear. Ending discrimination in American immigration law was not only a civil rights issue. It also helped advance US international relations as well. At a time when the United States emphasized its virtues of freedom and democracy over the totalitarianism of communism, the unequal treatment of immigrants based on race exposed the hypocrisy in American immigration regulation. Both the president and the state department warned that the national origins system seriously threatened the United States' strong relationship with many European allies and that the severe restrictions on immigrants from Asia was, according to secretary of state Dean Rusk, "indefensible from a foreign policy point of view."[19]

Public opinion was beginning to shift as well. During the 1964 presidential election, Republican Barry Goldwater tried to characterize Johnson's immigration reform plan as one that would "open the floodgates for any and all who would wish to come and find work in this country." But Goldwater ended up alienating Italian, Greek, Polish, and Hungarian American voters who supported immigration reform.[20] Johnson's landslide victory and Democratic control of Congress in 1964 gave him the necessary mandate to enact his Great Society reforms.

A growing rejection of racism worldwide and the civil rights movement at home also continued to erode racism's legitimacy and shift public opinion toward progress and equality. Global anti-racism and support for human rights had been growing since the end of World War II and increased international pressure on the United States to make a clear stand against racism, if only to support its foreign policy objectives.[21]

In the United States, the March on Washington brought a quarter million people from across the United States to demand passage of civil rights legislation. Over the next two years, the movement succeeded in garnering more and more public support, as well as growing backlash and devastating losses. Martin Luther King Jr. inspired a generation with his "I Have a Dream" speech at the march in August, but the next month, four young African American girls were killed when the 16th Street Baptist Church was bombed in Birmingham. In 1964, the Civil Rights Act outlawed discrimination on the basis of race, color, religion, sex, or national origin, and volunteers registered black voters in Mississippi during the Freedom Summer. But volunteers Michael Schwerner, James Chaney, and Andrew Goodman were murdered in Mississippi. Martin Luther King Jr. was awarded the Nobel Peace Prize in October 1964, but Malcolm X was assassinated four months later. Activists began a voting rights movement by marching from Selma to Montgomery in March 1965 but faced tear gas and brutal beatings by state and local police. By the time the Voting Rights Act became law on August 6, 1965, and prohibited discrimination in voter registration, the United States' blatantly discriminatory national origins quota system stood out as unacceptable and indefensible. Many Americans supported the position that all citizens should be accorded equal rights regardless of race, ethnicity, or ancestry. But not all Americans agreed, and the backlash against civil rights and immigration reform continued to grow.

As IMMIGRATION HEARINGS began in Congress, support for ending discrimination in US immigration laws was widespread in both houses. Lawmaker after lawmaker rose to denounce the national origins quotas as discriminatory and racist. Congressman Dominick V. Daniels of New Jersey called them "one of the last vestiges of racial and religious hatred." By acting on the premise that "some races and some ethnic groups make better Americans than others," he argued, current immigration policy "flew in the face of our national ideals." Congressman Jeffery Cohelan of California explained that the current system was not only racist, it was also detrimental to the United States. It had "arbitrarily denied us people with skills and talents that would benefit our way of life and our well-being." It was cruel in separating US citizens from their families. And it had weakened the United States both at home and in the eyes of the world. "How can the countries of the world believe that we are sincere in our concern for the elimination of prejudice and discrimination in the United States if we discriminate among them because of race or national origin?" he asked. Others made a direct connection between immigration reform and civil rights legislation. The United States needed an immigration policy that would reflect "America's ideal of equality of all men without regard to race, color, creed, or national origin," explained Representative Henry Helstoski of New Jersey. Congressman Daniels, his fellow lawmaker from New Jersey, put it more succinctly: "racism simply has no place in America in this day and age."[22]

Despite such broad and consistent support for immigration reform, many still opposed reform, testifying to the need for the race-based restrictions. In August 1964, Congressman Feighan introduced his own immigration bill that kept both the national origins quotas and the current ceiling on immigration but also reunited families, filled the country's need for certain jobs, and provided an asylum for a "fair share" of refugees fleeing communist countries. The bill received the support of many conservative and self-proclaimed patriotic organizations that wanted to maintain both the quotas and the current racial makeup of the United States dominated by northern and western European Americans. Most prominent among these was John B. Trevor Jr., chairman of the

Immigration Committee of the American Coalition of Patriotic Societies (ACPS), whose father had been instrumental in the passage of the 1924 Immigration Act. The ACPS had already made its anti-immigration position clear when President Kennedy had first proposed his immigration reform bill. In its June 1963 "Report to America," the ACPS asked readers, "Why Mutilate Our Immigration Policy?" It warned of immigrants coming in from "over-populated foreign countries," a veiled reference to countries in Africa, Asia, and Latin America, and claimed that it was "incomprehensible that any true American could favor an increase in the annual volume of immigrants arriving in the United States."[23]

During the May 1965 congressional hearings, Congressman Feighan welcomed ACPS president Trevor to Congress and allowed him to speak for a lengthy amount of time. Trevor claimed to represent three million members and called the national origins quota system "eminently fair" and good for the country. The quotas made sure that immigration into the United States conformed to the "composition to our own people," he explained. It also broke up ethnic enclaves and ensured the protection of "our standard of living" and "our ideals of government." He also criticized the Johnson proposal, specifically pointing out the alarming specter of increased immigration from the Western Hemisphere. His congressional appearance was followed by other witnesses testifying on behalf of other patriotic and conservative organizations, including the National Americanization Committee of the American Legion.[24]

In addition to this vocal opposition to immigration reform, there were also important limits to what Congress was willing to do. First, ending discrimination in immigration policy did not mean ending restrictions on immigration altogether. As the judiciary committee in the House of Representatives explained, the basic objective of the bill was to change the ways in which applicants for admission were chosen in a fair and equitable way "without proposing any substantial change in the number of authorized immigration." Support for immigration reform also did not mean that Congress supported less rigorous immigration enforcement. Liberal members, including Emanuel Celler, were some of the most vocal advocates of expanding the power and reach of the Border Patrol in the

1950s. One year prior to the immigration hearings, the United States had also ended the bracero agreement with Mexico, which was long criticized for subjecting Mexican workers to systematic exploitation by unscrupulous employers and corrupt Mexican officials. The end of the bracero program was couched in humanitarian language, but it also obscured lawmakers' intent to cut Mexican immigration and provide employment for white US workers.[25]

Lastly, support for immigration reform did not mean that Congress supported increased immigration from Asia, Latin America, and Africa that would alter the current ethnic and racial balance of American society. Ending discrimination was a legal formality, a political necessity, and an ethical and just action. But many concerns were raised about the consequences of the new law that belied Congress's professed commitment to racial equality. Indeed, the arguments in favor of immigration reform tilted heavily toward emphasizing the ways in which the current laws harmed just European immigrants. Officials on both sides of the immigration issue routinely cited examples of injustice involving Italian, Polish, Greek, and Hungarian Americans, all communities that, like the Irish a generation before them, had been safely assimilated into the United States and now yielded significant political power.[26]

Critics of the Johnson bill also vehemently opposed any increase in non-European migration. Subtly connecting immigration to the United States' existing race "problems" with African Americans and other racial minorities, Southern Democrats and their conservative allies fed into American anxieties about Latinx and black immigrants flooding into the country and displacing whites. Lawmakers supporting this position argued that European immigrants coming from what Senator Spessard Holland, a Democrat from Florida, called America's "mother countries" had helped create the United States and had made it possible to develop, expand, and thrive. (By excluding non-European countries from the list of mother countries, Holland of course implied that immigrants from Asia, Latin America, as well as Native Americans and African Americans, had done little to contribute to the making of America.) Shifting American immigration policy to reduce immigration from Europe

would be a "complete and radical departure" from what had been regarded as "sound principles" of immigration, he explained. "Why, for the
first time, are emerging nations of Africa to be placed on the same basis
as our mother countries—Britain, Germany, the Scandinavian nations,
France, and the other nations from which most Americans have come?"
he bluntly asked.[27]

Democrat Sam Ervin Jr. of North Carolina similarly used a comparison of Great Britain (with a quota of sixty-five thousand under the
national origins system) and Ethiopia (with a quota of a hundred) to
argue that a change in law would discriminate against British people.
Great Britain, Ervin explained, "gave us our language, they gave us our
common law, they give a large part of our political philosophy." Giving
Ethiopians the "same right to come to the United States under this bill
as the people of England, the people of France, the people of Germany,
the people of Holland . . . would be discriminatory," he explained, because "with all due respect to Ethiopia, I don't know of any contributions
that Ethiopia has made to the making of America." Ervin made similar
arguments concerning potential immigrants from Congo in later hearings. Others like Congressmen O. Clark Fisher from Texas, Clark Mac-
Gregor from Minnesota, and Michael Feighan from Ohio voiced similar
concerns. Testimony from anti-immigrant groups was even more blunt.
Some argued that without the quota system, "hordes of Red Chinese,
Indians, [and] Congolese cannibals" would enter the United States and
destroy the nation's identity.[28]

Many lawmakers agreed. Too many immigrants from "overpopulated
countries" in Asia, Africa, and the Western Hemisphere would "add to
the many social problems that now confront us across the Nation," Senator Robert Byrd of West Virginia predicted, in a thinly veiled reference
to African American protests and poverty. Representative Fisher from
Texas suggested that the new law would undoubtedly bring tens of thousands of politically dangerous immigrants from "Oriental Communist
countries." Senator John McClellan from Arkansas similarly alluded to
the United States' existing race problems with African Americans when
he suggested that the increase of "still more minority groups from all

parts of the world" would contribute to the "increasing racial tensions and violence we are currently witnessing on the streets of our major cities." On the topic of admitting more immigration from countries like Jamaica, Representative Frank Chelf from Kentucky was more blunt: "I really and truly think that we have got all the troubles that we can say grace over with our own American native-born colored people."[29]

Other lawmakers added that not only were non-European immigrants the wrong kind of immigrants; given the demographic conditions in the countries from which they would come, there would likely be too many of them as well. Lawmakers repeatedly pointed to the specter of a global "population explosion" that would send millions to the United States. Congressman MacGregor claimed, for example, that the population of Latin America would reach six hundred million people in the next thirty-five years. Chairman Feighan warned that immigration could rise to "floodgate proportions." Senator Ervin offered statistics purportedly confirming that the immigration explosion was already under way. Immigration from the Western Hemisphere had increased by a "fantastic 230% in the last five years," he claimed, "and by almost 400% in the last ten years." This immigration could easily "double each year" he predicted.[30] As a result of these concerns, lawmakers started calling for numerical limitations to be placed on immigration from the Western Hemisphere. Justifying these new restrictions within the context of the country's newfound commitment to nondiscrimination and civil rights, however, required the articulation of a new discourse of color blindness and reverse discrimination that would later become standard positions among conservatives in the post–civil rights era.

HOUSE SUBCOMMITTEE ON Immigration and Nationality chair Michael Feighan led the way in deftly framing the Western Hemisphere restrictions as a necessary antidiscriminatory measure in line with the civil rights mission of the larger immigration reform bill. The aggrieved parties in this case, he argued, would be all other countries outside the Western Hemisphere, notably those in Europe. "If a person is born in the Western Hemisphere by *accident of birth*, they come quota-free," he argued in committee hearings in March 1965, "whereas a person born in a country other than in the Western Hemisphere by accident of his birth is not quota-free." It would be discriminatory, Feighan argued, to practice "favoritism" toward countries of the Western Hemisphere. He further explained that *not* placing numerical limitations on immigration from the Western Hemisphere translated into a type of unearned privilege based on "accident of birth" and a type of reverse discrimination targeting potential immigrants from Europe. "Now *that* is a principle of discrimination," he emphatically concluded.[31]

Feighan would elaborate on his reverse discrimination argument in public speeches while hearings were taking place in Congress. Speaking before an audience at the Cleveland City Club, for example, Feighan explicitly argued that the nonquota system for the Western Hemisphere discriminated against "all people born outside the Western Hemisphere" while granting "prejudicial judgment in favor" of all people born in the Western Hemisphere. He then went on to use examples demonstrating how immigrants from European countries would have to wait years before they could be admitted, whereas "[a person] born in Panama, Guatemala, Dominican Republic, or Columbia . . . need only demonstrate that he is not likely to become a public charge, and pronto, he has an immigrant visa to the United States."[32]

Feighan's reverse discrimination argument gained traction in Congress. It successfully obscured the race-based intent of the restrictions while using the language of color blindness and nondiscrimination. In August 1965, Representative MacGregor from Minnesota introduced an amendment representing the xenophobic position spearheaded by Feighan and other hard-liners. MacGregor explained that without the restrictions, "we will be perpetuating and even increasing *a new form of discrimination*—discrimination based not upon race, which we eliminate in this bill and rightly so—but discrimination based upon national origin and the location of one's birth." Any immigrant from the Western Hemisphere, regardless of his station in life, he continued, would enjoy "a *preferential* position for admission over his counterpart across the Atlantic or Pacific Oceans." This result would be "a far cry from our declared policy of equal treatment for every immigrant." By not including numerical limitation of immigrants from the Western Hemisphere, MacGregor explained, "we would be extending an unjustifiable and obvious discrimination and an unjustified and unnecessary favoritism." Countries that would be adversely affected, MacGregor was quick to point out, included "our traditional friends and allies" from Europe.[33]

The MacGregor Amendment, as it was called, garnered much support in and out of Congress. Representative William M. McCulloch of Ohio declared that it would be "illogical and inconsistent to retain a form of discrimination by not including the Western Hemisphere under a numerical ceiling concept." Senator Ervin went further to claim that nonquota status of the Western Hemisphere was "the most apparent discrimination of all." In the Senate, testimony from xenophobic groups offered more support. Revealing the ways in which the reverse discrimination argument connected to nativism and white supremacy, one group even claimed that the Johnson immigration proposal even "robbed white citizens of their rights."[34]

Support for the MacGregor Amendment worked hand in hand with overall opposition to the Johnson bill and constituents' belief that it would bring millions of non-European immigrants to the United States. The conservative newspaper *The Independent American* distributed a pamphlet titled "Our Immigration Law Under Attack," which claimed that the Johnson bill invited foreigners to compete for US jobs, welcomed the "insane and diseased," imported "voting blocs," shuffled quotas to admit Asians, would lead to "unlimited, non-quota Orientals and Negroes," and would bring in "red spies disguised as refugees." The American Coalition of Patriotic Societies released a series of editorials that warned that President Johnson wanted to "let down the bars to swarms of Asiatics and Africans" as well as allow in a "Trojan horse at our gate . . . from whose dark bowels can emerge into our midst a million alien misfits a year!"[35]

The Johnson administration was put on the defensive. Bill co-sponsor Emanuel Celler called out the MacGregor Amendment for mischaracterizing the Western Hemisphere's nonquota status as "discrimination."

There was no discrimination, Celler insisted, because the policy had existed already for four decades as is. Neither the long string of Republican
administrations and lawmakers nor countries outside the Western Hemisphere had ever characterized the Western Hemisphere's status under US
immigration law as "discriminatory." Rather, he explained, exemption
was part of a long-standing policy of Western Hemisphere solidarity that
went back to the Monroe Doctrine.[36]

Others, like secretary of state Dean Rusk, repeatedly argued that immigration from the region should remain under existing policy in order to
recognize "the common bond" that united the Americas. Congressman
Richard McCarthy of New York further explained that the nonquota
policy was "a mark of mutual respect and friendship and a symbol of the
good neighbor policy." Senators Kennedy, Hart, and Javits also argued
that calls to limit immigration from the Western Hemisphere were misguided. There was no "real immigration problem," yet fellow lawmakers
wanted the United States to take a "historic step backward in our otherwise progressive Western Hemisphere policies," they argued. Celler concluded that any restrictions would have "very serious repercussions." They
"would alienate Latin America" and make "the conduct of our foreign
policy more difficult and more arduous" during a critical time when the
United States needed "all the friends we can muster." The United States
could not afford to "have any nations turn against us, particularly our
neighbors to the south of us," he argued.[37]

While these immigration reformers defended the exemption of the
Western Hemisphere from new restrictions, they did not challenge the
openly racist and xenophobic comments offered up by their colleagues
in Congress, nor did they point out how these bigoted statements con-
tradicted the representatives' alleged commitment to equality. Instead,
reformers unwittingly fed into the xenophobia and racism expressed by
their colleagues by using some of the same rhetoric. They assured lawmakers that the new policy would not substantially increase immigration or "open our gates to hordes of undesirable aliens . . . invading our
shores," as Congressman Robert D. Duncan claimed. Celler conceded
that there would be "shifts in countries other than those of northern and
western Europe." But he insisted that there would not be "many Asians or

Africans entering this country." Both the numerical caps and the quali-
tative controls would help keep those numbers down. And the law's family unification policy was meant to increase European immigration—not
immigration from outside Europe. "Since the people of Africa and Asia
have very few relatives here, comparatively few could immigrate from
those countries," he explained. There is "no danger whatsoever of an influx from the countries of Asia and Africa," Celler insisted.[38]

Senate immigration subcommittee chairman Ted Kennedy also gave
his assurances. "First, our cities will not be flooded with a million immigrants annually. Under the proposed bill, the present level of immigration
remains substantially the same," he began. "Secondly, the ethnic mix of
this country will not be upset." America's "ethnic pattern of immigration"
(i.e., European) would not "change as sharply as the critics seem to
think," he stated. Asian American senator Hiram L. Fong from Hawai'i
was enlisted to assure his colleagues that only a small number of people from Asia would enter the United States under the 1965 Act. Asians
made up just a tiny fraction of the total current US population, Fong
explained, and thus since the primary means of entering was through
family unification, only a small number of immigrants would likely come.
Asians would "never reach 1 percent of the population," he predicted, and
as a result, "our cultural pattern will never be changed as far as America
is concerned." These arguments did not sway the hard-liners, and restrictions on immigration from Latin America became a necessary precondi-
tion before any other changes could be made.[39] Reformers' arguments had
failed to demonstrate the economic need for Mexican immigrants and the
reality of US-Mexican economic interdependency that Mexican migration exemplified. They also failed to challenge the racist and xenophobic
language that conservatives used to justify their positions. In these compromised choices, Congress's liberals opted for reform, but not justice.

The policy of placing a ceiling on immigration from the Western
Hemisphere continued to gather support from traditional xenophobes in
Congress as well as from influential organizations and media outlets like
the AFL-CIO, the *Christian Science Monitor*, and the *New York Times*.
Even some liberal members of Congress supported them. Senator Ervin
introduced an immigration bill that reinstated a ceiling on immigration

from the Western Hemisphere and added additional restrictions on Mexican immigration by prohibiting the admission of unskilled labor unless the secretary of labor certified that no American workers would be displaced or negatively affected.[40]

President Johnson and his administration remained strongly opposed to any numerical limitations on immigration from the Western Hemisphere, but the president was also eager to get a bill passed. He instructed his cabinet officials to negotiate. He also began to apply his powers of persuasion to Feighan, whom he described as a "tough cookie" to Ted Kennedy.[41]

Feighan reluctantly agreed to support an end to the national origins quota system, but in exchange, he demanded an important concession from the president: immigration restrictions on the Western Hemisphere. This was a nonnegotiable issue to the congressman, and he was willing to hold the national origins quota system hostage to achieve this goal. He also forced through changes to the new visa preference system. Whereas the Johnson administration wanted to give first preference to immigrants with professional skills and training "advantageous" to the United States,

Congressman Michael Feighan (Democrat from Ohio) with President Lyndon B. Johnson. Courtesy of Public Policy Papers, Princeton University Library.

and second, to the relatives of US citizens and legal residents, Feighan negotiated a reversal of those priorities. If family unification was placed first in the list of preference categories, he rationalized, more European immigrants would come since European Americans were more numerous in the United States than other groups. Despite Feighan's public insistence that he only wanted to strengthen nondiscrimination in the law, his explicitly racist attempt to discourage nonwhite, non-European immigration and preserve the racial and ethnic composition of the US population (primarily European-descended) that the national origins quota system had facilitated in this way was clear.

Feighan allies in the American Legion certainly realized the importance of this maneuver. Writing in the *American Legion Magazine* in February 1966, Deane Heller and David Heller explained that although the new law had been "represented as a great liberal triumph" in ending discrimination, it in fact "preserved the bulk of the national-origins base of immigration to the United States, but keyed it to a system of preferences rather than quotas." The American Legion gave Feighan full credit for this aspect of the bill and for adding additional controls "to check immigration that is not in the best interest of the United States."[42]

Kennedy and Celler accepted Feighan's proposal, as did the president. Dismayed with the inclusion of the new restrictions on immigration from the Western Hemisphere in the bill, co-sponsor Hart distanced himself from the bill. The administration was successful in delaying the implementation of an annual Western Hemisphere ceiling until 1968, but it otherwise caved on the question of restrictions. In the end, a new intentional regime of restriction was established—but it was harder to spot immediately, hidden under the guise of nondiscrimination and civil rights. The Hart-Celler bill passed on September 22, 1965, and was approved by both chambers of Congress on September 30, 1965.[43]

WHEN THE PRESIDENT finally signed the bill on Liberty Island on October 3, 1965, he called it one of the "most important acts of this Congress and of this administration." The new bill, the president continued, overturned the "harsh injustice of the national origins quota system" and instead regulated immigration in a "fair and simple" way of admitting immigrants. "This bill says simply that from this day forth those wishing to immigrate to America shall be admitted on the basis of their skills and their close relationship to those already here," he declared. "The days of unlimited immigration are past," he continued. "But those who do come will come because of what they are, and not because of the land from which they sprung."[44]

Johnson was only partially right. The 1965 Immigration Act was an indelible part of the broader civil rights movement that sought to ensure equality and to eliminate race as a factor in public policy. However, it was imperfect in its design and in its execution. The Immigration Act and the new system of preference categories and ceilings was simultaneously less restrictive and more restrictive than the system it abolished. It ended formal racial discrimination and abolished the national origins quota system. But it allowed other forms of discrimination to persist, both overtly and covertly. Most noticeably, it prohibited people from receiving visas and gaining admission to the United States on the basis of sexual orientation. The immigration act also maintained restrictions based on nationality in its provisions pertaining to refugees—only people who came from "Communist or communist-dominated countr[ies]" or "the general area of the Middle East" qualified for refugee status.[45]

Despite its intent to treat all immigrant groups fairly and equally, the 1965 Immigration Act also ended up reinforcing inclusion for some and exclusion for others. In removing discriminatory national origins quotas that disadvantaged southern and eastern European immigrants, for example, the 1965 act extended both the civil rights rhetoric and the legal principle of nondiscrimination to all European immigrants—and signaled the total integration of all European Americans into America, including groups the Immigration Restriction League had been so hostile toward in the early twentieth century. This act of inclusion mirrored and helped energize European Americans' growing efforts to preserve and celebrate their ethnic heritage while also emphasizing their assimilation into American life and their bootstrap upward mobility. This white ethnic revival of the 1970s and 1980s rhetorically moved the site of the nation's roots away from Plymouth Rock and toward Ellis Island. In a dramatic turnaround in American thought and popular culture, the once "inferior races of Europe" had been rehabilitated as archetypal Americans by the 1980s. What one historian has called "Ellis Island whiteness," which emphasized overcoming hardship through struggle and hard work (and the denial of white privilege), became a dominant form of white identity in the United States and was celebrated and spread through films such as *Fiddler on the Roof* (1971) and the *Rocky* movies as well as the 1986 Statue of Liberty Centennial and the Ellis Island restoration project. The United States as a "nation of [European] immigrants" became entrenched as one of America's cherished myths and effectively obscured America's history of xenophobia.[46]

Much to the chagrin of conservatives like Feighan, post-1965 immigration from Europe, however, did not increase substantially. A postwar economic boom in Western Europe, greatly aided by financial assistance from the US Marshall Plan, diminished the need or desire for many to resettle abroad. Totalitarian governments in poorer nations in eastern and central Europe also blocked prospective migrants from leaving. Meanwhile, conditions in Latin America, Asia, and Africa increased the pressure to migrate. A series of economic crises in Mexico, for example, including unemployment, increased foreign debt, and inflation drove Mexicans first to the cities in search of jobs and then abroad. US involvement in Southeast Asia propelled millions out of the region as refugees. Growing numbers of educated and skilled professionals in Taiwan, South Korea, and India sought higher wages abroad, while Cubans came as refugees fleeing Fidel Castro's regime. Moreover, prospective migrants with relatives already in the United States took advantage of the family reunification clauses. Because spouses, minor children, and parents of American citizens were exempt from the numerical ceilings, the actual numbers of immigrants entering the United States in the decades after 1965 were actually much larger than the global ceiling of 290,000. Between 1976 and 1985, for example, recorded legal immigration averaged some 546,000 people entering per year.[47]

As a result of these larger geopolitical and economic forces, global migration patterns shifted. In 1960, the top ten largest US immigrant groups were, in order from largest to smallest: Italy, Germany, Canada, the United Kingdom, Poland, the Soviet Union, Mexico, Ireland, Hungary, and Austria (with a conglomeration of "other" countries making up the majority). By 1980, immigrants from Mexico outnumbered immigrants from European countries, and Cuba, the Philippines, and Korea had replaced Hungary, Austria, and Ireland in the top ten list of largest US immigrant groups. By 2000, the change was even more dramatic. Immigrants from Mexico made up nearly 30 percent of all immigrants, and only Germany and Canada remained in the top ten list. The other countries sending the largest number of immigrants to the US in 2000 were the Philippines, India, Vietnam, El Salvador, Cuba, China, and Korea.[48]

The act's stated policy of promoting family unification also had different impacts on different immigrant groups. Although it enabled millions of US citizens and legal permanent residents to bring their families to the United States, many others continued to be separated as a result of an ever-growing visa backlog. One result was the development of vastly unequal pathways into the United States. For example, the law eased restrictions and opened the door to new generations of immigrants from Asia, especially those with education and skills. Eligible for both the family reunification (through what became known as chain migration) and the professional skill preferences in the new law, Asian immigration grew exponentially. In 1970, there were 1.54 million Asians recorded in the US census. Ten years later, that number had doubled to 3.5 million, and ten years after that, it doubled again to 6.9 million. The 2010 census found that the Asian population had grown by 46 percent in the past ten years, faster than any other racial group in the country.[49]

The immigration act resulted in the reverse pattern for immigrants from Latin America, particularly Mexico. Combined with the nearly simultaneous termination of the bracero program, the act's numerical limits on immigration directly and dramatically reduced legal pathways for Mexican immigrants. In 1976, the United States applied the 20,000-immigrants-per-country limit to the Western Hemisphere. The separate hemispheric caps were folded together into one worldwide visa ceiling of 290,000 in 1978. In 1980, the ceiling was reduced to 270,000 and the per-country quota was further diminished to 18,200 legal immigrants, excluding quota exemptions such as spouses, parents, and children of US citizens. Mexico's quota was far below actual and historic numbers for Mexican migration. Having migrated north for generations, often directly recruited by American employers, Mexican workers suddenly faced new restrictions that made it much more difficult to come to the United States and reflected the anti-Mexican intent of the 1965 Immigration Act.[50]

The fact that these restrictions were intentionally enacted in a law designed to eliminate discrimination, sometimes using the civil rights language of equality to do so, pointed to another important impact and consequence of the 1965 Immigration Act: the creation and use of color-blind xenophobia, by which discrimination in immigration law was achieved under the guise of nondiscrimination. The 1965 Immigration Act established equal quotas for all nations and imposed ceilings on both the Eastern and Western Hemispheres in an attempt to establish a policy of formal equality. No nation and no hemisphere appeared to be favored over another.[51]

But equal quotas did not translate into immigration equality. This seemingly neutral and nondiscriminatory system had a disproportionate impact on certain countries that was significantly unequal. Some countries, for example, because of either geographical proximity, demand, or historical relationships, sent more people to the United States than others. Thus, granting Togo and Mexico the same quota of twenty thousand was unfair to Mexico given the latter country's long-standing history of migration, and geographical proximity, to the United States. Similarly, giving both Belgium and China a quota of twenty thousand immigration slots was unfair to China because of the vastly different sizes of the countries and the pools of potential immigrants. As legal experts pointed out, the one-size-fits-all approach did not fit "all nations well or equally."[52] Belgium and Togo may have never used up their annual quotas. Meanwhile, the demand for immigration from places like Mexico, India, the Philippines, and China was consistently greater than the available supply, resulting in visa backlogs that grew to be decades long. As a result, the number of transnational families and households separated by borders and oceans increased.

The 1965 act and its amendments also effectively eliminated most avenues for legal immigration for most Mexican immigrants. At the time of the act's passage, Mexico was the nation with the greatest demand for immigration to the United States. US recruitment of Mexican laborers under the bracero program had brought 4.6 million workers to the country in the previous twenty years. Some 445,000 had come in 1956 alone. The artificially low ceiling of 20,000 was far below the number of legal permanent residents and temporary workers who were admitted from Mexico each year in the decade prior to 1965. Beginning in 1968, the act also required labor certification specifying that no worker from the Western Hemisphere could enter the United States unless the secretary of labor certified that there were not sufficient able and qualified workers in the United States and that the immigrant worker would not adversely affect wages or working conditions of American workers. Moreover, the preferences for professional and skilled migrants left fewer options for unskilled and low-skilled workers just as global demand for such labor was increasing. Lastly, the Western and Eastern hemispheres were treated differently and unequally when it came to the provisions of quota-exempt family reunification. Relatives of both permanent residents (foreign-born individuals who are not US citizens but who have secured the right of permanent residency in the United States) and US citizens coming from the Eastern Hemisphere were given preferential treatment, whereas family members of only permanent residents from the Western Hemisphere were given preference.[53]

All three changes in immigration policy combined—the termination of the bracero program, the new Western Hemisphere ceiling imposed by the Immigration Act of 1965, and the labor certification system—effectively and abruptly decreased Mexican migration. However, the need and desire for immigrant laborers, especially from Mexico, kept demand for such immigrants high. Chaos ensued after the law was passed and the Western Hemisphere's new ceiling of 120,000 was imposed in 1968 and the per-country limitations were put in place in 1976. What had been a massive amount of legal immigration (200,000 braceros and 35,000 regular admissions for permanent residency) was reduced to the annual 20,000 quota. The 120,000 hemispheric quota represented a 40 percent reduction from pre-1965 levels. Put another way, in a span of just a few years, Mexican migration had been transformed from being almost unlimited to a quota of only 20,000.[54]

Mexicans could still apply for admission, most notably through family reunification, but the waiting list for visas was soon years long for applications of Mexican citizens. By July 1, 1969, the waiting period for a visa was nine months. A year later it was fourteen. By 1999, it was nine years long. In 2018, there were 1.2 million Mexicans waiting for a visa to enter the United States, compared to 314,000 Filipinos—the next largest group. China, fifth on the list of countries with the highest number of waiting list registrants, had 231,000 people waiting. Critics of unauthorized immigration often complained that unauthorized immigrants needed to "stand in line" like others. But by the early twenty-first century, the line was already nearly four million people long.[55]

Thus, in theory, the new law created a "fair" and "equal" system. In practice, however, countries in the Western Hemisphere were the most directly impacted by new restrictions and quotas that matched neither previous levels of migration nor historic ties and migration between the two countries. It served, as some legal scholars pointed out, as "a new and effective form of racial discrimination" that was even more sophisticated than the national origins quota system. Driven by racist and xenophobic fears, it was intentionally designed to restrict immigration from Latin America and compromised the promise of equality that the 1965 Immigration Act was supposed to embody.[56]

One result of this immigration inequality was an increase in undocumented immigration. American employers continued to rely on labor from Mexico, but with no legal way to enter the country to fill these jobs, Mexicans turned to entering without inspection. In many cases, migrants were returning to the same jobs and employers they had held before the new law went into effect. But now they were "illegal." At the same time, undocumented immigrants already in the United States began to remain in the country rather than risk multiple cross-border trips across an increasingly militarized border. Both trends resulted in record numbers of undocumented immigrants coming to, and staying in, the United States.[57]

THE 1965 IMMIGRATION Act and its consequences led to a new and divisive immigration debate focused on immigrants from Latin America, particularly from Mexico. This debate would reach a new climax in the 1990s, when states like California would begin to address the "illegal immigration problem" with new punitive measures. Color-blind xenophobia would continue to evolve as well. At a time when explicit racism was still taboo, xenophobes increasingly denounced immigrants' undocumented or "illegal" status rather than their race or national origin. But race and the specter of America's changing demographics was always lurking. Advocating for a "war on illegal immigration" became a primary way of channeling the racial anxiety and hostility that was consuming many white Americans. Over time, the war on "illegals" translated into a war that would impact all Mexican people in the United States.[58]

EIGHT

"SAVE OUR STATE"

In 1970, twenty-three-year-old Enrique Valenzuela crossed the US-Mexico border to join his father, a ranch hand working in northern San Diego County. He had grown up in a tiny village in the state of Puebla growing corn and beans. It was a precarious existence. "If it rains," he explained, "there is work [and food] for six months." If it didn't, there was neither. As an adult, he left the village and found work in Mexico City, where he earned 275 pesos a week (about US $22). He was making enough to eat and pay rent, but there was nothing left for anything else. He decided to follow in the footsteps of his father, a bracero who had been going to the United States to work for years. In 1964, the bracero program, which had brought 4.6 million temporary workers to the United States between 1942 and 1964, was terminated, but Mexican migration continued, and the demand for Mexican labor remained high. Indeed, much of the United States' agricultural system functioned on a built-in structural demand for immigrant workers. Undocumented immigrants and guest workers were especially popular hires with growers. With few rights or protections, both groups could be easily exploited, managed, and replaced.

Enrique's father continued to come to the United States and easily found work each time through his former employers. Enrique soon joined him, just as generations of Mexicans had done before him. Only now, the Valenzuelas were "illegal," the result of the new restrictions on immigration from the Western Hemisphere created in the 1965 Immigration Act and the end of the decades-long bracero program. In the late 1950s, 450,000 Mexican guest workers and 50,000 immigrants had entered the United States each year. But by 1976, only 20,000 visas were available to Mexicans hoping to come to the United States. The rest had to come without documentation.[1]

The Valenzuelas were just two of the millions of immigrants journeying to the United States during the late twentieth century. Between 1981 and 1990, 7.3 million immigrants entered the country as legal immigrants—a dramatic increase from the 2.5 million who entered between 1951 and 1960 before the passage of the 1965 Immigration Act. And they came from places that lawmakers had not expected. The numbers of immigrants from Europe fell. Meanwhile, those from Asia and Latin America accounted for nearly 85 percent of all admitted immigrants. From 1971 to 1990, some 1.5 million refugees from Cuba, Vietnam, Laos, Cambodia, and elsewhere also arrived in the United States.[2]

This was exactly what the xenophobic architects of the 1965 Immigration Act had tried to avoid. After all, Congressman Michael Feighan had advocated that family reunification be given priority status in the handing out of new immigrant visas because he assumed that mostly white Americans would send for their European relatives. The congressman and his allies did not expect that immigrants from Asia and Latin America would come to join their families in such great numbers. But they did. Underemployed at home, educated and skilled immigrants from Asia also sought professional opportunities in the United States through the special skills provision in the 1965 act. Poor economic conditions in Mexico and steady work in the United States continued to drive Mexican migrants northward whether there were enough visas or not. Meanwhile, economic growth in Europe kept many at home. From 1971 to 1980, 18 percent of immigrants were from Europe—but over 35 percent were from Asia and 44 percent were from the Americas. The next decade, European immigrants made up only 10 percent of total immigration; Asians constituted over 37 percent and immigration from the Americas was over

49 percent. In addition, more and more undocumented immigrants decided to stay in the United States as increased border enforcement made
remigration difficult and risky.[3]

A new debate over immigration surfaced in the 1980s and 1990s. As
in decades past, immigration became a flash point for culture wars and
other social, economic, and political anxieties. In the last two decades of
the twentieth century, these included a rapidly changing and deindustri-
alizing economy that was displacing millions of blue-collar workers; new
(and more radical) campaigns for social justice that challenged systemic
racism, sexism, and homophobia; rapid demographic change brought on
by increasing racial diversity; and the formal end of the Cold War, which
raised new questions about the role of American leadership in the world.

The epicenter of the debate was California, the entry point of many
of the new immigrants and where citizen activists, politicians, and other
leaders—many of them from conservative circles—resurrected the specter of an immigrant invasion, a border "out of control," and emphasized
the suffering of (white) Americans. They particularly identified undocumented Mexican immigration as a source of societal and economic woes.
But instead of proposing policy solutions that addressed the root causes
of immigration, including undocumented immigration, xenophobes relied on both explicit racism and fearmongering, as well as the newfound
weapon of color-blind xenophobia, to convince voters that an immigration "crisis" threatened their well-being. Many hard-line immigration
activists and politicians, for example, denounced immigrants' "illegal"
status rather than their race or national origin. They claimed that their
campaign against "illegal immigration" promoted public safety and fiscal
responsibility.[4]

But as in the past, race unmistakably and decisively fueled late-
twentieth-century xenophobia. The so-called war redeployed deep-rooted
stereotypes linking Mexicans to crime, poverty, and welfare dependency.
"Illegal aliens" were clearly understood to be *Mexican*, and the so-called
war on illegal immigration obscured a larger racial campaign that considered all Mexican immigration as a reconquest of the United States
by Mexican-descended peoples. It was also undeniably part of a larger

(white) backlash to the "browning of America," the demographic shift of the US population to a majority-minority society, and the perceived corresponding decline in white political and economic power. Accompanying the anti-Mexican discourse, for example, was a powerful nativist message of white victimization and white displacement that was already a central part of conservative political discourse on race.[5]

Like earlier anti-immigrant campaigns, xenophobes turned to state and federal laws to limit immigration and curb the rights of immigrants already in the country. In 1994, Californians passed Proposition 187, a voter-led ballot initiative informally known as "Save Our State." Its goal was to make the act of entering the country without authorization grounds for denying all public benefits, education, and health services to undocumented immigrants and to require all public employees to report anyone suspected of being in the United States without proper documentation to federal authorities.

Although the courts eventually ruled that most of Proposition 187's provisions were unconstitutional, much of the campaign's xenophobic ideology was later amplified by popular conservative writers and politicians and embraced by both major political parties. It also significantly influenced the overhaul of federal welfare and immigration policies later in the decade. Mass deportation and detention and the militarization of the US-Mexico border followed, while Mexican and Latinx-origin communities were subjected to widespread racial profiling and discrimination. By the early twenty-first century, the xenophobic message that Mexican immigration was endangering America had become so normalized that it helped propel Donald Trump to the White House in 2016.

As IMMIGRATION WAS transforming the United States in the decades following the 1965 Immigration Act, the public debate over immigration evolved. In the immediate post-1965 era, the mass media frequently celebrated immigrants as a positive and central aspect of American national identity and reaffirmed the United States as "a nation of immigrants." Media coverage in the 1970s often emphasized the role that America still played as the "promised land" to new immigrants and refugees. *Time* magazine, for example, celebrated the nation's two hundredth birthday in July 1976, with a brief history lesson detailing how yesterday's immigrants had contributed to the growth of the United States. It lovingly profiled Victor Valles Solan, a refugee from Castro's communist regime in Cuba, who praised the United States as "the place on earth where democracy is purest." It praised Bit Chuen Wu, a twenty-three-year-old from Hong Kong who worked twelve hours a day to support his widowed mother and younger brother without complaint. Wu, who expressed gratitude for the opportunity to be his "own boss" in the United States, was portrayed as the very model of the American work ethic, capitalism, and entrepreneurship.[6]

This optimistic and celebratory characterization of immigration lasted into the next decade. But new concerns about growing immigration, and increased levels of undocumented immigration in particular, began to surface across the political spectrum in the 1970s, along with anxiety caused by high unemployment and inflation. Labor unions and pro-union politicians denounced immigrants for taking jobs away from citizens and unfairly taxing state and federal welfare coffers. Federal officials like attorney general William Saxbe helped promote this scapegoating by describing undocumented immigration as a "severe national crisis" that cost jobs and increased crime and welfare costs. In 1974, he called for the deportation of one million Mexican "illegal aliens." That same year, US Immigration and Naturalization commissioner Leonard Chapman labeled undocumented immigration a "silent invasion" while testifying before Congress. Echoing the nativist calls for deportation made by government officials during the Great Depression, Chapman claimed that mass deportation could open up one million job vacancies "virtually overnight" for unemployed Americans. Some of this rhetoric was echoed in the media. *US News and World Report* printed sensationalist stories with headlines like "Rising Flood of Illegal Aliens: How to Deal with It" in February 1975, "Crisis Across the Borders: Meaning to US" in December 1976, and "Illegal Aliens: Invasion Out of Control?" in January 1979.[7]

By the late 1970s, the concept of an "illegal alien crisis" was firmly carved into the conversation of American politics, but little political action was taken. A new organization, the Federation for American Immigration Reform (FAIR), established in 1979 by Michigan doctor John Tanton, sponsored press conferences to promote the organization's campaign in support of immigration restriction, but these efforts drew scant attention or support. Immigration in general was only marginally important in American politics. US companies, especially those in agriculture-heavy California, depended on immigrant labor and lobbied politicians to make sure their access to immigrant workers remained open. Cold War US international relations and foreign policy interests in Asia and Latin America also dissuaded lawmakers from supporting any new restriction policies, lest they threaten US interests abroad. President Jimmy Carter unsuccessfully pushed for employer sanctions that would have punished employers who knowingly hired undocumented workers and a legalization program that would have allowed undocumented immigrants to adjust their legal status. He also supported enhanced border enforcement. Neither the Republican nor the Democratic Party supported major immigration restrictions, but the idea that the United States was experiencing an "immigration crisis" was slowly permeating American society and politics. FAIR released misleading data suggesting that Americans supported an all-out war on unauthorized immigration. Americans' xenophobic anxiety increased following an economic slump. It rose again when thousands of Cubans rushed to the United States following a surprise April 20, 1980, announcement by Fidel Castro that allowed Cubans to leave the country via the port of Mariel. Some 125,000 came during what became known as the Mariel Boatlift. The nearly simultaneous arrival of 15,000 Haitian asylum seekers, also known as "boat people," was additionally used to promote the idea of an out-of-control immigration crisis.[8]

News stories contributed to the growing hysteria. The *New York Times* warned against a "rising, ugly nativist sentiment," but it also criticized "illegal gate-crashers" in 1982. A *Time* magazine cover story that featured Los Angeles as the "new Ellis Island" in June 1983 described an "immigrant tide" and a "staggering influx of foreign settlers" from Asia and Latin America invading the city. "English (Sometimes) Spoken Here," claimed *US News and World Report* in March 1983, a reference to dark-skinned foreigners (and foreign languages) replacing white Americans and the English language.[9]

But late-twentieth-century xenophobia did not treat all new immigrants the same. Nowhere was the binary division of "good" and "bad" more apparent than in how immigrants from Asia were treated and discussed, versus immigrants from Latin America. Although some of the media discourse referred to the high levels of immigration from both places in generally negative ways, it was the threat from Latin America—and specifically Mexico—that became the near exclusive focus of xenophobes. On the other hand, Asian immigrants, once so despised that they had been largely excluded from the United States, were slowly being remade into supposed "model minorities," racial minorities who worked hard to overcome obstacles and achieve the American dream. Newspapers and magazines routinely praised Asian Americans for displaying the attributes most prized by American capitalism and its emphasis on achievement. In 1984, *Newsweek* reported that Asian Americans packed the honor rolls of "some of the country's most highly regarded schools" and routinely outscored other racial groups on the math portion of the Scholastic Aptitude Test (SAT). *Fortune* magazine's description of Asian Americans as "America's Super Minority" explained that Asian Americans were "smarter and better educated and make more money than everyone else" partly because of their upbringing, but also because of genetics. "Asian Americans," the magazine flatly declared, were simply "smarter than the rest of us." Even as it masked persistent racial discrimination and inequality that Asian Americans still faced, popular media discourse about the Asian American model minority in the 1980s was an effective way to compare Asian Americans to other minorities. (African Americans, in particular, had their own racially coded labels, such as "welfare queens" or "affirmative action babies.") The intent was to delegitimize claims of systemic racism and discrimination in the United States as the cause for educational and income gaps between whites and nonwhites and promote the idea of a color-blind society, in which opportunity was equal to all. If Asian Americans could succeed, proponents of the model minority discourse argued, why couldn't others?[10]

Simultaneously, American media outlets promoted another narrative about immigration, this one from Mexico. Researchers found that from 1965 to 1995, leading papers in the United States increasingly paired the terms *undocumented*, *illegal*, and *unauthorized* with *Mexico* or *Mexican immigrants* and *crisis*, *flood*, or *invasion*. One example was *US News and World Report*'s March 7, 1983, cover story, "Invasion from Mexico: It Just Keeps Growing." Other popular descriptions of undocumented immigrants labeled them "alien invaders" who "outgunned" the Border Patrol in their attempts to "defend" the border. But this "Latino threat" narrative was not just about undocumented immigration. It was about all immigration from Mexico. The high numbers of immigrants coming in were described as a "tidal wave" that would "inundate" the United States, "drown" its culture, and "flood" America. The twin themes of Mexican immigration as a reconquest of the United States and the creation of a separate Mexican homeland within the United States was the focus of another *US News and World Report* cover story in 1985 titled "The Disappearing Border: Will the Mexican Migration Create a New Nation?" Immigrants were described as "new conquistadors . . . rising in the land their forebears took from the Indians and lost to the Americans." They were

Newsweek reported on what it called the "immigration backlash" in this 1993 cover story. Courtesy Scott McKowen/copyright 1993 Newsweek, Inc. All rights reserved. Reprinted by permission.

an "unstoppable mass" with divided allegiances. Even US-born Mexicans were never truly American, writers implied. Repeated ad infinitum in the mass media through the 1970s and 1980s, these xenophobic ideas became a common and acceptable part of public discourse.[11]

Ronald Reagan tried to address these changing attitudes about immigration during his presidency. Just months after taking office in 1980, he offered a two-pronged message on immigration. It first reaffirmed the idea that America's strength came from "our own immigrant heritage and our capacity to welcome those from other lands," but he also conceded that there were limits. "No free and prosperous nation can by itself accommodate all those who seek a better life or flee persecution," Reagan declared. In reaffirming his commitment to the idea of the United States as a "nation of immigrants" while also recognizing its perceived limits, the president reflected the attitudes present in mass media: there were immigrants who were worth the price of admission, and there were others who would tax, even destroy, the country. Certain select immigrants would continue to be welcomed, but those who did not meet America's goals and those who challenged America's sovereignty by coming in without authorization would be met with increasing force. Reagan ordered Congress to study what many believed to be a growing immigration problem.[12]

President Reagan's Select Commission on Immigration and Refugee Policy completed its work in 1981 and put forth two new proposals. It suggested reducing all immigration, and it identified undocumented immigration as one of the nation's significant challenges. The president astutely used the issue of undocumented immigration to galvanize political support for "regaining control of our borders" and expanded the role and budget of the INS. Congress responded by increasing the agency's funding by 130 percent over the course of Reagan's two terms. As part of Reagan's growing drug war, too, the US-Mexico border also became a new site of enforcement where the battles against "illegal" drugs and "illegal" aliens merged to prompt a "border buildup." In 1986, President Reagan signed into law the Immigration Reform and Control Act (IRCA), which attempted to address flaws in the immigration system in a comprehensive way. It required employers to verify the eligibility of all newly hired employees to work in the United States, punished employers for hiring undocumented immigrants, and facilitated growers' efforts to bring foreign agricultural workers into the United States legally. In an attempt to, as Reagan called it, "humanely regain control of our borders," the law also provided amnesty for 2.73 million undocumented migrants, including two million Mexicans. This allowed them to apply for temporary resident status, permanent residency, and eventually, US citizenship.[13]

Although it had been designed to curb undocumented immigration, IRCA had a limited impact. There was still a high demand for immigrant laborers but few ways for them to enter the country. The employer sanctions were ineffective, and many agricultural, construction, and landscaping businesses evaded the paperwork rules and continued hiring undocumented workers. Despite increased funding for border security, the US-Mexico border also remained largely passable through the mid-1990s. Undocumented immigration continued, and the number of undocumented immigrants in the United States grew from an estimated 3.2 million in 1986 to an estimated five million in 1996.[14] Politicians and others seized on these numbers and stoked the coals of Americans' growing concern with new calls for action.

ON DECEMBER 10, 1991, Patrick Buchanan declared his candidacy for the presidency of the United States in Concord, New Hampshire. Before a crowd of supporters, the syndicated columnist, former Nixon speechwriter, and communications director for Ronald Reagan declared that the United States was "at a crossroads in our national history." The Cold War had been won, but the United States was being displaced in the new world order. The rise of "a European super state" (the European Union) and a "dynamic Asia" were imperiling the United States' dominance on the world's center stage. Meanwhile, a "chronic moral sickness" eroded the country from within. "Our western heritage" was being "dumped on to some landfill called multiculturalism," he claimed. He called for a new patriotism and nationalism that would "look out for the forgotten Americans right here in the United States" and "put America first."[15]

Immigration, especially undocumented immigration, was a major theme of Buchanan's campaign. Speaking to the California Republican Assembly at their April 1992 convention, he declared that undocumented immigration was "adding to the social and economic disasters in California." In the weeks following the L.A. riots, Buchanan falsely claimed that undocumented immigrants were responsible for much of the disorder that had ravaged the city. "Foreigners are coming into this country illegally and helping to burn down one of the greatest cities in America," he declared. Buchanan also went to the US-Mexico border to criticize the federal government for failing to halt what he called "an illegal invasion." Speaking to reporters at a border checkpoint, he blamed undocumented immigration for causing the nation's social, economic, and drug problems. He called for fortifying key sections of the border with ditches and concrete-buttressed fences. He also suggested doubling the size of the Border Patrol and deploying US military forces along the border.[16]

This public relations stunt had little impact. Reporters noted that a group of about twenty-five would-be border crossers waited patiently for Buchanan to finish talking so they could cross into the United States. Even in California, the entry point of most undocumented immigrants from Mexico, immigration was not yet a central issue. California state lawmakers who tried to pass anti-immigrant bills were regularly derided as "right-wing kooks." By the fall of 1993, however, the political landscape was starting to change. Citizens were mobilizing around the issue of undocumented immigration and turning into activists.[17]

One of the most important leaders in this new grassroots campaign was Barbara Coe. A crime analyst for the Anaheim Police Department, Coe recalled the exact moment when she realized how much damage immigration was causing to the state of California and its citizens. She was accompanying an elderly friend to a social services center in Orange County, California, when she came face-to-face with what appeared to be a takeover of the state by inassimilable foreigners. "I walked into this monstrous room full of people, babies and little children all over the place, and I realized nobody was speaking English," she later told a journalist. There were windows serving Spanish- and Vietnamese-speaking visitors, but the one serving English speakers, she remembered, was closed. "There was every language under the sun being spoken, and I am going, 'Where am I? What's happened here?'" she recalled thinking. Her shock quickly turned to anger when she learned from a welfare counselor that while her friend did not qualify for certain public benefits, undocumented immigrants did. "I went ballistic," said Coe. The visit was a wake-up call that turned Coe into a crusader in the new campaign against immigration.[18]

Coe would become a leader in the powerful new conservative movement reshaping both xenophobia and immigration politics in the United States. She started out by self-publishing an anti-immigration newsletter from her home in Huntington Beach. In early 1992, she joined forces with Bill King, a former US Border Patrol chief, to form Citizens for Action Now (CAN), an organization dedicated to stopping "illegal immigration." CAN placed ads in conservative magazines like the *National Review* to recruit members. Their xenophobic and nativist focus was clear from the beginning. "WANTED: TESTIMONY FROM U.S. citizens who have been victims of crimes either financial (welfare, unemployment, food stamps, etc.), educational (overcrowding, forced bilingual classes, etc.) or physical (rape, robbery assault, infectious disease, etc.) committed by illegal aliens," their July 5, 1993, advertisement read.[19] In other words, they defined immigrants as criminals and immigration as a crime committed against citizens.

Coe and King did not know if anyone would respond to their ads. On the day of their first meeting, they "made a big pot of coffee, crossed our fingers and waited," remembered Coe. To their surprise, almost forty people, primarily white, middle-aged residents of Orange County, showed up to the first CAN meeting in Tustin. Speaker after speaker complained of being "inundated" by lawbreaking "illegals" who were taking away benefits from law-abiding, hardworking taxpayers and transforming their neighborhoods into unrecognizably foreign spaces.[20]

In May 1992, CAN merged with other conservative groups to become the California Coalition for Immigration Reform (CCIR), a political advocacy group pledged to reduce all immigration and combat undocumented immigration to the United States. CCIR successfully recruited volunteers, expanded its reach, and soon claimed a collective membership of four thousand. In October, it invited ten people to the posh members-only Center Club of Orange County to write what would be called the Save Our State Initiative, or Proposition 187. The group included Coe; two former INS officials, Alan Nelson and Harold Ezell; Barbara Kiley, mayor of the wealthy suburb of Yorba Linda, and her husband Robert, a Republican political consultant and former chair of the Orange County Republican Party; Ron Prince, an accountant from Tustin who had previously launched a one-man fight against undocumented immigration in front of an Orange County supermarket; and state assemblyman Dick Mountjoy.

PROPOSITION 187'S OFFICIAL title in the 1994 California general election voter information guide was "Illegal Aliens. Ineligibility for Public Services. Verification and Reporting. Initiative Statute." This overly bureaucratic title obscured a roiling debate over what, if any, rights and benefits undocumented immigrants should have in the state of California. The opening paragraphs of the measure made clear what was at stake in the minds of the proponents. "The People of California find and declare as follows," it began, that they "suffered *economic hardship* caused by the presence of illegal aliens in this state"; that they "suffered *personal injury* and damage caused by the *criminal conduct of illegal aliens* in this state"; and that they had a "right to the *protection of their government* from any person or persons entering this country unlawfully."[21]

In defining a coming battle between innocent lawful citizens and lawbreaking alien intruders, CCIR hoped to persuade voters that undocumented immigration was a major threat to the state. It claimed that government benefits enticed and drew "people from around the world who ILLEGALLY enter our country." As a result, they cost California taxpayers more than $5 billion a year. Neither politicians in Washington, DC, nor in Sacramento were doing enough to protect Californians, the bill's proponents claimed. They promised that Proposition 187 would take back control of the situation and start a revolution. "California can strike a blow for the taxpayer that will be heard across America." The proposition's victory, they predicted, would "go down in history as the voice of the people against an arrogant bureaucracy." "WE CAN STOP ILLEGAL ALIENS," the measure's proponents pledged.[22]

Nothing like Proposition 187 had been made into state policy before. Immigrants and African Americans had lacked or had been informally denied access to social welfare programs for many years, but Proposition 187 proposed to formally deny all public benefits—including nonemergency health care and public education—to an entire group of people on the basis of their immigration status. It also imposed stricter penalties for false residency documents and mandated cooperation between local police and the INS. Lastly, it required all public employees, including staff and teachers in school districts, public colleges, and universities, to report anyone suspected of being in the country without authorization to the INS—meaning private citizens were required to act as agents of the government's immigration enforcement regime.

The debate over Proposition 187 was fierce. Would the measure actually stop undocumented immigrants from entering the state, or even save any taxpayers money? The state's legislative analyst examined how undocumented immigrants used public benefits and concluded that state and local governments might save up to $200 million annually if they denied these services to undocumented immigrants. But the costs incurred to verify citizenship or immigration status could potentially exceed $100 million. And the state risked the potential loss of up to $15 billion in annual funds for education, health, and welfare programs, due to conflicts with federal policies. Increased costs would likely come later if the denial of medical services led to the spread of contagious diseases among the general population and to the poor health of US-citizen infants whose mothers were denied prenatal care. The state analyst additionally pointed out that public education–related cost savings would never materialize because the law violated the Supreme Court case *Plyler v. Doe*, which stated that undocumented immigrants could not be denied public education.[23]

Proposition 187's proponents countered these legal and economic positions with both explicit race-based arguments and color-blind xenophobia. Ron Prince, one of the initiative's drafters, likened the Save Our

State campaign to a lynch mob when he told supporters, "You are the posse and SOS is the rope." Harold Ezell, the former INS official and another measure author, famously stated that "illegal aliens" should be "caught, skinned and fried" and that Californians were "tired of watching their state run wild and become a third world country." His colleague Barbara Kiley reportedly described the children of undocumented immigrants as "those little f--kers."[24]

These racist statements may have mobilized the measure's die-hard supporters. But implicit racial messages also made the measure appealing to the broader electorate, including those who rejected explicit racism. Continuing the use of color-blind xenophobia first used by conservatives in the debate over the 1965 Immigration Act, the Proposition 187 campaign relied on deploying two simultaneous rhetorical strategies: race-neutral language of fiscal conservatism and national security and racially coded messages that identified "illegal immigration" as an undeniably and exclusively Mexican problem.[25]

Statements regarding the race or national origin of the "illegal aliens" who were causing the alleged personal injury and damage to the "people of California," for example, were noticeably absent from the proposition's official wording. Also missing were explicitly racist conceptions about certain immigrants being inherently and biologically inferior or dangerous to Americans. Instead, the proposition focused attention on the language of fiscal conservatism and (white) taxpayer victimization in using labels such as "economic hardship," the "suffering" of the "people of California," "unlawful" entry, and "government protection." Ezell, for example, declared that California was "in big trouble due to illegal immigration." "Illegal immigration ain't *free*," he continued. "It costs all of us taxpayers." Congressman Ron Packard endorsed the initiative, citing taxpayer fairness. "Nothing will stop them," he explained, referring to undocumented immigrants. Government benefits were simply too enticing, and hardworking Californians were left paying the bills. "It's simply unfair to taxpayers," he concluded.[26]

California governor Pete Wilson was among the most high-profile politicians to promote the "war on illegal immigration" during the 1994 election season. The former mayor of San Diego and US senator had not always been a xenophobe. As senator, he had supported guest worker programs that brought 350,000 temporary workers into the country every year. As California's governor (elected in 1990), he was slow to focus on immigration. But under his watch, the state was experiencing a serious decline, and Wilson's popularity was dwindling. A devastating economic recession, the worst since the Great Depression, was bringing high unemployment rates, double-digit inflation, and soaring interest rates. A number of key military bases had recently closed, the large aerospace industry was losing contracts, and California was weighed down by a huge budget deficit. Race relations also seemed to be at a breaking point. New immigrants from Latin America and Asia had increased the state's overall population by 25 percent during the 1980s, and their transformation of neighborhoods, schools, and workplaces were leading to racial and ethnic tensions. At the same time, the state's African American population continued to face rampant discrimination and police brutality. After Los Angeles police officers accused of beating motorist Rodney King were acquitted in April 1992, the city erupted into riots.[27]

Facing a tough reelection and staggeringly low poll ratings, Wilson boarded the Proposition 187 bandwagon in the final months before election day. The governor could see that the strategy of linking undocumented immigration to economic decline, crime, and white victimization was a successful one. His message was simple and to the point: he blamed the state's economic woes on the cost of caring for undocumented immigrants. California would have a balanced budget, the governor claimed, if it did not have to pay to take care of all the people living in the state without authorization. Wilson's poll numbers began to rise, and he never looked back.[28]

On August 9, 1994, he wrote an "open letter on behalf of the people of California" to President Bill Clinton that was published in the *New York Times*, *USA Today*, and the *Washington Times*. "MASSIVE ILLEGAL IMMIGRATION WILL CONTINUE AS LONG AS THE FEDERAL GOVERNMENT CONTINUES TO REWARD IT . . . [BY] PROVIDING INCENTIVES TO ILLEGAL

IMMIGRANTS," he declared. And because the federal government was failing to enforce its borders, California was "under siege." "WHY EVEN HAVE A BORDER PATROL AND I.N.S. IF WE ARE GOING TO CONTINUE THE INSANITY OF PROVIDING IN-CENTIVES TO ILLEGAL IMMIGRANTS TO VIOLATE U.S. IMMIGRATION LAWS?" he asked.[29]

The next day, he traveled around Southern California, the state's big-gest Republican stronghold, to reiterate his message that undocumented immigration was damaging the state and contributing to the decline in California's quality of life for its citizens. He later followed up on his xenophobic message by proposing a state budget that relied on a $2.3 billion reimbursement from the federal government to cover the state's expenses for undocumented immigrants, according to his calculations. He then filed three lawsuits against the federal government in an effort to receive funds for incarcerating, educating, and providing emergency medical care for undocumented immigrants.[30]

The governor spread his message through a widely aired television campaign ad. It began with grainy black-and-white footage that looked like it was recorded off a surveillance camera. A dozen dark-skinned in-dividuals swarmed over a fence and ran past the border checkpoint on Interstate 5 in San Diego County. They passed the guard booths and nimbly wove in between the lines of cars waiting to enter the United States. They quickly hopped the freeway barrier before disappearing into the United States. No one pursued them, including the federal immigra-tion officers who were supposed to be guarding the border. "They keep coming," the deep-throated male narrator ominously told viewers. "More than two million illegal immigrants in California. The federal govern-ment won't stop them at the border, yet it requires us to pay billions to take care of them." Governor Wilson, the ad informed viewers, had sent the National Guard to help the Border Patrol. "But that's not all," the narrator continued before the governor himself appeared on camera. "For Californians who work hard, pay taxes, and obey the laws," Wilson de-clared, "I'm suing to force the federal government to control the border. And I'm working to deny state services to illegal immigrants. . . . Enough is enough." The message was clear. There were two types of Californians. There were the law-abiding Californians who worked hard and contributed to society. And there were the lazy lawbreakers who took from society. The federal government was failing in its duty to reward the law-abiding citizens of the state. But Wilson was stepping up. It was a matter of fairness, law and order, and fiscal responsibility, the governor claimed.[31]

But it was also clearly about race. The images of a swarm of dark-skinned trespassers brazenly entering the country at the San Diego checkpoint clearly identified undocumented immigration as a *Mexican* problem (despite the fact that only 39 percent of the undocumented immigrant population in the United States was from Mexico). The audacity of their entry also underscored the message that they were part of a larger foreign invasion of the United States. With such coded messages, explicit racial, national, or ethnic labels were completely unnecessary in the ad. It seeded racial fears without directly referencing race.[32]

With Governor Wilson now at the vanguard of the new anti-immigration campaign, national organizations like FAIR and the Republican Party began to help organize and fund the Save Our State initiative. They were not alone. Wilson's plan to sue the federal government received surprising support from California's two Democratic senators—Dianne Feinstein and Barbara Boxer. In fact, Feinstein had publicly endorsed the idea that unauthorized immigration posed a danger to the state's well-being two months before Wilson. Democratic gubernatorial candidate Kathleen Brown called for the deportation of all undocumented immigrants convicted of crimes in the United States. Meanwhile, members of the California Senate and Assembly introduced almost forty separate bills targeting both legal and undocumented immigration.[33]

Linking undocumented immigration to serious and violent crime was another Proposition 187 strategy that relied on thinly veiled racism and fear tactics. Ignoring innumerable studies that confirmed that immigrants were less likely to commit serious crimes than the native-born, Proposition 187 proponents claimed that violating immigration law (a civil offense) was a slippery slope, leading immigrants to commit acts of serious crime. "The mindset on the part of illegal aliens, is to commit crimes," explained Ron Prince. "The first law they break is to be here illegally. The attitude from then on is, I don't have to obey your laws." Barbara Coe similarly explained how undocumented immigrants preyed on Americans. "Illegal-alien gangs roam our streets, dealing drugs and searching for innocent victims to rob, rape and, in many cases, murder those who dare violate their turf," she explained in a 1994 op-ed. She also suggested that the "Third World cultures" from which the immigrants were coming were inherently dangerous and crime-prone. "You're not dealing with a lot of shiny face, little kiddies," she explained. "You're dealing with Third World cultures who come in, they shoot, they beat, they stab and they spread their drugs around in our school system. And we're paying them to do it."[34]

Once the idea that undocumented Mexican immigrants were criminals was established, a message of dehumanization followed. Immigrants who were criminals, the measure's supporters argued, were not worthy of entry into the United States, and they certainly were not worthy enough to receive basic social services like health care and education. It was therefore logical, they continued, to deny them these public benefits. And just as citizens were occasionally called upon to help law enforcement officers find and identify wanted criminals, so should they be recruited to do the same with undocumented immigrants. Thus, the measure required social service providers to report anyone they "suspected" of being undocumented to federal authorities for punishment.[35]

Justifying the need and morality of denying health care and public education to immigrant women and their children—an extraordinarily punitive proposal—required an additional level of racial messaging. This one equated Mexican immigrant women and their children, both documented and undocumented, with a larger "invasion" from Mexico that would eventually take over the state. Birthright citizenship and free education and health care provided incentive to come to the United States, proposition supporters argued. Take away the incentives and the flood would slow to a drip, they rationalized. Governor Wilson repeatedly argued that pregnant immigrant women were deliberately migrating to the

United States without authorization in order to give birth, receive free medical care, and gain US citizenship for their children.[36]

Seen as a whole, Proposition 187 and its explicit and implicit racial fearmongering was not only about addressing the economic costs of undocumented immigration; it was also about punishing and controlling Mexicans and their American-born children. Wilson and other Proposition 187 leaders made the larger goals of this racial campaign clear in their advocacy for core anti-immigrant positions long advocated for by FAIR. These were designed to restrict and deter new Mexican immigration and punish Mexicans already in the United States: a temporary halt to *all* legal immigration, the creation of a new tamperproof identification card for legal residents, the passage of state policies that denied public education and health care services to unauthorized residents, and a constitutional amendment denying citizenship to the US-born children of undocumented immigrants.[37]

Support for Proposition 187 was strong by the fall of 1994. But so was the opposition. Civil rights, immigrant rights, and taxpayer organizations; labor unions; and Democratic leaders all opposed the measure. But they were slow to mobilize. Some feared that publicizing the measure might inadvertently draw attention to it, help promote its message—and even help pass the proposal. Organized protest took place only after the Save Our State initiative qualified for the November ballot in late June 1994. With just over four months until the election, a No on S.O.S. group formed to raise funds, develop a network, and defeat the measure.[38]

Opponents struggled to clarify their message. Law enforcement officials, teachers, and medical professionals chose a strategy that endorsed and legitimized the message that undocumented immigrants were a threat to the state economy and quality of life, but that the proposition did nothing to fix it. "Something must be done to stop the flow of illegal immigrants coming across the border," one argument against the proposition explained in the voter's guide. "Illegal Immigration is a REAL PROBLEM, but Proposition 187 is NOT A REAL SOLUTION," it continued. Opponents also affirmed the pro-187 group's linkage between undocumented immigrants and crime. The measure would "kick 400,000 kids out of school and onto the streets," the group explained, presumably causing an uptick in crime (with so many immigrant kids on the streets, "CRIME AND GRAFFITTI [*sic*]" would increase). But it would not "result in their deportation," implying that deportation would in fact be the preferable course of action. The official statement against Proposition 187 ended with a clear indictment of undocumented immigration: "Illegal immigration is ILLEGAL." But it called for increased border enforcement and punishments for employers who hired undocumented immigrants, instead of the passage of Proposition 187.[39]

Other opponents like immigrant rights advocates focused on challenging the explicit racism and racial intent in the measure through a grassroots-based organization called Californians United Against 187. In their mass appeals to voters, the group took the following positions: Proposition 187 was discriminatory and unfair. If passed, it would lead to rampant racial profiling. Citizens and legal immigrants who looked or sounded "foreign" would be "burdened with proving their immigration status," opponents explained. It would turn teachers, nurses, doctors, and police officers into immigration agents by requiring them to report anyone suspected of being undocumented. It would endanger public health in California and place $15 billion in federal funds in jeopardy. It would create an underclass of uneducated and impoverished residents. The "No on Proposition 187" campaign succeeded in mobilizing a broad cross-section of voters against the initiative; many of these activists would go on to propel the immigrant rights movement forward in later decades. But they faced considerable obstacles, including a lack of experience organizing against a ballot initiative, limited funding, and an established network of local and national supporters.[40]

Moreover, a growing number of bipartisan elected officials and public leaders complicitly chose xenophobia over policy proposals that addressed the root causes of undocumented immigration. They didn't argue that immigration was a crisis that threatened the United States or that undocumented immigrants were criminals; they simply said that Proposition 187 wasn't the solution to this crisis. By refusing to deny the xenophobic roots of the debate, they lent credibility to the very rationale that fueled

Proposition 187. It was a masterful deflection of blame, too, for the state's current budget woes.[41]

On November 8, 1994, more than five million Californians (59 percent of the electorate) voted for Proposition 187; it was approved. The day after the election, civil rights groups—backed by school boards, city councils, unions, and religious and medical groups—filed successful legal challenges before the California Superior Court and the US District Court to block its implementation. The US District Court ruled it unconstitutional on the basis that immigration regulation was a federal, and not a state, responsibility. The state (under new Democratic governor Gray Davis) dropped the appeal. Proposition 187's most controversial provision—the one denying undocumented immigrants access to government services—was never implemented.[42]

Barbara Coe, one of the founders of the California Coalition for Immigration Reform and architects of Proposition 187, continued her campaign to reduce all immigration and end undocumented immigration to the United States long after Proposition 187 failed to become law in 1994. In 2001, she (wearing a flag-patterned jacket) joined other activists in Century City, California, to protest a visit by Mexican president Vicente Fox, a proponent of looser border restrictions between the United States and Mexico. Scott Nelson/AFP/Getty Images.

Proposition 187 may have failed to become policy in California. But it succeeded in many other ways. First, it helped crystallize and legitimize xenophobia as a powerful tool in late-twentieth-century American politics—first in conservative circles, and then in the mainstream. Second, its core policy components made their way into federal welfare and immigration laws that would overhaul both immigration to and immigrant rights in the United States. These policies supported the creation of an expanded immigration enforcement machine that identified, arrested, detained, and deported growing numbers of immigrants.

In the years following Proposition 187's successful passage, some of the country's most prominent conservative intellectuals, writers, media commentators, and politicians refined and mainstreamed an "anti-illegal immigration" campaign that was part of a larger political strategy to mobilize voters, gain political power, and attack the left. Among the most prominent were Peter Brimelow, a senior editor at *Forbes* and the *National Review*; former presidential candidate Patrick Buchanan; and Harvard political scientist Samuel Huntington. All argued that immigration was just one of the many forces eroding the nation: a cult of multiculturalism and diversity that had gone too far; the rise of group identities based on race, ethnicity, and gender that threatened a unified national identity; and globalization that siphoned away jobs from Americans. They agreed that immigration—especially immigration from Mexico—was the largest and most dangerous threat. Like previous generations of xenophobes, these conservatives also relied on, and helped expand, a key distinction between "old" (and European) immigration and "new" (and non-European) immigration, a distinction rooted in white supremacist understandings of the United States and what it meant to be American. Conservatives continued to deploy the framework of "good" immigrants, who helped build America, and "bad" ones, who were destroying the United States and its values.

As a central aspect of conservative politics and culture, this new brand of color-blind xenophobia sold books, mobilized voters, and justified new policies. Brimelow's, Buchanan's, and Huntington's widely read articles and best-selling books not only made the case for immigration restriction and rigorous enforcement but also promoted a white supremacist and nativist ("America First") vision of the United States.

Peter Brimelow's *Alien Nation: Common Sense About America's Immigration Disaster* was one of the first post–Proposition 187 books to hit the national market in 1995. With its plainspoken, "tell-it-like-it-is" approach, the British-born writer's alarmist, anti-immigrant manifesto became a national best seller. Like other conservatives, Brimelow railed against affirmative action and multiculturalism. But he reserved his strongest condemnation for immigrants, especially Mexicans, whom he blamed for all of America's economic, social, and political crises. He elaborated on the traditional economic argument that Mexican immigrants strained the US economy by driving down wages and taxing the public welfare system. He audaciously claimed that they also endangered public health, degraded the environment, and threatened US national unity.

Brimelow went even further to advocate for a return to America prior to 1965. He argued that the new mass migrations from Asia, Latin America, and Africa had been "accidentally triggered" by the 1965 Immigration Act. Articulating a white nationalist and white supremacist notion of the United States, he argued that it was time to turn America back to its "specific ethnic core. . . . And that core has been white." In the past, he explained, immigrants had come overwhelmingly from Europe, which he defined as the "historic homeland of America." The new immigration from Latin America and Asia, he argued, was "so huge and so systematically different from anything that had gone before" that it constituted "de facto *discrimination against* Europe."

Brimelow effectively used his foreign-born status to affirm his own credibility on the subject of immigration. He modestly explained that he was the right type of immigrant: educated, self-sufficient, English-speaking, and assimilated. Mexicans were the least assimilable of all immigrant groups, he claimed, without any proof. They were "symptomatic of the American anti-idea" and formed an inassimilable mass, or "anti-nation" inside the United States. Brimelow's book called not only for an end to all undocumented immigration, but also for a drastic reduction in legal immigration and an end to all payments and public education for all undocumented immigrants and their children as well.[43]

Patrick Buchanan lost his bid for the Republican nomination for the presidency in 1992 to President George H. W. Bush. But he would go on to refine and spread his "America First" message in a series of books that predicted the end of America and of the world: *The Death of the West: How Dying Populations and Immigrant Invasions Imperil Our Country and Civilization* (2001), *State of Emergency: The Third World Invasion and Conquest of America* (2006), and *Suicide of a Superpower: Will America Survive to 2025?* (2011). Buchanan promoted an alarmist vision of America being overrun by dangerous immigrants and declared that immigration was "the greatest invasion in history." If it continued "unresisted," he hysterically warned, the United States would fall. "We are entering upon the final act of our civilization," he declared ominously.[44]

Like Brimelow, Buchanan made it clear that not all immigration was contributing to the collapse of America. To him, "all the races of Europe" had proven themselves to be worthy American citizens; the problem was the "immigration tsunami" coming "from all the races of Asia, Africa, and Latin America." They were not assimilating, not "melting and reforming," he claimed. Buchanan singled out Mexicans for being particularly different and dangerous. They had "no allegiance to America" and were "not part of our family," he argued.[45]

Moreover, Buchanan asserted, immigration was just the tip of the iceberg of a much bigger problem: white displacement. Repeating early-twentieth-century xenophobes' claims that white Americans were committing "race suicide," Buchanan argued that Mexican immigrant women (and other minorities) were having too many children, while white American women were having too few. The "assault" was already under way in cities like Miami, Houston, Los Angeles, San Francisco, and Washington, DC, where whites were either already a minority or quickly becoming one. By 2050, Americans of European descent would be "a minority in the nation their ancestors created and built," he ominously predicted, something the country would not survive.[46]

Harvard political scientist Samuel Huntington gave Ivy League credibility to American xenophobia in the late twentieth and early twenty-first centuries. Beginning in the 1990s, Huntington began developing a new paradigm to understand global politics in the post–Cold War era.

Instead of conflicts between superpowers, he suggested, the world was now facing conflicts based on "civilizations" and cultural and religious divisions. He first laid out his provocative thesis in a 1993 article in *Foreign Affairs* and then expanded it in his 1996 book *The Clash of Civilizations and the Remaking of World Order*. Using *culture* in the same ways that early-twentieth-century race thinkers used *race* to separate and categorize humanity, Huntington argued that human beings were divided along cultural lines. Each major "civilization" ("Western," "Islamic," "Sinic" [Chinese], "African," "Latin American," etc.) was presented as fixed, uniform, and bound to clash with dissimilar cultures. In 1993, Huntington warned of a "clash of civilizations" in the United States resulting from what he called "the Hispanic Challenge." The "persistent inflow" of Hispanic immigrants threatened to divide the United States into two peoples, two cultures, and two languages, he argued. The United States ignored this challenge at its peril.[47]

As with Brimelow and Buchanan, Huntington's understanding of American history and identity was also based on white supremacist notions that the United States was a white nation whose creation and greatness stemmed from Europe. Huntington explained that America's creed, rule of law, and cherished ideals had all been the work of "17th- and 18th-century settlers who were overwhelmingly white, British, and Protestant." Huntington lumped all later generations of European immigrants into that great tradition.[48]

But Mexican immigration was different. In 1990, Mexicans accounted for 25 percent of total legal immigration, he reported, and although he conceded that these percentages did not match the even higher rates of Irish immigrants arriving between 1820 and 1840 or of German immigrants arriving in the 1850s and 1860s, Mexican immigration was not just a numbers problem, he explained. It was also a problem of persistence. Mexico, "a poor, contiguous country," had a never-ending supply of prospective immigrants that if left unchecked would completely overrun the United States. Moreover, unlike other immigrant groups, Mexicans and Mexican Americans, Huntington claimed, used immigration as a way of asserting "special rights" in the United States because most of the Southwest had at one time belonged to Mexico. Immigration, Huntington implied, was Mexico's revenge on the United States.[49]

Because he identified Mexican immigration and Mexican Americans as the source of nearly all problems plaguing modern America, Huntington recommended ending all Mexican immigration. Imagine, he instructed his readers, "what would happen if Mexican immigration abruptly stopped." The wages of low-income US citizen workers would rise. Divisive debates over bilingual education and welfare "would virtually disappear." And most important of all, he claimed, the country's "cultural and political integrity" would be preserved.[50]

Huntington's, Buchanan's, and Brimelow's books were highly influential, popular, and profitable, and along with the Proposition 187 campaign in California, they showed how xenophobia could unite various factions of conservatives—fiscal conservatives concerned about economic issues, and cultural conservatives concerned about demographic change and the loss of "traditional" (white) America. Xenophobia also brought in cold, hard cash. Foundations with a history of financing right-wing organizations like the Colcom, Scaife, and Weeden Foundations, were instrumental in supporting the work of major anti-immigrant groups like FAIR, which by the 1990s had become one of the most effective organizations lobbying for a reduction in all immigration. Often using racist and white supremacist arguments that the United States needed to maintain its "European-American majority" in order to preserve American culture, FAIR established a network of xenophobic organizations like the Center for Immigration Studies and NumbersUSA that helped it expand its national influence.[51]

And in the 1990s, xenophobia fostered the rise of conservative politics by mobilizing voters and electing lawmakers. The Republican Party benefited the most. For years, the party had attracted white voters by appealing to white racial anxieties over growing African American political power. Politicians and political operatives intentionally downplayed the existence of institutionalized discrimination, neutralized and eventually rolled back the equal rights protections gained in the civil rights movement, and stoked racial fears about emboldened African Americans. This

"Southern Strategy" successfully drew white voters away from the Democratic Party in the South and toward the Republican Party. It also worked in other parts of the country around the issue of immigration. Just as "law and order" were code words for the assertion of (white) control and force over African Americans, so did the "war on illegal immigration" mask a larger campaign to control, check, and reduce the numbers and power of immigrants from Latin America.[52]

By 1994, PUBLIC opinion polls reported that two-thirds of Americans agreed with the statement that "immigrants today are a burden on our country because they take our jobs, housing and health care." In contrast, only a third agreed with the contrasting statement that "immigrants today strengthen our country because of their hard work and talents." The idea that an "immigration crisis" threatened the United States and required radical action by the federal government was a popular position promoted by public officials across the political spectrum and around the country.[53] The "crisis" had three main components. The first framed undocumented immigrants as violent criminals who needed to be deported. The second was that immigrants were undeserving or less deserving than citizens and should be denied social services. The last was that the "crisis" could only be solved by militarizing the US-Mexico border. All built directly on the Proposition 187 campaign.

These positions on immigration would be turned into federal policy under President Bill Clinton. Known as the "first black president," Clinton, a Democrat, celebrated America's multicultural society and sought to bridge the racial divide separating whites and blacks. But on immigration, he helped legitimize the demonization of undocumented immigrants. Soon after the 1994 elections, Clinton called on Congress to form a new task force on immigration. Chaired by Republican Elton Gallegly of California, the group recommended adopting many of Proposition 187's goals at the federal level. The proposal received support from both Republicans and Democrats, and Congress soon followed with specific legislation.

In 1996, Clinton signed the Antiterrorism and Effective Death Penalty Act (AEDPA) and the Illegal Immigration Reform and Immigrant Responsibility Act (IIRIRA) as part of his "tough on crime" initiatives. These laws fundamentally changed the rights of all immigrants—both undocumented and legal permanent residents—in the United States. The IIRIRA barred undocumented immigrants from receiving most public health services and benefits, including federally sponsored loans, contracts, business licenses, retirement, welfare, health, disability, food assistance, and unemployment benefits. The law also required states to deny the same benefits unless they passed legislation specifically allowing undocumented immigrants to receive them. In one case, the law went further than Proposition 187 and prohibited legal immigrants from receiving Supplemental Security Income and food stamps until they became citizens. Some benefits were later restored to at-risk populations, like the elderly.[54]

Beginning with Clinton, the US government also increased the list of offenses that triggered deportation for all immigrants, regardless of legal status. AEDPA expanded the category of people designated as "criminal aliens" by making both violent crimes and nonviolent offenses punishable by deportation. The IIRIRA further expanded the list of offenses. This meant that immigrants could be detained and deported for even minor crimes and everyday legal infractions, such as drunk driving, failing to appear in court, filing a false tax return, passing bad checks, shoplifting, minor drug possession, and traffic violations. At the same time, violations of immigration law began to be punished through the criminal justice system more frequently. And federal programs that coordinated with state and local law enforcement officials expanded the government's ability to prosecute immigrants for both criminal acts and immigration violations.

The result has been what many have called *crimmigration*, the merging of criminal and immigration law. Immigrants, both undocumented and lawfully present, became subjected to a double standard that allowed the US government to inflict a far greater punishment (deportation) than the crime (traffic offenses, for example) merited and treated noncitizens far more harshly than citizens. By the first decade of the twenty-first century, immigration-related offenses constituted the largest share of prosecuted federal crimes in the United States. Over 60 percent of all deportations from the United States were triggered by criminal convictions, most of which were minor offenses like traffic violations, nonviolent drug crimes, and immigration violations.[55]

As US immigration laws created more and more "criminal aliens," the country also expanded the immigration enforcement dragnet to identify, arrest, detain, and deport growing numbers of immigrants. Beginning in 1996 and continuing over many years, the groundwork was laid for the creation of what critics have called a detention and "deportation regime" that accompanied the growth of mass incarceration in the United States in general. By the time George W. Bush became president in 2001, the federal government had increased funding for detention facilities and ramped up arrests and deportations of immigrants already in the United States.[56]

In the wake of the terrorist attacks of September 11, 2001, the US government's ability to keep track of, arrest, detain, and deport immigrants grew exponentially. Congress established the Department of Homeland Security (DHS) and folded what had been the INS, under the Justice Department, and the US Customs Service, part of the Treasury Department, into three new agencies that enjoyed increased powers and funding: Immigration and Customs Enforcement (ICE), US Citizenship and Immigration Services, and US Customs and Border Protection. In addition, the Bush administration's counterterrorism efforts (which included mandatory registration of certain groups, centralized data sharing capabilities, and increased capacity of local law enforcement officers to enforce federal immigration laws) netted more deportable aliens than ever before. In particular, the Criminal Alien Program and its "jail status check" programs deported growing numbers of immigrants, many of whom were never convicted of crimes. Formal deportations increased accordingly. From 1975 to 1995, there were an average 29,000 removals per year. In 2000, the United States formally deported 188,000 individuals. In 2012, that figure was 410,000. To put these figures in historical perspective, the number of people formally deported from the United States in the first decade of the twenty-first century was greater than the total number removed in the last 110 years. As in the past, formal deportation (and the criminalization of immigration) had a disparate impact on certain immigrant communities. By 2013, black and Hispanic immigrants, mostly men, from Latin America, made up 92 percent of all immigrants imprisoned for unlawful entry and reentry, causing some experts to label current deportation practices a "gendered racial removal program."[57]

The Proposition 187 campaign also helped fuel an increase in border policing and security that had long-lasting consequences. On July 27, 1993, President Clinton announced new border enforcement initiatives. The timing was important. Not only was California's Proposition 187 pushing him to act, but also the landing of the *Golden Venture*, a ship carrying 286 unauthorized immigrants from China onto a beach in Queens, New York, raised new public concerns about unprotected borders. Clinton stressed that legal immigration was a hallmark of US policy. But he added: "We must not, and we will not, surrender our borders to those who wish to exploit our history of compassion and justice. . . . We will make it tougher for illegal aliens to get into our country."[58]

On October 1, 1994—one month before California's vote on Proposition 187—Clinton's Operation Gatekeeper was launched. It followed the successful implementation of Operation Hold the Line in El Paso (originally named Operation Blockade) and used an enhanced border enforcement strategy designed to deter unauthorized immigration (rather than apprehend migrants after crossing). Operation Gatekeeper deployed increased numbers of Border Patrol agents and expanded the use of surveillance technologies. Other Border Patrol initiatives with military code names followed. Operation Rio Grande was based in Brownsville, Texas, and Operation Safeguard was established in Nogales, Arizona. From 1993 to 1997, the US Congress increased funding for enforcement efforts along the southwest US-Mexico border from $400 million to $800 million. The number of Border Patrol agents increased from 4,200 in 1994 to 9,212 in 2000.[59]

Far from deterring the entry of undocumented immigrants, these operations encouraged migrants to rely more heavily on smugglers who mercilessly exploited them and diverted migration to remote and deadly deserts and mountains. Twenty-three migrants died in 1995 in the San Diego and El Centro region trying to cross into the United States. The next year, 61 died. Eighty-nine migrants died in 1997 trying to cross the border, and the next year, 145 did. On March 22, 2000, the total death toll following Operation Gatekeeper reached the 500 mark.[60]

George W. Bush, Clinton's successor, ran as a "compassionate conservative" who embraced multiculturalism and understood the importance of the Latinx vote. He deliberately positioned himself as the ideological opponent to California governor Pete Wilson on immigration. Instead of running political ads that warned of an invasion from Mexico, Bush often spoke of America's ability to achieve racial harmony by showing mutual respect for each other. In a speech in Miami during the 2000 presidential campaign, Bush shared his vision of America, one that had "many accents" but "one national creed." He identified the fact that the United States was "now one of the largest Spanish-speaking nations in the world" and a "major source of Latin music, journalism, and culture" as positive symbols of a "New America." He ended up winning the support of many Latinx voters in 2000 and helped push the Republican Party toward outreach to Latinx communities. During his presidency, Bush made comprehensive immigration reform, including a pathway to citizenship for undocumented immigrants, a top domestic agenda priority.[61]

But the Bush administration also increased the use of detention as a primary method of immigration enforcement. Beginning in 2005, it launched Operation Streamline with the goal of apprehending people crossing the border and targeting them for detention and prosecution in order to deter undocumented border crossings. Additionally, the president increased investment in the Border Patrol and deployed six thousand National Guard troops to help with the effort.[62]

By the time President Barack Obama took the oath of office, he inherited what researchers at the Migration Policy Institute described as "a more legally robust and better-resourced immigration enforcement regime" than his predecessors had. The president abandoned some Bush-era immigration enforcement programs, but he retained many and even expanded others. Despite his administration's commitment to civil rights and his personal conviction that the United States had the ability to fully realize its potential as a nation of real equality, President Obama's record on immigration proved to be decidedly mixed. He began by relying on a carrot-and-stick approach to immigration reform. On the one hand he approved minor reforms to the immigration enforcement system and promised a comprehensive immigration reform bill. He moved away from aggressive worksite raids and replaced them with an online worker identification verification system. The Obama administration also stated that it would focus on deporting "high priority" migrants who were a threat to public safety or national security. And the Department of Justice brought charges against Arizona's Maricopa County sheriff Joseph Arpaio for violating the civil rights of Latinx groups.[63]

But at the same time, President Obama continued to increase immigration enforcement funding. During his tenure, spending increased to $18 billion in 2012, which was 24 percent higher than the funding allocated to all other principal federal criminal law enforcement agencies combined. The US government completed 651 miles of the 700-mile border fence approved by Congress and the 2006 Secure Fence Act signed by his predecessor, President George W. Bush. Immigrant detention expanded and was supported by a 2009 law mandating that 33,400 beds be filled per day in detention centers. By 2016, the United States was detaining 360,000 people a year in a system of over two hundred immigration jails across the country. The total detention budget for 2017 was a staggering $2.6 billion.[64]

Deportations also increased dramatically during the eight-year Obama administration. A total of 5,370,849 individuals were apprehended, 5,281,115 individuals were deported, and another 3,307,017 were apprehended at the US-Mexico border. In 2012, the DHS removed a record high of 419,000 people—ten times the number of people deported in 1991 and higher than the number of people deported during the entire decade of the 1980s. The president was famously labeled "Deporter-in-Chief" by critics, including the National Council of La Raza, the nation's largest Latinx advocacy organization. Like his predecessor, Obama did try to push comprehensive immigration reform through Congress, and when that failed, he announced a series of executive actions that granted temporary reprieve to millions of "Dreamers," immigrants who entered the United States without documentation when they were children, from deportation. The Deferred Action for Childhood Arrivals (DACA) eventually allowed approximately eight hundred thousand immigrants to temporarily stay in the United States and work.[65]

As a backlash to some of these measures, many conservative-led states responded with punitive immigration policies of their own, including a number of Proposition 187–like laws. In 2010, for example, Arizona's Support Our Law Enforcement and Safe Neighborhoods Act (also known as SB1070) surpassed all previous state immigration-control efforts by making it a crime to be an undocumented immigrant in the state and requiring police to determine the immigration status of people they stopped for other offenses if there was "reasonable suspicion" they were undocumented. Although the US Supreme Court eventually ruled that many of the law's provisions were unconstitutional, it did allow police to determine the immigration status of someone arrested or detained, a provision that became known as "show me your papers." Arizona's law also inspired copycat legislation in states across the country.[66]

BY THE TIME Donald Trump was running for president in 2015, the idea that Mexican immigration constituted an invasion of criminals who threatened the country had been well established and even normalized. "When Mexico sends its people, they're not sending their best," Trump declared when he announced his candidacy for the presidency in 2015. "They're sending people that have lots of problems, and they're bringing those problems with us," he continued. "They're bringing drugs. They're bringing crime. They're rapists. And some, I assume are good people." Throughout his campaign, he repeatedly characterized immigration as a cost, a burden, and a danger to the United States and its citizens. He promised to enact "immigration reform that will make America great again" by building a wall along the entirety of the US-Mexico border and deporting millions.

Many Americans expressed outrage at these explicitly racist and xenophobic positions. But in fact, Trump was just repeating a message that had been gaining traction for decades. Once popular only in the margins of the far right, the "war on illegal immigration" begun in the 1990s had steadily progressed to the center of American politics by the early twenty-first century. Trump effectively used xenophobia to rally disaffected voters to his unlikely campaign. According to Trump, immigrants—understood to be nonwhites who were growing in number and displacing white citizens—were the main cause of America's social, economic, and political problems.[67]

What was so curious about Trump's view of Mexican immigration was how outdated it was. Mexican immigration had indeed increased during the late twentieth century. But it was no invasion. In 2000, foreign-born Mexicans accounted for only 3 percent of the total US population. The total Hispanic population in the United States remained a relatively small proportion (13 percent). In fact, by the time Trump was calling for a border wall to stop undocumented immigration, net migration from Mexico was *below zero*, meaning that more immigrants were returning to Mexico than were heading to the United States. Moreover, undocumented entries across the border had plummeted to historic lows, and the undocumented population in the United States had declined to its lowest number since 2003, to 10.8 million.[68]

The necessity of building Trump's promised "great, great wall" on the southern border to prevent illegal drugs from entering the country was also heavily scrutinized. Data from US Customs and Border Protection showed that most drug smuggling occurred at legal ports of entry rather than in remote areas where a wall might be built. A wall would have little impact on this problem. But it would have many costs, experts argued. Stemming the migration of workers would limit US productivity and stunt contributions to the social security system, on which a growing number of aging Americans depended. Worsening relations with Mexico (the United States' third largest trade partner and the third largest supplier of US imports) would impact trade and investment. The wall would cut through the tribal homelands of indigenous nations and communities in the United States and Mexico, separating them from relatives and sacred sites on both sides of the border. And it would also erode binational environmental protections and cooperation to protect more than a hundred endangered or threatened species as well as the rich but fragile biodiversity in the borderlands.[69]

Trump blamed Mexico for "sending its people," but in fact, it had long been true that migration from Mexico to the United States was overwhelmingly shaped by US-backed policies like the North American Free Trade Agreement (NAFTA). Passed in 1994, NAFTA opened the Mexican and Canadian borders to the free flow of goods and capital. However, it had no provisions for the movement of labor, and in fact, proponents had predicted that the agreement would create economic opportunities in Mexico and reduce the pressure to emigrate. The opposite proved to be true. American agricultural companies flooded Mexican markets with corn and other grains. Unable to compete with US corporations, two million Mexican farmers and farmworkers were forced out of agriculture. They migrated first to large cities in Mexico, and then to the United States in search of economic survival. While some Mexicans became part of the growing workforce employed at *maquiladoras*, the multinational manufacturing plants along the US-Mexico border, others continued to migrate northward to employers and family members waiting for them in the United States.[70]

Trump's constant reference to Mexican immigrants as "they" also belied how much a part of "we" they had become. Mexican-born adults, and especially their US-born children, adopted English "at a very rapid pace." According to the 2000 census, less than 10 percent of the Hispanic population lived in households where no English was spoken; in households with children, it was just 2 percent. Longitudinal studies indicated that most Mexican-born people preferred English over Spanish, as did 96 percent of US-born Mexican Americans. Other research pointed to the positive impact that fluent bilingualism had on both academic achievement and intellectual development, as well as the positive impact that immigrant networks (as opposed to rapid cultural assimilation) had on integrating immigrants. And Trump's repeated claim that immigrants were lawbreakers committing serious crimes was also not supported by any facts. Empirical studies routinely found that immigrants did not increase local crime rates and were in fact less likely to cause crime than people born in the United States.[71]

Despite the many flaws, inaccuracies, and explicit racism in Trump's worldview of immigrants and immigration, Trump's xenophobic rhetoric and proposals were extremely popular among voters and became a centerpiece of his campaign. In addition to building the border wall, his official platform promised to order the mass deportation of undocumented immigrants, including all "criminal aliens," and establish a "deportation task force." Die-hard Trump supporters had no problem with Trump's explicit racism and xenophobia. They also understood his popular slogan to "make America great again" to be a coded message about race: a call to take America back to a time before so many dark-skinned foreigners had arrived (and before African Americans, women, and members of the LGBTQ community had gained so much power and influence). Pre-election surveys with registered Trump supporters overwhelmingly cited immigration as a "very big problem." They steadfastly supported Trump's xenophobic vision of America, telling pollsters that they often felt like "stranger[s] in their own land" and believed that the United States needed "protecting against foreign influence." More than six in ten believed that the growing number of newcomers from other countries threatened American culture. They also had acute economic anxiety. Despite strong economic growth and a low unemployment rate in 2016, most of these voters believed that the economy was stacked against them and favored the wealthy. Instead of supporting radical changes to America's unequal capitalist system, however, they favored fewer immigrants.[72]

Once in office, Trump turned his campaign promises into federal policy by issuing major executive orders on immigration. Signed on January 25, 2017, Executive Order 13767 ("Border Security and Immigration Enforcement Improvements") called for the construction of a multibillion-dollar border wall and additional detention facilities along the 1,900-mile US-Mexico border. It also mandated the hiring of five thousand additional Border Patrol agents. On the same day, the president signed Executive Order 13768 designed to "ensure the public safety of the American people . . . as well as to ensure that our Nation's immigration laws are faithfully executed." This order overturned many Obama-era immigration policies and entailed a massive expansion of interior immigration enforcement that prioritized all unauthorized immigrants

Supporters of US president Donald Trump gathered at a rally during his visit to see border wall prototypes on March 13, 2018, in San Diego, California. Their signs calling for the United States to "Deport All Illegals," "Build the Wall, Nice and Tall," and "Assimilate, Assimilate, Assimilate" repeated the xenophobic arguments that conservative politicians had been making for decades and that Trump had expertly marshaled to secure votes. Photo by David McNew/ Getty Images.

for removal, including longtime residents, families, and Dreamers. It allowed for the hiring of ten thousand more ICE agents and increased the use of state and local police to enforce immigration laws. It reinstated the controversial Secure Communities program, which required local law enforcement to share fingerprints of all those taken into custody with the DHS and created a new office for victims of violent crimes. And it pressured foreign countries to accept their deported nationals back into the country.[73]

That same week, the president signed another executive order that he claimed was necessary to protect America from another foreign threat, the threat of "foreign terrorists." The fulfillment of another one of Trump's xenophobic campaign pledges to implement a "complete and total shutdown" of Muslims to the United States, this order came to be known as the Muslim ban.

• NINE •

ISLAMOPHOBIA

On January 20, 2017, Hameed Khalid Darweesh was granted a special immigrant visa to come to the United States. An Iraqi citizen and electrical engineer, Darweesh had worked for the US military and government as an interpreter, engineer, and contractor for ten years beginning in 2003. He helped the American forces protect Iraqis from al-Qaeda terrorists; provide water and electricity; train local police; and rebuild roads, bridges, schools, and hospitals. It was work that Darweesh was proud to do. But it was also work that placed him at constant risk of being targeted by anti-American militias and insurgents. In 2005, two of his Iraqi colleagues were tracked down and killed in Baghdad. Darweesh was ambushed but he escaped. From that day, he lived in constant fear. After his attackers tracked him down again, Darweesh, his wife, and his three children fled Baghdad and relocated to the city of Kirkuk.

They were safe for a year and a half before they were found again. Once more, Darweesh and his family packed up their belongings and fled to Erbil in another region of the country. But they knew that they would never be safe in Iraq; they would have to seek refuge in the United States. With the help of the International Refugee Assistance Project, Darweesh applied for a special immigrant visa for people who worked with the US Armed Forces in Iraq or Afghanistan. It took three years, but the visas were finally granted to Darweesh and his family on January 20, 2017.

Halfway across the world on the same day, Donald Trump was taking the oath of office to become the forty-fifth president of the United States.[1]

Trump's xenophobia and his worldview that immigration—seemingly all immigration—threatened the United States had propelled him to the White House. Alongside his demonization of Mexican immigrants as rapists and criminals and his campaign pledge to build a wall along the entirety of the US-Mexico border was a powerful Islamophobia that functioned as a companion to the fear of "illegal" immigration. In October 2015, he used panic about the millions of refugees seeking entry into Europe to justify his anti-Muslim rhetoric and characterized Syrian refugees as members of ISIS. He claimed that letting any into the United States could be "the greatest Trojan horse." The next month he falsely proclaimed that "thousands of Muslims" in New Jersey had been "cheering as the World Trade Center came down" on September 11, 2001. Just days after a Muslim American couple carried out a deadly shooting attack in San Bernardino, California, Trump called for a "complete and total shutdown of Muslims entering the United States" on December 7, 2015.[2] Trump's proposal drew strong condemnation from not only immigrants, Muslim Americans, civil rights groups, and Democrats, but also from corporate America and other Republicans. Even Indiana governor Mike Pence, who would later become Trump's running mate and vice president, called the ban "unconstitutional" on Twitter when it was first announced.[3]

Trump's anti-Muslim sentiment drew from both the long history of xenophobia in the United States and a new political climate that allowed Islamophobia to flourish. Part of the new immigration transforming the United States after 1965, recent Arab and Muslim immigrants and refugees became targets of the growing backlash to immigration in the twentieth century. But they were also identified as national security threats as well, and America's ongoing war on terror following the terrorist attacks of September 11, 2001, were used to justify rising levels of violence, surveillance, and discrimination aimed at Muslims everywhere, similar to the treatment of Japanese Americans during World War II. Going to war "over there" after 9/11 and excluding and tracking immigrants "over here" worked in tandem to justify continued US intervention overseas and an expanded immigration enforcement regime at home. Cloaked in the language of national security, increased levels of Islamophobic hate-mongering became a standard form of religious bigotry and racism in America. First promoted by a fringe network of individuals allied with extreme conservative and religious right organizations after 9/11, Islam-ophobia eventually became part of the Republican Party and then main-stream media discourse. All of these factors conspired to make Trump's election possible.[4]

Once in office, Trump made good on his promise to ban Muslims. At the end of his first full week in office, he traveled to the Pentagon on Friday, January 27, 2017, to sign Executive Order 13769, "Protecting the Nation from Foreign Terrorist Entry into the United States." As he signed the order, the president announced that it would keep "radical Is-lamic terrorists out of the United States of America." The order, which took effect immediately, prohibited the entry of all aliens from Iran, Iraq, Libya, Sudan, Somalia, Syria, and Yemen for ninety days on the grounds that such entries were "detrimental to the interests of the United States." It suspended the Refugee Admissions Program for 120 days and imposed an indefinite ban on Syrian refugees. It also stated that no more than 50,000 refugees were to be admitted in 2017—a significant decrease from the 110,000 that President Obama had set for the year before—and that preference would be given to refugee claims based on "religious-based persecution, provided that the religion of the individual is a minority re-ligion" in the country.[5]

As chaos swirled around the news of the order, Hameed Khalid Dar-weesh, his wife, and his three children arrived in the United States at John F. Kennedy International Airport that evening at 5:45 p.m. The family waited for an hour to be processed by US Customs and Border Protection. Then Darweesh was moved into "secondary screening." He would ultimately be handcuffed and held in detention for eighteen hours, along with at least ten others, and was denied all requests to speak to his attorney.

Darweesh was crushed. "Over the course of those 18 hours, I had grown more and more disappointed," he later wrote. "They let me down by treating me as a criminal and putting handcuffs on me. . . . This was not the America I knew." Outside the airport, thousands of supporters were spontaneously gathering to protest the order. Darweesh's legal team rushed to file a lawsuit challenging the ban, and he was finally let go. As his lawyers escorted him from the airport, a crowd rushed in to celebrate the temporary legal victory and to welcome the family into the United States. For Darweesh, the moment was a vindication that his faith in the United States had not been misplaced after all. "I felt the greatness of America. Yes, this is the United States of America—this is the America I knew from my work in Iraq."[6] Darweesh's journey to the United States had concluded, but the legal challenges to what many called the Muslim ban would continue well into the next year. The Trump immigration era had begun.

ALONG WITH TWO other executive orders passed the same week to initiate the building of the border wall and increase deportations, the president's Muslim ban represented an unprecedented transformation of US immigration policy. During the first hundred days of his presidency, Trump signed another immigration-related executive order promoting a "buy American and hire American" proposal that tightened the rules that awarded visas to skilled foreign workers. He also endorsed the RAISE Act proposing dramatic cuts to legal permanent immigration and ended temporary protected status for 50,000 Haitians and 250,000 Salvadorans.[7]

Together, these orders and proposed legislation aimed to transform nearly every aspect of immigration to the United States from refugee resettlement to deportation. The changes were even more dramatic given that most were put into effect by executive action without congressional debate and approval. Previous administrations, from Ronald Reagan to Barack Obama, had adopted a more balanced approach to immigration by arresting and deporting undocumented immigrants and tightening border security at the same time that they maintained and increased certain aspects of legal and refugee migration. Trump's worldview on immigration was different. He was against not only undocumented immigration but *all* immigration.[8]

In many ways, Trump's xenophobia was both extreme and normal. In fact, the Trump administration's immigration policies were a logical evolution of America's xenophobic tradition. Beginning in the 1990s, American xenophobia, fueled by the "war on illegal immigration," had created a well-funded and highly resourced immigration enforcement regime that was supported and expanded by politicians in both major parties. Once xenophobia proved to be a viable political issue that mobilized voters and elected politicians, it remained a central aspect of American politics and media coverage. Presidents Bill Clinton, George W. Bush, and Barack Obama all built walls and fortified the US-Mexico border. They increased both the number of Border Patrol agents stationed along the southern border and the number of immigrants deported from the United States.

These federal policies did not always match the reality of changing immigration patterns on the ground. Long after undocumented immigration had stabilized and even dropped, for example, politicians and special interests continued to use xenophobia to mobilize voters, pass more anti-immigrant laws, and support a growing business of for-profit detention facilities. Each presidential administration was pressured into and willingly participated in expanding the government's immigration enforcement regime. By the end of the twentieth century, the idea that undocumented immigrants (and all Latinx people) constituted a clear and present danger to the nation was pervasive. Neither major political party challenged the increasingly alarmist and racist rhetoric; instead, many came to accept it as a truism. By the end of the twentieth century, the United States was well on its way to creating the largest "deportation machine" in American history.[9] Then, on September 11, 2001, terrorists attacked the United States, and Muslims became the latest targets of American xenophobia.

ON MARCH 9, 2016, Donald Trump sat down with CNN's Anderson Cooper and boldly stated, "I think Islam hates us." These remarks were

both extraordinary and mundane. On the one hand, he made no distinction between the entire religion of Islam (and the millions who practice it) and radical Islamic terrorism. The next day, Trump spokeswoman
Katrina Pierson had to clarify her boss's statement and told journalist
Wolf Blitzer that Trump should have referred to "radical Islamic extremists" rather than the blanket statement referring to all Muslims. On
the other hand, Trump was only articulating a sentiment and belief that
had become increasingly popular within the Republican Party and the
mainstream media. In 2015, a study reviewing 179 opinion polls over a
twenty-two-year period found that Islam was unfamiliar to most Americans and "unfavorable" to many. Americans also tended to see Islam as
"more violent" than other religions, and since 2001, one-quarter or more
of the population expressed support for specific measures that singled out
Muslims for special treatment like religious profiling, special IDs, surveillance, and internment.[10]

What these survey responses reflected was not only an increased
awareness to terrorism in the United States and around the world since
9/11, but also a barrage of media, popular culture references, and political
rhetoric that depicted Islam and Muslims in highly negative ways. The
Islamic faith was at odds with America and American institutions; Islam
was a violent religion and all Muslims identified with terrorism; Islam
oppressed women and forced them into subservient roles; Muslims in the
United States were a "new" and "foreign" population who were resistant
to assimilation; American Muslims were either radical terrorists themselves or complicit in shielding and protecting terrorists—all of these
messages were disseminated in the media and became persistent tropes
in American popular culture. In all cases, the underlying presumption
was that something about Islam and the people who practiced it made it
inherently dangerous.[11]

As a result, Islamophobia—an irrational hate and fear of Islam and
of Muslims that threatens eight million Muslim Americans today—
expanded in the years since 9/11. But Islamophobia also has a long history
in the United States that intersects with xenophobia. American Islamophobia is not only about religious intolerance; it is also a form of racism

that ascribes certain characteristics, tendencies, and beliefs to all Muslims and Muslim-appearing people. As a result, Islamophobia has led to hate-based violence, discriminatory government policies, and the de-Americanization of Arab and Muslim Americans in the United States.[12]

The West's denigration of Islam dates as far back as the Middle Ages and the Christian Crusades—a series of bloody, violent, and ruthless religious wars started by Pope Urban II to recapture the Holy Land from Muslim control and distract from the problems of the Church. The Crusades promoted religious intolerance and violence, resulting in the widespread massacre of Muslims, Jews, and other non-Christians; the lumping together of diverse peoples from the Arabian Peninsula; and categorizing them as inferior. It also helped establish a worldview in which Christianity and Islam, Christians and Muslims, and Europeans and "Saracens" were viewed as natural enemies, with Muslims being portrayed as dark and evil "others." This early form of racialization continued through the era of European colonization of the region, and the label *Saracen* gave way to *Arab, Moor, Muslim, Turk*, and *Oriental* to connote difference and inferiority. In the nineteenth century, the Middle East was exoticized as a region of fantastic riches and barbarism that was ruled by cruel despots with harems.[13]

Once they began migrating to the United States in sizable numbers during the nineteenth century, people from North Africa and Southwest Asia (i.e., the Middle East) continued to be lumped together as a racially distinct population. People who were identified as Middle Eastern, Arab, or Muslim based on appearance (dark skin, dark hair, mode of dress, use of Arabic, and type of name) were lumped together as a racial group that was considered inherently inferior, threatening, foreign, and violent.[14]

Contemporary Arab and Muslim migration to the United States has also been portrayed as a new phenomenon distinct from America's history of immigration. This emphasis on *foreignness* has been a powerful factor shaping contemporary Islamophobia and has helped connect the denigration of Muslims to other forms of xenophobia. In fact, people from the Middle East and others who are Muslim have been coming to the United States for centuries, even before the United States was a nation.

An estimated 10 to 15 percent of all enslaved Africans who were brought to the colonies and then, after the American Revolution, to the United States were Muslims. Some fought in the Civil War. Others, such as South Asian Muslims, migrated to the United States as part of the global mass migrations of the early twentieth century and worked as farmers, factory workers, and peddlers throughout the country.[15]

Between 1820 and 1924, an estimated 95,000 immigrants came from Greater Syria (present-day Syria, Lebanon, Jordan, and Palestine/Israel), with smaller numbers coming from Yemen, Iraq, Morocco, and Egypt. Most came from rural areas, were Christian, and had little formal education. Although men initially dominated the migration, eventually women came in equal and slightly larger numbers. Between 1965 and 2000, more than 630,000 Arabs immigrated to the United States. They mostly came through family reunification preferences, and some (particularly Egyptians) came on professional visas. Beginning in the 1990s, Iraqis, Somalis, and Sudanese started coming as refugees.[16]

An estimated six to seven million Americans now declare Islam as their faith. Despite false claims by Islamophobes that Muslims are another immigrant invasion from the Middle East, American Muslims are among the most racially diverse religious group in the United States, with African Americans making up the largest contingent of the population (35 percent). They are also at maximum only 2 percent of the US population (out of 321 million according to the US census in 2015); their small size underscores the irrationality and symbolic nature of Islamophobic rhetoric and politics.[17]

Just as Arab and Muslim Americans have a long history in the United States, so too does Islamophobia. Since the late nineteenth century, Islam has been perceived as an alien, threatening, and anti-Christian religion. This shaped numerous federal immigration policies. As early as 1891, the Supreme Court portrayed Islam as a threatening ideology and identified the "intense hostility of the people of Moslem faith to all other sects, and particularly to Christians." Beginning in 1910, Muslims were targeted for immigration exclusion. Islam, particularly the practice of polygamy, was considered incompatible with American values—and US immigration officials considered all Muslims potential or probable poly-gamists. Thus, the US Bureau of Immigration determined that simply adhering to the tenets of Islam served as sufficient grounds to deny ad-mission, a policy reflected in the exclusion of forty-three Muslims from the Ottoman Empire in 1910. Concerns over Muslim polygamy this same year also led to efforts to exclude, expel, or deport Muslims from the United States.[18]

In 1917, millions of Muslims and others who lived in what Congress called the Asiatic Barred Zone were prohibited from entering the United States as part of one of the most sweeping immigration laws passed in US history. The 1917 Immigration Act barred a number of "undesirable" immigrants, but the real targets were South Asians, including Sikhs and Muslims. The law prohibited immigrants from almost the entire Asian continent from entering the United States—an estimated population of five hundred million people, many of them Muslim, from modern-day India, Pakistan, Afghanistan, Iran, Saudi Arabia, and Indonesia.[19]

The next year, immigrants from the Ottoman Empire (about 250,000) who comprised a diverse group of Turks, Syrian Arabs, Kurds, Sephardic Jews, and Armenians, were effectively banned as part of World War I national security measures. A quarter of a million Ottomans were ensnared in a series of executive orders signed by President Woodrow Wilson to restrict the travel of "hostile aliens" to and from the United States. The travel ban affected immigrants of German, Austrian, and Ot-toman nationality, but the Ottomans were the only group to be included in the ban without being at war with America (the Ottoman Empire was considered a "neutral ally" of Germany, with whom the United States was at war, but the United States was not officially at war with the Ot-toman Empire). It was a ban that purposely targeted Muslims; Christian communities were gradually exempted from the ban, but it remained in place for Muslims. Seven years later, the 1924 Immigration Act granted only minimal quotas to many countries with sizable Muslim populations; Syria and Lebanon received quotas of only one hundred people per year, for example. Moreover, Asian Muslims were excluded outright as part of the law's ban on "aliens ineligible for citizenship."[20]

These early expressions of Islamophobia also impacted how easily Arab and Muslim immigrants could become naturalized American citizens. They were nominally recognized as white, but the privileges of whiteness were not uniform nor were they applied everywhere. The rights of Arabs and Muslims to become naturalized US citizens was challenged in places like Detroit, Buffalo, Cincinnati, St. Louis, and parts of Georgia and South Carolina, for example. Arabs like Christian Syrians who proved that they were Christians were allowed to become naturalized. However, Muslims were routinely disqualified from citizenship, a practice that persisted as late as 1942. And their not-quite-white status also made them vulnerable to the racial violence already directed at African, Asian, and Native Americans. In 1929, for example, Nicholas Romey, a Syrian immigrant described as white, was lynched by a mob after a dispute with the local chief of police in the town of Lake City, Florida.[21]

In the mid- and late twentieth century, American popular culture reinforced the stereotype that Arabs and Muslims were bloodthirsty and violent. In both movies and television, Arab and Muslim characters repeatedly engaged in suicide bombings and acts of terrorism. Analyses of television shows found that Arab characters were either power-hungry and barbaric oil sheiks or terrorists bent on mass violence. Both were portrayed as either potential or real enemies of the United States. Over the next decades, images of Arab terrorists proliferated in blockbuster films like *Back to the Future* (1985), *GI Jane* (1988), and *True Lies* (1994).[22]

The racialization of Arabs and Muslim Americans was also increasingly tied to US international relations and economic and military interests in the Middle East. During and after the 1967 Arab-Israeli War, for example, Arabness was portrayed as dangerous to the United States and to American interests in the Middle East. Images of Arabs as backward, defeated, and primitive showed up in newspapers and on TV. They were represented as a people who were inherently dangerous rather than as individuals who followed a dangerous ideology. These public perceptions only increased during the Iranian hostage crisis that began in 1979 and the 1993 bombing of New York City's World Trade Center. Anti-Arab racism became part of the larger xenophobic "clash of civilizations" framework promoted by intellectuals like Samuel Huntington and widely used by pundits, journalists, politicians, filmmakers, and the Christian right.[23]

By the mid-1990s, the stereotype of Arabs and Muslims as terrorists was so entrenched in American political and popular culture that when a bomb rocked the Murrah Federal Building in Oklahoma City, killing 168 people and injuring another 680 on April 19, 1995, there was a collective rush to blame Islamic extremists or Arab radicals for the attack. But the culprit was actually a white man and antigovernment terrorist named Timothy McVeigh. Nevertheless, Congress passed, and Bill Clinton signed, the Antiterrorism and Effective Death Penalty Act (AEDPA) in 1996 with provisions that allowed US immigration officials to arrest, detain, and deport noncitizens (but not white Christian radicals like McVeigh) on secret evidence if they were deemed to be national security threats. AEDPA led to the investigation of Muslim American political and social activity and the deportation of Muslims suspected of terrorist activity. Meanwhile, terrorist attacks abroad continued to influence American attitudes of Muslims at home. In 1998, the USS *Cole* was bombed in Yemen, as were the US embassies in Kenya and Tanzania in 2000. Then came the catastrophic attacks on the World Trade Center and the Pentagon in 2001.[24]

ON SEPTEMBER 11, 2001, Adam Soltani was just weeks into his freshman year at the University of Central Oklahoma. He proudly served as the president of the campus Muslim Student Association and though non-Muslims considered his faith with curiosity, he "didn't sense any fear in being Muslim at all." That morning, however, would transform Soltani's life and the lives of millions of Muslims in the United States. Terrorist followers of al-Qaida leader Osama bin Laden commandeered four passenger planes. Two were flown into the twin towers of Manhattan's World Trade Center. The third hit the Pentagon. The fourth crashed in Pennsylvania after passengers stormed the cockpit and redirected the plane. Altogether, almost three thousand people died.

Soltani's parents urged him to stay home from school once the news hit. But he brushed off their suggestion and decided to attend the weekly prayer service at the local mosque. Normally, the weekday service would be packed with 150 people. That day, no more than twenty showed up. Weeks after 9/11, Soltani and some Muslim friends were walking to the mosque after a university football game when a truck full of teenagers pulled up and yelled "Go back home, you sand-niggers." Soltani recalled this incident as the first time in his life that he had come face-to-face with an Islamophobic racial slur. "That's when I realized that things weren't the same or as safe as they used to be."[25] Soltani was not alone. Many American Muslims have identified 9/11 as a turning point in their lives in the United States.

Writer Shawna Ayoub Ainslie started keeping a list of the ways that 9/11 changed her life as an American Muslim. She stopped making eye contact with strangers in case she caught the attention of the large numbers of FBI agents and police officers she saw everywhere in the days and weeks after 9/11. A helicopter hovered above her apartment. The FBI was at her mosque for several months. She stopped wearing a headscarf. She stopped reading the Qur'an between classes. She stopped going to mosque. She hid all physical evidence that she was Arab or Muslim. In short, she "learned how to be invisible." Nevertheless, she also came to realize that she was still seen as a "Brown and Muslim or Other" and that Islamophobia would continue to shape her life no matter how hard she tried to hide her Muslim faith.[26]

Islamophobia's identification of Arab and Muslim Americans as a threat because of their religion, their "race," and their foreignness has made it particularly powerful and enduring. But Islamophobia has also treated and impacted men and women differently. Although Arab and Muslim American men, particularly working-class men, have been stereotyped as violent terrorists who threaten national security, women have been viewed as more of a cultural threat. Stereotyped as oppressed and lacking in personal freedom, Arab and Muslim women have come to symbolize backwardness and inassimilability. Women, especially those wearing hijabs or burkas, have been particularly vulnerable to racial violence. Muslim American women in the southwestern suburbs of Chicago, for example, reported experiencing hate acts at a rate more than double that of men—especially when wearing a hijab.[27] These private acts of violence have accompanied post-9/11 government programs singling out Arab and Muslim Americans for surveillance, detention, deportation, and exclusion.

On September 17, 2001, President George W. Bush traveled to the Islamic Center of Washington, DC, met with religious and community leaders, and quoted from the Qur'an in a widely publicized speech. "The face of terror is not the true face of Islam," the president declared. "That's not what Islam is all about. Islam is peace. These terrorists don't represent peace. They represent evil and war." In a widely praised move, the president emphatically called attention to the "millions of Muslims" who were American citizens and the "incredibly valuable contribution" they made to the United States. He also passionately condemned the rising number of hate crimes being committed in the wake of the terrorist attacks. "Those who feel like they can intimidate our fellow citizens to take out their anger don't represent the best of America, they represent the worst of humankind, and they should be ashamed of that kind of behavior."[28]

Despite these overtures, Bush-era policies in America's involvement in the war on terror ushered in a new wave of state-sanctioned discrimination against Muslims in the United States. While the global war on terror focused on eradicating al-Qaeda and the "axis of evil" abroad, the domestic war on terror targeted the "evil terrorist enemy within"— conflating the specter of radical Islamic terrorists abroad with suspect foreign Muslims in the United States. According to attorney general John Ashcroft, terrorists were lurking within (and were being concealed) by Arab and Muslim American populations, making it necessary to conduct vigorous counterterrorism efforts within these communities. In 2002, for example, Ashcroft framed the federal government's actions as a war against terrorists everywhere and anywhere. Using language similar to how Japanese Americans were described during World War II, Ashcroft explained that in the new war, "our enemy's platoons infiltrate our borders, quietly blending in with visiting tourists, students and workers."

They moved "unnoticed through our cities, neighborhoods and public spaces," expertly "evading recognition at the border and escaping detection within the United States."[29]

Ashcroft's description of dangerous Arab and Muslim American communities in the United States was echoed by conservative pundits. The Center for Immigration Studies' Mark Krikorian warned that Muslim immigrants would increase terrorism in the United States. In a 2002 *National Review* article titled "Muslim Invasion?" Krikorian argued that Muslim immigration helped facilitate terrorism. Most Muslim immigrants were not terrorists, he conceded, but they were dangerous nonetheless. Insular and protective, Muslim immigrant communities provided "unintentional cover for terrorists."[30]

Shaped by such beliefs, post-9/11 counterterrorism efforts implicated all Arab and Muslim Americans in the crimes of foreign terrorists. Experts found that even though government programs were ostensibly designed to catch terrorists without bias, they were "deeply flawed and often bigoted." As the war on terror increasingly maligned and criminalized Islam and Muslims in broad sweeps, Arab and Muslim Americans, regardless of citizenship or length of residence in the United States, were cast together, de-Americanized, and identified as dangerous and foreign. Entire communities came under suspicion, and racial profiling of all immigrants increased.[31]

In the days following the terrorist attacks, 1,200 men who matched an Arab/Middle Eastern/Muslim phenotype and were determined to be suspicious were arrested and detained under high security conditions. None were found to be connected with terrorist activity, but many were ordered deported on immigration violations and were referred to by the government as "terrorists." More than 11,000 individuals of Muslim, Arab, and South Asian descent were targeted for special scrutiny by the FBI and were interviewed. Government measures were almost exclusively directed against persons of Arab ethnicity or the Muslim faith: mass arrests, preventive and indefinite detention, FBI interviews, required registration and fingerprinting of tens of thousands of male foreign nationals, and domestic surveillance that included widespread wiretapping and reviews of private Internet, telecommunication, and financial records as well as surreptitious investigations of neighborhoods, places of worship, and community organizations.[32]

New government policies expanded these operations to form what one expert has called "the most aggressive national campaign of ethnic profiling since World War II." As in that conflict, the country's counter-terrorism programs were both motivated by and contributed to the racial profiling of specific communities perceived to be enemies or disloyal to the United States. For the post-9/11 programs, the US government acted on the premise that Arab and Muslim Americans were predisposed to violent extremism—without any evidence to support that conclusion. The 2001 USA Patriot Act included a range of provisions authorizing the detention and exclusion of noncitizens and undermining the rights of citizens. It also expanded the power of the US government to use surveillance and wiretapping without first showing probable cause, conduct secret searches, and access private records without oversight. All actions were principally used on Arabs and Muslims in the United States.[33]

One year after the terrorist attacks, the INS also implemented a "special registration" known as the National Security Entry-Exit Registration System, which also targeted Arab and Muslim American communities. It required all noncitizen men age sixteen and older from twenty-five Arab or Muslim majority countries, plus North Korea, to register with the US government. Between September 11, 2002, and June 1, 2003, 127,694 Arab and Muslim men registered at a US port of entry. In addition, 82,880 individuals already in the United States registered. Not one person was convicted of terrorism. But nearly 13,500 were ordered deported for being in the country without proper documentation. Called an unconstitutional religious registry by an Obama Justice Department official, the program was suspended in 2011 and was ended in December 2016, to prevent its use by the incoming Trump administration.[34]

Other programs called for mass deportation on the fallacy that it was done in the interest of national security. Launched in January 2002, the Absconders Initiative sought to deport 6,000 noncitizen males from Middle Eastern countries who had been ordered deported (usually for overstaying a visa) but had remained in the United States. These men made up less than 2 percent of the total population of so-called absconders (around 314,000, the majority from Latin America), but the department targeted them specifically as potential terrorists. One year later, 1,100 people had been detained under this initiative.[35]

Communities in and around New York City were also the subjects of a massive domestic spying operation run by the New York Police Department (NYPD). Run through the department's Demographics Unit, the operation used taxpayer funds to create an elaborate surveillance program monitoring the activities and movements in American Muslim communities in the New York metropolitan area. Concentrating on twenty-eight "ancestries of interest" that included people from Muslim-majority countries like Pakistan, Iran, Syria, Egypt, Uzbekistan, and Chechnya as well as "American Black Muslims," the NYPD used paid informants and spies, including so-called mosque crawlers, to monitor religious leaders, community and student organizations, businesses, soccer fields, and places of worship. The goal was to identify American Muslims who were "radicalized" and were recruiting others to their cause. Journalists found that the operation was so broad that it treated all individuals who identified as Muslim or engaged in Islamic religious practices with suspicion. Radicalization indicators were also ridiculously wide-ranging. They included wearing traditional Islamic clothing, growing a beard, abstaining from alcohol, and becoming involved in social activism. Over the years, the surveillance program targeted Muslim communities throughout New York City as well as every mosque within one hundred miles of New York City, including Pennsylvania, Connecticut, and New Jersey. The program even went so far as infiltrating college student whitewater-rafting trips.[36]

The domestic spying program operated for a decade following 9/11 before it was shut down. Investigators found that the program functioned far outside its own jurisdictional boundaries. It had received unprecedented help from the CIA in a "partnership that blurred the bright line between foreign and domestic spying." Plus, it was unconstitutional. The ACLU and the CLEAR Project at CUNY Law School charged that the spy program violated the Fourteenth Amendment's Equal Protection

Clause and the First Amendment right to the free exercise of religion and guarantee of government neutrality toward religion. Over 125 local and national organizations signed a joint letter to the US Department of Justice requesting a civil rights investigation into the program.[37]

Moreover, the illegal and unconstitutional spying was all for naught. It never generated a single lead or triggered a terrorism investigation. What it did do, however, was legitimize the vilification of all Muslims in the United States as dangerous terrorists and intensified the atmosphere of fear and mistrust within mosques and the Muslim community at large. Community leader Linda Sarsour put it bluntly: "the NYPD's spying program has created psychological warfare in the [American Muslim] community."[38]

For Arab and Muslim Americans, the NYPD domestic spying program was perhaps the most vivid example of both the state-sponsored and public Islamophobia they experienced daily following 9/11. Sociologists described a collective fear of quarantine among community members. But that sense of banishment was evident across the country. Arab and Muslim Americans in metropolitan Chicago who participated in one study from 2002 to 2003, for example, reported that they no longer felt at home in the United States. Even those who had lived for decades in the country or were born in the United States did not feel safe and protected; 9/11 and the US government's response had, in effect, de-Americanized them. As one young respondent told a researcher, "I see a black picture for the entire United States, not just for Muslims. The way that they are looking for these incidents, terror attacks, they are increasing culture clash, and bringing conflicts between races and religions."[39]

With government officials and pundits identifying Arab and Muslim American communities as dangerous hotbeds of terrorism, public support for this kind of profiling was strong, even if it meant discriminating against certain groups. In 2001, a Harvard polling researcher found that most Americans were willing to forgo cherished rights in order to support anti-terror campaigns. Sixty-eight percent supported letting the police randomly stop people who "might fit a terrorist profile." A majority also supported carefully scrutinizing Arabs and Arab Americans, and as many as one-third of those polled felt that Arab Americans should be "put under special surveillance." Five years later, a 2006 *USA Today*–Gallup poll found that less than half of the respondents believed that American Muslims were loyal to the United States. About 40 percent favored rigorous security measures for Muslims in the United States as a way to help prevent terrorism. They expressed support for programs requiring Muslims who were US citizens to carry a special ID and to undergo special, more intensive, security checks before boarding airplanes in the United States.[40]

Arab and Muslim American communities, as well as those who were believed to be Muslim, have also been victimized by a growing number of hate crimes. According to the FBI, anti-Muslim hate crimes grew by 1600 percent after 9/11. Mosques were vandalized and desecrated, and public displays of hatred and use of firepower became part of a "nationwide terror campaign directed at mosques and Islamic community centers." The Council on American-Islamic Relations (CAIR) also reported a dramatic rise in Islamophobic acts in all areas of American life: the private sector, the public sector, workplaces, schools, public spaces, and mosques.[41]

DOMESTIC AND INTERNATIONAL crises offer some explanation for the growth and persistence of Islamophobia in the early twenty-first century. In the first few years after the 9/11 attacks, much of the negativity was tied to the wars in Iraq and Afghanistan. The financial crisis, or Great Recession, of 2008 that caused the housing market to burst, banks to fail, and stock markets to plummet, also produced great economic instability and social tensions. A rise in nationalism and xenophobia followed, repeating earlier patterns. Both "illegal aliens" and "Muslim terrorists" became the receptacles for these anxieties. Terrorist attacks in the United States and abroad also increased public fears and anxieties about Islam and Muslims.[42]

As tragic as the attacks were, they did not represent an epidemic of radical Muslim terrorism in the United States, as some politicians and pundits professed. The Triangle Center on Terrorism and Homeland Security found that between 9/11 and 2011, eleven Muslim Americans had successfully executed terrorist attacks in the United States, killing thirty-three people. During the same amount of time, there had been 150,000 murders in the country. A 2015 report from the Southern Poverty Law Center similarly found that a domestic terror attack occurred (or was foiled) every thirty-four days in America. Muslim terrorists only accounted for a fraction of the total attacks. Still, negative views of Muslims and of Islam persisted and grew in the United States. In 2010, ABC News reported that just 37 percent of Americans held a favorable view of Islam, the lowest figure since October 2001. Even after the 2011 death of Osama bin Laden, anti-Muslim sentiment did not fall. Instead, it grew.[43]

There was a reason for this. Like other forms of xenophobia, Islamophobia has worked by design. It has been carefully and passionately promoted through a well-funded network, what CAIR has called a "U.S. Islamophobic network" of organizations and individuals who have promoted prejudice against and hatred of Islam and Muslims. In 2016, CAIR found seventy-four groups that had access to at least $205 million. Foundations funding conservative causes like the Scaife Foundation, the Carthage Foundation, and the Allegheny Foundation were part of this network, donating nearly $10.5 million combined to Islamophobic groups from 2001 to 2012. Groups identified by CAIR as falling within the "inner core" of the Islamophobic network included Stop Islamization of Nations and the David Horowitz Freedom Center, which sponsored an Islamo-Fascism Awareness Week every year to spread its message that Islam was a dangerous threat to the United States. Groups identified as being part of the "outer core" included media companies like the Christian Broadcast Network, Fox News Channel, *The Glenn Beck Program*, and HBO's *Real Time with Bill Maher.*[44]

There was also an active Islamophobia industry composed of right-wing bloggers, politicians, religious leaders, media personalities, and academics who spread their messages of fear and hate of Islam. Once operating on the fringe of American politics, right-wing, anti-Muslim groups and speakers filled a void in public knowledge about Islam and

offered impassioned, and often hysterical, warnings after the terrorist attacks of 9/11. Attention from mass media amplified and legitimized these
once-obscure actors and their message. As a result, they were able to expand their influence and financial resources. Islamophobia was carefully
nurtured and spread online, in rallies, and in the media and helped shift
public sentiment against Muslim Americans long after the 9/11 terrorist
attacks. Conservative politicians and a complicit media worked together
to offer a steady diet of misinformation and distorted news that was
played virtually on a loop. A growing number of Americans formed fears,
called for action, and contributed to the ongoing cycle of Islamophobia.[45]

Among the most active were right-wing leaders in the evangelical Christian community, who viewed their faith in terms of a religious war with Islam and its potential to threaten traditional Christian
(or Judeo-Christian) cultural influence and dominance in the United
States. Jerry Falwell, Pat Robertson, and John Hagee attached an anti-
Muslim fervor to their preaching. A new activist generation rose to lobby
for legislation, including Tony Perkins and his Family Research Council. They were joined by political conservatives like Daniel Pipes, considered by many to be one of the earliest founders of Islamophobia in
the United States. In a 1990 *National Review* article, Pipes combined
anti-immigrant xenophobia, racism, and Islamophobia into one seamless
discourse: "Western European societies are unprepared for the massive
immigration of brown skinned people cooking strange foods and not exactly maintaining Germanic standards of hygiene," he began, but Muslim
customs were "more troublesome" than most and they appeared "most
resistant to assimilation."[46]

Journalist Pamela Geller also became a prominent leader spreading
Islamophobia. Claiming to be an expert on Islam, she promoted the theory that an Islamic conspiracy was poised to destroy American values and
culture. In 2008, she helped spread the message that Barack Obama was
a Muslim. In 2010, she helped lead the charge against the Park51 Islamic
community center planned to be built in Lower Manhattan. Calling it a
"monster mosque . . . in [the] shadow of [the] World Trade Center," the
community center, she claimed, defamed the memory of those lost in the

fallen Twin Towers. Geller's public profile, and the number of visitors to her blog, shot up, and she published a book titled *Stop the Islamization of America: A Practical Guide to the Resistance* in 2011. Promising to provide "a much-needed wake-up call," the book argued that the United States was being transformed into an Islamic state through the creeping spread of Islamic law in the country. Echoing the scores of anti-Catholic writers who had warned of the need to protect the United States from the spread of Catholicism generations earlier, Geller passionately urged her readers to "fight back now to defend our nation and our civilization" from "Islamic supremacism."[47]

Geller teamed up with Robert Spencer, founder of the blog Jihad Watch and author of multiple books critical of Islam, to form Stop Islamization of America (SIOA). The organization intended to call attention to what its members believed was a vast Islamic conspiracy to destroy American values. Modeled after the European-based Stop Islamisation of Europe (SIOE) and Spencer's own worldview that terrorism was wholly unique to the religion of Islam, SIOA vilified the entire Islamic faith and all Muslims under the guise of fighting radical Islam. One way in which the "Islamic machine" operated, they argued, was through the spread of sharia, or Islamic law, in the United States. The US Constitution was "under attack from fundamentalist Islam and Shariah," SIOA claimed. Together, Geller and Spencer's Islamophobic blogging reached growing audiences and increased their influence (as well as their profits).[48]

While the work of Geller, Spencer, and Pipes continued to promote apocalyptic visions of America under Muslim rule, conservative media networks regularly participated in spreading and increasing public fear of Muslims. A network like Fox News was "at the heart of the public scaremongering about Islam" and, according to experts, regularly gave right-wing activists a prominent platform from which to push an anti-Muslim agenda. A ThinkProgress analysis of Fox News coverage in 2010–2011, for example, found that the network regularly used terms that reflected a negative view of Muslims (such as *radical Islam, jihad, sharia,* or *extremist Islam*) more than twice as often as its competitors.[49]

The American mainstream media also associated Arab and Muslim Americans with terrorism and a demonized, globalized Islam. Articles in the *New York Times*, for example, consistently differentiated American Muslims from other Americans. Immediately after 9/11, the paper portrayed American Muslims as uniformly devout, tied to their homelands, and resistant to assimilation. A 2001 story described Arab Americans in Dearborn, Michigan, as living in an insulated Muslim world where, despite the community's long history in the area, they remained resistant to assimilation. "Old-world ways" and un-American religious practices, including religiously mandated sex-segregated gym classes at a local middle school, were cited as evidence. Another 2002 article described American Muslims as having "hyphenated identities" and "divided loyalties" that split them between a (presumably) violent and fanatical homeland and religion and the peaceful and freedom-loving United States. A 2004 article focusing on Muslim taxi drivers essentially claimed that Muslims were programmed for religiosity. "They have an imprint of the city's mosques in their brains, at the ready wherever a fare may take them as prayer time closes in," the journalist described. Other stories in the *New York Times* linked American Muslims to international Muslims and Muslim movements, which were themselves racialized as dangerous and anti-Western. Through these rhetorical acts, media experts have argued, Arab and Muslim Americans were portrayed as requiring surveillance and regulation at the expense of their civil rights.[50]

As negative views about Muslim Americans and Islam became normalized in the mainstream media and public discourse, Islamophobia was embraced in mainstream American politics. The 2008 presidential campaign featuring African American Barack Obama unleashed a particularly effective surge of Islamophobia. A relative political newcomer, Obama was an easy target for those who sought to advance an anti-Muslim narrative. He was biracial, had a foreign-sounding name, had a Muslim father from Kenya, and had lived in Muslim-majority Indonesia. Denouncing Obama as Muslim, foreign, Arab, Kenyan, socialist, and un-American, his political enemies portrayed him as representing some of white Americans' greatest fears. Labeling him a Muslim was particularly intended as a slur and was a convenient and racially coded way to denigrate him and call into question his qualifications, fitness, and loyalty without citing race. It worked. Nearly one-third of Americans (and 43 percent of Republicans) believed that Obama was Muslim, despite his frequent invocations of his Christian faith.[51]

Republican candidates politicized Islamophobia as a way to mobilize voters with various anti-Muslim proposals and messages, including a requirement that Muslims take a loyalty oath before serving in government, a warning that Muslim immigrants wanted to come to the United States to "conquer us," and descriptions of Islam as "a religion that promote[d] the most murderous mayhem on the planet." Supporters of the Tea Party, the conservative populist social and political movement that emerged after the election, routinely equated all of Islam with terrorism through campaign rally signs like "All I Need to Know About Islam I Learned on 9/11."[52]

The election of the first African American to the presidency of the United States renewed many Americans' faith that the United States could indeed live up to its founding ideals of equality. Obama's own trust in the United States and its civic ideas inspired two hundred thousand people to gather in Grant Park in Chicago to celebrate his victory with him in 2008. Ten thousand charter buses brought some of the nearly two million people who gathered in the nation's capital for his inauguration.[53] For these Americans, Obama's presidency symbolized the realization of the American dream.

For others, though, it marked the beginning of an American nightmare, and the Obama election triggered a full-scale conservative backlash that would help send Donald Trump to the White House eight years later. Many objected to Obama's political positions and policies. Others objected to the very idea of an African American in the White House. They challenged his legitimacy to occupy the Oval Office by questioning his birth in the United States, calling him a liar during a speech to Congress, and diminishing his credentials. The backlash fed the populist rightward turn of the Republican Party led by the Tea Party movement and its largely older white constituency who opposed what they viewed as excessive taxation and government control, abortion, undocumented immigration, and health care reform. According to one poll, 92 percent of Tea Party supporters believed that President Obama's policies were moving the country toward socialism, and 30 percent believed he was born outside the United States. A majority thought that "too much" had been made of the problems facing black people.[54]

Once elected, President Obama faced an onslaught of unprecedented vitriol, part of a larger expression of what one historian described as "white rage," or white Americans' anger toward and opposition against the advancement of African Americans, including their demands for full and equal citizenship. To them, Obama's election, "the ultimate advancement," was the "ultimate affront." The anti-Obama backlash fit perfectly into the growing use of dog whistles and race baiting in American politics that gave new energy and legitimization to white nationalist and white supremacist organizations. On the policy front, it paved the way toward a rollback of civil rights victories, including voting rights, and policies that facilitated the mass incarceration of African American and Latinx people. Following the 2008 election, the GOP doubled down on building support among its mostly white base rather than broadening its support among nonwhites.[55]

The false charge that Obama was a Muslim who was not born in the United States represented more than a desperate attempt to discredit a political rival. It signaled how damaging the *foreign* and *Muslim* labels had become by the early twenty-first century. The civil rights revolution had made it politically difficult to challenge Obama's presidency on the basis of race, and being labeled a racist was still something that politicians sought to avoid even if they railed against "political correctness" in American society. But the *noncitizen* and *Muslim* labels were just as damaging when used as slurs to delegitimize and malign. Although Obama easily won reelection in 2012, he lost his Democratic majorities in the House (2010) and Senate (2014), and his legislative goals were met with Republican obstructionism at every turn.

During the Obama presidency, Republican politicians at both the state and federal levels adopted another Islamophobic approach and promoted the idea that so-called sharia law, which they defined as Islamic law, was infiltrating the United States and threatening its institutions. Echoing the calls of the Know Nothings who warned of Catholic influence in the United States through Irish Catholic immigration in the nineteenth century, both far-right and mainstream Republicans charged that Islam was similarly overtaking the United States through Muslim immigration. Some politicians began campaigning with a pledge to "root out Islamic law" from the country.[56]

These efforts had real consequences. In 2010, 70 percent of Oklahoma voters approved the Save Our State amendment to the state constitution, which explicitly rendered sharia law invalid in state courts. Like California's 1994 initiative of the same name, this act signaled a broader concern about dangerous foreigners and legitimized xenophobia in American politics. In 2011, Congressman Peter King, a Republican from New York and chair of the Homeland Security Committee, convened a hearing in the US House of Representatives on the domestic radicalization of American Muslims. With dramatic testimony and examples purportedly proving the grave threat that this group posed to the United States, the hearing served to cement Islamophobia as a central platform of the new Republican majority in the House. By 2016, there was also a growth in anti-Islam legislation in several states, a backlash against teaching the tenets of Islam in schools, armed anti-Islam demonstrations, and the establishment of so-called Muslim-free businesses.[57]

The 2016 presidential campaign of real estate mogul and reality TV star Donald Trump tapped into the common use of Islamophobia within the Republican Party. In 2011, Trump made his mark on national politics by jumping on the so-called birther bandwagon. He repeated the rumor that Obama was born overseas, was educated in an Indonesian madrassa, and was steeped in Islamist ideology from a young age. Trump repeatedly called on Obama to produce his birth certificate. During the election, he mobilized an already energized and organized conservative base of voters who had been nurtured on the politics of antiblack resentment, Islamophobia, and xenophobia for years. On November 8, 2016, they elected him president.[58]

ON ELECTION NIGHT in 2016, Khaled Beydoun, a law professor at the University of Detroit Mercy, watched the coverage alongside two hundred Muslim Americans in Dearborn, Michigan, the most concentrated Muslim American community in the country. As it became clear that Donald Trump was on his way to the White House, Beydoun remembers, the fear was palpable. "Adults cried. Young people led prayers." Beydoun predicted that Trump would be the country's first "Islamophobia President." There would be more hate crimes against Muslims and an expanded surveillance state. It would be more difficult for Muslims to freely exercise their faith. Come January, Islamophobia would become White House policy, he believed.[59]

Beydoun's prediction proved to be right. Anti-Muslim hate crimes increased in the months leading up to and directly after the 2016 presidential election, surpassing those that occurred after the 9/11 terrorist attacks. In 2015, the year that candidate Trump called for a "complete and total shutdown of Muslims," the United States experienced a spike in anti-Muslim hate crimes and physical assaults in the United States. It was the highest number reported since 2001. According to the Pew Research Center, ninety-one aggravated or simple assaults motivated by anti-Muslim bias were reported in 2015, just two shy of the ninety-three reported in 2001. The number of anti-Muslim intimidation crimes, defined as threatening bodily harm, also rose in 2015, with 120 reported to the FBI. CAIR also reported a record number (seventy-eight) of mosque incidents that same year, the highest since the organization began tracking such reports in 2009. The largest number of cases involving damage, destruction, vandalism, and intimidation were also reported in 2015. After the election, anti-Muslim hate crimes increased again by 19 percent. And the attacks continued into the first year of the Trump presidency. Between January 1 and September 30, 2017, CAIR identified 1,656 anti-Muslim incidents in the United States, including hate crimes, harassment, and intimidation. In the second half of 2018, anti-Muslim bias incidents had risen 83 percent in just a few months. These statistics, of course, did not include the number of incidents that were not reported.[60]

Trump does not deserve all the credit. By the time he began to lead the crowded pack of Republican presidential candidates in 2015,

One week after Donald Trump called for a "complete and total shutdown" of Muslims entering the United States, armed protesters from the so-called Bureau of American-Islamic Relations (BAIR) displayed signs in support of the candidate's proposal and demonstrated in front of the Islamic Association of North Texas mosque on December 12, 2015, in Richardson, Texas. Photo by John Moore/Getty Images.

Islamophobia had already been well entrenched in American life. As shocking as Trump's full-blown Islamophobia was to many voters, it resonated deeply with others. Demonizing Islam and vilifying Muslims proved to be a winning strategy.[61]

The Trump administration's Islamophobic agenda is not an aberration in American politics. Nor does it exist and flourish in a vacuum. It is best understood as an extension and intensification of American politics and policies that date back a century or more and were, more recently, institutionalized after 9/11. President George W. Bush built a national security regime that treated Arab and Muslim Americans as suspects in America's domestic war on terror. President Barack Obama let many of these policies stand.[62]

Nevertheless, Trump's vitriolic anti-Muslim campaign rhetoric set a new (low) standard for acceptable political discourse. And it became a preview for what the Brennan Center for Justice called an "unprecedentedly Islamophobic administration." From the president down to the

White House advisors and staff, the Trump administration explicitly targeted Muslims and tangibly harmed the American Muslim community, the center reported. Well-known Islamophobes like Steve Bannon, Michael Flynn, and Sebastian Gorka were elevated to key positions in the White House. Jeff Sessions, who said that he supported the passage of legislation like the 1920s quota laws to stem the growth of the foreign-born population in the United States and to put an end to the "indiscriminate acceptance of all races," was made attorney general. Xenophobe and white nationalist Stephen Miller became the president's top speechwriter and senior policy advisor, especially on immigration. And there was, of course, the executive order banning travel from Muslim-majority countries.[63]

The Muslim ban was challenged almost immediately in several courts on constitutional, statutory, and regulatory grounds. A federal judge in Washington state put the entire travel ban on hold, and a federal appeals court in San Francisco refused to lift the nationwide restraining order against the ban in February 2017. The Trump administration revised and reissued a second ban on March 6. Very similar to the first order, this was also subject to legal challenges and it never really went into effect. A third travel ban was announced by the administration on September 24, 2017, and added Chad, North Korea, and Venezuela, plus some additional changes. The last two countries were added, experts argued, to counter charges that the executive order discriminated against Muslims. This ban also faced legal challenges, but by then, the effects of the ban were obvious. Visitors and immigrants from targeted countries like Yemen, Libya, Somalia, Chad, and North Korea had dropped significantly. The number of refugees admitted into the country, including those who were Muslim, had fallen to the lowest levels since 1980.[64]

ON JUNE 26, 2018, the US Supreme Court upheld Trump's ban on travel from several predominantly Muslim countries in *Trump v. Hawaii*. The court's conservative majority agreed with the Trump administration's argument that the so-called Muslim ban was designed to protect the national security of the United States. They found no evidence of discrimination or religious prejudice. Instead, it ruled that it was an unbiased, facially neutral policy justified by national security concerns. The court's liberals denounced the decision, arguing that the ban was not informed by credible national security threats but by the president's own Islamophobic biases. They pointed to his many incendiary statements that Muslims were dangerous, including, most notably, his 2015 campaign pledge to establish a "complete and total shutdown" of Muslims coming to the United States.

Looming over the Supreme Court's division was a decision from 1944: *Korematsu v. United States*, the case initiated by Japanese American Fred Korematsu to challenge the government's forced removal and incarceration of Japanese Americans during World War II. Ever since the court had upheld these actions as a matter of "military necessity" in 1944, *Korematsu v. United States* stood as an egregious example of state-sanctioned racial discrimination in the name of national security. It was widely recognized as a shameful mistake, even by conservative justices like Antonin Scalia. In 1984, a federal district court judge vacated Korematsu's conviction after the discovery that the Roosevelt-era Justice Department had misled the judiciary about the need for the removal and incarceration. In 2011, the Justice Department issued a formal "confession of error" in the *Korematsu* case and acknowledged that government lawyers misled the court about the security threat. Four years later, declassified military documents including an internal report from the War Relocation Authority, the federal agency in charge of mass incarceration, showed that the government sought to remove and incarcerate Japanese Americans to boost—in the War Relocation Authority's words—"public morale," rather than for any evidence of spying or sabotage.[65]

Still, *Korematsu* remained law. No case presented a good vehicle for the Supreme Court to overturn the precedent, because the government had not tried to detain entire categories of people again. That changed in 2018 when the court's majority took the momentous step of overruling the *Korematsu* case when it decided on Trump's travel ban. Writing for the conservative majority, Chief Justice John G. Roberts Jr. explained that the forcible relocation of US citizens to concentration camps, solely and explicitly on the basis of race, "was objectively unlawful and outside the scope of presidential authority." Citing language used by then justice Robert H. Jackson in his dissent to the ruling, Chief Justice Roberts forcefully concluded that "*Korematsu* was gravely wrong the day it was decided, has been overruled in the court of history, and—to be clear—'has no place in law under the Constitution.'" Of course, this long-awaited repudiation of *Korematsu* came as the same court and the same chief justice upheld the travel ban. In reconciling these two actions, Chief Justice Roberts took pains to distinguish the *Korematsu* decision from *Trump v. Hawaii*. "It is wholly inapt to liken that morally repugnant order to a facially neutral policy denying certain foreign nationals the privilege of admission," he claimed.[66]

Justice Sonia Sotomayor vehemently dissented, arguing that the present decision was no better than *Korematsu*. Both invoked "an ill-defined national security threat to justify an exclusionary policy of sweeping proportion," she wrote. They relied on stereotypes about a particular group amid "strong evidence that impermissible hostility and animus motivated the government's policy." She pointed to Trump's many Islamophobic statements as the real motivation. Sotomayor further stated that while the court's formal overruling of *Korematsu* was a "silver lining," the majority's decision in *Trump v. Hawaii* would go down in Supreme Court history as a second coming of *Korematsu*. "By blindly accepting the government's misguided invitation to sanction a discriminatory policy motivated by animosity toward a disfavored group, all in the name of a superficial claim of national security," she explained, the court redeployed "the same dangerous logic underlying *Korematsu* and merely replaces one 'gravely wrong' decision with another."[67]

Karen Korematsu, daughter of Fred and founder and executive director of the Korematsu Institute, which advances racial equity, social justice, and human rights, agreed. Writing in the *New York Times*, she argued that although the court had "correctly rejected the abhorrent race-based relocation and incarceration of Japanese Americans, it failed to recognize—and reject—the rationale that led to that infamous decision."

The Supreme Court's 1944 decision in *Korematsu v. United States* upheld the constitutionality of the government's removal and incarceration of Japanese Americans during World War II. Long criticized, it was finally overturned in 2018. At the same time, the Court upheld the constitutionality of the Muslim ban, a law that many believed was similarly discriminatory. Karen Korematsu, posing with her brother Ken near a photograph of their father Fred at the National Portrait Gallery in 2012, vehemently condemned the court's decision. MANDEL NGAN/AFP/Getty Images.

In an interview with *Time*, Korematsu further explained, "In 1942, they talked about military necessity. Now, it's national security." In both cases, Korematsu believed these excuses justified discrimination against a group based on its ancestry. "The Supreme Court seemed to repeat the same bad logic of the 1940s decision by rubber stamping the Trump administration's bald assertions that the 'immigration travel ban' is justified by national security." Echoing Justice Sotomayor, Korematsu condemned the court for merely replacing "one injustice with another."[68]

Korematsu and Sotomayor may have been specifically referring to the two Supreme Court decisions. But their words were also an apt summary of the long history of xenophobia in the United States. Across the centuries, xenophobia has been an indelible part of America. The target of our xenophobia may have changed from decade to decade, but our fear and hatred of foreigners has not. From the colonial era to the present, xenophobia has been an American tradition.

CONCLUSION

On February 22, 2018, US Citizenship and Immigration Services (USCIS) changed its mission statement. Whereas it had previously included a description of its role in securing "America's promise as a nation of immigrants," the updated version offered a starkly different message: USCIS, it declared, "administers the nation's lawful immigration system, safeguarding its integrity and promise by efficiently and fairly adjudicating requests for immigration benefits." It would do so, it pledged, "while protecting Americans, securing the homeland, and honoring our values." Although director L. Francis Cissna did not explain why the agency dropped the words about the country's "promise" and its role as a home for and built by immigrants, he did describe the new mission statement as "simple, straightforward." It clearly defined the agency's role "in our country's lawful immigration system and the commitment we have to the American people," he explained.

The shift in language and tone was remarkable. Before, the USCIS mission had been framed around a worldview that considered immigration a positive American tradition. The agency's role was to be the guardian of that promise: to facilitate the immigration process and bestow "immigration and citizenship benefits." The agency served the immigrant. Now, USCIS's new mission was grounded in a worldview that considered immigration a threat to the United States and to Americans.

"Administering the lawful immigration system" and "safeguarding its integrity" came first. In other words, the agency no longer served the immigrant; it served the US nation-state. USCIS would still "fairly adjudicate" requests for immigration benefits, but this language and tone hinted at a reality in which few "requests" would actually be granted—and when they were, they would be granted to the few deemed worthy. Foremost in the agency's new mission was the work of "protecting Americans, securing the homeland, and honoring our values." Within the context of the Trump administration's reliance on white nationalism, racism, and xenophobia, there was little doubt as to which "Americans" needed protecting, whose "homeland" needed "securing," and which "values" needed to be honored.[1]

The mission statement followed President Donald Trump's first State of the Union address less than a month before. In that speech, immigration was a defining theme. Even though undocumented immigration from Mexico had fallen to its lowest level in nearly fifty years, the president described a United States under siege, vulnerable because of "open borders" that allowed "drugs and gangs" to "break into our country" and "pour into our most vulnerable communities." He warned of "millions of low-wage workers" who competed for jobs and wages against the "working poor." He blamed violent criminals who had first entered as "illegal, unaccompanied, alien minors" for brutally murdering innocent Americans.[2]

Many aspects of Trump's xenophobia were echoes from the past. Like xenophobia from earlier eras, Trump's was rooted in racism. A few weeks earlier, the president had referred to Haiti, El Salvador, and African nations as "shithole countries" in an Oval Office meeting with lawmakers. His xenophobia also drew on America's long tradition of white supremacy. In the same meeting, he suggested that the United States bring more people from countries like Norway. In his State of the Union speech, Trump stated that "Americans are dreamers too," a tagline already popular with white nationalists that redeployed undocumented immigrants' term *dreamer* to refer to (white) American citizens instead.[3]

The president, like others before him, also identified immigrants as economic and security threats to Americans. "My duty, and the sacred duty of every elected official in this chamber," he said, "is to defend

Americans, to protect their safety, their families, their communities, and their right to the American dream." And the president also repeated his brand of "American First" nativism by claiming that current immigration policies were not in the "best interest of American workers and American families"; that family reunification policies in the age of terrorism presented "risks we can just no longer afford"; and that immigration imperiled the "rights" of future generations "to the American dream."[4]

The president's address was, of course, just one example of the rampant xenophobia that characterized the Trump era. Since the 2016 presidential election, Trump and his allies had dramatically changed the conversation about immigration. Whereas predecessors from both political parties had at least paid lip service to the idea that immigration was something the United States should encourage in the abstract, President Trump framed all immigrants, including legal and undocumented immigrants, as well as refugees and asylum seekers, as threats to the United States.

His extreme xenophobia soon became implemented in a wide range of new policies: increased immigration enforcement in the interior of the country, the elimination of temporary protections for some noncitizens, the ban on nationals from seven Muslim-majority countries, the separation of families arriving at the US-Mexico border without documents, stricter requirements for those seeking asylum, and the reduction of refugee admissions to their lowest levels since the United States began its refugee resettlement program in 1980. Two years into his presidency, Trump demanded $5.7 billion in border wall funding as part of a spending bill and demonstrated his willingness to shut down the federal government until he received it. Congress refused, and the resulting government shutdown became the longest in US history. Less than a month later, he declared a national emergency to bypass Congress altogether and build his long-promised wall. When a record number of families, most of them from Central America, entered the country without papers in order to seek asylum in the spring of 2019, the president referred to them as an "invasion," threatened to close the southern border altogether, and adopted a blunt new message for asylum seekers hoping to find refuge in the United States, stating, "Our country is full." [5]

With Trump's anti-immigrant worldview and extremist policies constantly in the news, Americans were forced to recognize xenophobia's continuing relevance in twenty-first-century America. And this, in turn, led to a new realization that xenophobia had never gone away in the first place; it has always been an essential part of America.

HISTORY HAS SHOWN that xenophobia is not a contradiction to the United States' identity as a "nation of immigrants" or its tradition of immigration. It is not a matter of the United States being *either* a "nation of immigrants" *or* a "nation of xenophobia." It is also not a matter of the United States being a "nation of immigrants" during certain moments of its history and a "nation of xenophobia" during others. Rather, just as racial progress and racist progress can happen at the same time, Americans' embrace of immigrants and their fear and hatred of them have coexisted as equally strong forces shaping the United States.[6]

Xenophobia identifies and dehumanizes "bad immigrants" as those who come without authorization, take away jobs from Americans, do not assimilate, rely on welfare, and hate America. Meanwhile, the "nation of immigrants" identifies and disciplines "good immigrants" as those who come in the right way, behave, conform to American needs and desires, assimilate, and accept the status quo unquestioningly. There exists a fine line between the nation of immigrants and the nation of xenophobia, however, whereby the nation of immigrants has easily become a tool of xenophobia itself. This is because xenophobia includes, as it excludes. By celebrating the "good immigrant," the United States has more easily excluded the "bad" one; by demonizing one group, another has been protected. This involves trade-offs and transformations. Previously demonized communities (Germans, Irish, Italians, Chinese) have been remade into "good" immigrants while others have remained or become "bad" (Mexicans and Muslims).[7]

Our willful and purposeful historical amnesia regarding xenophobia has also helped it survive. Descendants of immigrants have been among the most effective in promoting flawed historical accounts to push contemporary xenophobic policies. Recently, these have included Tom Tancredo, Republican congressman from Colorado from 1999 to 2009, founder of the anti-immigration Congressional Immigration Reform Caucus, and unsuccessful candidate for the presidency and the governorship of Colorado. One of the country's most xenophobic politicians in the early 2000s, he introduced into Congress the 2003 Mass Immigration Reduction Act, which would have placed a five-year moratorium on all legal immigration to the United States. In 2007, he suggested that the United States bomb the holy sites in Mecca and Medina as a "deterrent" to terrorism. That same year when he was running for president, he boycotted a presidential debate hosted by Univision because candidates would be speaking Spanish.[8]

Tancredo framed many of his xenophobic positions on the well-trod argument that contemporary immigrants, especially from Mexico, were unlike the ones who had come in previous generations. He routinely drew on his own family's history to make these points but did so in ways that promoted mistruths and inaccuracies about the past. He proudly proclaimed himself the grandson of "legal" Italian immigrants, for example, while conveniently ignoring the fact that when his grandparents entered the country, in a time before general restriction laws, there was no such thing as an "illegal immigrant" (unless that immigrant was Chinese). Tancredo also cited his grandparents' love for the United States and their record of assimilation. "My grandparents, like most of their peers," Tancredo explained, "wanted to cut the ties that bound them to the old country and to connect to their new land." Today's immigrants, he claimed, wanted the opposite. They remained "loyal to their native countries" and took advantage of the United States. Conveniently missing from Tancredo's romanticized version of Italian immigration history was the fact that Italians did in fact maintain strong ties to their native country and often returned home. In fact, more Italians returned to Italy from the United States than any other national group in the late nineteenth and early twentieth centuries.[9]

Historical amnesia has also come in the form of historical monuments that erase or whitewash our violent history. The only public acknowledgment of the 1886 expulsion of Chinese immigrants from Seattle, for example, is a small interpretive panel located in the city's tourist-filled Pioneer Square. It blames "hard economic times" for turning white Seattle residents against immigrant Chinese workers. The good white citizens of Seattle's Home Guard tried to stop the "vigilante mob" and protect the Chinese residents, the panel explains, but the Chinese were still forced to leave the city. Nevertheless, it cheerily concludes, they "soon returned as their industrious nature and cheap labor proved essential for Seattle's economic structure."

In many ways, this account is almost completely useless as an accurate interpretation of the event. But it's actually highly instructive in another way: the panel unwittingly reveals some important truths about how we understand xenophobia in the United States. Too often, we have blamed violent anti-immigrant actions on "hard economic times" and discounted the power of racism in fueling xenophobia. In this retelling of the expulsion, anti-Chinese sentiment was a seemingly natural symptom of a brief economic downturn rather than a consequence of broader and systemic racism. The whitewashed story is oriented around the small number of good white defenders (who still supported the removal of Chinese) rather than on the much larger rioting mob that kicked down doors and torched Chinatown—or, indeed, the Chinese who were the victims of this mob. And the expulsion, while unfortunate, was just temporary, the panel implies. The Chinese eventually returned, apparently willing to absolve Seattle of its sins, and became the "good immigrants." Chinese Americans, with their "industrious nature," served as "cheap labor" and helped build the city into the economic success that it is today.

In Los Angeles, another historical marker offers a more honest portrayal of and reconciliation with the past. La Placita Olvera is still a gathering place for Angelenos. Weary workers, tourists, and the homeless rest on park benches amid landmarks that celebrate Los Angeles history and culture. There is a statue of Spain's King Carlos III, who ordered the founding of El Pueblo de la Reina de Los Angeles in 1781, and a marker of Lo Pobladores, the eleven families who were the first Spanish civilian settlers in Southern California. Across the plaza is Olvera Street, which L.A.'s tourist website describes as a "Mexican Marketplace that recreates a romantic 'Old Los Angeles'" with traditional foods, arts and crafts, strolling mariachi bands, and folk dancers.[10]

At first glance, it seems as if Los Angeles's violent forced deportation and repatriation of its Mexican and Mexican American citizens has been completely wiped from public memory. But tucked away next to La Plaza de Cultura y Artes, a Mexican American cultural center across the street from King Carlos's statue, one memorial remembers. Dedicated after the California state government held hearings and passed Senate Bill No. 670—"Apology Act for the 1930s Mexican Repatriation Program"—in 2005, the bilingual somber black marker describes the forced emigration of Mexican Americans during the Great Depression as the "clandestine removal of thousands of people" who were "denied their right to life, liberty, the pursuit of happiness, and the American dream in their country of birth." It also serves as the State of California's official public apology to victims of repatriation and for the "fundamental violations of their basic civil liberties and constitutional rights" committed against them. Nevertheless, the granite memorial obscures history in another way. Hidden away next to the cultural center, it is something that visitors must actively search for; it is not presented alongside the other memorials commemorating significant moments in the city's history across the street. The marker also fails to mention that no official apology has ever come from the federal government.[11]

Americans' historical amnesia of our xenophobic past is not just an example of bad history. It has real repercussions. By ignoring the deep roots of xenophobia in the past, we ignore the deep hold that xenophobia has on our present. By only celebrating and reaffirming the idea that the United States is a nation of immigrants, we drown out the constant drumbeat of xenophobia. In this way, we enable the United States to "replace one injustice with another," the charge made by Japanese American Karen Korematsu in her criticism of the Supreme Court's 2018 decision upholding the Muslim ban.[12]

OF COURSE, XENOPHOBIA has not been the only force shaping Americans' attitudes toward immigration, nor has its power been absolute. America's need for settlers and workers has often served as an effective counter-weight to growing anxiety over immigration. The desire to protect US international relations has also kept xenophobia in check. Throughout US history, immigrants and their allies have also challenged the most pernicious expressions and acts of xenophobia and appealed for modera-tion and justice. In doing so, they have embraced and embodied the core American ideals and values that xenophobia has threatened.

During the congressional debates over the Chinese Exclusion Act in 1882, for example, George Frisbie Hoar, a Republican senator from Mas-sachusetts, gave an extraordinary speech that denounced the discrim-inatory measure. Hoar, who had been a longtime defender of African American civil rights, Native American treaty rights, and women's suf-frage, argued that the exclusion of Chinese from America was nothing more than "the old race prejudice which has so often played its hateful and bloody part in history." The Declaration of Independence, he con-tinued, did not allow the government to interfere with an individual's desire "to go everywhere on the surface of the earth that his welfare may require."[13]

The next decade, John Fitzgerald, congressman for the 11th District in Boston, bristled as he listened to his colleagues condemn the "inferior" foreigners being allowed into the United States. He was further outraged when his colleague from Massachusetts, Senator Henry Cabot Lodge, in-troduced a literacy bill in 1896 that would have excluded Fitzgerald's own mother, an illiterate immigrant from Ireland. In a speech on the House floor, Fitzgerald registered his utter opposition to the bill. "It is fashion-able today to cry out against the immigration of the Hungarian, the Ital-ian, and the Jew," he declared, "but I think that the man who comes to this country for the first time—to a strange land without friends and without employment—is bound to make a good citizen." Lodge reportedly con-fronted him at the Capitol and asked him, "Do you think the Jews or the Italians have any right in this country?" "As much as your father or mine," Fitzgerald replied. "It was only a difference of a few ships."[14]

Writers and playwrights such as Israel Zangwill, Mary Antin, and Carlos Bulosan used their novels and plays to humanize immigrants and appeal to Americans' commitment to equality. Everyday Americans also condemned their elected officials for their xenophobic attitudes. After attending a 1913 speech by anti-Japanese politician James D. Phelan, Alice Brown of Elk Grove, California, was so incensed that she immediately sent off a letter of rebuke to the senator. "I cannot let your so called 'facts' go unchallenged," she began. "Your statements were falsehoods," she charged, influenced by "your race hatred [which] distorts your vision and the naked truth." She and her neighbors, she continued, "are perfectly certain that one law-abiding, industrious Japanese is worth to the community and to the state a dozen demagogues and the whole race of politicians put together."[15]

Social workers like Jane Addams worked tirelessly on behalf of immigrants and helped them integrate into American society. The American Committee for the Protection of Foreign Born challenged the repression, detention, and expulsion of immigrants from the 1930s to the 1980s. Lawyers from the ACLU defended the constitutional rights of Japanese Americans during World War II and fought to keep Japanese Peruvian deportees in the United States after the war. Immigrant advocacy and faith-based organizations like the American Jewish Committee, the Hebrew Immigrant Aid Society, the YWCA, Catholic Charities, and the International Institute pushed for the resettlement of refugees after World War II and the wars in Southeast Asia. Community activists like Luisa Moreno, a labor organizer in Los Angeles and San Diego with the Spanish-Speaking People's Congress, battled border enforcement policies. Chicano activists began addressing increasing violence from the Border Patrol in the 1960s.[16]

More recently, immigrant rights activists, along with unions, civil rights organizations, and faith leaders, have maintained a vociferous opposition to mass deportation and punitive immigration laws. Growing out of the campaign to oppose California's Proposition 187 in 1994, immigrant rights advocates have responded to anti-immigration legislation and increased arrests, detention, and deportation. In the spring of 2006, a series of massive protests took place across the country to oppose the draconian immigration bill (H.R. 4437) passed by the Republican majority in the US House of Representatives. It proposed to build seven hundred miles of border fencing, make undocumented entry a felony, increase interior enforcement, and make assisting undocumented immigrants by shielding them from detection a crime. *Mega marchas* organized by veteran Chicano movement organizers and student, labor, leftist, and community-based organizations signaled mass opposition to the bill. The May 1 march brought five hundred thousand people to the streets in Los Angeles and three hundred thousand in Chicago. Similarly, the sanctuary movement, first begun in the 1980s when churches opposed the federal government's refusal to accept Central American asylum seekers, reformed in the 2000s to oppose rising deportations of undocumented immigrants.[17]

Groups that had been unjustly discriminated against in earlier decades also came out in support of communities under threat. After 9/11, Fred Korematsu became an outspoken critic of the US government's national security measures that racially profiled Muslim and Arab Americans. He warned that such actions were reminiscent of civil liberties violations in the past. He argued that "even in times of crisis[,] we must

Protesters at Seattle's Sea-Tac Airport on the night of January 28, 2017, after the Muslim ban went into effect. Dennis Bratland [CC BY-SA 4.0 (https://creativecommons.org/licenses/by-sa/4.0)], from Wikimedia Commons.

guard against prejudice and keep uppermost our commitment to law and justice." For Fred, this transcended race, religion, and nationality. It was about civil rights for all Americans and human rights for all.[18]

Hours after President Donald Trump signed an executive order banning all foreign nationals from seven Muslim-majority countries, mass protests erupted at airports and city centers nationally and internationally, mostly organized via Facebook. By the next day, 120 planned protests were listed on the ThinkProgress website. Approximately two thousand people gathered at John F. Kennedy Airport in New York. Four thousand people were at LAX and three thousand more at Seattle's airport.[19]

Major US companies also joined in the protest. Google co-founder Sergey Brin participated in the protest at San Francisco International Airport Friday evening. Apple, whose founder Steve Jobs had a Syrian birth father, became one of the first companies to denounce the ban. "Apple would not exist without immigration, let alone thrive and innovate the way we do," wrote Apple chief Tim Cook in a memo to employees. Mark Parker, the CEO of Nike, denounced the order and described it as a "threat" to the company's values. The ride-sharing company Lyft donated $1 million to the ACLU, which actively challenged the ban. Starbucks pledged to hire ten thousand refugees. On January 30, 2017, approximately two thousand Google employees from across Google's global offices walked out in protest of the executive order.[20]

By 2018, the Trump administration's explicit xenophobia had led to an all-out assault on immigration and on immigrant and refugee communities. Immigration enforcement was up between 37 and 43 percent from the previous year. Those arrested included many people who had no criminal convictions, a change from how the Obama administration enforced immigration. Workplace raids increased, including an April 2018 raid at a meat-processing plant in rural Tennessee that was reportedly the largest since the George W. Bush administration.[21]

Trump officials worked to end the Obama-era DACA program and implemented policies designed to deter future unauthorized border crossers and to make life more difficult for those who did cross. Its "zero tolerance" policy at the US-Mexico border resulted in the separation of 2,500 migrant children from their parents when taken into custody. Many were subsequently lost within the system and were not reunited with their families for months. New rules also limited who was considered eligible for asylum, excluding from eligibility those who were fleeing domestic violence and gang violence. Aimed at Central Americans who commonly filed for asylum in the United States on these grounds, these rules drastically reduced the number of accepted asylum requests by individuals from these countries.[22]

The Trump administration also made historic reductions in refugee resettlement. Whereas President Obama raised the refugee admission ceiling to 110,000 in 2017, President Trump reduced it to 45,000 the next year. In 2019, he lowered it even more to 30,000, the lowest level since the United States began its refugee resettlement program in 1980. Meanwhile, new policies likened to "invisible walls" created additional barriers for legal immigrants and the companies that employed them. Applicants for the high-skilled H1-B visa faced more scrutiny and were deluged with requests for additional evidence critics deemed unnecessary. Spouses of high-skilled foreign workers already in the United States were additionally stripped of their work permits. Just before the 2018 midterm elections, President Trump announced that he would sign an executive order that would end the right of US birthright citizenship to children born in the United States to noncitizens.[23]

Both Trump's explicit xenophobia and his administration's wide-ranging policy changes terrorized immigrant and refugee communities. Undocumented immigrants and their children lived in fear of being deported and separated. Americans with families stuck in refugee camps despaired that they would never be reunited. A proposal to deport or deny legal permanent residence (i.e., a green card) to immigrants who used many popular and essential government programs such as the Supplemental Nutrition Assistance Program (SNAP), public housing (including the housing choice voucher program), Medicaid, and the Medicare Part D program led many families to withdraw from essential health programs.[24]

But Trump's inhumane policies also sparked an unprecedented backlash. As with the immediate response to the so-called Muslim ban, protests to these policies were highly visible, broad-based, and organized on a massive scale. Action included numerous legal challenges pursued by the ACLU, the Southern Poverty Law Center, the National Immigration Law Center, and many refugee resettlement and immigrant rights groups. There were nationwide marches and the spread of the "sanctuary movement" to cities and states across the country. By 2018, the State of California and about three hundred cities nationwide had sanctuary policies that either limited cooperation with ICE or symbolically opposed cooperation. State and local governments, attorneys, and community leaders organized to monitor ICE activities, develop response plans to protect targeted immigrants, and provide legal counsel. On June 30, 2018, more than six hundred marches occurred across the country under the banner "Families Belong Together" to protest the Trump administration's implementation of a zero-tolerance border policy. At the same time, calls to abolish ICE, the country's immigration enforcement agency tasked with identifying, detaining, and deporting people in the United States who violated immigration law, were being heard not only from progressive activists who had been fighting the expansion of immigration enforcement for years but also from a growing number of Americans. They were appalled by the images of screaming babies being wrested from their mothers' arms at the southern border and the arrests and deportation of longtime law-abiding residents in their own communities. By the time the president declared a national emergency to fund his border wall, politicians like California governor Gavin Newsom were condemning the "fear mongering from the White House" and identifying the border "emergency" as nothing more than a "manufactured crisis" and "political theater." Within a week of the president's declaration, sixteen states filed a lawsuit challenging the president over his plan to bypass Congress and use emergency powers to fund the wall.[25]

A growing number of interracial and interfaith coalitions also responded to the broad and expansive assault on so many types of immigrant communities. The Muslim ban, for example, was condemned by the American Friends Service Committee, the Anti-Defamation League, the Japanese American Citizens League, the Mexican American

Legal Defense and Education Fund, United We Dream, and many other organizations. Similarly, the Hebrew Immigrant Aid Society and CAIR joined an interfaith coalition led by the American Friends Service to stand in solidarity with the migrant caravan and those seeking asylum along the southern border in December 2018. Change came to politics as well. A record number of immigrants ran for public office in the 2018 midterm elections across the country, and many were successful, including two politicians who became the first Muslim women elected to Congress.[26]

It is too early to know whether today's protests will pave the way for real and lasting change beyond the Trump era. I fervently hope that they do. Unfortunately, the historical record reveals that just as it has been impossible to eradicate racism, xenophobia has been difficult to dismantle. Most of the challenge lies, of course, in the embeddedness of xenophobia in our institutions and in our worldview. But fault also lies with missed opportunities for radical change. Over the course of US history, xenophobia's opponents, including liberal and progressive lawmakers and advocates, have repeatedly compromised on major policy proposals that would have more completely altered the flawed political culture and legal system that promotes xenophobia. Or they have been complicit in helping to expand and justify xenophobia as an acceptable ideology and practice. This has happened when immigrants are blamed as the problem, while broken immigration laws and unequal economic policies are ignored. It has also happened when lawmakers have accepted only piecemeal reform without pushing for broader change, failed to establish broad-based and enduring coalitions across immigrant groups, and reaffirmed divisive narratives that pit certain "good" immigrants against "bad" ones.

Too often, reformers and advocates have only selectively denounced xenophobia as it has targeted certain, usually highly sympathetic populations, while leaving both the general acceptance of and the tools and machinery of xenophobia untouched. Members of Congress who opposed the 1924 Immigration Act, for example, denounced the explicit racism that identified southern and eastern European immigrants as inferior but acquiesced in the racial denigration of Japanese people, thereby reinforcing the very racism that they rejected for Europeans. And during the Cold War, Italian Americans tirelessly advocated for immigration reform for Italian immigrants but were ambivalent on advocating for equal immigration opportunities for all global migrants.[27]

More recently, pro-immigrant politicians, unions, and some advocacy groups have allowed an increasingly powerful bloc of government and nongovernmental xenophobes to set the terms of immigration reform in the late twentieth and early twenty-first centuries. Faced with extreme xenophobic proposals, these leaders have accepted moderate reform positions that offer some concessions like pathways to citizenship for so-called good immigrants while funding and expanding the nation's border security and deportation machine. Indeed, most comprehensive immigration reform bills that were introduced in the early twenty-first century contained massive enforcement provisions as nonnegotiable features. Critics contend that granting the federal government (and increasingly, local and state governments) this kind of authority only reinforces xenophobia, injustice, and state-sanctioned violence on immigrant communities. "Reform without justice," as one critic has argued, is no justice at all.[28] Xenophobia has thus never been fully excised from the United States. It has merely evolved.

As XENOPHOBIA HAS become increasingly embedded in American politics and life, we must fully understand its costs.

Xenophobia threatens American democracy. It allows the will of a vocal and mobilized minority to dictate policy for the majority. Public opinion polls consistently showed that most Americans rejected Donald Trump's divisive rhetoric and opposed his xenophobic policies before and after the 2016 presidential election and into the first year of the Trump presidency, for example. Americans were less concerned about immigrants' impact on the workforce than they were a decade before. A majority supported legal status for immigrants brought to the United States without documentation as children as well as an increase in legal immigration. What they did not support was a bigger border wall.[29]

American democratic processes and institutions have also been used to support, legalize, and facilitate xenophobia. Politicians have routinely scapegoated immigrants to mobilize voters for political gain or power. Xenophobic laws have granted the US government sweeping power over foreigners, sometimes resulting in practices that violate American laws, democratic principles, and human rights. But perhaps most damaging of all, attacks on immigrants have consistently threatened the core civil and political rights on which American democracy is built. The First Amendment to the US Constitution, for example, states that everyone in the United States has the right to practice their own religion, or no religion at all. But over the centuries, our attacks on Catholics, Jews, and Muslims and their houses of worship have threatened their freedom to practice their faith without harassment. The Fifth Amendment guarantees that "no person" shall be deprived of life, liberty, or property without due process of law. And the Fourteenth Amendment guarantees equal protection of the laws to "any person." Nevertheless, immigrants and refugees have consistently been treated unequally and denied due process and equal protection under the law. One of the most egregious examples includes the violent expulsions of Chinese immigrants in the nineteenth century, often while government officials passively looked on, or even participated. These policies have unfortunately continued. Since the US government began implementing the policy known as expedited removal in 1996, which allows for a sped-up deportation of some non–US citizens, for example, it has done so without extending the due process protections (such as legal counsel or an immigration court hearing) granted to other residents in the United States.[30]

Xenophobia ensnares and de-Americanizes long-term residents and US citizens by stigmatizing them as perpetual foreigners in—or even threats to—the United States, irrespective of their immigration or citizenship status. Mexican Americans who were prevented from voting in the US Southwest, for example, were de-Americanized. Japanese Americans were forcibly relocated and incarcerated during World War II in perhaps the best-known example of de-Americanization. But the process continues today. Since 9/11, Arab and Muslim Americans have been subjected to mass arrests, detention without charges, special registration, wiretapping, and spying without pretext. And as the United States has expanded its immigration enforcement into the interior of the country to target undocumented immigrants, deportation has resulted in the de facto deportation of US citizens as well as undocumented immigrants. These cases typically involve US-born citizen children in so-called mixed-status families who accompany a noncitizen parent deported back to their homeland. Described as "collateral victims" of a cruel deportation machine in the United States, these American citizens have become part of a growing deportation diaspora who have been effectively de-Americanized.[31]

Xenophobia threatens national unity. It allows white supremacy and white nationalism to come to the forefront of American politics and culture. It embraces only some as Americans, while others remain outsiders. It fosters a violent citizenship of exclusion, encouraging citizens to differentiate themselves from and pit themselves against the foreign-born. In recent years, for example, US citizens have been increasingly enlisted to enforce xenophobic policies. This was the intent behind California's Proposition 187. In 2011, Alabamans passed H.B. 56, which required teachers to verify the immigration status of their students, including those in elementary school. It also charged anyone found aiding or transporting undocumented immigrants with a felony. Although many provisions were ruled unconstitutional, some remain on the books, including a "show me your papers" policy.[32]

WITH SO MUCH at stake, understanding exactly how xenophobia works is fundamental to the future of American democracy and for the creation of a more humane global society. Part of this task is to reckon with the United States' violent history of xenophobia and recognize its tenacious grip on the United States today. Another urgent undertaking is to understand the limits of xenophobic policies that have led to building walls and banning immigrants. We are living in an era of unprecedented global migration as economic, political, social, and environmental forces continue to drive people from their homes. On our interconnected and warming planet, our future well-being will be inextricably connected to the well-being of those whom we might consider "strangers." As all of humanity faces limited resources and opportunities, we cannot afford to practice the closed-mindedness and isolation that xenophobia promotes.

In both the past and present, xenophobes have argued that immigrants are threats. But it is xenophobia, not immigration, that is our gravest threat today. It is time to reset the terms of the debate.

ACKNOWLEDGMENTS

IN THIS BOOK, I have tried to bring historical research and perspective to one of the most fundamental questions shaping the United States today: Is the United States a "nation of immigrants" or a nation of xenophobia? I began as I always have—by collecting and reading towers of books and articles; visiting archives and historical sites; identifying arguments, story lines, and evidence; and writing with both the scholar and the general reader in mind. None of this could have been possible without the help of many, many people.

My thank-you list is longer this time around, and the debt greater. This is because *America for Americans* is unlike any book I have written before. It was born out of the specific political moment of the 2016 US presidential election, and it was written in response to—and amid—the crisis of xenophobia that quickly followed. I felt compelled to answer the question "How did we get here?" not only for myself and other scholars, but also for my students, many of them immigrants and refugees, who shared with me their fears of being deported, being separated from their families, and being victims of hate crimes. Writing about xenophobia during this specific moment in the United States became an act of resistance and an urgent call for change. But it has also sometimes literally made me sick. I could not have finished without the many people who directly and indirectly helped, guided, and inspired me.

I first tested out new ideas and research before a group of brilliant K–12 teachers participating in the 2016 National Endowment for the Humanities Landmarks of American History and Culture Workshop organized by the great staff at the Wing Luke Museum in Seattle. Longtime activist and civil rights pioneer Betty Luke generously helped me locate specific sites marking the Chinese expulsion from Seattle in 1886 and shared with me the efforts of local activists to commemorate the expulsion and work toward social justice for all. The amazing Patricia Weaver Francisco was my writing coach during the early stages of researching and writing this book and helped me find new ways of looking at and writing history. She made writing fun again. Thank you, Patricia!

My amazing colleagues at the Immigration History Research Center and Archives stepped up to help us collectively respond to the dramatically changing public discourse around immigration during and after the 2016 presidential election. I am deeply proud that our efforts supported an increase in services to immigrant and refugee students, staff, and faculty on the University of Minnesota campus. We also created timely public programs and educational resources like Immigrant Stories and the #ImmigrationSyllabus that have been used around the world. Thank you, Saengmany Ratsabout, Liz Venditto, Bryan Pekel, Ellen Engseth, the amazing team from the University of Minnesota Libraries Publishing and eLearning Support Initiative, and the many scholars who co-organized and advised the #ImmigrationSyllabus project.

As always, I learned much from my students, who bravely shared their stories of how the new deportations and bans were impacting their own families and communities. Thank you for trusting me with these insights. An informal network of faculty formed to collectively respond to new Trump-era policies was an important source of information and inspiration. Elliott Young's initial question, "What are we going to do when the deportation trains start running again?" as well as Kelly Lytle Hernández's reply that "We know this history well" resonated with my own conviction of how high the stakes were and how historians could play a game-changing role.

My many visits to archives across the country were greatly facilitated by dedicated archivists who helped me identify sources, pulled and repulled boxes, and did so on short timelines. Staff at the Bancroft Library at UC Berkeley, the Center for the Study of Political Graphics, the UCLA Chicano Studies Research Center, the University of Minnesota Immigration History Research Center Archives, the Institute of Governmental Studies at UC Berkeley, the Massachusetts Historical Society, and Special Collections at UCLA were especially helpful.

Lectures and presentations at numerous conferences and institutions gave me the opportunity to share work in progress and receive valuable feedback. Thank you to the audiences and the organizers of my talks at the University of Illinois, Urbana-Champaign; Grinnell College; Google; UCLA; University of Otago (New Zealand); Williams College; the Society for Historians of the Gilded Age and Progressive Era; the University of Minnesota; La Trobe University (Australia); the Seattle Public Library; and Northwestern University. Panel discussions with activists and legal experts at Twin Cities Public Television and the Seattle Public Library were especially helpful and inspirational. A writing hunker with the Center for Writing Studies and the interdisciplinary collaborative workshop on migration at the University of Minnesota provided much needed camaraderie, time to write, and the opportunity to connect with a broad range of experts and professionals on and off campus.

This book would not be possible without my amazing team of research assistants at the University of Minnesota: Ben Hartmann, Bryan Pekel, Evan Taparata, and Kent Weber. They combed through multiple databases, scores of secondary sources, and dozens of news articles; identified new research materials; and expertly summarized findings. They also pushed me with their own insightful questions and perspectives.

I have gained so much from learning from my brilliant and generous colleagues whose own research has changed the way I think about my own. They offered reading suggestions, passed on helpful articles, patiently answered queries, and read chapter drafts, sometimes multiple times. Thank you to Doug Hartmann, Evan Taparata, Yuichiro Onishi, Adam Goodman, Jean O'Brien, Elaine Tyler May, Jimmy Patiño, Maddalena Marinari, Kent Weber, Jack DeWaard, and Ryan Allen. Thank you especially to Donna Gabaccia and Tyler Anbinder for reading a draft of the entire book and for offering many constructive suggestions and corrections.

I have been so fortunate to have Sandra Dijkstra as my literary agent. She has helped me turn vague ideas into award-winning books. She believed in this book and its importance from the very beginning. She and Elise Capron, and the rest of the team at the Dijkstra Agency, worked tirelessly to find just the right publishing house. Sandy's enthusiastic messages cheering me on throughout the writing of this difficult book always sustained me.

My editorial team at Basic Books has been an author's dream. Dan Gerstle was an early supporter and helped me fine-tune the book's structure, tone, and approach through many conversations and chapter reads. Brian Distelberg's first read of the completed manuscript resulted in thirty single-spaced pages of keen insights, razor-sharp questions, and concrete suggestions. They helped me articulate the book's arguments more clearly and make the book better and tighter. Claire Potter's line editing helped me improve the text even more, polished my prose and arguments, and brought much needed levity to the final writing stages with her enthusiasm and witticisms. Amy J. Schneider did an excellent job copyediting. Alex Colston and Melissa Veronesi expertly shepherded the final manuscript through to publication, and Kelsey Odorczyk and Liz Wetzel made sure that the book was well publicized.

Research and writing requires time and resources. I have been extremely fortunate to have received both. This book was made possible through generous financial support from a number of institutions, especially a two-year fellowship from the Carnegie Corporation of New York. (The statements made and viewed expressed are solely my responsibility.) Other crucial resources came from the University of Minnesota, where I have taught ever since I finished graduate school. My faculty colleagues and graduate students in the Department of History and the Asian American Studies Program inspire me and create a wonderful environment in which to research, teach, and serve. I follow in the footsteps of many other generations of immigration historians who have been equally committed to writing history that matters, and it is my great privilege to direct the Immigration History Research Center. The generous support and academic honors that the U of M has bestowed upon me have been crucial to my research and career, and I am most grateful to be a part of this tremendous public land-grant institution. These have included the Regent's Professorship, the Rudolph J. Vecoli Chair in Immigration History, the Distinguished McKnight Professorship, the Dean's Medal from the College of Liberal Arts, and a single-semester leave.

My family, sisters Laurel Lee-Alexander and Kristen Lee and father Howard Lee, deserve special thanks for their lifelong support. I have learned much from all of them. Laurel and Kristen continue to inspire me everyday. I cherish our amazingly strong bond and could not have survived the recent and heartbreaking loss of our mother without them. I am deeply grateful to my wonderful in-laws, Bill and Molly Buccella, whose interest in my work and love and support have meant so much.

My deepest thanks go to my amazing husband, Mark Buccella, and our wonderful sons, Ben and Billy, who daily provide a shelter from the storm. Ben and Billy have grown up amid the writing of three books. Nearly ten years ago, they accompanied me while I gave talks about Angel Island. They patiently drew in the back of the room and waited until we could do something really fun afterward. I realized that they were actually listening to me when they started telling me that I had skipped over their favorite stories in my presentations. Mark and I pushed them in a stroller during the 2006 *mega marchas* and walked alongside them during the 2018 marches. They now study race and immigration in their own ways. Ben and Billy—it is a great joy to be the one learning from you and to be inspired by your views of the world and how it should work. I am so proud to be your mom. Mark is my rock. He is an endless source of love and encouragement and a truly equal partner. Together, we keep two careers humming, raise two teenagers, support our families and communities, and weather life's ups and downs. He makes both small and big accomplishments possible and sustains me every day. Thank you, from the bottom of my heart, for your love and for valuing the work that I do. I could not have made it through this past year of devastating loss without your deep and constant support. I am so grateful for you and for what we have.

This book is dedicated in loving memory to my mother, Fay Huie Lee, who passed away as I was writing the last chapters. I wish that she had lived to see its publication. She was a devoted mother, beloved grandmother, and friend to many. To me, she was also a best friend and my greatest cheerleader. She always took a keen interest in my work, sent me links and news clippings, and was a constant source of love and encouragement. She instilled in my sisters and me a deep respect for others, a love and appreciation for diversity, and a keen sense of right and wrong. She lived by the belief that "there are no strangers in the world, only friends you haven't met yet." She herself had a gift of making anyone and everyone feel comfortable and she made friends wherever she went. In these pages, I have tried to demonstrate why making friends of strangers is so important today. Mom, this is for you.

ARCHIVES AND COLLECTIONS

Repositories

Bancroft Library, University of California Berkeley
California Historical Society
Center for Oral and Public History, California State University, Fullerton
Center for the Study of Political Graphics
Chicano Studies Research Center, University of California, Los Angeles
Densho Digital Repository
Ethnic Studies Library, University of California, Berkeley
Houghton Library, Harvard University
Immigration History Research Center Archives, University of Minnesota
Institute of Governmental Studies Library, University of California, Berkeley
Labor Archives and Research Center, San Francisco State University
Library of Congress
Massachusetts Historical Society
Special Collections, Princeton University Library
Special Collections, University of California, Los Angeles
Special Collections, University of Washington Libraries
US National Archives, Washington, DC
US National Archives at College Park, Maryland
Yale University

Government Records

General Records of the Department of State. RG 59. Decimal File, 1940–1944. US National Archives, College Park, Maryland
Records of the Office of Strategic Services. RG 226. Research and Analysis Branch Divisions. Intelligence Series, 1941–1945. US National Archives, College Park, Maryland

Manuscript and Digital Collections

A. Shibayama Family Collection, Densho Digital Repository

The American Committee on Italian Migration, Chicago Chapter (Ill.) Records, Italian American Collection, Immigration History Research Center Archives, Special Collections, University of Minnesota

American Party (Boston, MA) Records of the East Boston Chapter of the American Party, Massachusetts Historical Society

Angel Island Oral History Project, Ethnic Studies Library, University of California, Berkeley

Asiatic Exclusion League Records, 1906–1910, Labor Archives and Research Center, San Francisco State University

B. Shibayama Family Collection, Densho Digital Repository

Caesar Donnaruma Papers, Immigration History Research Center Archives, Special Collections, University of Minnesota

California General Election, 1994, Proposition 187 Campaign Ephemera and Newspaper Clippings, Institute of Governmental Studies Library, University of California Berkeley

California Joint Commission for Immigration Reform, 1924-1936, Bancroft Library, University of California, Berkeley

Charles B. Bagley Papers, Special Collections, University of Washington Libraries

Commission on Wartime Relocation and Internment of Civilians Collection, Densho Digital Repository

Densho Visual History Collection, Densho Digital Repository

Early Photographs Collection, Special Collections, University of Washington Libraries

Edmond S. Meany Papers, Special Collections, University of Washington Libraries

Edward N. Barnhart Papers, 1942-1952, Special Collections, University of California, Los Angeles Library

George P. Clements Papers, Special Collections, University of California, Los Angeles Library

Henry Ford Archive of American Innovation Digital Collections

Immigration Restriction League Records, Houghton Library, Harvard University

James D. Phelan Papers, Bancroft Library, University of California, Berkeley

Lyndon Baines Johnson Presidential Library

Mexican American Oral History Project, Center for Oral and Public History, California State University, Fullerton

Michael Feighan Papers, Special Collections, Princeton University Library

Papers of Benjamin Franklin, American Philosophical Society and Yale University

Proposition 187 Campaign Ephemera and Newspaper Clippings, Institute of Governmental Studies Library, University of California Berkeley

Ron Lopez Papers, Chicano Studies Research Center, University of California, Los Angeles

Watson C. Squire Papers, Special Collections, University of Washington Libraries

Wayne M. Collins Papers, 1918-1974, Bancroft Library, University of California, Berkeley

NOTES

Introduction

1. Marc Santora, "'We're Coming to Get You!' It's Vintage Giuliani at G.O.P. Convention," *New York Times*, July 19, 2016; Howard Koplowitz, "Jeff Sessions Republican Convention Speech 2016," Alabama Media Group, July 18, 2016, www.al.com /news/index.ssf/2016/07/jeff_sessions_republican_conve.html; Miriam Valverde, "Sen. Jeff Sessions Wrongly Says 350,000 People Succeed in Crossing the Border Every Year," Politifact, July 19, 2016, www.politifact.com/truth-o-meter/statements/2016/jul/19 /jeff-sessions/senator-jeff-sessions-says-about-350000-people-suc/; CNN's Reality Check Team, "Day 1 of GOP Convention Speeches: CNN Vets the Claims," CNN, July 19, 2016, www.cnn.com/2016/07/18/politics/gop-convention-speeches-fact-check/.

2. Valverde, "Sen. Jeff Sessions"; Jason L. Riley, "The Mythical Connection Between Immigrants and Crime," *Wall Street Journal*, July 14, 2016, www.wsj.com/articles /the-mythical-connection-between-immigrants-and-crime-1436916798.

3. Politico Staff, "Full Text: Donald Trump 2016 RNC Draft Speech Transcript," Politico, July 21, 2016, www.politico.com/story/2016/07/full-transcript-donald -trump-nomination-acceptance-speech-at-rnc-225974#ixzz4G10WS7fv; Patrick Healy and Jonathan Martin, "His Tone Dark, Donald Trump Takes G.O.P. Mantle," *New York Times*, July 21, 2016.

4. Kunal Parker, *Making Foreigners: Immigration and Citizenship Law in America, 1600–2000* (Cambridge, UK: Cambridge University Press, 2015), 2; US Department of Homeland Security, "2016 Yearbook of Immigration Statistics," December 18, 2017, www.dhs.gov/immigration-statistics/yearbook/2016/table1; Migration Policy Institute, "Legal Immigration to the U.S., 1820–Present," accessed April 2, 2019, www .migrationpolicy.org/programs/data-hub/charts/Annual-Number-of-US-Legal-Permanent-Residents; Pew Research Center, "Key Facts About Refugees to the U.S.," accessed March 31, 2019, www.pewresearch.org/fact-tank/2017/01/30/key-facts -about-refugees-to-the-u-s/; Jie Zong and Jeanne Batalova, "Refugees and Asylees in

the United States," Migration Policy Institute, June 7, 2017, www.migrationpolicy.org /article/refugees-and-asylees-united-states.

5. Adam Goodman, "Nation of Migrants, Historians of Migration," *Journal of American Ethnic History* 34, no. 4 (Summer 2015): 11.

6. Important exceptions include Kevin R. Johnson, *The "Huddled Masses" Myth: Immigration and Civil Rights* (Philadelphia: Temple University Press, 2004); Kelly Lytle Hernández, *City of Inmates: Conquest, Rebellion, and the Rise of Human Caging in Los Angeles, 1771–1965* (Chapel Hill: University of North Carolina Press, 2017); *Natalia Molina, How Race Is Made in America: Immigration, Citizenship, and the Historical Power of Racial Scripts* (Berkeley: University of California Press, 2014); Anna Sampaio, *Terrorizing Latina/o Immigrants: Race, Gender, and Immigration Politics in the Age of Security* (Philadelphia: Temple University Press, 2015).

7. See, for example, John Higham, *Strangers in the Land: Patterns of American Nativism, 1860–1925* (New Brunswick, NJ: Rutgers University Press, 2011), 3–11, 332–334, 340, 344; Peter Schrag, *Not Fit for Our Society: Nativism and Immigration* (Berkeley: University of California Press, 2010), 2; Roger Daniels, *Coming to America: A History of Immigration and Ethnicity in American Life* (New York: HarperCollins, 1990), 338; Gabriel J. Chin, "The Civil Rights Revolution Comes to Immigration Law: A New Look at the Immigration and Nationality Act of 1965," *North Carolina Law Review* 75, no. 1 (1996): 273–345; Nathan Glazer, "The Emergence of an American Ethnic Pattern," in *From Different Shores*, ed. Ronald Takaki (New York: Oxford University Press, 1987), 13.

8. Theodore Roosevelt, "America for Americans, Afternoon Speech of Theodore Roosevelt at St. Louis, May 31, 1916," in *The Progressive Party, Its Record from January to July, 1916* (New York: Mail and Express Job Print, 1916), 75; "America for Americans," 1920–1929, Item No. 214406, Kansas Historical Society, www.kansasmemory.org/item /display.php?item_id=214406&f=00734445; Roger Daniels, *Guarding the Golden Door: American Immigration Policy and Immigrants Since 1882* (New York: Hill and Wang, 2004), 27–58; Madison Grant, "America for Americans," Forum 74 (1925): 346–355.

9. Broadly speaking, psychologists tend to focus on the psychology of fear and view xenophobia as an exclusionary logic, a discriminatory ideology. Sociologists gravitate toward framing xenophobia as a social system that maintains and constructs social and cultural boundaries. Following the lead of historian John Higham, historians have tended to use more general definitions of xenophobia and have used it interchangeably with *nativism*. See, for example, Higham, *Strangers in the Land*, 3–11; John Higham, "Instead of a Sequel, or How I Lost My Subject," *Reviews in American History* 28, no. 2 (June 2000): 327–339; Tyler Anbinder, "Nativism and Prejudice Against Immigrants: An Historiographic Assessment," in *A Companion to American Immigration*, ed. Reed Ueda (Malden, MA: Blackwell, 2006), 177–201; Gary Gerstle, "The Immigrant as Threat to American Security: A Historical Perspective," in *From Arrival to Incorporation: Migrants to the U.S. in a Global Era*, ed. Elliott R. Barkan, Hasia Diner, and Alan M. Kraut (New York: New York University Press, 2008), 217–245. For a recent assessment of Higham's work and the ongoing relevance of xenophobia and nativism, see the special issue of the *Journal of the Gilded Age and Progressive Era* 11, no. 2 (April 2012). For more interdisciplinary frameworks that focus on xenophobia as structural discrimination, see Lilia Fernandez, "Nativism and Xenophobia," in *The Encyclopedia of Global*

Human Migration, ed. Immanuel Ness (Hoboken, NJ: Blackwell, 2013), http://dx.doi .org/10.1002/9781444351071.wbeghm386; Peter Hervik, "Xenophobia and Nativism," in *International Encyclopedia of the Social and Behavioral Sciences*, 2nd ed., ed. James D. Wright (Oxford, UK: Elsevier, 2015), 796–801; Oksana Yakushko, "Xenophobia: Understanding the Roots and Consequences of Negative Attitudes Toward Immigrants," *Counseling Psychologist* 37, no. 1 (January 2009): 36–66; David Haekwon Kim and Ronald R. Sundstrom, "Xenophobia and Racism," *Critical Philosophy of Race* 2, no. 1 (2014): 32–35; Tendayi Achiume, "Beyond Prejudice: Structural Xenophobic Discrimination Against Refugees," *Georgetown Journal of International Law* 45, no. 3 (2014): 325, 332; Tendayi Achiume, "Governing Xenophobia," *Vanderbilt Journal of Transnational Law* 51, no. 2 (March 2018): 338–342.

10. Evelyn Nakano Glenn, "Settler Colonialism as Structure: A Framework for Comparative Studies of U.S. Race and Gender Formation," *Sociology of Race and Ethnicity* 1, no. 1 (2015): 54–74.

11. Martha Gardiner, *The Qualities of a Citizen: Women, Immigration, and Citizenship, 1870–1965* (Princeton, NJ: Princeton University Press, 2005), 87–89; Douglas C. Baynton, *Defectives in the Land: Disability and Immigration in the Age of Eugenics* (Chicago: University of Chicago Press, 2016), 81–85; Margot Canaday, *The Straight State: Sexuality and Citizenship in Twentieth-Century America* (Princeton, NJ: Princeton University Press, 2009), 19–54; Eithne Luibhéid and Lionel Cantú, eds., *Queer Migrations: Sexuality, U.S. Citizenship, and Border Crossings* (Minneapolis: University of Minnesota Press, 2005); Eithne Luibhéid, *Entry Denied: Controlling Sexuality at the Border* (Minneapolis: University of Minnesota Press, 2002).

12. Kim and Sundstrom, "Xenophobia and Racism," 32–35; Achiume, "Beyond Prejudice," 325, 332; Achiume, "Governing Xenophobia," 338–342; Jean Pierre Misago, Iriann Freemantle, and Loren B. Landau, "Protection from Xenophobia: An Evaluation of UNHCR's Regional Office for Southern Africa's Xenophobia Related Programmes," African Centre for Migration and Society (University of Witwatersrand and the United Nations High Commissioner for Refugees, 2015), www.unhcr.org/research/evalreports /55cb153f9/protection-xenophobia-evaluation-unhcrs-regional-office-southern-africas .html; Eric Love, *Islamophobia and Racism in America* (New York: New York University Press, 2017), 1–34; #IslamophobiaIsRacismSyllabus, accessed March 31, 2019, https:// islamophobiaisracism.wordpress.com/; Michael Omi and Howard Winant, *Racial Formation in the United States*, 3rd ed. (New York: Routledge, 2015), 137; Charles W. Mills, *The Racial Contract* (Ithaca, NY: Cornell University Press, 1997), 3.

13. Myron Weiner, "The Global Migration Crisis," in *Global History and Migrations*, ed. Gungwu Wang (Boulder, CO: Westview Press, 1997), xx–xxi; Demetrios G. Papademetriou and Natalia Banulescu-Bogdan, "Understanding and Addressing Public Anxiety About Immigration," Migration Policy Institute, July 2016, 1–18, www .migrationpolicy.org/research/understanding-and-addressing-public-anxiety-about -immigration; R. G. Ratcliffe, "Appeals Court Upholds State 'Show Me Your Papers' Law," *Texas Monthly*, March 13, 2018, www.texasmonthly.com/news/appeals-court-up holds-state-show-papers-law/; Ronald H. Bayor, *Encountering Ellis Island: How European Immigrants Entered America* (Baltimore: Johns Hopkins University Press, 2014), 61; Erika Lee and Judy Yung, *Angel Island: Immigrant Gateway to America* (New York: Oxford University Press, 2010), 155–158.

14. Parker, *Making Foreigners*, 4–5; Johnson, *The "Huddled Masses" Myth*, 1–12.

15. Gary Gerstle, *American Crucible: Race and Nation in the Twentieth Century* (Princeton, NJ: Princeton University Press, 2018), 4; Higham, *Strangers in the Land*, 4; Steven Salaita, *Anti-Arab Racism in the USA: Where It Comes From and What It Means for Politics Today* (New York: Pluto Press, 2015), 83–84.

16. John Higham first defined *nativism* as "anti-foreign spirit" or "intense opposition to an internal minority on the ground of its foreign (i.e. 'un-American') connections" in his 1955 book. Higham, *Strangers in the Land*, 3–11. For works that identify subtle differences between nativism and xenophobia, see Kim and Sundstrom, "Xenophobia and Racism," 22, 31–32; Achiume, "Beyond Prejudice," fn14, 5.

17. Bringing the "native" back into discussions of nativism is an essential part of connecting immigration studies to settler colonialism. See Leti Volpp, "The Indigenous as Alien," *UC Irvine Law Review* 5, no. 289 (2015): 324; more generally, see Patrick Wolfe, "Settler Colonialism and the Elimination of the Native," *Journal of Genocide Research* 8, no. 4 (December 2006): 387–409; J. Kēhaulani Kauanui, "'A Structure, Not an Event': Settler Colonialism and Enduring Indigeneity," *Lateral* 5, no. 1 (2016), https://doi.org/10.25158/L5.1.7; Lorenzo Veracini, *Settler Colonialism: A Theoretical Overview* (New York: Palgrave Macmillan, 2010), 16–17. On nativism and the 2016 election, see Sarah Churchill, *Behold America: A History of America First and the American Dream* (New York: Bloomsbury Press, 2018); Evan Osnos, "The Fearful and the Frustrated," *New Yorker*, August 31, 2015, www.newyorker.com/magazine/2015/08/31/the-fearful-and-the-frustrated.

18. Molina, *How Race Is Made in America*, 2–11.

19. I base my definition of *color-blind xenophobia* on scholarship on color-blind racism. See, for example, Eduardo Bonilla-Silva, *Racism Without Racists: Color-Blind Racism and the Persistence of Racial Inequality in America*, 5th ed. (New York: Rowman and Littlefield, 2018), 2–3.

20. Nicholas De Genova, *Working the Boundaries: Race, Space, and "Illegality" in Mexican Chicago* (Durham, NC: Duke University Press, 2005), 8; Nakano Glenn, "Settler Colonialism," 70.

21. Robert Koulish, "Privatizing the Leviathan Immigration State," *MR Online*, July 20, 2007, https://mronline.org/2007/07/20/privatizing-the-leviathan-immigration-state/; Deepa Fernandes, *Targeted: Homeland Security and the Business of Immigration* (New York: Seven Stories Press, 2011), 169; Justin Akers Chacón, "The War on Immigrants," in Justin Akers Chacón and Mike Davis, *No One Is Illegal: Fighting Racism and State Violence on the U.S.-Mexico Border* (Chicago: Haymarket Books, 2006), 222; Leslie Berestein, "Detention Dollars: Tougher Immigration Laws Turn the Ailing Private Prison Sector into a Revenue Maker," *San Diego Union-Tribune*, May 4, 2008; Philip Mattera, Mafruza Khan, and Stephen Nathan, "Corrections Corporation of America: A Critical Look at Its First Twenty Years," Open Society Foundations, December 2003, www.opensocietyfoundations.org/reports/corrections-corporation-america-critical-look-its-first-twenty-years; Tanya Golash-Boza, *Immigration Nation: Raids, Detentions, and Deportations in Post 9/11 America* (Boulder, CO: Paradigm, 2012), 151–153; Sarah Macaraeg, "Inside a Private Prison's $150M Deal to Detain Immigrants in New Mexico," Reveal News (Center for Investigative Reporting), October 26, 2017, www.revealnews.org/article/inside-the-billion-dollar-industry-of-locking-up-immigrants/.

22. Bonnie Honig, *Democracy and the Foreigner* (Princeton, NJ: Princeton University Press, 2003), 80–81; Rich Karlgaard, "Immigrants Keep Capitalism Fresh," *Forbes*, October 26, 2016, www.forbes.com/sites/richkarlgaard/2016/10/04/immigrants -keep-capitalism-fresh/#5f0ec0fe1191.

23. My definition of "political xenophobia" is broader than just anti-immigrant politics; it is about gaining and maintaining power and institutionalizing discrimination. Meredith W. Watts similarly refers to the "desire or willingness to use public policy to discriminate against foreigners" as "political xenophobia." See Meredith W. Watts, "Political Xenophobia in the Transition from Socialism: Threat, Racism and Ideology Among East German Youth," *Political Psychology* 17, no. 1 (March 1996): 97–126. On xenophobia and state building, see David Scott FitzGerald and David Cook-Martín, *Culling the Masses: The Democratic Origins of Racist Immigration Policy in the Americas* (Cambridge, MA: Harvard University Press, 2014), 2–7, 333–334.

24. Donna Gabaccia, *Foreign Relations: American Immigration in Global Perspective* (Princeton, NJ: Princeton University Press, 2015), 1–12; Reginald Horsman, *Race and Manifest Destiny: The Origins of Racial Anglo-Saxonism* (Cambridge, MA: Harvard University Press, 1986); Paul Kramer, "The Geopolitics of Mobility: Immigration Policy and American Global Power in the Long Twentieth Century," *American Historical Review* 123, no. 2 (April 2018): 393–438.

25. Gerstle, "Immigrant as Threat," 217–245; Erika Lee, *The Making of Asian America: A History* (New York: Simon and Schuster, 2015), 125–136; FitzGerald and Cook-Martín, *Culling the Masses*, 25.

26. Erika Lee, *At America's Gates: Chinese Immigration During the Exclusion Era, 1882–1943* (Chapel Hill: University of North Carolina Press, 2003), 151–188; Clay Boggs, "Mexico's Southern Border Plan: More Deportations and Widespread Human Rights Violations," WOLA (Advocacy for Human Rights in the Americas), March 19, 2015, www.wola.org/analysis/mexicos-southern-border-plan-more-deportations -and-widespread-human-rights-violations/; Andreas E. Feldmann and Helena Olea, "New Formulas, Old Sins: Human Rights Abuses Against Migrant Workers, Asylum Seekers, and Refugees in the Americas," in *Human Rights from the Margins: Critical Interventions*, ed. N. Gordon (Lanham, MD: Lexington Books, 2004), 129–149.

Chapter 1: "Strangers to Our Language and Constitutions"

1. Benjamin Franklin, *Observations Concerning the Increase of Mankind, Peopling of Countries, &c.* (Boston: Kneeland, 1755), 10; Benjamin Franklin to James Parker, March 20, 1751, collected in American Philosophical Society and Yale University, *The Papers of Benjamin Franklin*, franklinpapers.org [hereafter cited as Franklin Papers].

2. Benjamin Franklin to Peter Collinson, May 9, 1753, Franklin Papers.

3. Franklin, *Observations*, 10; Benjamin Franklin to Peter Collinson, May 9, 1753, Franklin Papers [emphasis in original].

4. Michael C. LeMay and Elliott Robert Barkan, eds., *U.S. Immigration and Naturalization Laws and Issues: A Documentary History* (Westport, CT: Greenwood, 1999), 1–10; Emberson Edward Proper, *Colonial Immigration Laws: A Study of the Regulation of Immigration by the English Colonies in America* (New York: Columbia University Press, 1900), 21–37, 88; Leonard Dinnerstein, *Anti-Semitism in America* (New York: Oxford University Press, 1994), 5.

5. Ralph B. Strassburger, *Pennsylvania German Pioneers: A Publication of the Original Lists of Arrivals in the Port of Philadelphia from 1727 to 1808* (Norristown: Pennsylvania German Society, 1934), xv–xvi.

6. Roger Daniels, *Coming to America: A History of Immigration and Ethnicity in American Life* (New York: HarperCollins, 1990), 30, 103; Alan Taylor, *American Colonies: The Settling of North America, Vol. 1* (New York: Penguin, 2002), 317; Jon Butler, *Becoming America: The Revolution Before 1776* (Cambridge, MA: Harvard University Press, 2000), 29.

7. Marianne Wokeck, "The Flow and the Composition of German Immigration to Philadelphia, 1727–1775," *Pennsylvania Magazine of History and Biography* 105, no. 3 (July 1981): 249.

8. Donald F. Durnbaugh, "Christopher Sauer—Pennsylvania-German Printer: His Youth in Germany and Later Relationships with Europe," *Pennsylvania Magazine of History and Biography* 82, no. 3 (1958): 324; Marianne S. Wokeck, *Trade in Strangers: The Beginnings of Mass Migration to North America* (University Park: Pennsylvania State University Press, 1999), 29.

9. Marianne Wokeck, "Irish and German Migration to Eighteenth-Century North America," in *Coerced and Free Migration: Global Perspectives*, ed. David Eltis (Stanford, CA: Stanford University Press, 2002), 157, 173; Marilyn C. Baseler, *Asylum for Mankind: America, 1607–1800* (Ithaca, NY: Cornell University Press, 1999), 4, 6.

10. Sally Schwartz, *"A Mixed Multitude": The Struggle for Toleration in Colonial Pennsylvania* (New York: New York University Press, 1987), 23–24; James H. Merrell, *Into the American Woods: Negotiations on the Pennsylvania Frontier* (New York: Norton, 2000), 24; Aristide R. Zolberg, *A Nation by Design: Immigration Policy in the Fashioning of America* (Cambridge, MA: Harvard University Press, 2006), 33; Wokeck, *Trade in Strangers*, 25, 221; Baseler, *Asylum for Mankind*, 40.

11. Wokeck, *Trade in Strangers*, xxi–xxii, xxvii, 29, 59–60, 220–221; Farley Ward Grubb, *German Immigration and Servitude in America, 1709–1920* (New York: Routledge, 2011), 159.

12. Wokeck, "Irish and German Migration," 155; Grubb, *German Immigration*, 160; Marianne Wokeck, "German Settlements in the British North American Colonies: A Patchwork of Cultural Assimilation and Persistence," in *In Search of Peace and Prosperity: New German Settlements in Eighteenth-Century Europe and America*, ed. Hartmut Lehmann, Hermann Wellenreuther, and Renate Wilson (University Park: Pennsylvania State University Press, 2000), 191; Mark Häberlein, "Migrants in Colonial Pennsylvania: Resources, Opportunities, and Experience," *William and Mary Quarterly* 50, no. 3 (July 1993): 567, 574.

13. Gottlieb Mittelberger, *Journey to Pennsylvania*, ed. and trans. Oscar Handlin and John Clive (Cambridge, MA: Harvard University Press, 1960), 10–13, 15, 32.

14. Walter D. Kamphoefner, "Review of Andreas Brinck, *Die deutsche Auswanderungswelle in die britischen Kolonien Nordamerikas um die Mitte des 18 Jahrhunderts* (Studien zur modernen Geschichte number 45 (Stuttgart: Franz Steiner, 1993)," *American Historical Review* 100, no. 1 (February 1995): 227; Aaron Fogelman, "Migrations to the Thirteen British North American Colonies, 1700–1775: New Estimates," *Journal of Interdisciplinary History* 22, no. 4 (Spring 1992), 699–704; Häberlein, "Migrants in Colonial Pennsylvania," 561, 566, 568.

15. Schwartz, *"A Mixed Multitude,"* 86–87; Marie Basile McDaniel, "Processes of Identity Formation Among German Speakers, 1730–1760," in *A Peculiar Mixture: German-Language Cultures and Identities in Eighteenth Century North America*, ed. Jan Stievermann and Oliver Scheiding (University Park: Pennsylvania State University Press, 2013), 192–193; Proper, *Colonial Immigration Laws*, 192; James H. Kettner, *Development of American Citizenship, 1608–1870* (Chapel Hill: University of North Carolina Press, 1978), 109.

16. Strassburger, *Pennsylvania German Pioneers*, xx; Schwartz, *"A Mixed Multitude,"* 90; Taylor, *American Colonies*, 321.

17. McDaniel, "Processes of Identity Formation," 193; Strassburger, *Pennsylvania German Pioneers*, xx; Benjamin Franklin to Peter Collinson, May 9, 1753, Franklin Papers.

18. Jane T. Merritt, *At the Crossroads: Indians and Empires on a Mid-Atlantic Frontier, 1700–1763* (Chapel Hill: University of North Carolina Press, 2003), 12, 171; Grubb, *German Immigration*, 171; McDaniel, "Processes of Identity Formation," 193.

19. Merritt, *At the Crossroads*, 39, 8, 169; Taylor, *American Colonies*, 322; Kevin Kenny, *Peaceable Kingdom Lost: The Paxton Boys and the Destruction of William Penn's Holy Experiment* (New York: Oxford University Press, 2009), 3; McDaniel, "Processes of Identity Formation," 193.

20. Schwartz, *"A Mixed Multitude,"* 90.

21. Schwartz, *"A Mixed Multitude,"* 87; Kettner, *Development of American Citizenship*, 109; Baseler, *Asylum for Mankind*, 94; Strassburger, *Pennsylvania German Pioneers*, xx–xxxvi.

22. Schwartz, *"A Mixed Multitude,"* 87; Baseler, *Asylum for Mankind*, 73.

23. LeMay and Barkan, *U.S. Immigration and Naturalization Laws*, 5; Baseler, *Asylum for Mankind*, 62; FitzGerald and Cook-Martín, *Culling the Masses*, 87; Strassburger, *Pennsylvania German Pioneers*, xxvii; Wokeck, "The Flow," 254; Schwartz, *"A Mixed Multitude,"* 91; Fogelman, "Migrations," 698.

24. John Philip Meurer, "From London to Philadelphia, 1742," *Pennsylvania Magazine of History and Biography* 37, no. 1 (1913), 94–106; Strassburger, *Pennsylvania German Pioneers*, xxvi–xxvii.

25. Wokeck, "The Flow," 253; Wokeck, *Trade in Strangers*, 140; McDaniel, "Processes of Identity Formation," 194; Kettner, *Development of American Citizenship*, 86.

26. Strassburger, *Pennsylvania German Pioneers*, xxii; Proper, *Colonial Immigration Laws*, 51, n1; Baseler, *Asylum for Mankind*, 64–65.

27. Baseler, *Asylum for Mankind*, 40.

28. Peter Silver, *Our Savage Neighbors: How Indian War Transformed Early America* (New York: Norton, 2007), 8–9.

29. Philip Otterness, "The Palatine Immigrants of 1710 and the Native Americans," in *A Peculiar Mixture*, ed. Stievermann and Scheiding, 70, 75; Robert Middlekauff, *Benjamin Franklin and His Enemies* (Berkeley: University of California Press, 1998), 24.

30. Wokeck, "Irish and German Migration," 157; Daniel K. Richter, *Facing East from Indian Country: A Native History of Early America* (Cambridge, MA: Harvard University Press, 2001), 168.

31. Merritt, *At the Crossroads*, 237–238.

32. Merritt, *At the Crossroads*, 178–180.

33. Kenny, *Peaceable Kingdom Lost*, 75.

34. John B. Frantz, "Franklin and the Pennsylvania Germans," *Pennsylvania History: A Journal of Mid-Atlantic Studies* 65, no. 1 (Winter 1998): 25–27; Otterness, "Palatine Immigrants," 76; Merritt, *At the Crossroads*, 170; Kenny, *Peaceable Kingdom Lost*, 73–74.

35. Merritt, *At the Crossroads*, 4.

36. Merritt, *At the Crossroads*, 272–273.

37. Silver, *Our Savage Neighbors*, xix, 115; Merritt, *At the Crossroads*, 190.

38. Proper, *Colonial Immigration Laws*, 17; Kettner, *Development of American Citizenship*, 107, 110, 117–118, 197; Schwartz, *"A Mixed Multitude,"* 82.

39. Benjamin Franklin to Peter Collinson, May 9, 1753, Franklin Papers.

40. Benjamin Franklin to Peter Collinson, May 9, 1753, Franklin Papers; Frantz, "Franklin and the Pennsylvania Germans," 23.

41. Frantz, "Franklin and the Pennsylvania Germans," 28.

42. Silver, *Our Savage Neighbors*, 220; Frantz, "Franklin and the Pennsylvania Germans," 28.

43. Silver, *Our Savage Neighbors*, 222.

44. Frantz, "Franklin and the Pennsylvania Germans," 28–29; Silver, *Our Savage Neighbors*, 223.

45. Silver, *Our Savage Neighbors*, 298.

46. Kettner, *Development of American Citizenship*, 78–79.

47. Parker, *Making Foreigners*, 36–38.

48. Parker, *Making Foreigners*, 39; Matthew Desmond and Mustafa Emirbayer, *Race in America* (New York: Norton, 2015), 60–61, 63.

49. Zolberg, *A Nation by Design*, 83–87; FitzGerald and Cook-Martín, *Culling the Masses*, 88.

50. Paul Spickard, *Almost All Aliens: Immigration, Race, and Colonialism in American History and Identity* (New York: Routledge, 2007), 101–102; Grubb, *German Immigration*, 391; Daniels, *Coming to America*, 30, 103; Jason Horowitz, "For Donald Trump's Family, an Immigrant's Tale with 2 Beginnings," *New York Times*, August 21, 2016.

Chapter 2: "Americans Must Rule America"

1. Leslie Ann Harper, "Lethal Language: The Rhetoric of George Prentice and Louisville's Bloody Monday," *Ohio Valley History* 11, no. 3 (Fall 2011): 24, 33; Charles E. Deusner, "The Know Nothing Riots in Louisville," *Register of the Kentucky Historical Society* 61 (April 1963): 139–142, 144–145; Carl Fields, "The Know-Nothing Party in Louisville" (PhD diss., University of Louisville, 1936), 43–83; Sister Agnes Geraldine McGann, "Nativism in Kentucky to 1860" (PhD diss., Catholic University of America, 1944), 66–70; Evan Taparata, "An Anti-Immigrant Political Movement That Sparked an Election Day Riot—150 Years Ago," PRI's *The World*, March 5, 2016, www.pri.org/stories/2016-03-05/anti-immigrant-political-movement-sparked-election-day-riot-150-years-ago.

2. Ray Allen Billington, *The Protestant Crusade, 1800–1860: A Study of the Origins of American Nativism* (New York: Rinehart, 1938).

3. "The Irish Refugee, or Poor Pat Must Emigrate" (New York: De Marsan, n.d.), American Song Sheets Library of Congress Rare Books and Special Collections, Library of Congress.

4. Kevin Kenny, "Diaspora and Comparison: The Global Irish as a Case Study," *Journal of American History* 90, no. 1 (June 2003): 43–44.

5. Hidetaka Hirota, *Expelling the Poor: Atlantic Seaboard States and the Nineteenth-Century Origins of American Immigration Policy* (New York: Oxford University Press, 2017), 21.

6. *Illustrated London News*, October 18, 1845, Views of the Famine, https://views ofthefamine.wordpress.com/illustrated-london-news/the-potato-disease/.

7. Jay P. Dolan, *The Irish Americans: A History* (New York: Bloomsbury Press, 2008), 71.

8. *Cork Examiner*, December 28, 1846, Views of the Famine, https://viewsofthe famine.wordpress.com/1846/12/.

9. "Hundreds frantically . . . " from *Cork Examiner*, December 17, 1846, Views of the Famine, https://viewsofthefamine.wordpress.com/1846/12/; Hasia Diner, *Erin's Daughters: Irish Immigrant Women in the Nineteenth Century* (Baltimore: Johns Hopkins University Press, 1983), 31; Jon Gjerde, *Catholicism and the Shaping of Nineteenth-Century America*, ed. S. Deborah Kang (Cambridge, UK: Cambridge University Press, 2012), 138–139; Dolan, *Irish Americans*, 82; Andrew Urban, "Irish Domestic Servants, 'Biddy' and Rebellion in the American Home, 1850–1900," *Gender and History* 21, no. 2 (August 2009), 265; Tyler Anbinder, *City of Dreams: The 400-Year Epic History of Immigrant New York* (Boston: Houghton Mifflin Harcourt, 2016), 132; William G. Bean, "Puritan Versus Celt, 1850–1860," *New England Quarterly* 7, no. 1 (March 1934): 71.

10. Lyman Beecher, *Autobiography, Correspondence, Etc., of Lyman Beecher, DD*, vol. 2, ed. Charles Beecher (New York: Harpers, 1865), 277–281.

11. Lyman Beecher, *A Plea for the West* (Cincinnati, OH: Truman & Smith, 1835), 11.

12. Billington, *Protestant Crusade*, 7–10, 21; Gjerde and Kang, *Catholicism*, 31–32.

13. Billington, *Protestant Crusade*, 241.

14. Samuel F. B. Morse, *Foreign Conspiracy Against the Liberties of the United States* (New York: American and Foreign Christian Union, 1855), 7–10, 117, 115, 127; Samuel F. B. Morse, *Imminent Dangers to the Free Institutions of the United States Through Foreign Immigration and the Present States of the Naturalization Laws* (New York: Clayton, 1835); Tyler Anbinder, *Nativism and Slavery: The Northern Know Nothings and the Politics of the 1850s* (New York: Oxford University Press, 1992), 9.

15. Billington, *Protestant Crusade*, 98, 53, 90–93, 345–379.

16. Maria Monk, *The Awful Disclosures of Maria Monk, as Exhibited in a Narrative of Her Sufferings During a Residence of Five Years as a Novice and Two Years as a Black Nun, in the Hotel Dieu Nunnery in Montreal* (New York: Howe and Bates, 1836), 30–31; Billington, *Protestant Crusade*, 99–108, 361–362.

17. Beecher, *Plea for the West*, 70, 15–16, 52–54, 59, 49.

18. Beecher, *Plea for the West*, 12–13, 161; Lyman Beecher to Dr. Albert Barnes, July 11, 1842, in Beecher, *Autobiography*, ed. Beecher, 453–454.

19. Leo Hershkowitz, "The Native American Democratic Association in New York City, 1835–1836," *New York Historical Society Quarterly* 46, no. 1 (January 1962), 41–60;

Anbinder, *Nativism*, 10, 77; Reverend M. D. Lichliter, *History of the Junior Order United American Mechanics* (Philadelphia: Lippincott, 1908); Ira M. Leonard, "The Rise and Fall of the American Republican Party in New York City, 1843–1845," *New York Historical Society* 40 (1966): 151–192; Billington, *Protestant Crusade*, 131, 201–204, 223.

20. Gjerde and Kang, *Catholicism*, 144–156; Anbinder, *Nativism*, 10–11.

21. Lichliter, *History*; Billington, *Protestant Crusade*, 336–337; Dale T. Knobel, *Paddy and the Republic: Ethnicity and Nationality in Antebellum America* (Middletown, CT: Wesleyan University Press, 1988), 143.

22. Billington, *Protestant Crusade*, 249, 337.

23. Billington, *Protestant Crusade*, 382.

24. Vols. 1 and 2, American Party (Boston, MA), Records of the East Boston Chapter of the American Party, 1853, 1856, MS N-1762, Massachusetts Historical Society [hereafter cited as American Party Records, MHS].

25. Statement of Party Principles, July 11, 1855, Minutes of Subordinate Council No. 5 of the American Party of Massachusetts, American Party Records, MHS; "Examiner's Questions for Admittance to the American (or Know-Nothing) Party," July 1854, American Party Collection, Library of Congress, https://memory.loc.gov /cgi-bin/query/r?ammem/mcc:@field(DOCID+@lit(mcc/062)); Billington, *Protestant Crusade*, 386.

26. *Principles and Objects of the American Party* (New York: American Party, 1855), 17; Anbinder, *Nativism*, 104, 107, 110.

27. *Principles and Objects*, 14; Anbinder, *Nativism*, 107, 109; *The Know Nothing Almanac and True Americans' Manual, for 1855* (New York: De Witt and Davenport, 1854), 19; Hirota, *Expelling the Poor*, 103; Billington, *Protestant Crusade*, 200.

28. John R. Mulkern, *The Know Nothing Party in Massachusetts: The Rise and Fall of a People's Movement* (Boston: Northeastern University Press, 1990), 7–8, 12–13, 67.

29. Billington, *Protestant Crusade*, 334.

30. *Principles and Objects*, 13; Anbinder, *Nativism*, 105, 144–145.

31. Kevin Kenny, *The American Irish: A History* (Harlow, UK: Routledge, 2000), 66–71; Knobel, *Paddy and the Republic*, 91, 88.

32. Urban, "Irish Domestic Servants," 264, 274, 272.

33. "Ireland," *North American Review* 51, no. 108 (July 1840): 205; Knobel, *Paddy and the Republic*, 56.

34. Theodore Parker, *A Sermon on the Moral Condition of Boston*, (Boston: Crosby and Nichols, 1849), 26; Knobel, *Paddy and the Republic*, 22, 86–87.

35. Knobel, *Paddy and the Republic*, 80, 100, 121; Matthew Frye Jacobson, *Whiteness of a Different Color: European Immigrants and the Alchemy of Race* (Cambridge, MA: Harvard University Press, 1998), 48.

36. Hirota, *Expelling the Poor*, 18; Urban, "Irish Domestic Servants," 268; David R. Roediger, *How Race Survived U.S. History: From Settlement and Slavery to the Obama Phenomenon* (London: Verso, 2008), 149; Knobel, *Paddy and the Republic*, 87.

37. "Most impoverished . . . " from Anbinder, *City of Dreams*, 149; Billington, *Protestant Crusade*, 194; Hirota, *Expelling the Poor*, 124.

38. Hirota, *Expelling the Poor*, 45–46.

39. Anbinder, *Nativism*, 108; Hirota, *Expelling the Poor*, 45–46, 48, 104, 124–125.

40. Billington, *Protestant Crusade*, 196–197, 222–223; Anbinder, *City of Dreams*, 123; Gjerde and Kang, *Catholicism*, 222–223, 4–5; "Race war" from *New York Daily Times*, June 6, 1854, cited in Knobel, *Paddy and the Republic*, 88.

41. Billington, *Protestant Crusade*, 386–387.

42. Gjerde and Kang, *Catholicism*, 255; Bean, "Puritan Versus Celt," 80–81; Theodore Parker, *A Sermon of the Dangers Which Threaten the Rights of Man in America*, (Boston: Mussey, 1854), 23.

43. Frederick Douglass, *My Bondage and My Freedom* (New York: Miller, Orton, 1857), 454; Kenny, *American Irish*, 67; Dolan, *Irish Americans*, 98.

44. Anbinder, *Nativism*, 89; Hirota, *Expelling the Poor*, 112–113.

45. Bean, "Puritan Versus Celt," 80; *Principles and Objects*, 22, 8; Anbinder, *Nativism*, 123, 125; Billington, *Protestant Crusade*, 413; Mulkern, *Know Nothing Party*, 87, 108, 64.

46. Mulkern, *Know Nothing Party*, 65.

47. Philip J. Deloria, *Playing Indian* (New Haven, CT: Yale University Press, 1998), 58, 61–68; Cécile R. Ganteaume, "Introduction," in Cécile R. Ganteaume, *Officially Indian: Symbols That Define the United States* (Washington, DC: Smithsonian Institution/National Museum of the American Indian, 2017), 21.

48. Anbinder, *Nativism*, fn1, 20; Dale T. Knobel, "Know-Nothings and Indians: Strange Bedfellows?" *Western Historical Quarterly* 15, no. 2 (April 1984): 175–198; Dale T. Knobel, "To Be an American: Ethnicity, Fraternity, and the Improved Order of Red Men," *Journal of American Ethnic History* 4, no. 1 (Fall 1984): 62–87.

49. Mulkern, *Know Nothing Party*, 15.

50. Bean, "Puritan Versus Celt," 71; Susan E. Gray, *The Yankee West: Community Life on the Michigan Frontier* (Chapel Hill: University of North Carolina Press, 1996), 6; Mulkern, *Know Nothing Party*, 12.

51. "Writing Indians . . . " from Jean M. O'Brien, *Firsting and Lasting: Writing Indians Out of Existence in New England* (Minneapolis: University of Minnesota Press, 2010), xi–xv, 120–130; "Cradle of national liberty" from *Appeal to Democrats and Union Men Against Northern Fusion and Sectionalism: From the Democracy of Boston and Suffolk, Adopted by the Ward and County Committees, in Convention, October 1855* (Boston: Hinks, 1855).

52. Vols. 1, 3, and 4, American Party Records, MHS.

53. Anbinder, *Nativism*, 125.

54. Anbinder, *Nativism*, 121; "Examiner's Questions."

55. *Principles and Objects*, 8; Anbinder, *Nativism*, 123, 125.

56. Billington, *Protestant Crusade*, 387, 391; Hirota, *Expelling the Poor*, 102.

57. Anbinder, *Nativism*, 89; Mulkern, *Know Nothing Party*, 5, 61; "Platform of the American Party of Massachusetts," August 7, 1855, MHS.

58. Dolan, *Irish Americans*, 97; Mulkern, *Know Nothing Party*, 68, 76; Anbinder, *Nativism*, 93; Billington, *Protestant Crusade*, 396.

59. Mulkern, *Know Nothing Party*, 88–89; Billington, *Protestant Crusade*, 413.

60. "State-sponsored . . . " from Mulkern, *Know Nothing Party*, 102, 104, 111.

61. Mulkern, *Know Nothing Party*, 102–103; Hirota, *Expelling the Poor*, 105, 79.

62. Hirota, *Expelling the Poor*, 75, 79–80, 3–4, 8, 126–127.

63. Hirota, *Expelling the Poor*, 181–182.

64. Anbinder, *Nativism*, xiii, xv.

65. Roediger, *How Race Survived U.S. History*, 151.

66. Knobel, *Paddy and the Republic*, 176; Jason Silverman, "Lincoln's 'Forgotten' Act to Encourage Immigration," President Lincoln's Cottage, July 1, 2016, www.lincoln cottage.org/lincolns-forgotten-act-to-encourage-immigration/.

67. Stuart Creighton Miller, *The Unwelcome Immigrant: The American Image of the Chinese, 1785–1882* (Berkeley: University of California Press, 1969), 199–200.

Chapter 3: "The Chinese Are No More"

1. *San Francisco Bulletin*, April 7, 1876; Andrew Gyory, *Closing the Gate: Race, Politics, and the Chinese Exclusion Act* (Chapel Hill: University of North Carolina Press, 1998), 78.

2. *San Francisco Bulletin*, April 7, 1876; Gyory, *Closing the Gate*, 78; Elmer Clarence Sandmeyer, *The Anti-Chinese Movement in California* (Urbana: University of Illinois Press, 1939), 59.

3. California Senate, Committee on Chinese Immigration, *Chinese Immigration: The Social, Moral, and Political Effect of Chinese Immigration. Report of the California State Senate of the Special Committee on Chinese Immigration* (Sacramento: State Printing Office, 1878), 29, 32 [hereafter cited as California, *Chinese Immigration*].

4. Karen J. Leong, "'A Distant and Antagonistic Race': Constructions of Chinese Manhood in the Exclusionist Debates, 1869–1878," in *Across the Great Divide: Cultures of Manhood in the American West*, ed. Laura McCall and Matthew Basso (New York: Routledge, 2000), 131–148; US Congress, Joint Special Committee to Investigate Chinese Immigration, "Report of the Joint Special Committee to Investigate Chinese Immigration" (Washington, DC: US Government Printing Office, 1877), 11 [hereafter cited as US Congress, "Joint Report"].

5. California, *Chinese Immigration*, 17; *San Francisco Bulletin*, April 7, 1876.

6. *San Francisco Bulletin*, April 7, 1876; Gyory, *Closing the Gate*, 78.

7. California, *Chinese Immigration*, 275, 4; Gyory, *Closing the Gate*, 78; Gwendolyn Mink, *Old Labor and New Immigrants in American Political Development: Union, Party, and State, 1875–1920* (Ithaca, NY: Cornell University Press, 1986), 73.

8. California, *Chinese Immigration*, 55, 65, 3.

9. California, *Chinese Immigration*, 46–54.

10. *San Francisco Call*, November 22, 1901.

11. Tin-Yuke Char, *The Sandalwood Mountains: Readings and Stories of the Early Chinese in Hawaii* (Honolulu: University of Hawai'i Press, 1975), 67; Judy Yung, Gordon Chang, and Him Mark Lai, eds., *Chinese American Voices: From the Gold Rush to the Present* (Berkeley: University of California Press, 2006), 8; Ronald T. Takaki, *Strangers from a Different Shore: A History of Asian Americans* (Boston: Little, Brown, 1998), 79, 34; Xiao-huang Yin, *Chinese American Literature Since the 1850s* (Urbana: University of Illinois Press, 2000), 14.

12. Edwin Legrand Sabin, *Building the Pacific Railway: The Construction-Story of America's First Iron Thoroughfare* (Philadelphia: Lippincott, 1919), 111; Takaki, *Strangers from a Different Shore*, 84–85.

13. Victor Nee, *Longtime Californ': A Documentary Study of an American Chinatown* (Boston: Houghton Mifflin, 1974), 16; Erika Lee, *The Making of Asian America: A History* (New York: Simon and Schuster, 2015), 66, 90.

14. Erika Lee, *At America's Gates: Chinese Exclusion During the Exclusion Era, 1882–1943* (Chapel Hill: University of North Carolina Press, 2003), 25.

15. Robert G. Lee, *Orientals: Asian Americans in Popular Culture* (Philadelphia: Temple University Press, 1999), 27–43; Najia Aarim-Heriot, *Chinese Immigrants, African Americans, and Racial Anxiety in the United States, 1848–1882* (Urbana: University of Illinois Press, 2003), 8.

16. Samuel Gompers, *Some Reasons for Chinese Exclusion—Meat vs. Rice—American Manhood Against Asiatic Coolieism—Which Shall Survive?* (Washington, DC: US Government Printing Office, 1902).

17. Richard Samuel West, *The San Francisco Wasp: An Illustrated History* (Easthampton, MA: Periodyssey Press, 2004), 11, 15, 17, 19, 86; Gray Brechin, "The Wasp: Stinging Editorials and Political Cartoons," *Bancroftiana* 121 (Fall 2002): 1, 8; Nicholas Sean Hall, "The Wasp's 'Troublesome Children': Culture, Satire, and the Anti-Chinese Movement in the American West," *California History* 90, no. 2 (2013): 42–63, 74–76.

18. Charles J. McClain, "The Chinese Struggle for Civil Rights in Nineteenth Century America: The First Phase, 1850–1870," *California Law Review* 72, no. 4 (1984): 544, 555; Lucy Salyer, *Laws Harsh as Tigers: Chinese Immigrants and the Shaping of Modern Immigration Law* (Chapel Hill: University of North Carolina Press, 1995), 8; Charles J. McClain, *In Search of Equality: The Chinese Struggle Against Discrimination in Nineteenth-Century America* (Berkeley: University of California Press, 1996), 17–18.

19. Sandmeyer, *Anti-Chinese Movement*, 50–52.

20. Moon-Ho Jung, *Coolies and Cane: Race, Labor, and Sugar in the Age of Emancipation* (Baltimore: Johns Hopkins University Press, 2008), 5, 33–38; Page Act (March 3, 1875) (18 Stat. 477); George Anthony Peffer, *If They Don't Bring Their Women Here: Chinese Female Immigration Before Exclusion* (Urbana: University of Illinois Press, 1999), 28; Salyer, *Laws Harsh as Tigers*, 5.

21. Gyory, *Closing the Gate*, 28, 15.

22. Fu-ju Liu, "A Comparative Demographic Study of Native-Born and Foreign-Born Chinese Populations in the United States" (PhD diss., University of Michigan, 1953), 223; Sandmeyer, *Anti-Chinese Movement*, 57.

23. Sandmeyer, *Anti-Chinese Movement*, 59; Gyory, *Closing the Gate*, 79.

24. Oscar Lewis and Carroll D. Hall, *Bonanza Inn: America's First Luxury Hotel* (New York: Knopf, 1939), 4, 23–29.

25. Gerald Stanley, "Frank Pixley and the Heathen Chinese," *Phylon* 40, no. 3 (1979): 224–228; Theodore R. Copeland, "Men of the Day," *Californian Illustrated Magazine* 5 (1893): xviii–xix.

26. US Congress, "Joint Report," 10.

27. US Congress, "Joint Report," 13, 15, 10.

28. US Congress, "Joint Report," 17–18.

29. US Congress, "Joint Report," 34, 10.

30. Rhoda F. Milnarich, "The Public Career of Aaron Augustus Sargent" (MA thesis, University of Texas, El Paso, 1961), 44–45, 74–80; Lucile Eaves, *A History of California Labor Legislation*, vol. 2 (Berkeley: University of California Press, 1910), 163;

Constitution and By-Laws of the Anti-Chinese Union of San Francisco, Appendix F, US Congress, "Joint Report," 1169.

31. US *Congressional Globe*, 37th Cong., 2d Sess., June 25, 1862, 2938; Christopher Shepard, "No Chinese Wanted: Aaron Sargent and Chinese Immigration, 1862–1886," *Journal of the West* 51, no. 1 (Winter 2012): 52.

32. Gyory, *Closing the Gate*, 82; US Congress, "Joint Report," v, vii.

33. Gyory, *Closing the Gate*, 223–226.

34. Gyory, *Closing the Gate*, 224–227, 238.

35. Lee, *At America's Gates*, 6–12; *Chae Chan Ping v. United States* (1889).

36. Chinese Exclusion Act (May 6, 1882) (22 Stat. 58) [emphasis added].

37. Lee, *At America's Gates*, 30–43; Madeline Hsu, *The Good Immigrants: How the Yellow Peril Became the Model Minority* (Princeton, NJ: Princeton University Press, 2015), 4–11.

38. Adam McKeown, *Melancholy Order: Asian Migration and the Globalization of Borders* (New York: Columbia University Press, 2008), 13; David FitzGerald and David Cook-Martín, *Culling the Masses: The Democratic Origins of Racist Immigration Policy in the Americas* (Cambridge, MA: Harvard University Press, 2014), 25; Aristide Zolberg, "The Great Wall Against China: Responses to the First Immigration Crisis, 1885–1925," in *Migration, Migration History, History: Old Paradigms and New Perspectives*, ed. Jan Lucassen and Leo Lucassen (Bern: Peter Lang, 1999), 291–316; Kathy Paupst, "A Note on Anti-Chinese Sentiment in Toronto," *Canadian Ethnic Studies* 9, no. 1 (1977): 55; Patricia Roy, *A White Man's Province: British Columbia Politicians and Chinese and Japanese Immigrants, 1858–1914* (Vancouver: University of British Columbia Press, 1989), 62–63.

39. Royal Commission on Chinese Immigration, "Report of the Royal Commission on Chinese Immigration: Report and Evidence" (Ottawa: Order of the Commission, 1885), cxxvii, xix, lxxx; *Pacific Commercial Advertiser* (Honolulu, HI), October 28, 1889.

40. Act to Restrict and Regulate Chinese Immigration into Canada, July 20, 1885, cha. 71, 1885, S.C. 207-12 (Can); Peter S. Li, *The Chinese in Canada* (New York: Oxford University Press, 1988), 38.

41. Evelyn Hu-DeHart, "Racism and Anti-Chinese Persecution in Sonora, Mexico, 1876–1932," *Amerasia* 9, no 2 (1982): 1–27; Wilfley and Bassett, *Memorandum on the Law and the Facts in the Matter of the Claim of China Against Mexico for Losses of Life and Property Suffered by Chinese Subjects at Torreon on May 13, 14, and 15, 1911* (San Francisco: American Book and Print, 1911), 3, 4–7; Robert Chao Romero, *The Chinese in Mexico, 1882–1940* (Tucson: University of Arizona Press, 2011), 147–155.

42. Ching Chieh Chang, "The Chinese in Latin America: A Preliminary Geographical Survey with Special Reference to Cuba and Jamaica" (PhD diss., University of Maryland, 1956), 32, 73; "Restrictive international . . ." from Zolberg, "Great Wall," 292.

43. Lee, *At America's Gates*, 40–41.

44. Immigration Act of 1924 (43 Stat. 153).

45. Geary Act, Section 7 (May 5, 1892) (27 Stat. 25); McCreary Amendment, Section 2 (November 3, 1893) (28 Stat. 7); Alien Registration Act of 1940, (54 Stat. 670).

46. Act of May 6, 1882 (22 Stat. 58); Act of March 3, 1891 (26 Stat. 1084); Act of August 18, 1894 (28 Stat. 390); "Deportation nation" from Daniel Kanstroom, *Deportation Nation: Outsiders in American History* (Cambridge, MA: Harvard University Press, 2010).

47. Jean Pfaelzer, *Driven Out: The Forgotten War Against Chinese Americans* (New York: Random House, 2007); Beth Lew-Williams, *The Chinese Must Go: Violence, Exclusion, and the Making of the Alien in America* (Cambridge, MA: Harvard University Press, 2018).

48. Art Chin and Doug Chin, *The Chinese in Washington State* (Seattle: OCA Greater Seattle, 2013), 42.

49. Carlos A. Schwantes, "Protest in a Promised Land: Unemployment, Disinheritance, and the Origin of Labor Militancy in the Pacific Northwest, 1885–1886," *Western Historical Quarterly* 13, no. 4 (October 1982): 373–390; *Seattle Daily Post-Intelligencer*, September 22, 1885; Edmond S. Meany, "The Chinese Riots in Seattle," Edmond S. Meany Papers, Box 6, Folder 40, Special Collections, University of Washington Libraries [hereafter cited as Meany Papers].

50. *Seattle Daily Post-Intelligencer*, September 24, 1885.

51. Pfaelzer, *Driven Out*, 261, 265.

52. Chang Yen Hoon to the Secretary of Washington Territory, June 28, 1886, Box 1/5, Watson C. Squire Papers, Special Collections, University of Washington [hereafter cited as Squire Papers]; *Report of the Governor of Washington Territory to the Secretary of the Interior, 1886* (Washington, DC: US Government Printing Office, 1886), 866.

53. *Seattle Daily Post-Intelligencer*, September 29, 1885.

54. *Seattle Daily Post-Intelligencer*, September 29, 1885; John H. McGraw, "The Anti-Chinese Riots of 1885," *Washington State Historical Society Publications* 2 (1915): 389–390.

55. Anonymous to Henry L. Yesler, c. 1885, Box 5, Charles B. Bagley Papers, Special Collections, University of Washington; *Report of the Governor of Washington Territory*, 870.

56. Henry Shih-shan Tsai, *The Chinese Experience in America* (Bloomington: Indiana University Press, 1986), 71; Edmond S. Meany, "Summary of Riots," Folder 40: 7, Box 6, Meany Papers; Jules Alexander Karlin, "The Anti-Chinese Outbreaks in Seattle, 1885–1886," *Western Historical Quarterly* 39, no. 2 (April 1948), 109–110.

57. Chin and Chin, *Chinese in Washington State*, 48.

58. Pfaelzer, *Driven Out*, xv–xvi; "Committee of Fifteen in Charge of Organizing the Expulsion of Chinese, Tacoma, Washington, ca. 1885," Special Collections, University of Washington, accessed March 31, 2019, http://digitalcollections.lib.washington.edu/cdm/singleitem/collection/social/id/897/rec/15.

59. *Report of the Governor of Washington Territory*, 875; Chin and Chin, *Chinese in Washington State*, 53; Herbert Hunt, *Tacoma: Its History and Its Builders, A Half Century of Activity*, vol. 1 (Chicago: Clarke, 1916), 355, 373–374; Pfaelzer, *Driven Out*, 219, 252–290.

60. Clayton D. Laurie, "'The Chinese Must Go': The United States Army and the Anti-Chinese Riots in Washington Territory, 1885–1886" *Pacific Northwest Quarterly* 81, no. 1 (1990): 25; "November 9, 1885 Ammunition Order for King County Sheriff,"

Folder 26, Box 5, Bagley Papers, Special Collections, University of Washington Libraries; McGraw, "Anti-Chinese Riots of 1885," 390; George Kinnear, "Anti-Chinese Riots at Seattle, WN, February 8th, 1886" (Seattle: George Kinnear, 1911) 5.

61. Chin and Chin, *Chinese in Washington State*, 54–55; Karlin, "Anti-Chinese Outbreaks," 116–118.

62. Laurie, "'Chinese Must Go,'" 26; Meany, "Chinese Riots in Seattle," 10; Karlin, "Anti-Chinese Outbreaks," 119.

63. Owyang Ming and Colonel F. A. Bee to Watson C. Squire, February 7, 1886, Box 1/35, Squire Papers; Meany, "Chinese Riots in Seattle," 10; Ida Remington Squire account, February 7–14, 1886, 1, Squire Papers; Karlin, "Anti-Chinese Outbreaks," 120; McGraw, "Anti-Chinese Riots of 1885," 393.

64. US Department of Commerce and Labor, *Annual Reports of the Commissioner-General of Immigration* (Washington, DC: US Government Printing Office, 1903), 32; "Hundred kinds . . . " from Him Mark Lai, Genny Lim, and Judy Yung, eds., *Island: Poetry and History of Chinese Immigrants on Angel Island, 1910–1940*, 2nd ed. (Seattle: University of Washington Press, 1991), 162.

65. *San Francisco Morning Call*, September 14, 1892, 8.

66. Robert Barde, *Immigration at the Golden Gate: Passenger Ships, Exclusion, and Angel Island* (Westport, CT: Praeger, 2008), 56–59.

67. Lee, *At America's Gates*, 189–220; Erika Lee and Judy Yung, *Angel Island: Immigrant Gateway to America* (New York: Oxford University Press, 2010), 4, 69.

68. Interview with Ted Chan by Judy Yung and Him Mark Lai, April 17, 1977, San Francisco, Interview 23, Angel Island Oral History Project, Ethnic Studies Library, University of California, Berkeley; Lee, *At America's Gates*, 189.

69. Mary Roberts Coolidge, *Chinese Immigration* (New York: Holt, 1909), 328.

70. Lee and Yung, *Angel Island*, 70; Ronald H. Bayor, *Encountering Ellis Island: How European Immigrants Entered America* (Baltimore: Johns Hopkins University Press, 2014), 39–40.

71. Lai, Lim, and Yung, *Island*, 162.

72. Act of October 1, 1888 (25 Stat. 504, section 2); Act of May 5, 1892 (27 Stat. 25); Act of April 29, 1902, "Chinese Immigration Prohibited" (32 Stat. 176).

73. *San Francisco Examiner*, June 16, 1910; *San Francisco Post*, May 24, 1910.

Chapter 4: The "Inferior Races" of Europe

1. Barbara Solomon, *Ancestors and Immigrants: A Changing New England Tradition* (Boston: Northeastern University Press, 1989), 99–102; Neil Swidey, "Trump's Anti-Immigration Playbook Was Written 100 Years Ago," *Boston Globe Magazine*, February 8, 2017, https://apps.bostonglobe.com/magazine/graphics/2017/01/immigration/.

2. Noel Ignatiev, *How the Irish Became White* (New York: Routledge, 2008); David Roediger, *The Wages of Whiteness: Race and the Making of the American Working Class* (New York: Verso, 1991).

3. Matthew Frye Jacobson, *Whiteness of a Different Color: European Immigrants and the Alchemy of Race* (Cambridge, MA: Harvard University Press, 1998), 42–43, 77; Douglas C. Baynton, *Defectives in the Land: Disability and Immigration in the Age of Eugenics* (Chicago: University of Chicago Press, 2016), 12–13.

4. Solomon, *Ancestors and Immigrants*, 106.

5. John B. Weber, *Autobiography of John B. Weber* (Buffalo, NY: Clement, 1924), 127–128.

6. Roger Daniels, *Coming to America: A History of Immigration and Ethnicity in American Life* (New York: HarperCollins, 1990), 124, 189, 224.

7. Lucyle Irby Hall, *Immigration and Other Interests of Prescott Farnsworth Hall* (New York: Knickerbocker Press, 1922), 119, 102, xxv.

8. Jacobson, *Whiteness of a Different Color*, 59; Solomon, *Ancestors and Immigrants*, 43; Madison Grant, "Foreword," in Hall, *Immigration and Other Interests*, ix–x.

9. Prescott F. Hall, "The Future of American Ideals," *North American Review* (January 1912): 94–95; IRL, "The Present Aspect of the Immigration Problem" (Boston, 1894), IRL Records, Houghton Library, Harvard University [unless otherwise noted, all IRL publications and records are from Harvard University].

10. IRL, "Present Aspect," 3–4, 6–7; Hall, "Future of American Ideals," 94–95; Prescott F. Hall, "Immigration and the Educational Test," *North American Review* (October 1897): 395.

11. IRL, "Present Aspect," 4, 6, 7; Josiah Strong, *Our Country: Its Possible Future and Its Present Crisis* (New York: Baker and Taylor, 1885); Thomas Bailey Aldrich, *Unguarded Gates, and Other Poems* (New York: Houghton Mifflin, 1895), 13–17.

12. Francis Walker, "Restriction of Immigration," *The Atlantic* (June 1896); Solomon, *Ancestors and Immigrants*, 71.

13. John Higham, *Strangers in the Land: Patterns of American Nativism, 1860–1925* (New Brunswick, NJ: Rutgers University Press, 2011), 54–55.

14. *New York Times*, December 8, 1905; Linda Kerber, *The Second Coming of the KKK: The Ku Klux Klan of the 1920s and the American Political Tradition* (New York: Liveright, 2017), 35; Higham, *Strangers in the Land*, 286–299; "A Klansman's Creed," c. 1922, from the Collections of Henry Ford, www.thehenryford.org/collections-and-research/digital-collections/artifact/326607.

15. Vince Cannato, *American Passage: The History of Ellis Island* (New York: HarperCollins, 2009), 103; Florence Balgarnie, "Home-Seekers in Western Lands; a Day in Ellis Island, the New 'Castle Garden' of New York," *English Illustrated Magazine* 13 (May 1895): 155–161.

16. IRL, "Annual Report of the Executive Committee for 1895."

17. Cannato, *American Passage*, 103–104; IRL, "Immigration: Its Effects" (Boston, 1897); IRL, Annual Report for 1895; Hall, "Immigration and the Educational Test," 393–402; *New York Times*, April 21, 1896.

18. IRL, "Various Facts and Opinion Concerning the Necessity of Restricting Immigration" (Boston, 1894); IRL, "Twenty Reasons Why Immigration Should Be Further Restricted Now" (Boston, 1894); IRL, "Study These Figures and Draw Your Own Conclusions" (Boston, 1894).

19. IRL, "The Present Italian Influx, Its Striking Illiteracy" (Boston, 1896); Hall, "Future of American Ideals," 95; Higham, *Strangers in the Land*, 66; Charlotte Adams, "Italian Life in New York," *Harper's New Monthly Magazine* (April, 1881): 676; Jacobson, *Whiteness of a Different Color*, 56–57; James Barrett and David Roediger, "Inbetween Peoples: Race, Nationality and the 'New Immigrant' Working Class," *Journal of American Ethnic History* 16 (1997): 3–44; David R. Roediger, *How Race Survived U.S.*

History: From Settlement and Slavery to the Obama Phenomenon (London: Verso, 2008), 156–157.

20. *New York Times*, March 15, 1891, and March 16, 1891; Thomas A. Guglielmo, *White on Arrival: Italians, Race, Color, and Power in Chicago, 1890–1945* (New York: Oxford University Press, 2004), 77–78.

21. Donna Gabaccia, "The 'Yellow Peril' and the 'Chinese of Europe': Global Perspectives on Race and Labor, 1815–1930," in *Migration, Migration History, History: Old Paradigms and New Perspectives*, ed. Jan Lucassen and Leo Lucassen (Bern: Peter Lang, 1999): 177–179; J. H. Patten to Unions, October 15, 1908, IRL Scrapbooks, IRL Records.

22. Hall, "Immigration and the Educational Test," 401–402.

23. Henry Cabot Lodge, "The Restriction of Immigration," *North American Review* 152 (1891): 27–36.

24. Grover Cleveland, "Veto Message," March 2, 1897, American Presidency Project, www.presidency.ucsb.edu/documents/veto-message-31; Solomon, *Ancestors and Immigrants*, 124.

25. Jonathan Spiro, *Defending the Master Race: Conservation, Eugenics, and the Legacy of Madison Grant* (Burlington: University of Vermont Press, 2008), 199; Matthew Pratt Guterl, *The Color of Race in America, 1900–1940* (Cambridge, MA: Harvard University Press, 2002), 28.

26. Henry Fairfield Osborn, Preface to Madison Grant, *The Passing of the Great Race or The Racial Basis of European History*, 4th rev. ed. (New York: Scribner, 1921), xxviii–xxix; Grant, *Passing of the Great Race*, 263.

27. Grant, *Passing of the Great Race*, 20, 42, 27, 298.

28. Grant, *Passing of the Great Race*, 229, 20–21.

29. Grant, *Passing of the Great Race*, 82, 18; Guterl, *Color of Race*, 47, 64.

30. Roger Daniels, *Guarding the Golden Door: American Immigration Policy and Immigrants Since 1882* (New York: Hill and Wang, 2004), 45.

31. Spiro, *Defending the Master Race*, 32.

32. Grant, *Passing of the Great Race*, xxviii, 32.

33. Carole R. McCann, *Birth Control Politics in the United States, 1916–1945* (Ithaca, NY: Cornell University Press, 1999), 17, 100, 107; Theodore Roosevelt, "On American Motherhood," March 13, 1905, excerpted in Melody Rose, *Abortion: A Documentary and Reference Guide* (Westport, CT: Greenwood, 2008), 24–27; Spiro, *Defending the Master Race*, 99.

34. Madison Grant to Prescott F. Hall, August 27, 1920, Folder 3, 468, Correspondence to and from the IRL, IRL Records; Paul Spickard, *Almost All Aliens: Immigration, Race, and Colonialism in American History and Identity* (New York: Routledge, 2007), 123; Dinnerstein, *Antisemitism*, 15, 22, 40, 46, 49; Kerber, *Second Coming of the KKK*, 52.

35. Spiro, *Defending the Master Race*, 94–95; Hall, "Future of American Ideals," 95; Dinnerstein, *Antisemitism*, 65, 59; Katherine Benton-Cohen, *Inventing the Immigration Problem: The Dillingham Commission and Its Legacy* (Cambridge, MA: Harvard University Press, 2018), 151–159; Baynton, *Defectives in the Land*, 32–36, 40–42, 125.

36. Burton J. Hendrick, "The Great Jewish Invasion," *McClure's Magazine* 28 (January 1907): 307–321. See also Burton J. Hendrick, "The Jewish Invasion of America," *McClure's Magazine* 40 (March 1913): 125–165.

37. Grant, *Passing of the Great Race*, 91, xxxi.

38. Osborn, Preface to Grant, *Passing of the Great Race*, ix.

39. Guterl, *Color of Race*, 33; Spiro, *Defending the Master Race*, 166–168.

40. US Immigration Commission, 61st Cong., 3d Sess., "Dictionary of Races or Peoples," Document No. 602 (Washington, DC: US Government Printing Office, 1911); Tom Gjelten, *A Nation of Nations: A Great Immigration Story* (New York: Simon and Schuster, 2015), 85; Benton-Cohen, *Inventing the Immigration Problem*, 1, 6; US Immigration Commission, 61st Cong., 3rd Sess., *Reports of the Immigration Commission*, vol. 1 (Washington, DC: US Government Printing Office, 1911), 45–48; Spickard, *Almost All Aliens*, 278.

41. James Murphy Ward, *The Immigration Problem, or America First* (n.p., 1917); Theodore Roosevelt, "America for Americans, Afternoon Speech of Theodore Roosevelt at St. Louis, May 31, 1916," in *The Progressive Party, Its Record from January to July, 1916* (New York: Mail and Express Job Print, 1916); Higham, *Strangers in the Land*, 204–212.

42. Gary Gerstle, "The Immigrant as Threat to American Security: A Historical Perspective," in *From Arrival to Incorporation: Migrants to the U.S. in a Global Era*, ed. Elliott R. Barkan, Hasia Diner, and Alan M. Kraut (New York: New York University Press, 2008), 226.

43. Frederick C. Luebke, *Germans in the New World: Essays in the History of Immigration* (Champaign: University of Illinois Press, 1990), 41; Kathleen Neils Conzen, *Germans in Minnesota* (St. Paul: Minnesota Historical Society Press, 2003), 67; Sara Egge, "How Midwestern Suffragists Used Anti-Immigrant Fervor to Help Gain the Vote," Zócalo Public Square, "What It Means to Be American" Project, September 17, 2018, www.zocalopublicsquare.org/2018/09/17/midwestern-suffragists-used-anti -immigrant-fervor-help-gain-vote/ideas/essay/; "Nov. 16, 1919: Tarred and Feathered," *Star Tribune* (Minneapolis–St. Paul, MN), November 18, 2015; "Prussianizing Wisconsin," *Atlantic Monthly* 11, no. 1 (January 1919): 101–102; Higham, *Strangers in the Land*, 216; Gerstle, "Immigrant as Threat," 226–228.

44. Madison Grant, "The Racial Transformation of America," *North American Review* 219 (March 1924): 343.

45. Canaday, *Straight State*, 19–54; Eithne Luibhéid and Lionel Cantú, eds., *Queer Migrations: Sexuality, U.S. Citizenship, and Border Crossings* (Minneapolis: University of Minnesota Press, 2005), xii; Atticus Lee, "Sexual Deviants Need Not Apply: LGBTQ Oppression in the 1965 Immigration Act Amendments," in *The Immigration and Nationality Act of 1965: Legislating a New America*, ed. Gabriel J. Chin and Rose Cuison Villazor (New York: Cambridge University Press, 2015), 250–253.

46. Immigration Act of 1917 (39 Stat. 874).

47. Swidey, "Trump's Anti-Immigration Playbook."

48. Edwin Palmer Hoyt, *The Palmer Raids, 1919–1920: An Attempt to Suppress Dissent* (New York: Seabury Press, 1969), 105–108; Robert K. Murray, *Red Scare: A Study in National Hysteria, 1919–1920* (Minneapolis: University of Minnesota Press, 1955), 15–17, 84–95; Higham, *Strangers in the Land*, 221; Gerstle, "Immigrant as Threat," 231–232.

49. Quota Act of 1921, Section 2 (42 Stat. 5).

50. Grant, *Passing of the Great Race*, xxviii, xviii; Spiro, *Defending the Master Race*, xi.

51. Emanuel Celler, *You Never Leave Brooklyn: The Autobiography of Emanuel Celler* (New York: Day, 1953), 5–7, 82–83, 4.

52. Immigration Act of 1924 (43 Stat. 153); Mae M. Ngai, *Impossible Subjects: Illegal Aliens and the Making of Modern America* (Princeton, NJ: Princeton University Press, 2014, 3; Jacobson, *Whiteness of a Different Color*, 86.

53. Quota information from *Statistical Abstract of the United States* (Washington, DC: US Government Printing Office, 1929), 100, from History Matters, George Mason University, http://historymatters.gmu.edu/d/5078; Gjelten, *Nation of Nations*, 90. "White American race" from Ngai, *Impossible Subjects*, 25.

54. Gjelten, *Nation of Nations*, 90; Calvin Coolidge, "Whose Country Is This?" *Good Housekeeping* 72, no. 2 (February 1921), 13–14, 109; Calvin Coolidge, "First Annual Message," December 6, 1932, American Presidency Project, www.presidency.ucsb .edu/ws/index.php?pid=29564; "Statement Issued to the Press by President Coolidge," May 26, 1924, in Carnegie Endowment for International Peace, *International Conciliation: Documents for the Year 1924* (Washington, DC: Carnegie Endowment for International Peace, 1924), 445–446.

55. Celler, *You Never Leave Brooklyn*, 4.

56. Daniels, *Coming to America*, 291; James Q. Whitman, *Hitler's American Model: The United States and the Making of Nazi Race Law* (Princeton, NJ: Princeton University Press, 2017), 12, 46–47; Spiro, *Defending the Master Race*, xi, 355–361; Timothy W. Ryback, *Hitler's Private Library: The Books That Shaped His Life* (New York: Vintage, 2008), 94–115; Spickard, *Almost All Aliens*, 268.

57. David Wyman, *Paper Walls: America and the Refugee Crisis 1938–1941* (New York: Pantheon, 1985), 75–98; Alan Kraut, *Silent Travelers: Germs, Genes, and the "Immigrant Menace"* (Baltimore: Johns Hopkins University Press, 1994), 256.

58. Wyman, *Paper Walls*, 75–98; "Immigration to the United States, 1900–1945," US Holocaust Memorial Museum, https://exhibitions.ushmm.org /americans-and-the-holocaust/us-immigration-from-1900-1945.

59. Sarah Ogilvie and Scott Miller, *Refuge Denied: The St. Louis Passengers and the Holocaust* (Madison: University of Wisconsin Press, 2006), x.

Chapter 5: "Getting Rid of the Mexicans"

1. Abraham Hoffman, *Unwanted Mexicans in the Great Depression: Repatriation Pressures, 1929–1939* (Tucson: University of Arizona Press, 1974), 61; Francisco E. Balderrama and Raymond Rodríguez, *Decade of Betrayal: Mexican Repatriation in the 1930s* (Albuquerque: University of New Mexico Press, 2006), 73–74.

2. "Get rid . . . " from Carey McWilliams, "Getting Rid of the Mexican," *American Mercury* (March 1933): 322–324; US Citizenship and Immigration Services, "INS Records for 1930s Mexican Repatriations," March 3, 2014, www.uscis.gov/history-and -genealogy/our-history/historians-mailbox/ins-records-1930s-mexican-repatriations; Balderrama and Rodríguez, *Decade of Betrayal*, 67.

3. Cybelle Fox, *Three Worlds of Relief: Race, Immigration, and the American Welfare State from the Progressive Era to the New Deal* (Princeton, NJ: Princeton University Press, 2012), 187; Balderrama and Rodríguez, *Decade of Betrayal*, 67; Mae M. Ngai, *Impossible Subjects: Illegal Aliens and the Making of Modern America* (Princeton, NJ: Princeton

University Press, 2004), 75; Alex Wagner, "America's Forgotten History of Illegal Deportations," *The Atlantic*, March 6, 2017, www.theatlantic.com/amp/article/517971/.

4. David J. Weber, ed., *Foreigners in Their Native Land: Historical Roots of the Mexican Americans* (Albuquerque: University of New Mexico Press, 2003).

5. George Sánchez, *Becoming Mexican American: Ethnicity, Culture, and Identity in Chicano Los Angeles, 1900–1945* (New York: Oxford University Press, 1995), 18–19, 281; Balderrama and Rodríguez, *Decade of Betrayal*, 9.

6. California Development Association, "Survey of the Mexican Labor Problem in California" (San Francisco, 1928), 11; Mark Reisler, *By the Sweat of Their Brow: Mexican Immigrant Labor in the United States, 1900–1940* (Westport, CT: Greenwood, 1976), 128, 67; Lawrence Cardoso, *Mexican Emigration to the United States, 1897–1931: Socio–Economic Patterns* (Tucson: University of Arizona Press, 1980), 120–122; Hoffman, *Unwanted Mexicans*, 10; Vicki Ruiz, *From Out of the Shadows: Mexican Women in Twentieth-Century America* (New York: Oxford University Press, 1998), 29.

7. California Development Association, "Survey," 10.

8. David G. Gutiérrez, *Walls and Mirrors: Mexican Americans, Mexican Immigrants, and the Politics of Ethnicity* (Berkeley: University of California Press, 1995), 49; California Development Association, "Survey," 11–12; George Clements to Governor C. C. Young, December 28, 1927, Folder 1, Part 2, Box 62 [emphasis added]; California Development Association, "Mexican Indian or Porto [*sic*] Rican Indian Casual Labor?" Folder 1, Box 62, George P. Clements Papers, Special Collections, UCLA Library [hereafter cited as Clements Papers].

9. Balderrama and Rodríguez, *Decade of Betrayal*, 101.

10. Gutiérrez, *Walls and Mirrors*, 46–47.

11. California Development Association, "Survey," 9; George P. Clements, "Notes for Talk Before Annual Conference of the Friends of the Mexicans," 3, Pomona College, November 13, 1926, Folder 1, Part 2, Box 62, Clements Papers.

12. "Conference Held in the Los Angeles Chamber of Commerce Room, October 5, 1927. Re: Bill to Include Mexico in the Immigration Quota Law," 3–5, Folder 1, Part 1, Box 62, Clements Papers; California Development Association, "Survey," 7–9.

13. Cardoso, *Mexican Emigration*, 71; Sánchez, *Becoming Mexican American*, 39, 67, 19; Reisler, *By the Sweat of Their Brow*, 11; Gutiérrez, *Walls and Mirrors*, 44–45; Hoffman, *Unwanted Mexicans*, 7; Molina, *How Race Is Made in America*, 21.

14. Luis Valdez and Stan Steiner, eds., *Aztlan: An Anthology of Mexican American Literature* (New York: Vintage, 1972), 133.

15. Sánchez, *Becoming Mexican American*, 20–23; Balderrama and Rodríguez, *Decade of Betrayal*, 14; Cardoso, *Mexican Emigration*, 12.

16. Balderrama and Rodríguez, *Decade of Betrayal*, 12, 14; Sánchez, *Becoming Mexican American*, 20.

17. Balderrama and Rodríguez, *Decade of Betrayal*, 8–9; Immigration Act of 1917 (39 Stat. 874); Sánchez, *Becoming Mexican American*, 19–20, 61, 52, 133; S. Deborah Kang, *The INS on the Line: Making Immigration Law on the U.S.-Mexico Border, 1917–1954* (New York: Oxford University Press, 2017), 36–61.

18. Samuel Bryan, "Mexican Immigrants in the United States," *The Survey* 20, no. 23 (September 1912).

19. Gutiérrez, *Walls and Mirrors*, 52–53; Molina, *How Race Is Made*, 20.

20. US Congress, House Committee on Immigration and Naturalization, H.R. 6465, H.R. 7358, H.R. 11687, 70th Cong., 1st Sess. (1928), 20.

21. Gutiérrez, *Walls and Mirrors*, 54; US Congress, House Committee on Immigration and Naturalization, Western Hemisphere Immigration, H.R. 8523, H.R. 8702, 71st Cong., 2nd Sess. (1930), 436.

22. Frederick Russell Burnham, "The Howl for Cheap Mexican Labor," in *The Alien in Our Midst or Selling Our Birthright for a Mess of Pottage*, ed. Madison Grant and Charles Stewart Davison (New York: Galton, 1930), 48, 45; Neil Foley, *The White Scourge: Mexicans, Blacks, and Poor Whites in Texas Cotton Culture* (Berkeley: University of California Press, 1997), 55, 53; Chester Rowell, "Why Make Mexico an Exception?" *Survey*, 1 (May 1, 1931): 180.

23. Molina, *How Race Is Made*, 53–55; California Joint Immigration Commission, "Is the Mexican Indian Eligible?" December 11, 1931, California Joint Immigration Commission Collection, 1924–1936, Bancroft Library, University of California, Berkeley [hereafter cited as CJIC Collection]; Gutiérrez, *Walls and Mirrors*, 55; Alexandra Minna Stern, *Eugenic Nation: Faults and Frontiers of Better Breeding in Modern America* (Berkeley: University of California Press, 2005), 69.

24. Weber, *Foreigners in Their Native Land*, 225; Roy L. Garis, "Report on Mexican Immigration," submitted to House Committee on Immigration and Naturalization, in House Committee on Immigration, *Immigration from Countries of the Western Hemisphere: Hearings*, 1930, 424–428, 436; F. Arturo Rosales, ed., *Testimonio: A Documentary History of the Mexican American Struggle for Civil Rights* (Houston: Arte Pública, 2000), 93–95.

25. California Department of Industrial Relations, Department of Agriculture, and Department of Social Welfare, *Mexicans in California: Report of Governor C. C. Young's Mexican Fact-Finding Committee* (San Francisco: California State Printing Office, 1930), 206; Molina, *How Race Is Made*, 82.

26. Remsen Crawford, "The Menace of Mexican Immigration," *Current History* 31 (February 1930): 902–907; Garis, "Report," 424–428.

27. Stern, *Eugenic Nation*, 62.

28. Chris Frazer, *Bandit Nation: A History of Outlaws and Cultural Struggle in Mexico, 1810–1920* (Lincoln: University of Nebraska Press, 2006).

29. Hoffman, *Unwanted Mexicans*, 30–32.

30. Hoffman, *Unwanted Mexicans*, 30–32; Emory Bogardus, "Current Problems of Mexican Immigrants," *Sociology and Social Research* 25 (November 1940): 167; Ngai, *Impossible Subjects*, 60.

31. Hidetaka Hirota, *Expelling the Poor: Atlantic Seaboard States and the Nineteenth-Century Origins of American Immigration Policy* (New York: Oxford University Press, 2017), 180–183, 191–192; Ngai, *Impossible Subjects*, 57, 59, 67–70.

32. Ngai, *Impossible Subjects*, 82–83.

33. Nicholas De Genova, "Mexican/Migrant 'Illegality,'" *Latino Studies* 2, no. 2 (July 2004): 161; Hoffman, *Unwanted Mexicans*, 84; Kelly Lytle Hernández, *Migra! A History of the U.S. Border Patrol* (Berkeley: University of California Press, 2010), 19–69, 109); Lytle Hernández, *City of Inmates*, 76–81, 139.

34. Isaac Marcosson, "The Alien and Unemployment," *Saturday Evening Post* (June 14, 1930), 6–7; Roy L. Garis, "The Mexican Conquest," *Saturday Evening Post* (June 22, 1929), 26.

35. Balderrama and Rodríguez, *Decade of Betrayal*, 83–87; Roy L. Garis, "The Mexicanization of American Business," *Saturday Evening Post* (February 8, 1930), 46.

36. Interview of Mrs. Emilia Castañeda de Valenciana, September 8, 1971, Mexican American Oral History Project, California State University, Fullerton.

37. Balderrama and Rodríguez, *Decade of Betrayal*, 90.

38. Balderrama and Rodríguez, *Decade of Betrayal*, 91, 121.

39. Hoffman, *Unwanted Mexicans*, 36–37.

40. Hoffman, *Unwanted Mexicans*, 128–129; Robert N. McLean, "The Mexican Return," *The Nation* (August 24, 1932), 135, 165–167.

41. Roger W. Babson, *Washington and the Depression, Including the Career of W. N. Doak* (New York: Harper, 1932), 101–105; Robert S. Allen, "One of Mr. Hoover's Friends," *American Mercury* (January 1931): 57.

42. *New York Times*, January 6, 1931; *Los Angeles Times*, April 11, 1931; *New York Times*, April 22, 1932.

43. President Herbert Hoover, "Annual Message to the Congress on the State of the Union," December 2, 1930, American Presidency Project www.presidency.ucsb.edu /ws/index.php?pid=22458; *New York Times*, February 10, 1931.

44. *New York Times*, February 16, 1931.

45. Marin Dies, "The Immigration Crisis," *Saturday Evening Post*, (April 20, 1935); *New York Times*, February 24, 1931; *Los Angeles Times*, April 11, 1931; Rosales, *Testimonio*, 96–97; Balderrama and Rodríguez, *Decade of Betrayal*, 69.

46. Balderrama and Rodríguez, *Decade of Betrayal*, 76; Fox, *Three Worlds*, 127.

47. Hoffman, *Unwanted Mexicans*, 47.

48. Hoffman, *Unwanted Mexicans*, 43.

49. Hoffman, *Unwanted Mexicans*, 44.

50. Charles P. Visel to Colonel Arthur Woods, January 19, 1931, Folder 15, Box 80, Clements Papers.

51. Hoffman, *Unwanted Mexicans*, 47.

52. Hoffman, *Unwanted Mexicans*, 53.

53. Hoffman, *Unwanted Mexicans*, 47, 57; Balderrama and Rodríguez, *Decade of Betrayal*, 70; Mr. Arnoll to Dr. Clements, "Mexican and Alien Question," January 21, 1931, and Mr. George C. Clements to Mrs. Robert A. Woods, February 2, 1931, Folder 1, Part 1, Box 62, Clements Papers; "Los Deportados" from Gutiérrez, *Walls and Mirrors*, 73.

54. Hoffman, *Unwanted Mexicans*, 58.

55. Hoffman, *Unwanted Mexicans*, 64–65.

56. Hoffman, *Unwanted Mexicans*, 73–75, 67–68; W. M. Creekbaum, Manager, Xth Olympic Games, Los Angeles, 1932 to Mr. Clarence H. Matson, April 22, 1931, Box 80, Clements Papers; Gutiérrez, *Walls and Mirrors*, 100.

57. Hoffman, *Unwanted Mexicans*, 67; Balderrama and Rodríguez, *Decade of Betrayal*, 71, 82.

58. McWilliams, "Getting Rid of the Mexican," 323.

59. Fernando Saúl Alanís Enciso, *They Should Stay There: The Story of Mexican Migration and Repatriation*, trans. Russ Davidson (Chapel Hill: University of North Carolina Press, 2017), 51–73.

60. Balderrama and Rodríguez, *Decade of Betrayal*, 121; Kang, *INS on the Line*, 66–70.

61. Fox, *Three Worlds of Relief*, 75; Stern, *Eugenic Nation*, 111.

62. Sánchez, *Becoming Mexican American*, 99; Fox, *Three Worlds of Relief*, 80, 74, 82; California, "Mexicans in California," 192.

63. Charles Goethe, "Other Aspects of the Problem," *Current History* 28 (1928): 768.

64. Balderrama and Rodríguez, *Decade of Betrayal*, 94–95.

65. Fox, *Three Worlds of Relief*, 187.

66. Hoffman, *Unwanted Mexicans*, 86; Balderrama and Rodríguez, *Decade of Betrayal*, 129; McWilliams, "Getting Rid of the Mexican," 322–324.

67. John Anson Ford interview with Christiane Valenciana, September 4, 1971, Mexican American Oral History Project, Center for Oral and Public History, California State University, Fullerton; Clements to Arnoll, August 13, 1931, Folder 118, Box 62, Clements Papers; Fox, *Three Worlds of Relief*, 163; Emory Bogardus, "Mexican Repatriates," *Sociology and Social Research* 17 (November 1933): 174.

68. W. H. Holland to Los Angeles Board of Supervisors, February 15, 1931, "Repatriation Correspondence as Authorized by the County Clerk 1931–1937," Folder 9, Box 18, Ron Lopez Papers, Chicano Studies Research Center, University of California, Los Angeles [hereafter cited as Lopez Papers] [emphasis added]; Paul S. Taylor, *A Spanish-Mexican Peasant Community, Arandas in Jalisco, Mexico* (Berkeley: University of California Press, 1933), 55–63.

69. W. H. Holland to Los Angeles Board of Supervisors, February 15, 1931.

70. H. A. Payne to W. H. Holland, February 10, 1931, W. H. Holland to Los Angeles County Board of Supervisors, February 10, 1931, and W. H. Holland to Los Angeles County Board of Supervisors, April 24, 1931, "Repatriation Correspondence as Authorized by the County Clerk 1931–1937," Folder 9, Box 18, Lopez Papers; Hoffman, *Unwanted Mexicans*, 87–88, 94.

71. George Clements to Mr. Arnoll, August 17, 1931, Folder 1, part 1, Box 62, Clements Papers.

72. George Clements to Mr. Arnoll, August 17, 1931, Folder 1, part 1, Box 62, Clements Papers.

73. Fox, *Three Worlds of Relief*, 163–164; *New York Times*, July 9, 1932; Pablo Guerrero to L.A. County, May 28, 1934, in "Los Angeles Board of Supervisors—Mexican Repatriation 1928–1938," Folder 23, Box 27, Lopez Papers.

74. Fox, *Three Worlds of Relief*, 163–164.

75. Hoffman, *Unwanted Mexicans*, 98–99, 113; Fox, *Three Worlds of Relief*, 167; "Trains to Take Mexicans Home," *Los Angeles Times*, January 12, 1932; Sánchez, *Becoming Mexican American*, 210.

76. Hoffman, *Unwanted Mexicans*, 120, 123, 117; Dionicio Nodín Valdés, *Barrios Norteños: St. Paul and Midwestern Mexican Communities in the Twentieth Century* (Austin: University of Texas Press, 2000), 100.

Chapter 6: "Military Necessity"

1. Unless otherwise noted, my account of Morita family history and Betty Shibayama's life history in this chapter relies on Betty Morita Shibayama Interview, October 27, 2003, Densho Digital Repository, https://ddr.densho.org/media/ddr-densho-1000/ddr-densho-1000-152-transcript-f4a84a79ac.htm.

2. Unless otherwise noted, my account of Shibayama family history and Art Shibayama's life history in this chapter relies on Art Shibayama Interview, Segment 1, October 26, 2003, Densho Digital Repository, http://ddr.densho.org/interviews /ddr-densho-1000-151-1/.

3. Roger Daniels, "Words Do Matter: A Note on Inappropriate Terminology and the Incarceration of the Japanese Americans," in *Nikkei in the Pacific Northwest: Japanese Americans and Japanese Canadians in the Twentieth Century*, ed. Louis Fiset and Gail Nomura (Seattle: University of Washington Press, 2005), 183–207, fn22, 209; Roger Daniels, *Prisoners Without Trial: Japanese Americans in World War II* (New York: Hill and Wang, 1993).

4. Casey Peek and Irum Shiekh, "Hidden Internment: The Art Shibayama Story," Peek Media, 2004; US Commission on Wartime Relocation and Internment of Civilians, *Personal Justice Denied* (Seattle: University of Washington Press, 1997), 305 [hereafter cited as USCWRIC, *Personal Justice*].

5. Daniel M. Masterson and Sayaka Funada-Classen, *The Japanese in Latin America* (Urbana: University of Illinois Press, 2004), 122, 141–146; Japanese Peruvian Oral History Project, "Japanese Latin Americans: The Hostage Exchange Program During WWII," accessed April 1, 2019, www.campaignforjusticejla.org/resources/pdf /hostageFAQ.pdf.

6. Yuji Ichioka, *The Issei: The World of the First Generation Japanese Immigrants, 1885–1924* (New York: Free Press, 1988), 42–46.

7. Ronald T. Takaki, *Paul Hana: Plantation Life and Labor in Hawaii, 1835–1920* (Honolulu: University of Hawai'i Press, 1984), 43, 45; Yamato Ichihashi, *Japanese in the United States* (New York: Arno Press, 1969), 66.

8. Ichioka, *The Issei*, 150.

9. Ayumi Takenaka, "The Japanese in Peru: History of Immigration, Settlement, and Racialization," *Latin American Perspectives* 31, no. 3 (2004): 80, 83–86.

10. Robert E. Hennings, *James D. Phelan and the Wilson Progressives of California* (New York: Garland, 1985), 3, 6, 41, 152; Robert W. Cherny, "City Commercial, City Beautiful, City Practical: The San Francisco Visions of William C. Ralston, James D. Phelan, and Michael M. O'Shaughnessy," *California History* 73, no. 4 (Winter 1994/1995), 304.

11. Hennings, *James D. Phelan*, 15; *San Francisco Call*, November 22, 1901; James D. Phelan, "Why the Chinese Should Be Excluded," *North American Review* 173 (November 1901): 633.

12. Homer Lea, *The Valor of Ignorance: The Inevitable Japanese-American War* (New York: Harper, 1909), 115, 157–159, 192, 264–278, 249–251, 343; V. S. McClatchy, "Brief in Opposition to Quota for Japan," 1931, 6, CJIC Collection; Roger Daniels, *The Politics of Prejudice* (Berkeley: University of California Press, 1962), 20–21, 25–26.

13. Asiatic Exclusion League, *Proceedings of the First International Convention* (San Francisco, 1908), 68, Asiatic Exclusion League Records, 1906–1910, Labor Archives and Research Center, San Francisco State University, San Francisco, California; Executive Order 589 (March 14, 1907); Daniels, *Politics of Prejudice*, 43–44, 130, fn42.

14. *New York Times*, May 30, 1907.

15. Daniels, *Politics of Prejudice*, 63, 88.

16. Hennings, *James D. Phelan*, 7, 77.

17. *San Francisco Call*, March 6, 1919, *San Francisco Chronicle*, March 7, 1919, *Riverside Press*, March 19, 1919, *San Francisco Call*, April 16, 1920, Scrapbook, Carton 18, James D. Phelan Papers, 1857–1941, Bancroft Library, University of California Berkeley [hereafter cited as Phelan Papers]; Hennings, *James D. Phelan*, 183.

18. Daniels, *Politics of Prejudice*, 70; James D. Phelan, "The Japanese Menace," October 25, 1914, Folder 14, Box 120, Phelan Papers; Hennings, *James D. Phelan*, 113.

19. Randall Phillips to James D. Phelan, August 4, 1919, and Brayton Horton to James D. Phelan, July 3, 1920, Folder 5, Box 120, Phelan Papers.

20. Hennings, *James D. Phelan*, 179–180; Daniels, *Politics of Prejudice*, 84–85.

21. CJIC, "California's Answer to Japan," December 23, 1924, CJIC Collection.

22. Lothrop Stoddard, *The Rising Tide of Color Against White World-Supremacy* (New York: Scribner, 1920), 14.

23. Stoddard, *Rising Tide*, 251, 221, 282, 255, 276.

24. "Rising tide . . . " from Jun Kodani, "The Japanese Peruvians of Lima and Anti–Japanese Agitation, 1900–1940," (MA thesis, University of California, Berkeley, 1984), 65, 72–73; "The Japanese Infiltration" from Amelia Morimoto, *Los Inmigrantes Japoneses en el Perú* (Lima: Taller de Estudios Andinos Universidad Nacional Agraria Departamento de Ciencias Humanas, 1979), 69; João Frederico Normano et al., *The Japanese in South America; An Introductory Survey with Special Reference to Peru* (New York: Day, 1943), 78.

25. "Compatible races" from Marisol de la Cadena, *Indigenous Mestizos: The Politics of Race and Culture in Cuzco, Peru, 1919–1991* (Durham, NC: Duke University Press, 2000), 16; Kodani, "Japanese Peruvians," 17.

26. Takenaka, "Japanese in Peru," 83, 85–86; Kodani, "Japanese Peruvians," 29, 31, 42; C. Harvey Gardiner, *The Japanese and Peru, 1873–1973* (Albuquerque: University of New Mexico Press, 1975), 31; Molinari Morales, *El Fascismo en el Peru: La Unión Revolucionaria 1931–36* (Lima: Fondo Editorial de la Facultad de Ciencias Sociales, 2006), 224–230, 237–238, 240–242.

27. Francisco García Calderón, *Latin America: Its Rise and Progress* (London: Unwin, 1913), 324, 329–330; Gardiner, *Japanese and Peru*, 65; *El Comercio*, May 29, 1924; Morales, *El Fascismo*, 233–234; *La Prensa*, November 30, 1934.

28. Normano et al., *Japanese in South America*, 8, 113–115; Gardiner, *Japanese and Peru*, 77, 114–116; Takenaka, "Japanese in Peru," 87.

29. Kodani, "Japanese Peruvians," 77; Seiichi Higashide, *Adios to Tears: The Memoirs of a Japanese-Peruvian Internee in U.S. Concentration Camps* (Seattle: University of Washington Press, 2000), 105–110; Normano et al., *Japanese in South America*, 52–53.

30. Peter H. Smith, *Talons of the Eagle: Latin America, the United States, and the World* (New York: Oxford University Press, 2000), 29–30, 36, 63–64, 68–69, 75, 80–81, 85.

31. USCWRIC, *Personal Justice*, 55, 61; Daniels, "Words Do Matter," 195.

32. USCWRIC, *Personal Justice*, 54; Greg Robinson, *A Tragedy of Democracy: Japanese Confinement in North America* (New York: Columbia University Press, 2009), 47–48.

33. Daniels, *Prisoners Without Trial*, 25–26; "Memorandum on C. B. Munson's Report 'Japanese on the West Coast,'" November 7, 1941, Commission on Wartime Relocation and Internment of Civilians Collection, Densho Digital Repository, ddr.densho.org/ddr-densho-67-11; Robinson, *Tragedy of Democracy*, 32–33.

34. USCWRIC, *Personal Justice*, 66.

35. Daniels, *Prisoners Without Trial*, 29; USCWRIC, *Personal Justice*, 82 [emphasis added].

36. Robinson, *Tragedy of Democracy*, 93, 113–119; Ronald T. Takaki, *Strangers from a Different Shore: A History of Asian Americans* (Boston: Little, Brown, 1998), 382; Daniels, *Prisoners Without Trial*, 51.

37. Cordell Hull, *The Memoirs of Cordell Hull*, vol. 1 (New York: Macmillan, 1948), 602; H. L. Keenleyside, "The Canada–United States Permanent Joint Board of Defence, 1940–1945," *International Journal* 16 (1960–1961); Robinson, *Tragedy of Democracy*, 43; Patricia Roy, *Mutual Hostages: Canadians and Japanese During the Second World War* (Toronto: University of Toronto Press, 1990), 36, 38–39, 45–46; Roger Daniels, "The Decisions to Relocate the North American Japanese: Another Look," *Pacific Historical Review* 51, no. 1 (1982): 75.

38. Max Paul Friedman, *Nazis and Good Neighbors: The United States Campaign Against the Germans of Latin America in World War II* (Cambridge, UK: Cambridge University Press, 2003), 77–78; C. Harvey Gardiner, *Pawns in a Triangle of Hate: The Peruvian Japanese and the United States* (Seattle: University of Washington Press, 1981), 10.

39. S. H. Sherrill to Orme Wilson, December 11, 1941, Telegram from US Department of State to American Embassy, Panama, December 12, 1941, and Orme Wilson to Sumner Welles, December 12, 1941, File 740.00115 PACIFIC WAR/11 and 12, Decimal File, 1940–1944, RG59, US State Department Records, National Archives [hereafter cited as US State Department Records]; USCWRIC, *Personal Justice*, 307.

40. Boaz Long to US Secretary of State, January 2, 1942, and Stephen E. Aguirre to US Secretary of State, January 14, 1942, File 740.00115 PACIFIC WAR/59 and 77, US State Department Records; Jan Jarboe Russell, *The Train to Crystal City: FDR's Secret Prisoner Exchange Program and America's Only Family Internment Camp During World War II* (New York: Scribner, 2015), xvii.

41. John K. Emmerson, "Japanese in Peru," October 9, 1943, iv, 16, 54, 58, 23, 64, 65, 78; John K. Emmerson to Henry Norweb, April 18, 1942, File 894.20223/196 and 124; Undersecretary of State to Francis Biddle, August 20, 1942, File 740.00115/ PACIFIC WAR 1002 2/6; Henry Norweb, "The Japanese Problem in Peru," File 894.20210/198, US State Department Records.

42. Friedman, *Nazis and Good Neighbors*, 104–105; Gardiner, *Pawns in a Triangle of Hate*, 13–14.

43. "Making the Western Hemisphere . . . " from "Rio Exposes Fifth Columns," February 1, 1942, and "Rio Parley Closes in Unity as Brazil Breaks with Axis," *New York Times*, January 29, 1942; "Not exercised . . . " and "heterogeneous collection . . . " from "Japanese Activities in Peru: Summary of FBI Report," June 27, 1942, File 894.20223/154; John K. Emmerson to Henry Norweb, April 18, 1942, File 894.20223/124, US State Department Records.

44. "In the interest . . . " from Department of State Telegram, August 12, 1942, File 740.00115/PACIFIC WAR 1001 2/6, US State Department Records; Friedman, *Nazis and Good Neighbors*, 121–122; Gardiner, *Pawns in a Triangle of Hate*, 16–18; USCWRIC, *Personal Justice*, 307, 310.

45. J. Edgar Hoover to William Donovan, March 6, 1942, File 13280, US OSS Records, NARA; Gardiner, *Pawns in a Triangle of Hate*, 14–16.

46. Memo, October 13, 1942, File 740.00115 PACIFIC WAR/1140 2/7, US State Department Records; "Subversive activities" from Ambassador Norweb to Secretary of State, February 11, 1942, File 701.0023/24; "Very Much" from Henry Norweb to Mr. Sumner, July 20, 1942, File 740.00116 PACIFIC WAR/1002 2/6; "Ideal" from Memo, October 13, 1942, File 740.00115 PACIFIC WAR/1140 2/7, US State Department Records; Friedman, *Nazis and Good Neighbors*, 238, n19, 190–191.

47. John K. Emmerson, "Japanese in Peru," October 9, 1943, 22, 40, 68–75, and Henry Norweb to Secretary of State, July 7, 1943, File 894.20223/196, US State Department Records; Higashide, *Adios to Tears*, 119, 125; Gardiner, *Pawns in a Triangle of Hate*, 27.

48. Edward N. Barnhart, "Japanese Internees from Peru," *Pacific Historical Review* 31, no. 2 (1962): 172; USCWRIC, *Personal Justice*, 312.

49. Fred Korematsu–Kathryn Korematsu interview, May 14, 1996, Densho Digital Repository, https://encyclopedia.densho.org/media/encyc-psms/en-denshovh -kfred_g-01-0002-1.htm; Roger Daniels, *The Japanese American Cases: The Rule of Law in Time of War* (Lawrence: University Press of Kansas, 2013), 34–36, 49, 51, 55–59, 62–63, 67–76, 78–79; *Toyosaburo Korematsu v. United States*, 323 U.S. 214 (1944).

50. USCWRIC, *Personal Justice*, 195, 208; Robinson, *Tragedy of Democracy*, 192.

51. Gardiner, *Pawns in a Triangle of Hate*, 29; Elsa Kudo Interview, Segment 14, February 6, 2012, Densho Visual History Collection, Densho Digital Repository, ddr .densho.org/interviews/ddr-densho-1000-388-14/.

52. US Department of Justice, Immigration and Naturalization Service, "Alien Enemy Detention Facility," Motion Picture Films, c. 1942–1943, RG85, Motion Picture, Sound, and Video Records LICON, Special Media Archives Services Division, National Archives, College Park, MD.

53. Gardiner, *Pawns in a Triangle of Hate*, 59–61; Higashide, *Adios to Tears*, 168, 170.

54. Dillon S. Meyer, Director of the War Relocation Authority, "Problems of Evacuee Resettlement in California," Address given at Eagle Rock, California, June 19, 1945, Folder 2, Box 49, Edward N. Barnhart Papers, UCLA [hereafter cited as Barnhart Papers].

55. Masterson and Funada-Classen, *Japanese in Latin America*, 171, 174–178; Gardiner, *Pawns in a Triangle of Hate*, 112.

56. Higashide, *Adios to Tears*, 173; File of Yuzo Shibayama and Family, Folder 11, Box 19, Wayne M. Collins Papers, 1918–1974, Bancroft Library, UC Berkeley.

57. Wayne M. Collins to George C. Marshall, February 7, 1947, Folder 2, and Wayne Collins to Mr. Harold Ickes, July 7, 1947, Folder 7, Box 49, Barnhart Papers.

58. In the Matter of Yuzo Shibayama," June 3, 1949, File of Yuzo Shibayama and Family, 1949–1954, Folder 11, Box 19, Collins Papers; Higashide, *Adios to Tears*, 179, 223–224; Memorandum from Wayne M. Collins, October 7, 1954, Folder 14, Box 49, Barnhart Papers.

59. Erika Lee, *The Making of Asian America: A History* (New York: Simon and Schuster, 2015), 311–313; Martha Nakagawa, "Obituary: Art Shibayama," *Rafu Shimpo*, August 8, 2018, www.rafu.com/2018/08/obituary-art-shibayama-fighter-for -japanese-latin-american-redress/; Sam Roberts, "Isamu Shibayama Dies at 88, His Quest for Reparations Unfulfilled," *New York Times*, August 17, 2018.

Chapter 7: Xenophobia and Civil Rights

1. Tom Gjelten, *A Nation of Nations: A Great Immigration Story* (New York: Simon and Schuster, 2015), 88.

2. Edward M. Kennedy, "The Immigration Act of 1965," *Annals of the American Academy of Political and Social Science* 367 (1966): 138.

3. Immigration-related correspondence, Box 25, and Immigration Speeches, February to September, 1965, Box 65, Michael A. Feighan Papers, Special Collections, Princeton University Library [hereafter cited as Feighan Papers]; Wolfgang Saxon, "Ex-Rep. Michael A. Feighan, 87; Architect of '65 Immigration Law," *New York Times*, March 20, 1992.

4. Immigration and Nationality Act (Pub.L. 89–236); Muzaffar Chishti, Faye Hipsman, and Isabel Ball, "Fifty Years On, the 1965 Immigration and Nationality Act Continues to Reshape the United States," Migration Policy Institute, October 15, 2015, www.migrationpolicy.org/article/fifty-years-1965-immigration-and-nationality -act-continues-reshape-united-states; Douglas S. Massey and Karen A. Pren, "Unintended Consequences of US Immigration Policy: Explaining the Post-1965 Surge from Latin America," *Population and Development Review* 38, no. 1 (2012): 1.

5. "President Lyndon B. Johnson's Remarks at the Signing of the Immigration Bill, Liberty Island, New York, October 3, 1965," *Public Papers of the Presidents of the United States: Lyndon B. Johnson, 1965*, vol. 2 (Washington, DC: US Government Printing Office, 1966), 1037–1040.

6. American Immigration and Citizenship Conference to Michael A. Feighan, October 22, 1965, "Immigration" Folder, Box 27, Feighan Papers; Gabriel J. Chin, "The Civil Rights Revolution Comes to Immigration Law: A New Look at the Immigration and Nationality Act of 1965," *North Carolina Law Review* 75, no. 1 (1996): 273–345; Bill Ong Hing, *Making and Remaking Asian America Through Immigration Policy, 1850– 1990* (Stanford, CA: Stanford University Press, 1993): 18.

7. Kevin R. Johnson, "The Beginning of the End: The Immigration Act of 1965 and the Emergence of the Modern U.S.-Mexico Border State," in *The Immigration and Nationality Act of 1965: Legislating a New America*, ed. Gabriel J. Chin and Rose Cuison Villazor (New York: Cambridge University Press, 2015), 116–170; Eithne Luibhéid and Lionel Cantú, eds., *Queer Migrations: Sexuality, U.S. Citizenship, and Border Crossings* (Minneapolis: University of Minnesota Press, 2005), xiii–xv; Atticus Lee, "Sexual Deviants Need Not Apply: LGBTQ Oppression in the 1965 Immigration Act Amendments," in *The Immigration and Nationality Act of 1965*, 259, 267–269.

8. Maddalena Marinari, Madeline Y. Hsu, and María Cristina García, "Introduction," in Maddalena Marinari, Madeline Y. Hsu, and María García, eds., *A Nation of Immigrants Reconsidered: U.S. Society in an Age of Restriction, 1924–1965* (Urbana: University of Illinois Press, 2018), 1–24.

9. Marinari, Hsu, and García, "Introduction," 8; Erika Lee, *The Making of Asian America: A History* (New York: Simon and Schuster, 2015), 270–271; S. Deborah Kang, *The INS on the Line: Making Immigration Law on the U.S.-Mexico Border, 1917–1954* (New York: Oxford University Press, 2017), 161–165; Kelly Lytle Hernandez, "Largest Deportation Campaign in U.S. History Is No Match for Trump's Plan," The Conversation, March 8, 2017, https://theconversation.com/largest-deportation-campaign-in-us

-history-is-no-match-for-trumps-plan-73651; Pew Research Center, "U.S. Foreign-Born Population Trends," September 28, 2015, www.pewhispanic.org/2015/09/28/chapter-5-u-s-foreign-born-population-trends/.

10. Gary Gerstle, *American Crucible: Race and Nation in the Twentieth Century* (Princeton, NJ: Princeton University Press, 2018), 261.

11. Gjelten, *Nation of Nations*, 101.

12. John F. Kennedy, *A Nation of Immigrants* (New York: Harper and Row, 1964).

13. Roger Daniels, *Guarding the Golden Door: American Immigration Policy and Immigrants Since 1882* (New York: Hill and Wang, 2004), 129; Caesar L. Donnaruma to Senator John F. Kennedy, January 23, 1958, Box 1, Caesar Donnaruma Papers, Immigration History Research Center Archives, Special Collections, University of Minnesota; Center for Immigration Studies, "The Legacy of the 1965 Immigration Act: Three Decades of Mass Immigration," Center for Immigration Studies, September 1, 1995, https://cis.org/Report/Legacy-1965-Immigration-Act.

14. Posters Demanding New United States Immigration Law, accessed April 1, 2019, https://umedia.lib.umn.edu/item/p16022coll137:1021; Victor J. Lezza, "An Open Letter to All Americans and Organizations with Members of Southern European Ancestry," April 10, 1964, File 42, Address by Judge Juvenal Marchisio, National Chairman, ACIM, February 16, 1958, File 35, American Committee on Italian Migration, Chicago Chapter (Ill.) Records, Immigration History Research Center Archives, Special Collections, University of Minnesota, [hereafter cited as ACIM Records].

15. White House Press Release, July 23, 1963, File 39, ACIM Records; US House of Representatives Judiciary Committee, "Report to Accompany H.R. 2580 Amending the Immigration and Nationality Act" (Washington, DC, August 6, 1965), 11; Gjelten, *Nation of Nations*, 105.

16. "Remarks of Honorable Michael A. Feighan Before the American Immigration and Citizenship Conference," April 16, 1965, in "Immigration, Statement of Policy," Box 38, Feighan Papers; Gjelten, *Nation of Nations*, 106.

17. US House of Representatives Judiciary Committee, "Report to Accompany H.R. 2580," 11; Gjelten, *Nation of Nations*, 109; Lyndon Baines Johnson, "Annual Message to the Congress on the State of the Union, January 8, 1964," LBJ Presidential Library, www.lbjlibrary.net/collections/selected-speeches/november-1963-1964/01-08-1964.html; "Statement by Robert F. Kennedy Before Subcommittee No. 1 of the House Judiciary Committee Regarding H.R. 7700, A Bill to Amend the Immigration and Nationality Act, July 22, 1964," in "Immigration, Statement of Policy," Box 38, Feighan Papers.

18. Gjelten, *Nation of Nations*, 109–110.

19. Maddalena Marinari, "'Americans Must Show Justice in Immigration Policies Too': The Passage of the 1965 Immigration Act," *Journal of Policy History* 26, no. 2 (2014): 226.

20. Gjelten, *Nation of Nations*, 113.

21. FitzGerald and Cook-Martín, *Culling the Masses*, 64–81.

22. *Congressional Record*, August 25, 1965, 21783, 21787, 21786.

23. "Feighan Argues Merits of His Immigration Bill," *Cleveland Plain Dealer*, August 13, 1964; "Cong. Feighan Pushes His Bill on Immigration," *Cleveland Press*, August

12, 1964, in Box 5, "Immigration" Folder, and ACPS, "Report to America," September 1963, in "Immigration, Statement of Policy," Box 38, Feighan Papers.

24. "Transcript of Proceedings," House of Representatives Committee on the Judiciary, Subcommittee No. 1, H.R. 2580, Washington, DC, May 20, 1965, 457–518, Box 25, Feighan Papers.

25. US House of Representatives Judiciary Committee, "Report to Accompany H.R. 2580," 13; Mae M. Ngai, *Impossible Subjects: Illegal Aliens and the Making of Modern America* (Princeton, NJ: Princeton University Press, 2004), 248; Kang, *INS on the Line*, 144–147.

26. "Statement by Robert F. Kennedy" and "Basic Principles for a Selective Immigration Reform—Address of Honorable Michael A. Feighan Delivered to the 4th National Biennial Symposium of the American Committee for Italian Migration," May 18, 1965, in "Immigration, Statement of Policy," Box 38, Feighan Papers.

27. *Congressional Record*, September 22, 1965, 24779 and 24776.

28. Gjelten, *Nation of Nations*, 120; *Congressional Record*, August 25, 1965, 21773; Marinari, "'Americans Must Show Justice,'" 232, 225, 234.

29. Gabriel Chin, "Were the Immigration and Nationality Act Amendments of 1965 Antiracist?" in *Immigration and Nationality Act of 1965*, ed. Chin and Villazor, n140, n141, 33; *Congressional Record*, August 25, 1965, 21761 and 21774 and September 21, 1965, 24557; Center for Immigration Studies, "Legacy of the 1965 Immigration Act."

30. *Congressional Record*, August 25, 1965, 21761; William G. Hartley, "United States Immigration Policy: The Case of the Western Hemisphere," *World Affairs* 135, no. 1 (1972): 58.

31. "Transcript of Proceedings, House of Representatives, Committee on the Judiciary, Subcommittee No. 1, H.R. 2580," March 8, 1965, Washington, DC, 77–82, Box 25 [emphasis added], and Press Release, February 4, 1965, "Immigration" Folder, Box 27 [emphasis added], Feighan Papers.

32. "Immigration—Fact and Fiction," Address of Honorable Michael A. Feighan Delivered at the City Club, Cleveland, Ohio, May 14, 1965, "Cleveland Hearings," Box 38, Feighan Papers.

33. *Congressional Record*, August 25, 1965, 21759 and 21761, 21760 [emphasis added]; Marinari, "'Americans Must Show Justice,'" 232; US House of Representatives Judiciary Committee, "Report to Accompany H.R. 2580," 49.

34. *Congressional Record*, August 25, 1965, 21759; US Senate, "Report Amending the Immigration and Nationality Act and for Other Purposes" (Washington, DC, September 15, 1965), 58; Marinari, "'Americans Must Show Justice,'" 234.

35. "Our Immigration Law Under Attack," *Independent American*, n.d., 1965, in "Cleveland Hearings"; American Coalition of Patriotic Societies, "Time to Hold Fast" and "Trojan Horse at Our Gate," n.d., "Immigration, 1961–1964," Box 38, Feighan Papers.

36. *Congressional Record*, August 25, 1965, 21762, 21810, 21763.

37. Marinari, "'Americans Must Show Justice,'" 227; *Congressional Record*, August 25, 1965, 21007, 21762, and September 22, 1965, 24782; "Separate Views of Mr. Kennedy of Massachusetts, Mr. Hart, and Mr. Javits," in US Senate, "Report Amending the Immigration and Nationality Act and for Other Purposes," 59.

38. *Congressional Record*, August 25, 1965, 21758.

39. Center for Immigration Studies, "Legacy of the 1965 Immigration Act"; Desmond S. King, *Making Americans: Immigration, Race, and the Origins of the Diverse Democracy* (Cambridge, MA: Harvard University Press, 2000), 244; Johnson, "Beginning of the End," 136–137.

40. Marinari, "'Americans Must Show Justice,'" 231–232; Johnson, "Beginning of the End," 123.

41. Gjelten, *Nation of Nations*, 117.

42. Deane Heller and David Heller, "Our New Immigration Law," *American Legion Magazine*, February 1966, 8–9.

43. Ngai, *Impossible Subjects*, 257; Marinari, "'Americans Must Show Justice,'" 220–221.

44. "President Lyndon B. Johnson's Remarks."

45. Lee, "Sexual Deviants Need Not Apply," 248–272; Brian Soucek, "The Last Preference: Refugees and the 1965 Immigration Act," in *Immigration and Nationality Act of 1965*, ed. Chin and Villazor, 171–196.

46. Matthew Frye Jacobson, *Whiteness of a Different Color: European Immigrants and the Alchemy of Race* (Cambridge, MA: Harvard University Press, 1998), 6, 7, 245.

47. Roger Daniels, *Coming to America: A History of Immigration and Ethnicity in American Life* (New York: HarperCollins, 1990), 343; Marinari, Hsu, and García, "Introduction," 10–11; Ana Raquel Minian, *Undocumented Lives: the Untold Story of Mexican Migration* (Cambridge, MA: Harvard University Press, 2018), 28.

48. Migration Policy Institute, "Largest U.S. Immigrant Groups over Time, 1960–Present," www.migrationpolicy.org/programs/data-hub/charts/largest-immigrant-groups-over-time.

49. Johnson, "Beginning of the End," 144; Lee, *Making of Asian America*, 1, 284–285.

50. Johnson, "Beginning of the End," 120, 170.

51. Eithne Luibhéid, "The 1965 Immigration and Nationality Act: An End to Exclusion?" *Positions: East Asia Cultures Critique* 5, no. 2 (Fall 1997): 510; Marinari, "'Americans Must Show Justice,'" 220.

52. Johnson, "Beginning of the End," 146.

53. Chishti, Hipsman, and Ball, "Fifty Years On"; Luibhéid, "1965 Immigration and Nationality Act," 508; Charles B. Keely, "Effects of the Immigration Act of 1965 on Selected Population Characteristics of Immigrants to the United States," *Demography* 8, no. 2 (1971): 157–169; Nicholas De Genova, "Mexican/Migrant 'Illegality,'" *Latino Studies* 2, no. 2 (July 2004), 170.

54. Ngai, *Impossible Subjects*, 261; Minian, *Undocumented Lives*, 68–69.

55. Hartley, "United States Immigration Policy," 66; *Time*, November 21, 1969; Kevin R. Johnson, "Race, the Immigration Laws, and Domestic Race Relations: A Magic Mirror into the Heart of Darkness," *Indiana Law Journal* 73, no. 4 (1998): 1134; US Department of State, Bureau of Consular Affairs, "Annual Report of Immigrant Visa Applicants in the Family-Sponsored and Employment-Based Preferences Registered at the National Visa Center as of November 1, 2018," https://travel.state.gov/content/dam/visas/Statistics/Immigrant-Statistics/WaitingList/WaitingListItem_2018.pdf.

56. Johnson, "Beginning of the End," 119, 170.

57. Johnson, "Beginning of the End," 139; Douglas S. Massey, "How a 1965 Immigration Reform Created Illegal Immigration," *Washington Post*, September 25, 2015.

58. Minian, *Undocumented Lives*, 67; David R. Roediger, *How Race Survived U.S. History: From Settlement and Slavery to the Obama Phenomenon* (London: Verso, 2008), 170–171.

Chapter 8: "Save Our State"

1. Douglas S. Massey, "The Real Hispanic Challenge," *Pathways* (Spring 2015): 4.

2. Roger Daniels, *Coming to America: A History of Immigration and Ethnicity in American Life* (New York: HarperCollins, 1990), 404.

3. Paul Spickard, *Almost All Aliens: Immigration, Race, and Colonialism in American History and Identity* (New York: Routledge, 2007), 342; Douglas Massey, Jorge Durand, and Nolan Malone, *Beyond Smoke and Mirrors: Immigrants in an Era of Economic Integration* (New York: Russell Sage, 2002), 43–47.

4. Ian Haney López, *Dog Whistle Politics: How Coded Racial Appeals Have Reinvented Racism and Wrecked the Middle Class* (New York: Oxford University Press, 2014), 3–5; Robin D. Jacobson, *The New Nativism: Proposition 187 and the Debate over Immigration* (Minneapolis: University of Minnesota Press, 2008), 19, 24.

5. Ronald Sundstrom, "Racism and the Political Romance of the Browning of America," *Philosophy*, Paper 47 (2008): 295, http://repository.usfca.edu/phil/47; Ronald Sundstrom, *The Browning of America and the Evasion of Social Justice* (Albany: State University of New York Press, 2008).

6. Leo Chavez, *Covering Immigration: Popular Images and the Politics of the Nation* (Berkeley: University of California Press, 2001), 84; "The New Immigrants: Still the Promised Land," *Time*, July 5, 1976, 18.

7. Ana Raquel Minian, *Undocumented Lives: the Untold Story of Mexican Migration* (Cambridge, MA: Harvard University Press, 2018), 71; Joseph Nevins, *Operation Gatekeeper: The Rise of the "Illegal Alien" and the Remaking of the U.S.-Mexico Boundary* (New York: Routledge, 2001), 63–64; Chavez, *Covering Immigration*, 92–99.

8. Daniel Martinez HoSang, *Racial Propositions: Ballot Initiatives and the Making of Postwar California* (Berkeley: University of California Press, 2010), 171; Carl Lindskoog, *Detain and Punish: Haitian Refugees and the Rise of the World's Largest Immigration Detention System* (Gainesville: University of Florida Press, 2018); Cindy Hahamovitch, *No Man's Land: Jamaican Guestworkers in America and the Global History of Deportable Labor* (Princeton, NJ: Princeton University Press, 2013), 202.

9. "Immigration and Purity," *New York Times*, December 16, 1982, www.nytimes.com/1982/12/16/opinion/immigration-and-purity.html; "English (Sometimes) Spoken Here: Our Big Cities Go Ethnic," *US News and World Report*, March 21, 1983; "Los Angeles: America's Uneasy New Melting Pot," *Time*, June 13, 1983; Chavez, *Covering Immigration*, 112.

10. Dennis William et al., "A Formula for Success," *Newsweek*, April 23, 1984; Anthony Ramirez, "America's Super Minority," *Fortune*, November 24, 1986.

11. Douglas S. Massey and Karen A. Pren, "Unintended Consequences of US Immigration Policy: Explaining the Post-1965 Surge from Latin America," *Population and Development Review* 38, no. 1 (2012): 6; Leo Chavez, *The Latino Threat: Constructing*

Immigrants, Citizens, and the Nation (Stanford, CA: Stanford University Press, 2013), 24, 28, 31–33; Massey, Durand, and Malone, *Beyond Smoke and Mirrors*, 3; Otto Santa Ana, *Brown Tide Rising: Metaphors of Latinos in Contemporary American Public Discourse* (Austin: University of Texas Press, 2002), 77.

12. *The Papers of the Presidents, Ronald Reagan, 1981*, vol. 1 (Washington, DC: US Government Printing Office, 1982), 676–677; Michael C. LeMay and Elliott Robert Barkan, eds., *U.S. Immigration and Naturalization Laws and Issues: A Documentary History* (Westport, CT: Greenwood, 1999), 276–277; Spickard, *Almost All Aliens*, 392–393.

13. Daniels, *Coming to America*, 219–220; Nevins, *Operation Gatekeeper*, 67–68; López, *Dog Whistle Politics*, 58–59; HoSang, *Racial Propositions*, 166; Minian, *Undocumented Lives*, 210; Walter Ewing, Daniel E. Martínez, and Rubén G. Rumbaut, "The Criminalization of Immigration in the United States," American Immigration Council, July 13, 2015, 13, www.americanimmigrationcouncil.org/research /criminalization-immigration-united-states.

14. Minian, *Undocumented Lives*, 183.

15. "Pat Buchanan Presidential Campaign Announcement," C-SPAN, December 10, 1991, www.c-span.org/video/?23289-1/pat-buchanan-presidential -campaign-announcement; Jeff Greenfield, "Trump Is Pat Buchanan with Better Timing," Politico, September/October 2016, www.politico.com/magazine/story/2016/09 /donald-trump-pat-buchanan-republican-america-first-nativist-214221.

16. *Los Angeles Times*, April 4, 1992; *Los Angeles Times*, May 14, 1992.

17. HoSang, *Racial Propositions*, 168–172; Kevin R. Johnson, "An Essay on Immigration Politics, Popular Democracy, and California's Proposition 187: The Political Relevance and Legal Irrelevance of Race," *Washington Law Review* 70, no. 3 (1995): 655–656.

18. Elaine Woo, "Barbara Coe Dies at 79," *Los Angeles Times*, September 4, 2013, http://articles.latimes.com/2013/sep/04/local/la-me-barbara-coe-20130905.

19. *National Review*, July 5, 1993, 60 [emphasis in original]; Johnson, "Essay on Immigration Politics," n141, 658.

20. HoSang, *Racial Propositions*, 167; Andrew Wroe, *The Republican Party and Immigration Politics: From Proposition 187 to George W. Bush* (New York: Palgrave Macmillan, 2008), 58.

21. *California Ballot Pamphlet, General Election, November 8, 1994* (Sacramento: California Secretary of State, 1994), 91 [emphasis in original].

22. *California Ballot Pamphlet*, 54 [emphasis in original].

23. *California Ballot Pamphlet*, 52–53.

24. "You are the posse . . . " from *Los Angeles Times*, August 10, 1994; "Caught, skinned and fried" from Daniel B. Wood, "Ballot Vote on Illegal Immigrants Set for Fall in California," *Christian Science Monitor*, June 1, 1994, 1, 18; "Those little . . . " from Elizabeth Kadetsky, "Bashing Illegals in California: 'Save Our State' Initiative," *The Nation*, October 17, 1994, 418.

25. Nevins, *Operation Gatekeeper*, 13; HoSang, *Racial Propositions*, 140, 176.

26. "In big trouble . . . " from *Los Angeles Times*, January 12, 1994; "Illegal immigration ain't *free* . . . " from Letter to the Editor, *Los Angeles Times*, March 27, 1994, B14 [emphasis in original]; "Nothing will stop them" from *Los Angeles Times*, February 17, 1994.

27. HoSang, *Racial Propositions*, 161; Jacobson, *New Nativism*, xx.

28. HoSang, *Racial Propositions*, 170; Jacobson, *New Nativism*, xvi–xvii; Wroe, *Republican Party*, 3; Mark Z. Barabak, "Pete Wilson Looks Back on Proposition 187," *Los Angeles Times*, March 23, 2017, www.latimes.com/politics/la-me-on-politics-column -20170323-story.html.

29. Nevins, *Operation Gatekeeper*, 87 [emphasis in original]; Anthony Lewis, "Abroad at Home, The Politics of Nativism," *New York Times*, January 14, 1994.

30. Jacobson, *New Nativism*, xvi–xvii; Wroe, *Republican Party*, 47–48.

31. "Pete Wilson 1994 Campaign Ad on Illegal Immigration," YouTube, February 15, 2010, www.youtube.com/watch?time_continue=8&v=lLIzzs2HHgY.

32. Robert Warren, "Estimates of the Unauthorized Immigrant Population Residing in the United States, by Country of Origin and State of Residence" (Washington, DC: INS Statistics Division, October 1992), 28–29.

33. Wroe, *Republican Party*, 7, 44, 51, 63, 56–57, 84; Nevins, *Operation Gatekeeper*, 89; HoSang, *Racial Propositions*, 172, 176, 166, 169.

34. Ewing, Martínez, and Rumbaut, "The Criminalization of Immigration"; "The mindset . . . " from Marc Cooper, "The War Against Illegal Immigrants Heats Up," *Village Voice*, October 4, 1994, 28; "Illegal-alien gangs . . . " from Barbara Coe, "Keep Illegals Out of State," *USA Today*, October 12, 1994; Johnson, "Essay on Immigration Politics," 657–658.

35. Johnson, "Essay on Immigration Politics," 653; Jacobson, *New Nativism*, 64.

36. Johnson, "Essay on Immigration Politics," 653; Suzanne Espinosa, "Attacks by White Supremacists," *San Francisco Chronicle*, August 13, 1993.

37. Nevins, *Operation Gatekeeper*, 87; Lewis, "Abroad at Home."

38. HoSang, *Racial Propositions*, 178–179.

39. California Voter Information Guide for 1994, 55; HoSang, *Racial Propositions*, 180–181.

40. Californians United Against Proposition 187, "15 Billion Reasons Why Californians Should Oppose Proposition 187" and "Who Will Pay?" Folder 1, California General Election, 1994, Proposition 187 Campaign Ephemera and Newspaper Clippings, Institute of Governmental Studies Library, UC Berkeley; Howard F. Chang, "Shame on Them, Picking on Children: Banning Illegal Immigrants and Their U.S.-Born Offspring from School and Clinics Is Malicious and Foolhardy," *Los Angeles Times*, September 6, 1994, http://articles.latimes.com/1994-09-06/local/me-35187_1 _undocumented-immigrants; HoSang, *Racial Propositions*, 182.

41. HoSang, *Racial Propositions*, 186–187.

42. Jacobson, *New Nativism*, xiv.

43. Peter Brimelow, *Alien Nation: Common Sense About America's Immigration Disaster* (New York: HarperPerennial, 1995), xvi, xvii, 79, 219 [emphasis in original].

44. Patrick Buchanan, *State of Emergency: The Third World Invasion and Conquest of America* (New York: St. Martin's Press, 2006), 5–6.

45. "Melting and reforming" from Patrick Buchanan, *The Death of the West: How Dying Populations and Immigrant Invasions Imperil Our Country and Civilization* (New York: St. Martin's Press, 2001), 3; "No allegiance . . . " from Buchanan, *State of Emergency*, 13, 28.

46. "Assault" from Buchanan, *Death of the West*, 12; "a minority . . . " from Buchanan, *State of Emergency*, 12.

47. Samuel P. Huntington, "The Hispanic Challenge," *Foreign Policy* (March–April 2004): 30.

48. Huntington, "Hispanic Challenge," 31–32.

49. Huntington, "Hispanic Challenge," 34, 36.

50. Huntington, "Hispanic Challenge," 32.

51. Jacobson, *New Nativism*, xxiii; Anti-Defamation League, "Funders of the Anti-Immigrant Movement," January 27, 2014, www.adl.org/news/article/funders-of-the-anti-immigrant-movement; Alfonso Gonzales, *Reform Without Justice: Latino Migrant Politics and the Homeland Security State* (Oxford, UK: Oxford University Press, 2014), 33–34; Gjelten, *Nation of Nations*, 241–254; HoSang, *Racial Propositions*, 139; Jason DeParle, "The Anti-Immigration Crusader," *New York Times*, April 17, 2011, www.nytimes.com/2011/04/17/us/17immig.html; Peter Schrag, *Not Fit for Our Society: Nativism and Immigration* (Berkeley: University of California Press, 2010), 178–180; Southern Poverty Law Center, "John Tanton," accessed April 1, 2019, www.splcenter.org/fighting-hate/extremist-files/individual/john-tanton; Southern Poverty Law Center, "Federation for American Immigration Reform," accessed April 1, 2019, www.splcenter.org/fighting-hate/extremist-files/group/federation-american-immigration-reform; Carly Goodman, "The Shadowy Network Shaping Trump's Anti-Immigration Policies," *Washington Post*, September 27, 2018, www.washingtonpost.com/outlook/2018/09/27/shadowy-network-shaping-trumps-anti-immigration-policies/.

52. Carol Anderson, *White Rage: The Unspoken Truth of Our Racial Divide* (New York: Bloomsbury Press, 2016), 98–137; Maris Abrajano and Zoltan L. Hajnal, *White Backlash: Immigration, Race, and American Politics* (Princeton, NJ: Princeton University Press, 2015), 61–112, 183–200; Jessica Brown, "The 'Southwestern Strategy': Immigration and Race in GOP Discourse," Working Paper No. 2015-01 (Kinder Institute for Urban Research, Rice University, 2015), 1–36.

53. Elizabeth Fussell, "Warmth of the Welcome: Attitudes Toward Immigrants and Immigration Policy," *Annual Review of Sociology* 40 (July 2014): 481–482.

54. Spickard, *Almost All Aliens*, 394; Chavez, *Latino Threat*, 9; López, *Dog Whistle Politics*, 52.

55. Juliet Stumpf, "The Crimmigration Crisis: Immigrants, Crime, and Sovereign Power," *American University Law Review* 56, no. 2 (December 2006): 367–419; Ewing, Martínez, and Rumbaut, "Criminalization of Immigration," 10; Suzy McElrath, Rahsaan Mahadeo, and Stephen Suh, eds., "'Crimmigration,' with Tanya Golash-Boza, Ryan King, and Yolanda Vázquez," The Society Pages, February 24, 2014, https://thesocietypages.org/roundtables/crimmigration/; Jennifer M. Chacón, "Overcriminalizing Immigration," *Journal of Criminal Law and Criminology* 102, no. 3 (Summer 2012): 613–652; César Cuauhtémoc García Hernández, *Crimmigration Law* (Washington, DC: American Bar Association, 2015); Kelly Lytle Hernández, "Amnesty or Abolition? Felons, Illegals, and the Case for a New Abolition Movement," *Boom: A Journal of California* 1, no. 4 (Winter 2011): 63.

56. Nicholas De Genova and Nathalie Peutz, eds., *The Deportation Regime: Sovereignty, Space, and the Freedom of Movement* (Durham, NC: Duke University Press, 2010).

57. Katie McDonough, "A Short, Brutal History of ICE," Splinter, February 2, 2018, https://splinternews.com/a-short-brutal-history-of-ice-1822641556; American Immigration Council, "The Criminal Alien Program (CAP): Immigration Enforcement in Prisons and Jails," August 1, 2013, www.americanimmigrationcouncil.org/research

/criminal-alien-program-cap-immigration-enforcement-prisons-and-jails; Massey, "Real Hispanic Challenge," 3–7; Gonzales, *Reform Without Justice*, 2; "Gendered racial . . . " from Tanya Golash-Boza and Pierrette Hondagneu-Sotelo, "Latino Immigrant Men and the Deportation Crisis: A Gendered Racial Removal Program," *Latino Studies* 11, no. 3 (2013): 271–292.

58. "Clinton Demands Tighter Borders," *New York Times*, July 28, 1993.

59. Nevins, *Operation Gatekeeper*, 4.

60. Nevins, *Operation Gatekeeper*, 145.

61. Gary Gerstle, *American Crucible: Race and Nation in the Twentieth Century* (Princeton, NJ: Princeton University Press, 2018), 381, 383; John O'Sullivan, "Bush's Latin Beat," *National Review* 53, no. 14 (July 23, 2001): 35–37.

62. Donald Kerwin and Kristen McCabe, "Arrested on Entry: Operation Streamline and the Prosecution of Immigration Crimes," Migration Policy Institute, April 29, 2010, www.migrationpolicy.org/article/arrested-entry-operation-streamline-and -prosecution-immigration-crimes; "George W. Bush on Immigration," On the Issues, June 17, 2017, www.ontheissues.org/celeb/George_W__Bush_Immigration.htm.

63. Muzaffar Chishti, Sarah Pierce, and Jessica Bolter, "The Obama Record on Deportations: Deporter in Chief or Not?" Migration Policy Institute, January 26, 2017, www.migrationpolicy.org/article/obama-record-deportations-deporter-chief-or-not; Nick Corasaniti, "A Look at Trump's Immigration Plan, Then and Now," *New York Times*, August 31, 2016; Alex Nowrasteh, "President Trump's Immigration Plans," Cato Institute, November 9, 2016, www.cato.org/blog/president-trumps-immigration-plans; Gonzalez, *Reform Without Justice*, 147.

64. Chishti, Pierce, and Bolter, "Obama Record"; Gonzalez, *Reform Without Justice*, 147–149; Ted Robbins, "Little-Known Immigration Mandate Keeps Detention Beds Full," NPR, November 19, 2013, www.npr.org/2013/11/19/245968601/little-known -immigration-mandate-keeps-detention-beds-full; Jennifer Chan, "Immigration Detention Bed Quota Timeline," National Immigrant Justice Center, January 13, 2017, www .immigrantjustice.org/staff/blog/immigration-detention-bed-quota-timeline.

65. Chishti, Pierce, and Bolter, "Obama Record"; McElrath, Mahadeo, and Suh, "'Crimmigration'"; Tom K. Wong, Greisa Martinez Rosas, Adam Luna, Henry Manning, Adrian Reyna, Patrick O'Shea, Tom Jawetz, and Philip. E. Wolgin, "DACA Recipients' Economic and Educational Gains Continue to Grow," Center for American Progress, August 28, 2017, www.americanprogress.org/issues/immigration/news /2017/08/28/437956/daca-recipients-economic-educational-gains-continue-grow/.

66. National Conference of State Legislatures, "State Laws Related to Immigration and Immigrants," August 6, 2017, www.ncsl.org/research/immigration/state-laws -related-to-immigration-and-immigrants.aspx.

67. Donald Trump's Presidential Announcement Speech, *Time*, June 16, 2016, http://time.com/3923128/donald-trump-announcement-speech/; "Immigration Reform That Will Make America Great Again," Donald Trump 2016 Campaign Website, https://assets.donaldjtrump.com/Immigration-Reform-Trump.pdf; Corasaniti, "Look at Trump's Immigration Plan."

68. Woodrow Wilson International Center for Scholars and the Migration Policy Institute, "The Hispanic Challenge? What We Know About Latino Immigration" (Washington, DC: Woodrow Wilson International Center for Scholars and the Migration Policy Institute, 2004), 7, 12, 14; Ana Gonzalez-Barrera, "More Mexicans

Leaving Than Coming to the U.S.," Pew Hispanic Center, November 19, 2015, www
.pewhispanic.org/2015/11/19/more-mexicans-leaving-than-coming-to-the-u-s/; Robert
Warren, "The U.S. Undocumented Population Fell Sharply During the Obama Era:
Estimates for 2016," Center for Migration Studies, February 22, 2018, http://cmsny
.org/publications/warren-undocumented-2016/; Rob Warren, "Sharp Multiyear Decline in Undocumented Immigration Suggests Progress at U.S.-Mexico Border, Not a
National Emergency," Center for Migration Studies, February 27, 2018, http://cmsny
.org/publications/essay-warren-022719/.

69. Vanda Felbab-Brown, "The Wall: The Real Costs of a Barrier between the
United States and Mexico," August 22, 2017, www.brookings.edu/essay/the-wall-the
-real-costs-of-a-barrier-between-the-united-states-and-mexico/; Linda Qiu, "Rationale
for a Wall on Flimsy Foundations," *New York Times*, February 16, 2019.

70. Schrag, *Not Fit for Our Society*, 167.

71. Woodrow Wilson International Center and the Migration Policy Institute,
"Hispanic Challenge?" 5, 23, 24; Michelangelo Landgrave and Alex Nowrasteh,
"Criminal Immigrants: Their Numbers, Demographics, and Countries of Origin," Cato
Institute, March 15, 2017, www.cato.org/publications/immigration-reform-bulletin
/criminal-immigrants-their-numbers-demographics-countries#full.

72. Corasaniti, "Look at Trump's Immigration Plan"; Nowrasteh, "President
Trump's Immigration Plans"; Stanley Greenberg and Nancy Adunkewicz, "Macomb
County in the Age of Trump," Roosevelt Institute, March 9, 2017, http://roosevelt
institute.org/wp-content/uploads/2017/03/Dcor_Macomb_FG-Memo_3.9.2017_v8-2
.pdf; Thomas B. Edsell, "How Immigration Foiled Hillary," *New York Times*, October
5, 2017; Carroll Doherty, "5 Facts About Trump Supporters' Views of Immigration,"
Pew Research Center, August 25, 2016, www.pewresearch.org/fact-tank/2016/08/25/5
-facts-about-trump-supporters-views-of-immigration/; Daniel Cox and Robert P.
Jones, "Beyond Economics: Fears of Cultural Displacement Pushed the White Working Class to Trump," PRRI/The Atlantic Report, May 9, 2017, www.prri.org/research
/white-working-class-attitudes-economy-trade-immigration-election-donald-trump/;
Julia Young, "Making America 1920 Again? Nativism and U.S. Immigration, Past and
Present," *Journal on Migration and Human Security* 5, no. 1 (2017): 217–235.

73. White House Office of the Press Secretary, "Executive Order: Border Security and Immigration Enforcement Improvements," January 25, 2017, www
.whitehouse.gov/the-press-office/2017/01/25/executive-order-border-security-and
-immigration-enforcement-improvements; "Summary of Executive Order 'Border Security and Immigration Enforcement Improvements,'" American Immigration
Council, February 27, 2017, www.americanimmigrationcouncil.org/research/border
-security-and-immigration-enforcement-improvements-executive-order; "Summary
of Executive Order 'Enhancing Public Safety in the Interior of the United States,'"
American Immigration Council, May 19, 2017, www.americanimmigrationcouncil.org
/immigration-interior-enforcement-executive-order.

Chapter 9: Islamophobia

1. Hameed Darweesh, "I Risked My Life for the U.S. Army in Iraq," *Washington Post*, February 10, 2017, www.washingtonpost.com/posteverything/wp/2017/02/10
/i-worked-for-the-u-s-army-in-iraq-but-when-i-landed-in-america-i-was-detained.

2. Corasaniti, "Look at Trump's Immigration Plan;" Jenna Johnson, "Trump Calls for a Complete and Total Shutdown," *Washington Post*, December 7, 2015, www .washingtonpost.com/news/post-politics/wp/2015/12/07/donald-trump-calls-for-total -and-complete-shutdown-of-muslims-entering-the-united-states/.

3. Avi Selk, "Pence Once Called Trump's Muslim Ban 'Unconstitutional,'" *Washington Post*, January 28, 2017, www.washingtonpost.com/news/the-fix/wp/2017/01/28 /mike-pence-once-called-trumps-muslim-ban-unconstitutional-he-just-applauded-the -order/.

4. Arsalan Iftikhar, *Scapegoats: How Islamophobia Helps Our Enemies and Threatens Our Freedoms* (New York: Skyhorse, 2016), xviii, vi, 11; Nadine Naber, "Look, Mohammed the Terrorist Is Coming!': Cultural Racism, Nation-Based Racism and the Intersectionality of Oppressions After 9/11," in *Race and Arab Americans Before and After 9/11*, ed. Amaney Jamal and Nadine Naber (Syracuse, NY: Syracuse University Press, 2008), 281; Christopher Bail, *Terrified: How Anti-Muslim Fringe Organizations Became Mainstream* (Princeton, NJ: Princeton University Press, 2015), 3–15.

5. White House Press Secretary, "Executive Order No. 13769 of January 27, 2017, Protecting the Nation from Foreign Terrorist Entry into the United States," 82 Fed. Reg. 8, 977, January 27, 2017, www.whitehouse.gov/the-press-office/2017/01/27 /executive-order-protecting-nation-foreign-terrorist-entry-united-states; "Trump-O-Meter," Politifact, April 20, 2017, www.politifact.com/truth-o-meter/promises /trumpometer/promise/1401/establish-ban-muslims-entering-us/.

6. Darweesh, "I Risked My Life."

7. Sela Cowger, Jessica Bolter, and Sarah Pierce, "The First 100 Days: Summary of Major Immigration Actions Taken by the Trump Administration," Migration Policy Institute, April 24, 2017, www.migrationpolicy.org/research/first-100-days-summary -major-immigration-actions-taken-trump-administration; Julia Gelatt, "The RAISE Act: Dramatic Change to Family Immigration, Less So for the Employment-Based System," Migration Policy Institute, August 4, 2017, www.migrationpolicy.org/news /raise-act-dramatic-change-family-immigration-less-so-employment-based-system; Catherine E. Shoichet, "Decision Could Spell Deportation for These 250,000 Immigrants," CNN, January 8, 2018, www.cnn.com/2018/01/06/politics/el-salvador-tps -immigration/index.html.

8. "The Trump Effect," Reuters, accessed April 1, 2019, http://fingfx .thomsonreuters.com/gfx/rngs/TRUMP-EFFECT-IMMIGRATION/010050 ZX28W/index.html; Angilee Shah, ed., "We've Been Here Before: Historians Annotate and Analyze Immigration Ban's Place in History," PRI, February 1, 2017, www .pri.org/stories/2017-02-01/we-ve-been-here-historians-annotate-and-analyze -immigration-bans-place-history.

9. Massey and Pren, "Unintended Consequences," 6, 13; Marisa Franco and Carlos Garcia, "The Deportation Machine Obama Built for President Trump," *The Nation*, June 27, 2016, www.thenation.com/article/the-deportation-machine-obama -built-for-president-trump/.

10. Theodore Shleifer, "Donald Trump: 'I Think Islam Hates Us,'" CNN, March 10, 2016, www.cnn.com/2016/03/09/politics/donald-trump-islam-hates-us/index .html; "The Super Survey: Two Decades of Americans' Views on Islam and Muslims," Georgetown University's Bridge Initiative, April 2015, http://bridge.georgetown.edu /the-super-survey-two-decades-of-americans-views-on-islam-muslims/.

11. Kareeda Kabir, "5 Common Stereotypes About Muslims, Debunked," Huffington Post, July 19, 2016, www.huffingtonpost.com/entry/five-common-stereotypes -about-muslims-debunked_us_578e6d9ae4b004b4c9a37e78; Southern Poverty Law Center, "Debunking Stereotypes About Muslims and Islam," Teaching Tolerance, www.tolerance.org/classroom-resources/tolerance-lessons/debunking-stereotypes -about-muslims-and-islam; Anti-Defamation League, "Myths and Facts About Muslim People and Islam," accessed April 2, 2019, www.adl.org/education/resources /tools-and-strategies/myths-and-facts-about-muslim-people-and-islam.

12. Reza Aslan, Foreword to Iftikhar, *Scapegoats*, vii; Erik Bleich, "Defining and Researching Islamophobia," *Review of Middle East Studies* 46, no. 2 (2012): 180–189; Council on American-Islamic Relations (CAIR) and UC Berkeley Center for Race & Gender (UCBCRG), "Same Hate New Target: Islamophobia and Its Impact in the United States, January 2009–December 2010," 6, www.cair.com/islamophobia_report _islamophobia_and_its_impact_in_the_united_states_same_hate_new_target; Love, *Islamophobia and Racism*, 2–34; Junaid Rana, "The Story of Islamophobia," *Souls* 9, no. 2 (2007), 148–161; #IslamophobiaIsRacismSyllabus, accessed March 31, 2019, https:// islamophobiaisracism.wordpress.com/.

13. Khaled Beydoun, "Between Muslim and White: The Legal Construction of Arab American Identity," *New York University Annual Survey of American Law* 69, no. 1 (2003): 29–76.

14. Louise Cainkar, *Homeland Insecurity: The Arab American and Muslim American Experience After 9/11* (New York: Russell Sage, 2011), 66, 67, 72; Iftikhar, *Scapegoats*, xv, xviii; Amaney, "Civil Liberties and the Otherization of Arab and Muslim Americans," in *Race and Arab Americans*, ed. Jamal and Naber, 116.

15. Mark Nuckols, "The New Dangers of Immigration: Are Muslim Immigrants Different?" Townhall, August 18, 2015, https://townhall.com/columnists/marknuckols /2015/08/18/the-new-dangers-of-immigration-are-muslim-immigrants-different -n2039757; Evan Taparata, "More American Than Apple Pie, Muslims Have Been Migrating to the United States for Centuries," PRI, April 4, 2016, www.pri.org/stories /2016-04-04/more-american-apple-pie-muslims-have-been-migrating-us-centuries; Vivek Bald, *Bengali Harlem and the Lost Histories of South Asian America* (Cambridge, MA: Harvard University Press, 2013).

16. Cainkar, *Homeland Insecurity*, 73.

17. CAIR and UCBCRG, "Confronting Fear: Islamophobia and Its Impact in the United States," 4.

18. *Ross v. McIntyre* (140 U.S. 453, 463 [1891]), cited in Beydoun, "Between Muslim and White," 8; Erika Lee and Judy Yung, *Angel Island: Immigrant Gateway to America* (New York: Oxford University Press, 2010), 158; Deirdre M. Moloney, "The Muslim Ban of 1910," UNC Press Blog, April 4, 2017, https://uncpressblog.com/2017/04/04 /deirdre-m-moloney-muslim-ban-1910/.

19. Immigration Act of 1917 (39 Stat. 874).

20. Executive Order 2932 (August 8, 1918); John Torpey, "The Great War and the Birth of the Modern Passport System," in Jane Caplan and John Torpey, eds., *Documenting Individual Identity: The Development of State Practices in the Modern World* (Princeton, NJ: Princeton University Press, 2001), 265; Stacy Fahrenthold, "What We Can Learn from America's Other Muslim Ban (Back in 1918),"

Tropics of Meta, February 8, 2017, https://tropicsofmeta.wordpress.com/2017/02/08 /what-we-can-learn-from-americas-other-muslim-ban-back-in-1918/.

21. Cainkar, *Homeland Insecurity*, 73–74, 77; Khaled Beydoun, "America Banned Muslims Long Before Donald Trump," Islamophobia Research and Documentation Project, August 20, 2016, https://irdproject.com/america-banned-muslims-long-before -donald-trump/; Sarah Gualtieri, "Strange Fruit? Syrian Immigrants, Extralegal Violence and Racial Formation in the Jim Crow South," *Arab Studies Quarterly* 26, no. 3 (Summer 2004): 63.

22. Cainkar, *Homeland Insecurity*, 89; Nadine Naber, "Introduction: Arab Americans and U.S. Racial Formation," in *Race and Arab Americans*, ed. Jamal and Naber, 37.

23. Amaney, "Civil Liberties and the Otherization of Arab and Muslim Americans," in *Race and Arab Americans*, ed. Jamal and Naber, 119–122; Steven Salaita, *Anti-Arab Racism in the USA: Where It Comes From and What It Means for Politics Today* (New York: Pluto Press, 2015), 12–13; Cainkar, *Homeland Insecurity*, 84–85, 88; Naber, "Introduction," 51.

24. Khaled Beydoun, "Islamophobia: New Name, Old Fear," BBC News, September 29, 2015, www.bbc.com/news/magazine-34385051.

25. Lydia O'Connor, "How 9/11 Changed These Muslim Americans' Lives Forever," Huffington Post, September 10, 2016, www.huffingtonpost.com/entry/post -911-islamophobia_us_57d075dfe4b0a48094a75bc1; Aliyah Frumin and Amanda Sakuma, "Hope and Despair: Being Muslim in America After 9/11," NBC News, September 11, 2016, www.nbcnews.com/storyline/9-11-anniversary/hope-despair -being-muslim-america-after-9-11-n645451.

26. Shawna Ayoub Ainslie, "20 Ways 9/11 Changed My Life as an (American) Muslim," Huffington Post, December 6, 2017, www.huffingtonpost.com/shawna -ayoub-ainslie/20-ways-911-changed-my-life_b_8111518.html.

27. Cainkar, *Homeland Insecurity*, 231–235, 241.

28. White House Press Secretary, "'Islam Is Peace' Says President: Remarks by the President at the Islamic Center of Washington, DC," George W. Bush White House Archives, September 17, 2001, https://georgewbush-whitehouse.archives.gov/news /releases/2001/09/20010917-11.html.

29. US Justice Department, "Attorney General Prepared Remarks on the National Security Entrance and Exit Registration System," June 6, 2002, www.justice.gov /archive/ag/speeches/2002/060502agpreparedremarks.htm.

30. Mark Krikorian, "Muslim Invasion? What Increased Muslim Immigration Could Mean for U.S. Israeli Policy—and American Jews," *National Review*, April 17, 2002, https://cis.org/Muslim-Invasion-What-increased-Muslim-immigration -could-mean-US-Israeli-policyand-American-Jews.

31. "Deeply flawed . . . " from Love, *Islamophobia and Racism*, 10–11; Cainkar, *Homeland Insecurity*, 231–232, 119; Bill Ong Hing, "Vigilante Racism: The De-Americanization of Immigrant America," *Michigan Journal of Race and Law* 7 (Spring 2002): 1–16; Tram Nguyen, *We Are All Suspects Now: Untold Stories from Immigrant Communities After 9/11* (Boston: Beacon Press, 2005).

32. Cainkar, *Homeland Insecurity*, 119, 232.

33. "The most aggressive . . . " from David Cole, *Enemy Aliens: Double Standards and Constitutional Freedoms in the War on Terrorism* (New York: New Press, 2003), 17; Cainkar, *Homeland Insecurity*, 112, 123; Love, *Islamophobia and Racism*, 11.

34. Cainkar, *Homeland Insecurity*, 123, 128, 139–141; Kevin Liptak and Shachar Peled, "Obama Administration Ends Program Once Used to Track Mostly Arab and Muslim Men," CNN, December 22, 2016, www.cnn.com/2016/12/22/politics /obama-nseers-arab-muslim-registry/index.html.

35. Cainkar, *Homeland Insecurity*, 127.

36. Matt Apuzzo and Adam Goldman, "The NYPD Division of Un-American Activities," NYMag.com*New York Magazine*, August 25, 2013, http://nymag.com/news /features/nypd-demographics-unit-2013-9/; American Civil Liberties Union, "Factsheet: The NYPD Muslim Surveillance Program," accessed April 1, 2019, www.aclu .org/other/factsheet-nypd-muslim-surveillance-program; Chris Boyette, "New York Police Department Disbands Unit That Spied on Muslims," CNN, April 16, 2014, www .cnn.com/2014/04/15/us/nypd-muslims-spying-ends/index.html; Colin Moynihan, "A New York City Settlement on Surveillance of Muslims," *New Yorker*, January 7, 2016, www.newyorker.com/news/news-desk/a-new-york-city-settlement-on-surveillance-of -muslims; Garrett Epps, "The NYPD Fails to Learn the Lessons of Past Bigotries," *The Atlantic*, October 20, 2015, www.theatlantic.com/politics/archive/2015/10 /muslims-have-a-discrimination-case-against-the-nypd/411370/; Corinne Segal, "NYPD Settles Two Lawsuits over Post-9/11 Surveillance of Muslims," *PBS NewsHour*, January 7, 2016, www.pbs.org/newshour/nation/nypd-lawsuits-surveillance-muslims -911.

37. Azmat Khan, "AP Documents Expansion of NYPD into "Domestic CIA," *Frontline*, August 24, 2011, www.pbs.org/wgbh/frontline/article/ap-documents -expansion-of-nypd-into-domestic-cia/; Iftikhar, *Scapegoats*, 86, 80.

38. Iftikhar, *Scapegoats*, 81–82, 85; Matt Apuzzo and Joseph Goldstein, "New York Drops Unit That Spied on Muslims," *New York Times*, April 15, 2014, www.nytimes .com/2014/04/16/nyregion/police-unit-that-spied-on-muslims-is-disbanded.html ?_r=0.

39. Cainkar, *Homeland Insecurity*, 3, 267.

40. Cainkar, *Homeland Insecurity*, 68–69; John L. Esposito, Foreword in Nathan Lean, *Islamophobia Industry: How the Right Manufactures Fear of Muslims* (New York: Pluto Press, 2012), xii.

41. CAIR and UCBCRG, "Confronting Fear," vii–viii; "History of Hate: Crimes Against Sikhs Since 9/11," Huffington Post, August 7, 2012, www.huffingtonpost .com/2012/08/07/history-of-hate-crimes-against-sikhs-since-911_n_1751841.html.

42. Iftikhar, *Scapegoats*, 6, 36–37.

43. Iftikhar, *Scapegoats*, 77; Lean, *Islamophobia Industry*, 8–9.

44. CAIR and UCBCRG, "Confronting Fear," 1–2; Robert G. Kaiser and Ira Chinoy, "Scaife: Funding Father of the Right," *Washington Post*, May 2, 1999, www .washingtonpost.com/wp-srv/politics/special/clinton/stories/scaifemain050299.htm; Cainkar, *Homeland Insecurity*, 271.

45. Lean, *Islamophobia Industry*, 10, 12, 13, 41–58; Bail, *Terrified*, 28–31, 35, 68, 75–78, 83–85; Iftikhar, *Scapegoats*, 40.

46. Daniel Pipes, "The Muslims Are Coming, the Muslims Are Coming," *National Review*, November 19, 1990.

47. Lean, *Islamophobia Industry*, 41, 55, 57; Pamela Geller, *Stop the Islamization of America: A Practical Guide to the Resistance* (Washington, DC: WND Books, 2011) [quotes are from the book jacket].

48. American Defamation League, "Stop Islamization of America," September 19, 2012, www.adl.org/news/article/stop-islamization-of-america-sioa; Lean, *Islamophobia Industry*, 57.

49. Lean, *Islamophobia Industry*, 69; Umer Mahmood, "Islamophobia in the Media," Islamophobia Research and Documentation Project, December 6, 2016, https://irdproject.com/islamophobia-in-the-media/; Hatem Bazian, "American Muslims and the Specter of Fear," November 24, 2016, Islamophobia Research and Documentation Project, https://irdproject.com/american-muslims-specter-fear/.

50. Jodi Wilgoren, "Struggling to Be Both Arab and American," *New York Times*, November 4, 2001; Matthew Purdy, "On Arab-America's Main Street, New Flags and Old Loyalties," *New York Times*, April 7, 2002; Daniel Wakin, "Even Muslims on the Move Stop at Prayer Time," *New York Times*, May 28, 2004, cited in Suad Joseph and Benjamin D'Harlingue, with Alvin Ka Hin Wong, "Arab Americans and Muslim Americans in the New York Times, Before and After 9/11," in *Race and Arab Americans*, ed. Jamal and Naber, 233–234, 244–246, 250–251.

51. Sarah Pulliam Bailey, "A Startling Number of Americans Still Believe President Obama Is a Muslim," *Washington Post*, September 14, 2015, www.washingtonpost.com/news/acts-of-faith/wp/2015/09/14/a-startling-number-of-americans-still-believe-president-obama-is-a-muslim/; Carol Anderson, *White Rage: The Unspoken Truth of Our Racial Divide* (New York: Bloomsbury Press, 2016), 156; Bail, *Terrified*, 97–99.

52. Arsalan Iftikhar, "Being a Muslim in Trump's America Is Frightening. Here's What We Can Do in Response," *Washington Post*, November 9, 2016, https://www.washingtonpost.com/posteverything/wp/2016/11/09/being-a-muslim-in-trumps-america-is-frightening-heres-how-we-can-survive/; Deepa Kumar, "Islamophobia: A Bipartisan Project," *The Nation*, July 2, 2012, www.thenation.com/article/islamophobia-bipartisan-project/; Matthew Rothschild, "Xenophobia Runs Rampant," *The Progressive*, August 19, 2010, https://progressive.org/op-eds/xenophobia-runs-rampant/.

53. Lena H. Sun, "Where Do You Park 10,000 Charter Buses?" *Washington Post*, September 15, 2015, www.washingtonpost.com/wp-dyn/content/article/2008/12/08/AR2008120803650.html; Michael E. Ruane and Aaron C. Davis, "D.C.'s Inauguration Head Count," *Washington Post*, January 22, 2009, www.washingtonpost.com/wp-dyn/content/article/2009/01/21/AR2009012103884_2.html?sid=ST2009012102519.

54. "Tea Party Supporters," CBS News, December 14, 2012, www.cbsnews.com/news/tea-party-supporters-who-they-are-and-what-they-believe/.

55. Michael Eric Dyson, *The Black Presidency: Barack Obama and the Politics of Race in America* (Boston: Houghton Mifflin, 2016), 5; "White rage" from Anderson, *White Rage*, 3, 5, 160.

56. Katherine Lemons and Joshua Takano Chambers-Letson, "Rule of Law: Sharia Panic and the U.S. Constitution in the House of Representatives," *Cultural Studies* 28, no. 5–6 (2014): 1051.

57. Lemons and Chambers-Letson, "Rule of Law," 1048–50, 1052, 1055; CAIR and UCBCRG, "Confronting Fear," vii–viii.

58. Anderson, *White Rage*, 169.

59. Khaled Beydoun, "Donald Trump: The Islamophobia President," Al Jazeera, November 9, 2016, www.aljazeera.com/indepth/opinion/2016/11/donald-trump-islamophobia-president-161109065355945.html.

60. Katayoun Kishi, "Anti-Muslim Assaults Reach 9/11-Era Levels, FBI Data Show," Pew Research Center, November 21, 2016, www.pewresearch.org/fact -tank/2016/11/21/anti-muslim-assaults-reach-911-era-levels-fbi-data-show/; US Department of Justice, Federal Bureau of Investigation, Criminal Justice Information Services Division, "2016 Hate Crime Statistics," accessed April 1, 2019, https://ucr .fbi.gov/hate-crime/2016/topic-pages/incidentsandoffenses; Katayoun Kishi, "Assaults Against Muslims in U.S. Surpass 2001 Level," Pew Research Center, November 15, 2017, www.pewresearch.org/fact-tank/2017/11/15/assaults-against-muslims-in-u-s -surpass-2001-level/; CAIR, "Civil Rights Data Quarter One Update: Anti-Muslim Bias Incidents January–March 2017," accessed April 1, 2019, www.islamophobia.org /images/pdf/Quarter-1-Data-Report-Final.pdf; CAIR, "Civil Rights Data Quarter Two Update: Anti-Muslim Bias Incidents April–June 2018," https://d3n8a8pro7vhmx .cloudfront.net/cairhq/pages/1125/attachments/original/1531335495/07.09.18_-_Q2 _Report_%281%29.pdf?1531335495; CAIR, "CAIR 3rd Quarter Civil Rights Report," October 17, 2017, www.cair.com/cair_3rd_quarter_civil_rights_report_shows_rise_in _hate_crimes_over_same_period_last_year_moderate_decline_in_total_cases; CAIR, "Anti-Muslim Bias Incidents and Hate Crimes, 2018," accessed April 1, 2019, www.cair .com/cair_report_anti_muslim_bias_incidents_hate_crimes_spike_in_second _quarter_of_2018.

61. Beydoun, "Donald Trump"; Iftikhar, "Being a Muslim in Trump's America Is Frightening."

62. Faiza Patel and Rachel Levinson-Waldman, "The Islamophobic Administration," April 19, 2017, www.brennancenter.org/publication/islamophobic -administration.

63. Adam Serwer, "Jeff Sessions's Unqualified Praise for a 1924 Immigration Law," *The Atlantic*, January 10, 2017, www.theatlantic.com/politics/archive/2017/01 /jeff-sessions-1924-immigration/512591/; Patel and Levionson-Waldman, "Islamophobic Administration"; Farid Hafez, "Trump's Politics Is Institutionalized Islamophobia at the Highest Level," Islamophobia Research and Documentation Project, March 27, 2017, https://irdproject.com/trumps-politics-institutionalized-islamophobia-highest -level; McKay Coppins, "Trump's Right-Hand Troll," *The Atlantic*, May 28, 2018, www.theatlantic.com/politics/archive/2018/05/stephen-miller-trump-adviser/561317/; David S. Glosser, "Stephen Miller Is an Immigration Hypocrite," Politico, August 13, 2018, www.politico.com/magazine/story/2018/08/13/stephen-miller-is-an -immigration-hypocrite-i-know-because-im-his-uncle-219351; Andrew Kragie, "Stephen Miller as MAGA's Angry Id," *The Atlantic*, December 17, 2018, www.theatlantic .com/politics/archive/2018/12/stephen-miller-appeared-scripted-and-angry-sunday /578293/.

64. Adam Liptak and Michael D. Shear, "Trump's Travel Ban Is Upheld by Supreme Court," *New York Times*, June 26, 2018; Alicia Parlapiano, "The Travel Ban Has Been Upheld," *New York Times*, June 27, 2018.

65. Charlie Savage, "Korematsu, Notorious Supreme Court Ruling on Japanese Internment, Is Finally Tossed Out," *New York Times*, June 26, 2018; Josh Gerstein, "Supreme Court Repudiates Infamous Korematsu Ruling," Politico, June 26, 2018, www .politico.com/story/2018/06/26/supreme-court-overturns-korematsu-673846; Jeff Guo, "Before People Start Invoking Japanese American Internment, They Should

Remember What It Was Like," *Washington Post*, November 18, 2016, www.washingtonpost .com/news/wonk/wp/2015/11/18/before-people-start-invoking-japanese-american -internment-they-should-remember-what-it-was-like/; War Relocation Authority, "Background for the Relocation Program," Topaz Internment Camp Documents, 1942– 1943, MSS COLL 170, Special Collections and Archives, Utah State University, http:// digital.lib.usu.edu/cdm/ref/collection/Topaz/id/5297.

66. Savage, "Korematsu"; US Supreme Court, "*Trump v. Hawaii*," 38, October 2017, www.supremecourt.gov/opinions/17pdf/17-965_h315.pdf.

67. US Supreme Court, "*Trump v. Hawaii*," 27.

68. Karen Korematsu, "How the Supreme Court Replaced One Injustice with Another," *New York Times*, June 27, 2018, www.nytimes.com/2018/06/27/opinion /supreme-court-travel-ban-korematsu-japanese-internment.html; Abigail Simon, "The Supreme Court Finally Said Her Father Was Right About Japanese Internment," *Time*, June 28, 2018, http://time.com/5324434/supreme-court-travel-ban-karen-korematsu/.

Conclusion

1. US Citizenship and Immigration Services, "Mission Statement," accessed April 1, 2019, www.uscis.gov/aboutus; Richard Gonzales, "America No Longer a 'Nation of Immigrants,'" NPR, February 22, 2018, www.npr.org/sections/thetwo -way/2018/02/22/588097749/america-no-longer-a-nation-of-immigrants-uscis-says.

2. "Fact Check: Trump's State of the Union Address," NPR, January 30, 2018, www.npr.org/2018/01/30/580378279/trumps-state-of-the-union-address-annotated.

3. Josh Dawsey, "Trump Derides Protections for Immigrants from 'Shithole' Countries," *Washington Post*, January 12, 2018, www.washingtonpost.com/politics /trump-attacks-protections-for-immigrants-from-shithole-countries-in-oval-office -meeting/2018/01/11/bfc0725c-f711-11e7-91af-31ac729add94_story.html; "Fact Check," NPR.

4. "Fact Check," NPR.

5. Sarah Pierce, Jessica Bolter, and Andrew Selee, "U.S. Immigration Policy Un- der Trump: Deep Changes and Lasting Impacts," Migration Policy Institute (July 2018), www.migrationpolicy.org/research/us-immigration-policy-trump-deep-changes -impacts; "Stopgap Bill to End Government Shutdown Passes Congress," *New York Times*, January 22, 2019; Linda Qiu, "Rationale for a Wall on Flimsy Foundations," *New York Times*, February 16, 2019; Colby Itkowitz and John Wagner, "Trump Says White Nationalism Is Not a Rising Threat After New Zealand Attacks: 'It's a Small Group of People,'" *Washington Post*, March 15, 2019, www.washingtonpost.com/politics/trump -offers-us-assistance-after-horrible-massacre-in-new-zealand/2019/03/15/931833d2 -4712-11e9-aaf8-4512a6fe3439_story.html; Dara Lind, "Trump's Threats to Close the US-Mexico Border, Explained," Vox, March 29, 2019, www.vox .com/2019/3/29/18287101/trump-close-border-us-mexico-tweets; Katherine Faulders and John Santucci, "Trump Ordered Part of Border Closed, His Administration Pushed Back: Sources," ABC News, April 8, 2019, https://abcnews.go.com/Politics/trump -ordered-part-border-closed-administration-pushed-back/story?id=62260303; Neil Ir- win and Emily Badger, "Trump Says the U.S. Is 'Full.' Much of the Nation Has the Opposite Problem," *New York Times*, April 9, 2019.

6. Bonnie Honig, *Democracy and the Foreigner* (Princeton, NJ: Princeton University Press, 2003), 76; Ibram X. Kendi, "Racial Progress Is Real. But So Is Racist Progress," *New York Times*, January 21, 2017; Gary Gerstle, *American Crucible: Race and Nation in the Twentieth Century* (Princeton, NJ: Princeton University Press, 2018), xiv.

7. Honig, *Democracy and the Foreigner*, 76; Alfonso Gonzales, *Reform Without Justice: Latino Migrant Politics and the Homeland Security State* (Oxford, UK: Oxford University Press, 2014), 6–7.

8. H.R. 946, Mass Immigration Reduction Act of 2003, www.congress.gov /bill/108th-congress/house-bill/946/text; Marc Santora, "Tancredo Takes a Tough Stance," *New York Times*, August 6, 2007, https://thecaucus.blogs.nytimes .com/2007/08/06/tancredo/?_r=0; Amanda Terkel, "Tancredo to Boycott Tomorrow's Univision Debate," ThinkProgress, December 8, 2007, https://thinkprogress.org /tancredo-to-boycott-tomorrows-univision-debate-d27d1b19bbb9/; Josh Israel, "The Eight Most Xenophobic Stances of Tom Tancredo," ThinkProgress, May 23, 2013, https://thinkprogress.org/the-eight-most-xenophobic-stances-of-tom-tancredo -candidate-for-colorado-governor-ed40c109a6c4/.

9. Tom Tancredo, *In Mortal Danger: The Battle for America's Border and Security* (Nashville: WND Books, 2006), 15, 22, 23, 203; Dino Cinel, *The National Integration of Italian Return Migration, 1870–1939* (New York: Cambridge University Press, 1991), 2; Donna Gabaccia and Fraser M. Ottanelli, *Italian Workers of the World: Labor Migration and the Formation of Multiethnic States* (Urbana: University of Illinois Press, 2005), n3, 15; Peter Schrag, *Not Fit for Our Society: Nativism and Immigration* (Berkeley: University of California Press, 2010), 3, 212, 226.

10. "Olvera Street," Discover Los Angeles, accessed April 1, 2019, www.discover losangeles.com/what-to-do/activities/olvera-street.

11. Francisco E. Balderrama and Raymond Rodríguez, *Decade of Betrayal: Mexican Repatriation in the 1930s* (Albuquerque: University of New Mexico Press, 2006), 299–342.

12. Korematsu, "How the Supreme Court."

13. Charles Frisbie Hoar, speech on the floor of the US Senate, February 28, 1882, reprinted in C. M. Whitman, *American Orators and Oratory* (Chicago: Fairbanks, Palmer, 1884), 988–989.

14. Doris Kearns Goodwin, *The Fitzgeralds and the Kennedys: An American Saga* (New York: Simon and Schuster, 2001), 102.

15. Israel Zangwill, *The Melting Pot* (New York: Macmillan, 1921); Mary Antin, *The Promised Land* (New York: Houghton Mifflin, 1912); Carlos Bulosan, *America Is in the Heart* (Seattle: University of Washington Press, 1946); Alice M. Brown to James D. Phelan, May 20, 1913, Folder 5, Box 120, Phelan Papers.

16. Rachel Buff, *Against the Deportation Terror: Organizing for Immigrant Rights in the Twentieth Century* (Philadelphia: Temple University Press, 2018); Jimmy Patiño, *Raza Si, Migra No: Chicano Movement Struggles for Immigrant Rights in San Diego* (Chapel Hill: University of North Carolina Press, 2017), 28–29, 150–200.

17. Alfonso Gonzales, "The 2006 *Mega Marchas* in Greater Los Angeles: Counter-Hegemonic Movement and the Future of *El Migrante* Struggle," *Latino Studies* 7, no. 1 (2009), 47; Schrag, *Not Fit for Our Society*, 175–177; A. Naomi Paik, "Abolitionist Futures and the U.S. Sanctuary Movement," *Race and Class* 59, no. 2 (2017): 3–25.

18. Korematsu Institute for Civil Rights and Education, "Fred T. Korematsu," www
.korematsuinstitute.org/fred-t-korematsu-lifetime; Nat Hentoff, "Fred Korematsu v.
George W. Bush," *Village Voice*, February 17, 2004, www.villagevoice.com/2004-02-17
/news/fred-korematsu-v-george-w-bush/.

19. Adrienne Mahsa Varkiani, "Here's Your List of All the Protests Happening
Against the Muslim Ban," ThinkProgress, January 28, 2017, https://thinkprogress.org
/muslim-ban-protests-344f6e66022e/; Mike Lindblom, "Light-Rail Trains Loaded
with Protesters," *Seattle Times*, January 30, 2017, www.seattletimes.com/seattle-news
/transportation/light-rail-trains-loaded-with-protesters-skipped-sea-tac-briefly-on
-saturday-but-why.

20. Adam Chandler, "Cars, Shoes, Tech: An Array of Corporations Protest the Immigration Ban," *The Atlantic*, January 31, 2017, www.theatlantic.com/business/archive
/2017/01/corporations-protest-immigration-ban/515076/; "Message from Howard
Schultz to Starbucks Partners: Living Our Values in Uncertain Times," January 29, 2017,
https://news.starbucks.com/news/living-our-values-in-uncertain-times; "Google Employees Stage Worldwide Walkout over Trump Edict," *USA Today*, January 30, 2018,
www.usatoday.com/story/tech/talkingtech/2017/01/30/googlers-stage-worldwide-walk
out-trump-immigration-ban-rally-mountain-view-serge-brin-sundar-pichai/97265938/.

21. Pierce, Bolter, and Selee, "U.S. Immigration Policy," 3; Maria Sacchetti, "ICE
Raids Meatpacking Plant in Rural Tennessee," *Washington Post*, April 6, 2018, www
.washingtonpost.com/local/immigration/ice-raids-meatpacking-plant-in-rural-tennes
see-more-than-95-immigrants-arrested/2018/04/06/4955a79a-39a6-11e8-8fd2
-49fe3c675a89_story.html.

22. Muzaffar Chishti and Jessica Bolter, "Family Separation and 'Zero Tolerance' Policies Rolled Out to Stem Unwanted Migrants," Migration Policy Institute, May 24, 2018, www.migrationpolicy.org/article/family-separation-and-zero
-tolerance-policies-rolled-out-stem-unwanted-migrants-may-face; Dara Lind, "The
Migrant Caravan, Explained," Vox, October 25, 2018, www.vox.com/2018/10/24
/18010340/caravan-trump-border-honduras-mexico; Scott Pelley, "The Chaos Behind
Trump's Policy of Family Separation at the Border," CBS News, November 26, 2018,
www.cbsnews.com/news/trump-family-separation-policy-mexican-border-60-minutes
-investigation-greater-in-number-than-trump-administration-admits/; Shannon Dool-
ing, "What Is Asylum? Who Is Eligible? Why Do Recent Changes Matter?" WBUR,
December 3, 2018, www.wbur.org/news/2018/12/03/asylum-explainer.

23. Pierce, Bolter, and Selee, "U.S. Immigration Policy," 3; Dara Lind, "Trump
Slashed Refugee Levels This Year. For 2019, He's Slashing Them Even Further,"
Vox, September 18, 2018, www.vox.com/2018/9/17/17871874/refugee-news-record
-history-asylum; Tracy Jan, "The Wall Does Not Exist Yet, But Trump Has Already Erected New Barriers for Foreign Workers," *Washington Post*, March 21, 2018,
www.washingtonpost.com/news/wonk/wp/2018/03/21/the-wall-does-not-exist-yet
-but-trump-has-already-erected-new-barriers-for-foreign-workers/; John Wagner,
Josh Dawsey, and Felicia Sonmez, "Trump Eyeing Executive Order to End Birthright Citizenship, A Move Most Legal Experts Say Would Run Afoul of the Constitution," *Washington Post*, October 30, 2018, www.washingtonpost.com/politics/trump
-eyeing-executive-order-to-end-citizenship-for-children-of-noncitizens-born-on-us
-soil/2018/10/30/66892050-dc29-11e8-b3f0-62607289efee_story.html.

24. "'Public Charge' Changes Could Mean Fewer Children Receiving Medicaid and CHIP," KUT (Austin, TX), December 4, 2018, www.kut.org/post/public-charge-changes-could-mean-fewer-children-receiving-medicaid-and-chip-study-says; Randy Capps, Mark Greenberg, Michael Fix, and Jie Zong, "Gauging the Impact of DHS' Proposed Public-Charge Rule on U.S. Immigration," Migration Policy Institute, November 2018, www.migrationpolicy.org/research/impact-dhs-public-charge-rule-immigration.

25. Randy Capps, Muzaffar Chishti, Julia Gelatt, Jessica Bolter, and Ariel G. Ruiz, "Revving up the Deportation Machinery: Enforcement and Pushback Under Trump," Migration Policy Institute, May 2018, 3–4, www.migrationpolicy.org/sites/default/files/publications/ImmigrationEnforcement_ReportinBrief_FINAL.pdf; "How States Took Action on Immigration in 2018," American Immigration Impact, American Immigration Council, November 27, 2018, http://immigrationimpact.com/2018/11/27/states-immigration-in-2018/; Liora Danan, Elizabeth Venditto, Robbie Wilson, and Georgette Mulheir, "On the Frontlines of the Family Separation Crisis: City Response and Best Practices for Assisting Families," Cities for Action, September 24, 2018, https://d3n8a8pro7vhmx.cloudfront.net/citiesforaction/pages/29/attachments/original/1537804683/Family_Separation_Crisis_Report_WEB-SINGLES_21SEP18.pdf?1537804683; Peter L. Markowitz, "Trump Can't Stop the Sanctuary Movement," *New York Times*, March 9, 2018; Vann R. Newkirk II, "Family Separation Protests Shift the Narrative," *The Atlantic*, June 30, 2018, www.theatlantic.com/politics/archive/2018/06/a-rally-for-families-by-families/564239/; "Thousands Across U.S. Join 'Keep Families Together' March," NBC News, June 30, 2018, www.nbcnews.com/news/us-news/thousands-across-u-s-join-keep-families-together-march-protest-n888006; Dara Lind, "The Trump Administration's Separation of Families at the Border, Explained," Vox, June 15, 2018, www.vox.com/2018/6/11/17443198/children-immigrant-families-separated-parents; Maria Sachetti, "Still Separated," *Washington Post*, August 31, 2018, www.washingtonpost.com/local/immigration/still-separated-nearly-500-separated-migrant-children-remain-in-us-custody/2018/08/30/6dbd8278-aa09-11e8-8a0c-70b618c98d3c_story.html; Dara Lind, "'Abolish ICE,' Explained," Vox, June 28, 2018, www.vox.com/policy-and-politics/2018/3/19/17116980/ice-abolish-immigration-arrest-deport; Sean McElwee, "It's Time to Abolish ICE," *The Nation*, March 9, 2018, www.thenation.com/article/its-time-to-abolish-ice/; Office of Governor Gavin Newsom, "Governor Newsom Delivers State of State Address," February 12, 2019, CA.gov, www.gov.ca.gov/2019/02/12/state-of-the-state-address/; Charlie Savage and Robert Pear, "States' Lawsuit Aims to Thwart Emergency Bid," *New York Times*, February 19, 2019.

26. Naaz Modan, "CAIR Action Alert Demanding That Congress Repeal Trump's Muslim Ban," September 5, 2018, www.cair.com/action_alert_sign_petition_demanding_that_congress_repeal_trump_s_muslim_ban; "Love Knows No Borders," American Friends Service Committee, December 2018, https://migrantjustice.afsc.org; Carol Kuruvilla, "Quakers, Rabbis, Imams Protest for Migrant Rights," Huffington Post, December 12, 2018, www.huffingtonpost.com/entry/interfaith-border-protest-migrants_us_5c112943e4b0ac53717af2ce; Ibrahim Hirsi, "Immigrants Have a Long History of Taking Their Issues to the People—as Political Candidates," PRI, November 1, 2018, www.pri.org/stories

/2018-11-01/immigrants-have-long-history-taking-their-issues-people-political
-candidates; "After an Ugly Campaign for Immigrants, Some Midterm Wins Spark
a Glimmer of Hope," PRI, November 7, 2018, www.pri.org/stories/2018-11-07
/after-ugly-campaign-immigrants-some-midterm-wins-spark-glimmer-hope.

27. Gerstle, *American Crucible*, 117–122, 127; Danielle Battisti, *Whom We Shall
Welcome: Italian Americans and Immigration Reform, 1945–1965* (New York: Fordham
University Press, 2019), 82.

28. Gonzales, *Reform Without Justice.*

29. Anna Brown, "Americans Less Concerned Than a Decade Ago over Immigrants' Impact on Work Force," October 7, 2016, Pew Research Center FactTank, www
.pewresearch.org/fact-tank/2016/10/07/americans-less-concerned-than-a-decade
-ago-over-immigrants-impact-on-workforce/; Alec Tyson, "Public Backs Legal Status
for Immigrants Brought to U.S. Illegally as Children, But Not a Bigger Border Wall,"
January 19, 2018, www.pewresearch.org/fact-tank/2018/01/19/public-backs-legal
-status-for-immigrants-brought-to-u-s-illegally-as-children-but-not-a-bigger-border
-wall/; "Shifting Public Views on Legal Immigration into the U.S.," Pew Research
Center, June 28, 2018, www.people-press.org/2018/06/28/shifting-public-views-on
-legal-immigration-into-the-u-s/; Matt Barreto, "Even for Trump, There Is Such a
Thing as Too Far," *New York Times*, October 24, 2018.

30. On the impact of the 1996 policy, see American Immigration Council, "A
Primer on Expedited Removal," February 3, 2017, www.americanimmigrationcouncil
.org/research/primer-expedited-removal.

31. Hing, "Vigilante Racism," 443–444; Tanya Golash-Boza, *Immigration Nation:
Raids, Detentions, and Deportations in Post-9/11 America* (New York: Routledge, 2012),
5–6, 9, 47, 111–112; Daniel Kanstroom, *Aftermath: Deportation Law and the New American Diaspora* (New York: Oxford University Press, 2012).

32. Connor Sheets, "Alabama's 2011 Anti-Immigrant Law H.B. 56 Still on Books,"
Alabama Media Group, March 24, 2017, www.al.com/news/birmingham/index
.ssf/2017/03/hb_56_alabamas_2011_anti-immig.html.

INDEX

Absconders Initiative, 303–304
African Americans
  citizenship status of, 72–73
  criticism of immigration reform
    and race problems with, 235,
    236–237
  immigrants compared to, 8, 57–58,
    81, 125, 156
  and interracial mixing, 130
  Muslim, 296
  and national origin quotas,
    142–143
  Republican Party appeals to white
    racial fears of, 277–278,
    310–312
  segregation of, 122, 130, 143
African immigrants, quotas for, 142–143,
  236
agricultural labor
  Chinese immigrants supplying,
    89
  Japanese immigrants supplying,
    186–187
  Mexican immigrants supplying,
    150–151, 153, 154, 155, 286
  undocumented immigrants supplying,
    251, 260
Ainslie, Shawna Ayoub, 300

Alabama, xenophobic legislation in, 337
alcohol abuse, immigrants blamed for, 39,
  54, 55
Aldrich, Thomas Bailey, 120
Alien Land Law (1913), 193
Alien Nation: Common Sense About
    America's Immigration Disaster
    (Brimelow), 274
Alien Registration Act (1940), 201
"America for Americans" article (Grant,
    1925), 6
"America for Americans" pamphlet
    (KKK), 6
"America for Americans" speech
    (Roosevelt, 1916), 6
American Civil Liberties Union (ACLU),
    211, 217, 304–305, 329, 331
American Coalition of Patriotic Societies
    (ACPS), 144, 234, 239
American Committee for the Protection of
    Foreign Born, 329
American Committee on Italian
    Migration (ACIM), 229, *230*
American Eugenics Society, 158
American Federation of Labor (AFL), 81,
    122, 241
American Legion, 144, 157, 234, 243
American Legion Magazine, 243

American Party (Order of the Star-
  Spangled Banner; Know
  Nothing Party)
  anti-Catholicism of, 53–54, 55, 67
  anti-party sentiment/distrust of
    professional politicians, 51,
    61–62
  anti-pauperism of, 59–60
  attacks on voters by, 39–41
  blamed immigrants for crime, 54
  blamed immigrants for economic
    conditions, 54–55
  decline of, 71–72
  East Boston chapter of, 52–53, 65–66
  establishment of, 52–53
  ideology of, 53–63
  nativism of, 43–44, 62–63, 65–67
  political victories of, 67–71
  promoted racial stereotypes of Irish,
    56–58
  and slavery, 60–61, 69, 71
  and women's rights, 69
American Protestant Society, 52
American Republican Party, 51
anarchists, 115, 137, 139–140
Angel Island Immigration Station,
  107–108, 109–110
Anti-Asian Association, 197
anti-Catholicism, 8
  and anti-immigrant organizations,
    50–52
  Catholic immigrants as threat to
    democracy, 48–49, 50, 53–54, 55
  Catholicism as conspiracy to take over
    US, 42, 47, 48, 49–50, 54, 55
  in colonial America, 18, 28, 47
  dehumanization of Irish Catholics,
    57–58
  and economic pressure, 54–55
  and fear of displacement, 119
  Irish Catholics as unable to assimilate,
    56–57
  and Know Nothings, 52–53, 53–54,
    55, 69–70
  in media, 49
  and poverty, 59–60

and Protestant Crusade, 42, 46–47
and slavery debate, 60
stereotypes of Irish Catholics, 56,
  57–58
and violence, 39–41, 49
Anti-Chinese Congress, 101
Anti-Chinese Union, 85–86, 89, 90
anti-Chinese xenophobia, 75–111
  anti-Chinese legislation, 83–84
  arguments against Chinese
    immigrants, 75–76, 77, 88, 89,
    92, 191
  in Canada, 94–95
  Congressional Committee
    to Investigate Chinese
    Immigration, 86, 87–89
  dehumanization of Chinese
    immigrants, 82–83, 90
  and economic pressure, 326
  exclusion efforts, 86–99, 138–139
  expulsion efforts, 99–106, 326
  extended to other Asian immigrants,
    111, 138, 191
  and gender/sexuality, 76
  in media, 82–83
  in Mexico, 95–96
  and nativism, 78
  other groups compared to Chinese
    immigrants, 58, 125–126
  Phelan's, 191
  political tactics of, 78
  as profitable, 82
  and race, 76, 78–79, 81, 111
  racial stereotypes of Chinese
    immigrants, 82–83
  rise in to become national issue,
    85–86
  San Francisco meeting on, 75–77
  Sargent's, 89–92
  and violence, 99, 100–101, 102–103,
    326
anti-German xenophobia, 17–37
  Germans as about to outnumber the
    English, 18, 24–25
  Germans as racially different from the
    English, 18

and Native Americans, 25–26, 30–32

public opposition to German immigrants, 24–26

regulation of German immigrants, 26–28

as threat to peace and security, 18

as unable to assimilate, 17, 25

and violence, 39–41, 121

during WWI, 37, 135–136

anti-Japanese xenophobia, 183–219

  anti-Japanese organizations, 195

  compared to anti-Chinese xenophobia, 191

  and economic pressure, 197

  exclusion efforts, 192, 196

  and government surveillance, 201, 205–206

  Japanese as invasion, 191, 192, 194, 198, 202–203

  Japanese as unassimilable, 184, 207

  "Keep California White" campaign, 189–190

  in Peru, 184, 186, 188, 196–199, 206–210

  rebuke of, 329

  and violence, 193, 199

anti-Mexican xenophobia, 146, 147–181

  and conservative movement against immigration, 273–275

  deportation campaign, 10, 161–162, 166–172

  draws on other racisms, 156–157

  and economic pressure, 146, 156, 163, 287

  Mexicans as invasion, 158–159, 253, 258, 269–270, 275

  Mexicans as unassimilable, 157, 274, 275

  and nativism, 163, 164–165, 254

  politicians' arguments, 155–159

  repatriation campaign, 172–180, 327

  and Trump, 284–285

  and undocumented immigration, 258–259, 265, 268, 269

and US territorial expansion, 149, 276–277

anti-Semitism, 8, 18, 117, 132–133, 144–145

Antiterrorism and Effective Death Penalty Act (AEDPA) (1996), 279, 299

Arab Americans

  long immigration history of, 296

  in media, 310

  race of, 298

  racial profiling of, 302–303, 305–306

  See also Islamophobia; Muslim Americans

Arizona, 164–165, 180, 193, 284

Arpaio, Joseph, 283

Ashcroft, John, 301–302

Asian immigrants

  exclusion of, 78–79, 85, 117, 138, 142, 196, 297

  increase in, 245, 246, 252

  as model minorities, 257

  numbers of, 241, 252

  quotas for, 226

  See also anti-Chinese xenophobia; Chinese immigrants; Japanese immigrants

Asiatic Barred Zone, 117, 138, 297

assimilation

  of Arabs/Muslims, 294, 308

  of Chinese immigrants, 76, 88, 191

  of German immigrants, 17, 25, 33, 136

  of Irish Catholics, 56–57

  of Japanese immigrants, 184, 207

  of Mexicans, 157, 274, 275

asylum seekers, 256, 323, 330, 332, 334

Austria, immigration from, 246

Awful Disclosures of Maria Monk, The (book), 49

Beecher, Lyman, 46, 49–50

benefits, public

  opposition to immigrants receiving, 332

  opposition to Mexican immigrants receiving, 163, 174–176

benefits, public *(continued)*
  opposition to undocumented
    immigrants receiving, 254, 262,
    264, 269, 279
bilingualism, 286
birthright citizenship
  Chinese immigrants claiming, 108
  and deportation, 337
  and Mexican immigrants, 269–270
  and repatriation of Mexican
    Americans, 176–177, 179
  and Trump presidency, 332
Bloody Monday (August 6, 1855),
    39–41
Bogardus, Emory, 161
border. *See* US Border Patrol; US-Mexico
    border
Boston, Massachusetts, 45–46, 52–53, 61,
    64, 68, 118
Box, John C., 156–157, 159
Boxer, Barbara, 268
bracero program, 226, 235, 248, 251
Brazil, 198
Brimelow, Peter, 273, 274
Brin, Sergey, 331
Bryan, Samuel, 155
Bryant, Andrew Jackson, 75, 86
Buchanan, Patrick, 14, 260–261, 273, 275
Bureau of Immigration, 96, 166–167, 170,
    171, 297
Burlingame Treaty (1868), 77, 85
Burns, Anthony, 61
Bush, George W., 280, 282, 301
Byrd, Robert, 236

California
  alien land laws in, 193
  anti-Chinese movement in, 75–77,
    83–84
  deportation of Mexicans in, 168–172
  historical markers in, 326–327
  Japanese immigrants in, 187
  "Keep California White" campaign,
    189–190
  Mexican Americans in, 150
  Mexican immigrant labor in, 153

repatriation of Mexicans in, 175–180,
    327
  sanctuary movement in, 333
  See also Proposition 187; San
    Francisco, California
California Coalition for Immigration
    Reform (CCIR), 262–263
California Development Association, 152
California Federation of Labor, 195
California Joint Immigration Commission,
    195
Californians United Against 187, 271
California Workingmen's Party, 81
Canada, 15, 16, 94–95, 204–205, 246
Canada–United States Permanent Joint
    Board of Defense, 204–205
capitalism, 13–14, 54–55, 121, 257. *See
    also* economic pressure; labor/
    workers; socialism
Carter, Jimmy, 256
Catholicism. *See* anti-Catholicism; Irish
    Catholics
Celler, Emanuel, 141, 143
  on hemispheric restrictions, 239–240,
    240–241
  on opposition to 1924 Immigration
    Act, 141
  and immigration reform, 228
  and passage of Immigration Act of
    1965, 221, 222, *223*
Central Intelligence Agency (CIA), 304
Chapman, Leonard, 255
Chelf, Frank, 237
Cherokees, 48
Chicago Tribune, 60
China
  immigration from, 80, 246, 249
  labor recruiters in, 79–80
  treaties with, 85, 96
  as unthreatening to US, 191
Chinese Exclusion Act (1882-1943), 4, 10,
    79, 226
  effects around the world, 94–96
  effects in US, 92–93, 96–99
  length of, 110
  protests of, 106, 328

Chinese Exclusion Convention, 191

Chinese exclusion efforts, 86–99, 138–139

Chinese expulsion efforts, 99–106

Chinese immigrants
    citizenship status of, 226
    and Communist Revolution, 226
    mistreated as workers, 80
    numbers of, 81, 106
    race of, 76, 81
    reasons for leaving China, 79–80
    recruitment of, 79–80, 85
    surveillance/registration of, 96–97, *98*
    women, 9, 84, 85
    See also anti-Chinese xenophobia;
        Chinese Exclusion Act
        (1882-1943)

Christian Arabs, 296, 298

Christianity, and Islamophobia, 295, 296, 308

Cissna, L. Francis, 321

Citizens for Action Now (CAN), 262

citizenship status
    for children, 269–270, 337
    of Chinese immigrants, 226
    in colonial America, 14–15, 35, 36
    denied to Asian immigrants, 189, 195, 196
    of Irish immigrants, 59
    of Mexican Americans, 148, 149–150, 176–177, 179
    and xenophobic campaigns, 10–11
    See also birthright citizenship;
        naturalization

civil rights, 5, 13, 221–225, 232, 244. *See also* immigration reform

Civil Rights Act (1964), 232

Clark, Victor S., 152

Clash of Civilizations and the Remaking of World Order, The (Huntington), 276

class, 93, 121. *See also* economic pressure; poverty

Clements, George P., 150, 151, 152, 176, 178–179

Cleveland, Grover, 127

Clinton, Bill, 278–279, 281

Coe, Barbara, 261–262, 263, 269, *272*

Collins, Wayne M., 217

colonial America
    anti-Catholicism in, 18, 28, 47
    anti-German arguments in, 17–18
    diversity of immigrants to, 20
    movements of people in, 19
    recruitment of European immigrants to, 20–22
    See also Pennsylvania, colonial

colonial expansion, 19
    and anti-Mexican xenophobia, 149–150, 155, 276–277
    and recruitment of immigrants to American colonies, 21–22, 29–30, 42
    US overseas territories, 122
    See also settler colonialism

Colorado, alien land laws in, 193

color blindness
    and hemispheric caps, 237–238

color-blind xenophobia, 13
    and illegal immigration, 250
    and Immigration Act of 1965, 225, 247
    and model minority discourse, 257–258
    and Proposition 187, 265

Commissioners of Alien Passengers and Paupers (Massachusetts), 70

Commission on Immigration and Naturalization, 228

Committee on Public Information, 135–136

communists, 139–140, 226, 229, 236

Connecticut, anti-Catholicism in, 47

conservatives
    backlash to Obama, 311–313
    call for hemispheric caps, 236–237
    Islamophobia promoted by, 307–308
    movement against undocumented immigrants, 261–263, 273–278

Coolidge, Calvin, 143

Coolie Trade Act (1862), 84–85

Cork Examiner, 45

Corrections Corporation of America
(CCA), 14
Council on American-Islamic Relations
(CAIR), 306, 307, 314, 334
Crawford, Remsen, 158
crime
Chinese immigrants blamed for, 75
immigrants less likely to commit, 2,
286
Italians stereotyped as criminals, 124,
125
Know Nothings blamed immigrants
for, 39, 54
Mexicans blamed for, 159, 286
undocumented entry linked to, 167,
168, 262, 268–269
Criminal Alien Program, 280
crimmigration (merging of criminal and
immigration law), 279–280
Crusades, 295
Crystal City detention camp, 213–214
Cuba, 145, 246, 256
Current History (Crawford), 158

Darweesh, Hameed Khalid, 289,
291–292
de-Americanization, 336–337
of Japanese Americans, 184
of Mexican Americans, 179, 180–181
of Muslim Americans, 295, 302,
305–306
Dearborn Independent, 133
Declaration of Lima (1938), 205
Deferred Action for Childhood Arrivals
(DACA), 284, 331
democracy
Catholic immigrants as threat to,
48–49, 50, 53–54, 55
and immigration reform, 231
southern/eastern Europeans as threat
to, 115
xenophobia's impact on, 14–15,
335–337
Democratic Party, 71
Department of Homeland Security
(DHS), 280, 283

deportation
and anti-Chinese xenophobia, 98–99
and anti-Mexican xenophobia,
166–172, 293
of citizen children, 337
expedited, 336
increases in, 279–280, 280–281, 283
and Islamophobia, 302, 303–304
of Japanese Latin Americans, 185,
206–210, 215–216
and Know Nothing party, 69–70
legislation affirming, 161
of Mexicans, 147–149, 161–162
opposition to, 329, 330
and political radicalism, 139–140
and race, 162, 281
detention
of Chinese immigrants, 107, 109–110
increases in, 280, 282, 283
and Islamophobia, 302
of Japanese Americans, 200–201,
210–213, 215, 317–318
of Japanese Peruvians, 213–215
profitability of, 13–14
DeWitt, John, 202, 203
Díaz, Porfirio, 153–154
Dillingham, William P., 134
Dillingham Commission (1911), 134–135,
152
Displaced Persons Act (1948), 226
Doak, William N., 166, 167–168
Douglass, Frederick, 61
Dreamers (immigrants who entered
undocumented as children), 284,
288
drugs, 259, 261, 269, 284, 285
Duncan, Robert D., 240

eastern Europeans
decrease in immigration of, 145
inclusion of in white American
identity, 244–245
increase in immigration of, 117–118
as invasion, 115, 120, 131–132
and literacy test, 123
and national origin quotas, 140

as racially different, 114–115, 130
and Red Scare, 139–140
restrictions on/quotas for, 142
economic pressure
and anti-Catholicism, 54–55
and anti-Chinese xenophobia, 326
and anti-Japanese xenophobia, 197
and anti-Mexican xenophobia, 146,
156, 163, 287
and Islamophobia, 306
Ecuador, Japanese residents of, 206
Egypt, immigration from, 296
Eisenhower, Dwight, 37, 228
El Comercio (Lima), 198
Ellis Island, 1, 2–3, 110, 123–124, 245
El Salvador, 246, 292, 322
Emergency Quota Act (1921), 140
Emmerson, John K., 207
Emmons, Delos, 203
employment
and deportation campaign, 167–168,
169
restricted to citizens, 164–165
See also labor/workers
enforcement. *See* immigration
enforcement
environmental protections, impact of
Trump's wall on, 285–286
equality, and one-size-fits-all policy, 247,
249
Ervin, Sam Jr., 236, 237, 239, 241–242
Ethiopia, national origin quota of, 236
eugenics, 9, 114, 115, 131–132, 137,
174, 196, 197. *See also* Grant,
Madison
European immigrants. *See* eastern
Europeans; German
immigrants; Irish Catholics;
Italian immigrants; southern
Europeans; whiteness
Examiner, 170
Executive Order 589 (1907), 192
Executive Order 9066 (1942), 183, 203,
211
Executive Order 13767 (2017), 287
Executive Order 13768 (2017), 287–288

Executive Order 13769 (2017) (Muslim
travel ban), 288, 290, 291,
316–319
protests of, *330*–331, 333–334
Ezell, Harold, 263, 265

family reunification
in Feighan's immigration bill, 233
in Immigration Act of 1965, 224,
242–243, 246, 248, 252
immigration of Arabs through, 296
and increase in immigration, 245
through War Brides Acts, 226
and white supremacy, 241
Federal Bureau of Investigation (FBI),
199–200, 201, 205, 208, 302, 306
Federation for American Immigration
Reform (FAIR), 256, 277
Feighan, Michael A., 222–223, *223*, 230,
233, 237–238, *242*, 242–243, 252
Feinstein, Dianne, 268
Fillmore, Millard, 71
Fisher, O. Clark, 236
Fitzgerald, John F., 227, 328
Fong, Hiram L., 241
Ford, Henry, 133
*Foreign Conspiracy Against the Liberties of
the United States* (Morse), 48–49
Foreign Miners' License Tax (1852), 83
foreign relations, US, 15–16
foreign policy in Latin America,
184–185, 199, 205
and immigration reform, 231
and Islamophobia, 298
and Trump's wall, 285
during WWII, 184–185
Fortune, 257
Fox News, 309
Franklin, Benjamin, 17–18, 25, 33, 34–35

Gardner, Henry, 66
Garfield, James, *91*
Garis, Roy, 156, 158–159
Geary Act (1892), 110
Geisel, Theodor Seuss, *202*
Geller, Pamela, 308–309

gender
    anti-Chinese arguments about, 76
    and deportation, 281
    and Islamophobia, 300–301
    and targets of xenophobia, 8–9,
        137–138
    See also women; women's rights
genealogy, 64, 66
Gentlemen's Agreement (1908), 193
George I (England), 29
German Americans, 37, 135–136, 204. *See
    also* German immigrants
German immigrants
    assimilation of, 17, 25, 33, 119, 136
    demographics of, 22
    as hard workers, 17
    Jewish, 144–145
    naturalization of, 19
    number of, 36–37
    political clout of, 33–35
    recruitment of, 20–22, 29–30
    travel conditions for, 22–23
    whiteness of, 32, 35
    See also anti-German xenophobia
Germany, 143–144, 246
Giuliani, Rudy, 2
Goethe, Charles, 174
gold rush, 79
Goldwater, Barry, 231–232
Gompers, Samuel, 81, 122
"good immigrants vs bad immigrants" idea,
        11, 12, 14, 273, 324, 334–335
Gordon, Patrick, 24–25
Grant, Madison, 128–130
    anti-Semitism of, 132
    Hitler's admiration for, 143
    and Immigration Act of 1924, 143
    and immigration restriction, 6, 140
    The Passing of the Great Race, 14, 128,
        129, 134, 140, 143
    on race, 129–130, 131, 133–134
    on WWI, 136
Great Depression, 162–163
    and anti-Mexican xenophobia, 148,
        149, 163, 164–165, 175, 180
    and anti-Semitism, 144

Haiti and Haitian immigrants, 256, 292,
        322
Hall, Prescott Farnsworth, 113, 118,
        119–120, 123, 125, 127, 133
Hart, Philip A., 228, 240, 243
Hart-Celler Act. *See* Immigration and
        Nationality Act (1965)
hate crimes. *See* violence
Hawai'i, Japanese in, 187, 203–204
Haymarket Square riots, 121
H.B. 56 (Alabama, 2011), 337
health services, opposition to immigrants
        receiving, 254, 264, 269, 279,
        332. *See also* public health
Heller, David, 243
Heller, Deane, 243
hemispheric caps
    conservative calls for, 236–237
    framed as antidiscriminatory measure,
        237–239
    liberals' support for, 241–242
    and Mexican immigrants, 225,
        246–247
    replaces national origins quotas, 224
hemispheric security, 184–185, 199,
        204–205, 207–208
Hendrick, Burton J., 133
historical amnesia, 324–327
Hitler, Adolf, 143
Hoar, George Frisbie, 328
Holland, W. H., 176, 177
homosexuality, 9, 137–138, 225, 244
Hoover, Herbert, 166–167
hostage shopping, 185
Houghteling, Laura Delano, 144
H.R. 4437 (2006), 329–330
Hungary, immigration from, 120, 123,
        246
Huntington, Samuel, 273, 275–277

Idaho, alien land laws in, 193
illegal immigration. *See* undocumented
        immigrants
Illegal Immigration Reform and
        Immigrant Responsibility Act
        (IIRIRA) (1996), 279

immigrant rights advocacy, 328–330,
332–334
immigrants
misleading statements about, 2, 124
(*See also* Trump, Donald)
numbers in US, 3, 81, 131, 227,
245–246, 252
immigration
public opinion of, 231–232, 278, 335
Immigration Act (1882), 71
Immigration Act (1891), 99
Immigration Act (1917), 136–139, 161,
297
Immigration Act (1924), 97, 141–143, 196,
198, 297
Immigration Act (1929), 160
Immigration and Customs Enforcement
(ICE), 280, 288, 333
Immigration and Nationality Act (1952)
(McCarran-Walter Act),
226–228
Immigration and Nationality Act (1965)
(Hart-Celler Act), 221–225
criticism of, 235–237
defense of, 239–241
effects of, 244–250, 252
hemispheric caps in, 224, 237–240,
241–242, 243
MacGregor Amendment, 238–239
signing of, 221–224, *223*, 243–244
visa preference system in, 224, 241,
242–243
Immigration and Naturalization Service
(INS), 201, 213, 259, 264, 280,
303
"immigration crisis," 253, 255–257, 278
immigration enforcement
under Bush administration, 282
citizens called on for, 254, 264, 269,
337
under Clinton administration,
279–281
increases in, 293
by Know Nothing party, 69–70
under Obama administration,
282–283

and Proposition 187, 264
protests of, 333
and surveillance, 154, 267, 281
under Trump administration,
287–288, 323, 331–332
and undocumented immigrants, 253,
281–282, 284
at US-Mexico border, 281–282, 283,
323, 329, 331–332
See also deportation; Immigration and
Naturalization Service (INS);
US Border Patrol
immigration inspections, 107, 109
immigration papers, fraudulent, 108–109
Immigration Problem, or America First
(Ward), 135
immigration raids, 147
immigration reform, 221–250
backlash against, 232
Bush approach to, 282
Congressional support for, 233,
234–235
defense of as complicit in xenophobia,
239–241, 335
Feighan bill, 233–234
as foreign policy position, 231
Johnson bill (Act of 1965), 221–225,
230–232, 239
Kennedy proposal, 229–230, 234
Kennedy's call for, 228, 229–230
Obama approach to, 283
opposition to, 233–234, 235–239
as political necessity, 235
Immigration Reform and Control Act
(IRCA) (1986), 259–260
Immigration Restriction League (IRL)
academics involved in, 115–116
anti-Italian rhetoric, 124, 125–126
and eugenics, 115
formation of, 113
influence of, 116
laws promoted by, 117
and literacy test, 127, 139
and nativism, 119, 131, 134
opposed to Jewish refugees, 144
and race, 114–115

Immigration Restriction League (IRL)
  (continued)
  recommends increasing head tax,
    126–127
  visits to Ellis Island immigration
    station, 123–124
immigration restrictions
  on Chinese immigrants, 84–85
  justified in name of national security,
    93
  on Mexican immigrants, 159–161,
    246–247, 248–249
  set by Immigration Act of 1965, 224
  taxes on immigrants, 27, 83–84, 95,
    99, 126–127, 136
  See also Chinese Exclusion Act;
    hemispheric caps; national origin
    quotas
Independent American, 239
India, immigration from, 246
Indian Removal Act (1830), 47–48
indigenous peoples. *See* Native Americans
Inter-American Emergency Advisory
    Committee for Political Defense,
    208
International Conference of American
    States, 205
International Jew, The (Ford), 133
International Refugee Assistance Project,
    289
interracial mixing (miscegenation), 76, 130
invasion, immigrants as, *126*
  in anti-Catholicism, 39–40, 48–49
  in anti-Chinese xenophobia, 77, 88,
    92, 95, 111
  in anti-German xenophobia, 18,
    24–25
  in anti-Japanese xenophobia, 191,
    192, 194, 198, 202–203
  in anti-Mexican xenophobia,
    158–159, 253, 258, 269–270,
    275
  in anti-Semitism, 133–134
  eastern/southern Europeans as
    invasion, 115, 120, 131–132
  in Islamophobia, 308–309

  undocumented immigrants as
    invasion, 253, 255–257, 258–259,
    269–270
  See also nativism
Iranian immigrants, 291, 297
Iraqi immigrants, 289, 291–292, 296
Ireland, immigration from, 246
Irish Catholics, 12, 37
  acceptance of, 72, 114, 118, 119
  number of immigrants, 44
  and potato famine, 44–45
  race of, 43, 57–58, 60, 72, 76, 114
  racism of, 60–61, 73, 81
  See also anti-Catholicism
Irwin, William, 75
Islam, 8, 294. *See also* Islamophobia;
    Muslims
Islamophobia, 8, 289–319
  conservative network promoting,
    307–308
  and domestic spying on American
    Muslims, 302–303, 304–306
  and economic pressure, 306
  and fears of terrorism, 294, 298,
    306–307, 309
  history of, 295, 296–297
  in media, 307–310
  Muslims as unassimilable, 294, 308
  and 9/11, 299–300
  and Obama, 310–312
  Republican Party appeals to, 310–313
  and Trump, 313–317
  and war on terror, 290–291, 301–305
  women's oppression, 294, 300–301
issei. *See* Japanese immigrants
Italian Americans, 78, 125, 204, 229, 335
Italian immigrants
  as cheap labor, 125–126
  compared to Chinese immigrants,
    125–126
  historical mistruths about, 325
  numbers of, 118
  racial stereotypes of, 124–126
  as threat to peace and security,
    124–125, 139
Italy, immigration from, 142, 229, 246

jails. *See* detention
Japan
    deportation of Japanese Latin
        Americans to, 185, 216
    Gentlemen's Agreement with, 193
    as threat to US, 191–192, 194
Japanese Americans, 11, 183–219
    arrests of, 199–200
    experiences of, 183, 185–186, 187–
        188, 189, 200–201, 210–211,
        213, 215
    incarceration of, 183–184, 200–201,
        203–204, 210–213, 317–318
    loyalty of, 201–202, 212–213
    redress for, 218
    as security threat, 200–203
Japanese immigrants
    citizenship status of, 212
    loyalty of, 212–213
    numbers of, 194
    recruitment of, 186–187
    See also anti-Japanese xenophobia
Japanese-Korean Exclusion League, 192
Japanese Peruvians
    deportation and incarceration of,
        184–185, 206–209, 213–215,
        217
    experiences of, 184, 188–189,
        205–206, 210, 213, 216,
        217–218, *218*
    repatriation to Japan, 216
    US surveillance of, 205–206
    violence against, 199
Javits, Jacob, 228, 240
Jewish immigrants, 18, 117, 130, 132–133.
    See also anti-Semitism
Jewish refugees, 144–145, 226
Jobs, Steve, 331
Johnson, Albert, 140, 143
Johnson, Edwin C., 164
Johnson, Lyndon Baines, *242*
    and Immigration Act of 1965, 221,
        223, 224, 242–243, 243–244
    and immigration reform, 230–231
Journey to Pennsylvania (Mittelberger), 23
Judge Magazine, *126*

Kansas-Nebraska Act (1854), 60
Keith, William, 18, 24, 27, 29
Keller, George Frederick, 82
Kennedy, John F., 227, 228, 229–230
Kennedy, Robert F., 231
Kennedy, Ted, 221–222, 241
Kiley, Barbara, 263, 265
Kiley, Robert, 263
King, Bill, 262
King, Cameron H., 87, 88, 89
King, Martin Luther, Jr., 232
King, Peter, 313
Knights of Labor, 100, 101, 105
Know Nothing Party. *See* American Party
Know Nothing Soap, 63, *64*
Korbel, Francis, 82
Korean immigrants, 13, 111, 192, 246,
    303, 316
Korematsu, Fred, 211–212, 317, *319*,
    330–331
Korematsu, Karen, 318–319, *319*
Korematsu v. United States (1944), 211–212,
    317–318, *319*
Krikorian, Mark, 302
Ku Klux Klan (KKK), 6, 122, 133

labor/workers
    bracero program, 226, 235, 248, 251
    Chinese immigrants blamed for
        undercutting, 75, 81, 85–86, 89,
        92
    immigrant scapegoating for troubles
        in, 121, *255*
    and Immigration Act of 1965, 248
    Irish Catholic immigrants blamed for
        poor conditions of, 54–55
    labor unions in Peru oppose Japanese
        immigration, 197
    and limitations on Mexican
        immigrants, 248
    and Mexican immigrants, 286
    Mexicans as cheap labor, 150–153
    mistreatment of Chinese immigrants
        as cheap labor, 80
    recruitment of Chinese immigrants
        for, 79–80, 85

labor/workers *(continued)*
　　recruitment of Japanese immigrants
　　　for, 186–187
　　See also economic pressure
La Prensa (Lima), 197, 198
La Raza, 283
Latin America
　　Asian immigration to, 85, 96,
　　　184–185
　　and Immigration Act of 1965, 241,
　　　246
　　immigration from, 246, 252
　　immigration policies in, 16
　　US foreign policy in, 184–185, 199,
　　　205
　　See also hemispheric caps; Japanese
　　　Peruvians; Mexico
Laughlin, Harry H., 15–16, 140
Lea, Homer, 192
Lebanon, 297
legislation
　　anti-Chinese, 83–84, 99, 104–105
　　discrimination in immigration
　　　legislation, 225–226
Lenni Lenapes (Delawares), 26, 30, 31
Liberal League, 100
Libya, 291, 316
"likely to become public charges" law,
　　10
Lincoln, Abraham, 71, 72
literacy, 119–120, 124, 160
literacy test, 117, 123, 127–128, *138*,
　　139
local histories, and New Englander
　　nativism, 64–65
Lodge, Henry Cabot, 127, 128, 134, 227,
　　328
Logan, James, 24, 25, 26
London Illustrated News, 45
Los Angeles, California, 168–172,
　　175–180, 326–327
Los Angeles Bar Association, 171
Los Angeles Evening Herald and Express,
　　177–178
Los Angeles Illustrated Daily News, 169–170
Los Angeles Times, 180

Louisiana, anti-German xenophobia in,
　　136
Louisiana Purchase (1803), 47
Louisville, Kentucky, anti-immigrant riots
　　in, 39–41

MacGregor, Clark, 236, 237, 238–239
MacGregor Amendment, 238–239
Magnuson Act (1943), 226
Manifest Destiny, 47–48. *See also* colonial
　　expansion
marriage
　　arranged between picture brides and
　　　issei, 187–188, 194, 195
　　polygamy as grounds for exclusion,
　　　115, 127, 137, 296–297
Massachusetts, 47, 59, 63–64, 68–70
Mass Immigration Reduction Act, 325
McCarran, Patrick, 227
McCarran-Walter Act (Immigration
　　and Nationality Act) (1952),
　　226–228
McCarthy, Richard, 240
McClatchy, V. S., 192
McClellan, John, 236–237
McClure's Magazine, 133
McCoppin, Frank, 87, 88
McCulloch, William M., 239
McLean, Robert N., 165–166
McWilliams, Carey, 149, 173
media
　　anti-Catholicism in, *41*, 49
　　anti-Chinese xenophobia in, 82–*83*,
　　　91
　　anti-Italian xenophobia in, 125
　　anti-Japanese xenophobia in, 197,
　　　202
　　anti-Mexican xenophobia in,
　　　258–259
　　anti-Semitism in, 133
　　Asian immigrants in, 257
　　celebrations of immigration in,
　　　254–255
　　detention camps in, 214
　　immigration as threat in, *126*,
　　　258–259

Islamophobia in, 294, 298, 307–308, 309–310
literacy test in, *138*
undocumented immigrants in, 255, 258
medical examinations, 109
mentally ill population, 124, 137
Mexican Americans
citizenship status of, 149–150, 176–177, 179
languages spoken by, 286
welfare population of, 175
See also anti-Mexican xenophobia; Mexican immigrants
Mexican-American War, 62, 149
Mexican immigrants, 147–181
birth rate among, 158
bracero program, 226, 235, 248, 251
as cheap labor, 150–153
compared to other groups, 156, 157, 158
de-Americanization of, 149, 155, 156, 158, 162
deportation of, 10, 147–149, 161–162, 172
enforcement targeting, 227
expulsion of, 148
and hemispheric caps, 241, 242, 246–247
and Immigration Act of 1965, 246–247, 248–249
legislation targeting, 161, 225
and literacy test, 160
numbers of, 150, 160, 246, 276, 285
racial stereotypes of, 151–152, 155, 156–157, 173, 174, 253
repatriation of, 172–180, 327
restriction of, 159–161, 246–247, 248–249
as seasonal/transient migrants, 151, 155
undocumented, 251–252
and US border policy, 154–155
women, 9, 173–174, 269–270, 275
See also anti-Mexican xenophobia

Mexicans
race of, 155, 156
unemployment among, 165
Mexico
anti-Chinese movement in, 95–96
bracero agreement with, 226, 235, 248, 251
immigration from, 246, 286
Japanese residents of, 206
quota for, 247
reasons for leaving (pressure to emigrate from), 153–154, 245
US border policing, 16
the Middle East, 244, 295, 298. *See also* Islamophobia
Migration Policy Institute, 282
Miller, John F., 92
Miller, Stephen, 316
Minnesota, anti-German xenophobia in, 136
model minorities, 257–258
Morita, Betty May Chieko, 183, 188, 189, 200, 210–211, 213, 218, *218*
Morita, Kashichi, 185–186, 200
Morita, Masano (Sakakiyama), 187–188, 189
Morita, Mototsugu, 187–188, 189, 199–200
Morse, Samuel F. B., 48–49
Morse, Solomon Bradford, Jr., 52–53, 65–66
Mountjoy, Dick, 263
Muslim Americans
experiences of, 299–300
in media, 310
race of, 296, 298
racial profiling of, 302–303, 305–306
See also Islamophobia
Muslims
long history of immigration to US, 295–296
negative stereotypes of, 294, 295, 298, 300–301
numbers of, 296
public opinion of, 294, 305–306
See also Islamophobia

Muslim travel ban (Executive Order 13769) (2017), 288, 290, 291, 316–319
  protests of, *330*–331, 333–334
Muslim women, 9, 300–301, 334

The Nation, 172
National Club of America for Americans, Inc., 163
national origin quotas
  and calls for immigration reform, 227–230, 233–234
  and Emergency Quota Act of 1921, 140
  in Feighan's immigration bill, 233
  and Immigration Act of 1924, 142, 196
  and Immigration Act of 1952, 226–227
  and Immigration Act of 1965, 223, 247
  and IRL, 117
  and Mexican immigration, 159
  and Muslim countries, 297
National Review, 302, 308
National Security Entry-Exit Registration System, 303
Nation of Immigrants, A (Kennedy), 228
Native American Association, 50
Native American Democratic Association, 50
Native Americans
  in colonial America, 25–26, 29–32, 30–32, 35
  forced migration of, 19, 47–48
  immigrant groups compared to, 8, 57, 81, 125, 156
  impact of Trump's wall on, 285
  and interracial mixing, 130
  and nativism, 12, 35, 62–63, 64–65
  Wounded Knee massacre, 121–122
nativism
  and anti-Chinese xenophobia, 78
  and anti-Mexican xenophobia, 163, 164–165, 254
  definition of, 11–12
  distinct from xenophobia, 11

  and Great Depression, 163, 164–165
  and immigration reform, 235, 239
  and IRL rhetoric, 119, 131, 134
  and Know Nothings, 43, 62–63, 65–67
  and Native Americans, 12, 35, 62–63, 64–65
  in New England, 63–65
  roots of, 11
  and white supremacy, 11–12, 65, 274
naturalization
  and anti-Chinese xenophobia, 90
  and anti-Japanese xenophobia, 189, 195, 196
  and anti-Mexican xenophobia, 157–158
  of Asian immigrants, 226
  of immigrants in colonial America, 19, 28–29, 36
  and Islamophobia, 298
  Know Nothings' proposed waiting period for, 67, 69
Naturalization Act (1790), 15, 36
Nazis, admiration for US race-based lawmaking, 143
Nelson, Alan, 263
Newsweek, 257, *258*
New York, New York, 45, 50–51, 131
New York Police Department (NYPD), 304
New York state, poor laws in, 59
New York Times, 125, 165, 167, 179, 223, 256, 310, 318
nisei. *See* Japanese Americans
Norris, Isaac, 25
North American Free Trade Agreement (NAFTA), 286
North American Review, 56, 191
Norweb, R. Henry, 207, 209

Obama, Barack
  conservative backlash to, 311–313
  immigration enforcement under, 282–283
  rumored to be Muslim, 308, 310–311, 312, 313
Office of Naval Intelligence, 201

Oklahoma, Islamophobic legislation in, 313
Oklahoma City bombing (1995), 299
Operation Gatekeeper (1994), 281, 282
Operation Rio Grande (1997), 281
Operation Safeguard (1994), 281
Operation Streamline (2005), 282
Operation Wetback (1954), 227
Order of the Star-Spangled Banner. *See* American Party
Order of United American Mechanics, 51
Oregon, alien land laws in, 189, 193
Osborn, Henry Fairfield, 134
Ottoman Empire, immigration from, 297

Packard, Ron, 265
Page Act (1875), 85
Paine, Robert Treat, Jr., 123
Palace Hotel, San Francisco, California, 86–87
Palmer, A. Mitchell, 139–140
Panama, Japanese residents of, 206
paper sons, 108–109
Parker, Theodore, 45, 57, 60
Parkman, Francis, 119
Passing of the Great Race, The (Grant), 14, 128, 129, 134, 140, 143
Pence, Mike, 290
Penn, Thomas, 26
Penn, William, 21
Pennsylvania, colonial
    anti-German xenophobia in, 18, 24–26
    anti-Native American sentiment in, 30–32
    German vote in, 33–35
    and movements of people in colonial America, 19
    race in, 32
    regulation of immigration to, 26–29
    settlement of German immigrants in, 20–21, 29–30
Peru, anti-Japanese xenophobia in, 184, 186, 188, 196–199, 206–210. *See also* Japanese Peruvians

Phelan, James D.
    anti-Asian activism of, 189–191
    condemnation of, 329
    "Keep California White" campaign, 189–190, 195
    as mayor of San Francisco, 190–191
    opposes Japanese immigration, 189–190, 194, 195
    scrapbooks of, 193–194
Philadelphia, Pennsylvania
    anti-immigrant movements in, 41, 50, 51
    German immigrants to, 23–24, 24–25, 27
the Philippines, 139, 226, 246, 249
picture brides, 187–188, 194, 195
Pierson, Katrina, 294
Pipes, Daniel, 308
Pixley, Frank M., 87–88, 88–89
Plea for the West, A (Beecher), 49–50
Poland, immigration from, 246
political radicalism, of southern/eastern Europeans, 115, 139–140
political xenophobia, 15, 43, 53, 55, 336. *See also* nativism
polygamy, as grounds for exclusion, 115, 127, 137, 296–297
Pontiac's Rebellion (1763), 32
poor laws, 59
Populist Party, 132
potato famine, 44–45
poverty, 54, 59–60, 70, 115, 121, 124
Prado, Manuel, 208
Prince, Ron, 263, 264–265, 269
professional skill preferences, 224, 233, 242–243, 246, 248, 296, 332
Proposition 187 ("Save Our State") (1994), 254, 263–273
    and border policing, 281
    and color-blind xenophobia, 265
    effects of, 273
    goals of become federal policy under Clinton administration, 278–279
    opposition to, 270–272
    and Pete Wilson's campaign, 265–268
    and racism, 264–265, 268–269
    requirements of, 264, 337

The Protestant (weekly newspaper), 49
Protestant Crusade, 42, 46–47
Protestantism, 11, 21, 29, 42, 44,
    53–54
public health, 23, 27, 89, 109, 137, 159,
    264
Public Law 1018, 160–161
Puck magazine, *91*, *138*

quota system, 5, 9

race
    and anti-Chinese xenophobia,
        78–79
    and anti-Japanese xenophobia,
        195–196, 197
    exclusion based on, 93
    and immigration reform, 235–237
    interracial mixing, 76, 130
    and Irish immigration, 43, 60
    and Islamophobia, 298
    of Mexicans, 155, 156
    and slavery in colonial America,
        35–36
    and targets of xenophobia, 9
    See also racism; whiteness
race suicide argument, 120–121, 131–132,
    275
Racial Integrity Law (1925), 130
racial profiling, 10, 254, 271, 302–303,
    305–306, 330
racism
    growing rejection of, 232
    by Irish Americans, 60–61
    and Obama, 310–311, 312
    and Proposition 187, 264–265
    Republican Party appeals to,
        277–278, 310–312
    scientific racism, 9, 43, 57–58,
        114–115, 129–130, 132–133
    Trump appeals to, 287, 322
    xenophobia as form of, 9
    See also scientific racism; white
        supremacy
railroads, 80, 152, 153
RAISE Act, 292
Reagan, Ronald, 259–260

Red Scare (1919–1920), 139–140
Refugee Act (1953), 217
refugees
    from Asia and Latin America, 245
    in Feighan's immigration bill, 233
    in Immigration Act of 1965, 244
    Irish immigrants as, 44–45
    and Islamophobia, 290
    Jewish, 144–145, 226
    and Muslim travel ban, 316
    resettlement in US, 3, 329, 332
    Syrian, 290, 291
    Trump opposes, 323, 332
registry of immigrants, 27–28, 96–97, *98*
regulation of immigration, 26–28, 96–97.
        See also Immigration Acts
religion
    anti-Semitism, 8, 18, 117, 132–133,
        144–145
    and refugee claims, 291
    of southern/eastern Europeans, 115
    xenophobia focuses away from with
        anti-Chinese movement, 79
    See also anti-Catholicism;
        Islamophobia
repatriation, of Mexicans, 148, 164,
    165–166, 172–180, 327
Republican National Convention (2016),
    1–2
Republican Party
    appeals to racism, 277–278,
        310–312
    benefits from xenophobia, 277–278
    and Islamophobia, 311, 312–313
    pro-immigration plank, 72
    and slavery, 71
reverse discrimination, 237–239
Ripley, William, 133
*Rising Tide of Color Against White World-
        Supremacy, The* (Stoddard), 128,
    196
Roberts, John G., Jr., 317–318
Roosevelt, Franklin Delano, 144, 203
Roosevelt, Theodore, 6, 132, 135, 192,
    193
Ross, Edward, 125, 128, 133
Rowell, Chester H., 157

Rusk, Dean, 231, 240
Russian Jews, 117

Sakakiyama, Masano, 187–188
sanctuary movement, 330, 333
San Francisco, California
   anti-Chinese xenophobia in, 75, 76,
      84
   anti-Japanese xenophobia in, 192–193,
      204
   Palace Hotel, 86–87
   Phelan as mayor of, 190–191
San Francisco Illustrated Wasp (magazine),
      82–83
Sargent, Aaron A., 87, 89–92
Sarsour, Linda, 305
Saturday Evening Post, 163
Save Our State amendment (Oklahoma),
      313
Save Our State Initiative. *See* Proposition
      187
Saxbe, William, 255
scareheading tactics, 148, 168–169, 173
schools, public, 51, 69, 192, 264
scientific racism, 9, 43, 57–58, 114–115,
      129–130, 132–133
Scott Act (1888), 110
Seattle, Washington, anti-Chinese
      movement in, 100, 101–102,
      104–106, 326
Secure Communities program, 288
Secure Fence Act (2006), 283
segregation, 122, 130, 143, 149–150, 192
September 11, 2001 (9/11) terrorist
      attacks, 280, 290–291, 299–300,
      301, 302–303
Sessions, Jeff, 2, 316
settler colonialism
   and anti-Chinese rhetoric, 78–79,
      81
   and closing of frontier, 121–122
   and nativism, 62, 65, 78–79
   and recruitment of European
      immigrants, 72
   See also colonial expansion
Seven Years' War (1756-1763), 31–32

sexuality
   anti-Chinese arguments about, 76, 88
   homosexuality, 9, 137–138, 225, 244
   and targets of xenophobia, 8–9,
      137–138
sharia law, 309, 313
Shaw, Frank L., 175–176
Shibayama, Betty. *See* Morita, Betty May
      Chieko
Shibayama, Isamu (Art), 184, 188–189,
      205–206, 210, 213, 216,
      217–218, *218*
"show me your papers" policy, 284, 337
slaves and slavery
   and anti-Chinese movement, 81
   in colonial America, 35–36
   emancipation and white supremacy,
      72–73
   forced migration of, 19
   Know Nothings' position on, 60, 69,
      71
   Muslim, 296
socialism, 115, 139–140, 166, 312
Somalia, 291, 296, 316
songs of emigrants/immigrants, 44, 79,
      153, 170
Sotomayor, Sonia, 318
South America. *See* Latin America; Peru
South Dakota, anti-German xenophobia
      in, 136
Southern Border Program, 16
southern Europeans
   decrease in immigration, 145
   inclusion of in white American
      identity, 244–245
   as invasion, 115, 120, 131–132
   and literacy test, 123
   and national origin quotas, 140
   as racially different, 114–115, 130
   and Red Scare, 139–140
   restrictions on/quotas for, 142, 229
   rise in immigration of, 117–118
Southern Poverty Law Center, 307
the Southwest, disenfranchisement of
      Mexicans in, 149–150
Soviet Union, immigration from, 246

Spencer, Robert, 309
Squire, Watson C., 100, 101, 102, 103
St. Louis (ocean liner), 145
Stoddard, Lothrop, 128, 196
Stop Islamization of America (SIOA), 309
Stop the Islamization of America: A Practical Guide to the Resistance (Geller), 309
Strong, George Templeton, 58
Strong, Josiah, 120
Sudan, 291, 296
Support Our Law Enforcement and Safe Neighborhoods Act (SB1070) (2010), 284
surveillance
　　and anti-Japanese xenophobia, 201, 206
　　and border enforcement, 154, 267, 281
　　of Chinese immigrants, 96–97, *98*
　　and Islamophobia, 302–303, 304–305, 306
Syrian immigrants, 291, 296, 297, 298
Syrian refugees, 290, 291

Tacoma, Washington, anti-Chinese movement in, 102–104
Tancredo, Tom, 325
Tanton, John, 256
taxes on immigrants, 27, 83–84, 95, 99, 126–127, 136
Tea Party, 311–312
terrorism, and Islamophobia, 294, 298–299, 306–307
Texas, 150, 157, 180, 193
Time magazine, 255, 256–257, 319
transatlantic migration, 21–24
Treaty of Guadalupe Hidalgo, 149
Trevor, John B., 140
Trevor, John B., Jr., 233–234
Triangle Center on Terrorism and Homeland Security, 307
Truman, Harry S., 215, 228
Trump, Donald
　　German heritage of, 37

immigration policy under, 292–293, 321–323, 331–332
and Islamophobia, 290–291, 293–294, 313–317
on Mexican immigration, 284–285, 286
and Muslim travel ban, 290, 316–317
xenophobic messages of, 1–2, 5, 284–285, 287, 290, 322–323
Trump v. Hawaii (2018), 316–317, 317–318
"Twenty Reasons Why Immigration Should Be Further Restricted Now" (IRL), 124

"undesirable" immigrants, 126–127, 136–138
undocumented immigrants, 251–288
　　amnesty for, 260
　　and anti-Mexican xenophobia, 159, 161, 166–167, 168, 227, 251–252, 253–254, 258–259, 269–270, 293
　　and border enforcement, 253, 281–282, 284
　　and Buchanan campaign, 261
　　and Chinese exclusion laws, 4, 97–99, 108–109
　　and Clinton presidency, 278–279
　　conservative movement against, 261–263, 273–278
　　criminalization of, 97–99, 160–161
　　dehumanization of, 269
　　increase in due to Immigration Act of 1965, 249–250, 252
　　as invasion, 253, 255–257, 258–259, 269–270
　　Japanese Latin Americans classified as by INS, 213, 215, 217
　　numbers of, 260, 285
　　and Obama presidency, 283–284
　　and Reagan presidency, 259–260
　　and Trump presidency, 331–332
　　See also Proposition 187
Unión Revolucionaria (Peru), 197
United Kingdom/Great Britain, immigration from, 236, 246
USA Patriot Act (2001), 303

US Border Patrol
creation of, 161–162
expansions of, 281, 282, 287
and Mexican immigration, 154–155,
162, 227
US Citizenship and Immigration Services
(USCIS), 280, 321–322
US Constitution, 336
US Customs and Border Protection, 280,
285
US Immigration Commission (1911), 125
US-Mexico border
benign neglect policy at, 154–155
Buchanan speech at, 261
and drug war, 259
increased enforcement at, 281–282,
283, 323, 329, 331–332
in Pete Wilson TV ad, 267
Trump's wall, 284, 285–286, 287,
323, 333
US News and World Report, 255, 257, 258
US Supreme Court
and Chinese exclusion laws, 84,
92–93, 161
and Islamophobia, 296, 316–319
Korematsu case in, 211–212, 215,
317–318, *319*
and Native American removal, 48
and undocumented immigrants, 284

*Valor of Ignorance, The: The Inevitable
Japanese-American War* (Lea), 192
"Various Facts and Opinion Concerning
the Necessity of Restricting
Immigration" (IRL), 124
Vestal, Albert H., 155
Vietnam, immigration from, 246
violence
anti-Catholic, 39–41, 49
anti-Chinese, 95–96, 99, 100–101,
102–103
anti-German, 136
anti-Japanese, 193, 199
anti-Mexican, 150, 165
anti-Muslim, 295, 298, 301, 306, 314
in backlash against civil rights, 232

immigrant groups stereotyped as
violent, 8, 56, 124, 125, 136, 159,
268–269, 294
visa preference system (prioritizing family
unification and professional
skills), 224, 242–243, 246, 248,
296
Visel, Charles P., 168–169, 171
voting
attacks on Catholic/immigrant voters
by Know Nothings, 39–41
by German community in
Pennsylvania, 33–35
by Irish immigrants, 59
and Mexican Americans, 150
withheld from Chinese, 99
withheld from free and enslaved
blacks, 36, 73
Voting Rights Act (1965), 232

Walker, Francis, 120–121
"Walking Purchase" (1737), 26
Ward, James Murphy, 135
Ward, Robert DeCourcy, 113
War Relocation Authority, 215, 317
Warren, Charles, 113, 123
Washington
alien land laws in, 193
anti-Chinese movement in Seattle,
100, 101–102, 104–106, 326
Wasp magazine, 14, 82–83
WASPs (white Anglo-Saxon Protestants).
See nativism
Weisbach, Robert Jacob, 103
welfare. *See* benefits, public
the West
and anti-Chinese movement, 78–79,
99–101
migration of New Englanders to, 62,
64
and Protestant Crusade, 46–48
See also California
Western Hemisphere
deportation from, 215–216
and family reunification preferences,
248

Western Hemisphere *(continued)*
    open immigration from, 146, 240
    opposition to increased immigration
        from, 234, 236, 237
    US hegemony in, 199
    See also hemispheric caps; hemispheric
        security
whiteness
    of Arab and Muslim immigrants, 298
    in colonial America, 14–15, 18, 19,
        32, 35, 36
    and deportation policy, 162
    extended to all Europeans, 78–79,
        119, 244–245
    and Immigration Act of 1924, 142
    of the Irish, 43, 58, 72, 76, 114
    and race suicide argument, 120–121,
        131–132, 275
    See also white supremacy
white supremacy
    and colonial expansion, 19, 155
    and "colored peril," 195–196
    and conservative anti-immigrant
        movement, 273–277
    and emancipation, 72–73
    and immigration reform, 234,
        235–236, 239, 243
    and nativism, 11–12, 65, 274
    and reverse discrimination argument,
        239, 274
    Trump appeals to, 287, 313, 316, 322
    See also nativism; racism
white victimization, 254, 262, 263, 265,
        266. *See also* nativism; white
        supremacy
Wilson, Pete, 265–268
Wirin, A. L., 217
women
    Chinese women, 9, 84, 85
    and Islamophobia, 294, 300–301
    Japanese women (picture brides),
        187–188, 194, 195
    Mexican women, 9, 173–174,
        269–270, 275

    Muslim women, 9, 300–301, 334
    and race suicide argument, 131–132
    as targets of xenophobia, 8–9, 137
women's rights, 69, 122, 131–132, 136
World War I
    and anti-German xenophobia, 15, 37,
        135–136
    and anti-Japanese xenophobia, 194
    immigration bans during, 297
World War II, and anti-Japanese
        xenophobia, 15, 183–184,
        184–185, 199–200, 201–203

xenophobia
    and American democracy, 14–15,
        335–337
    arguments against immigrants, 3–4
    as defining feature of American life,
        7, 324
    and foreign relations, 15–16
    "good immigrants vs bad immigrants"
        idea, 11, 12, 14, 273, 324,
        334–335
    historical amnesia about, 324–327
    "liberals" complicit in, 239–241,
        270–272, 334–335
    meaning of term, 7–8
    opposition to, 328–331, 332–334
    persistence of, 12–13, 334–335
    and power, 11
    as profitable (and American
        capitalism), 13–14, 82, *94*,
        277
    reasons for, 4–5
    viewed as episodic, 4–5
    viewed as exception to US
        immigration tradition, 5,
        324–325

yellow peril, Japanese immigration as,
        191–192, 197–198. *See also* anti-
        Japanese xenophobia
Yemen, 291, 296, 316
Yesler, Henry L., 102

Credit: Eric Mueller

Erika Lee is a Regents Professor, the Rudolph J. Vecoli Chair in Immigration History, director of the Immigration History Research Center at the University of Minnesota, and an Andrew Carnegie Fellow. The author of *The Making of Asian America* and other award-winning books, Lee lives in Minneapolis, MN.